History of the Ancestors, Families and Descendants of
Paris Patrick Comisford

William D. Comisford, Jr.

HERITAGE BOOKS
2007

HERITAGE BOOKS
AN IMPRINT OF HERITAGE BOOKS, INC.

Books, CDs, and more—Worldwide

For our listing of thousands of titles see our website
at
www.HeritageBooks.com

Published 2007 by
HERITAGE BOOKS, INC.
Publishing Division
65 East Main Street
Westminster, Maryland 21157-5026

Copyright © 2007 William D. Comisford, Jr.

All rights reserved. No part of this book may be reproduced or transmitted in any form or by any means, electronic or mechanical, including photocopying, recording or by any information storage and retrieval system without written permission from the author, except for the inclusion of brief quotations in a review.

International Standard Book Number: 978-0-7884-4243-8

Dedication

This book on the history of the ancestors, families, and descendants of Paris Patrick Comisford is respectfully dedicated to my grandmother and grandfather, Mildred Ada (McKinley) and Homer Whitcome Comisford.

This project started early on, when my great-grandmother, Jessie Helen (Davis) Comisford drew a tree on a piece of paper and started putting names on the limbs of the tree. Then during the mid 1970's, my grandmother started scouring through family records, old pictures, census information, church records, cemeteries, newspaper clippings, and all sorts of information to trace the family roots. During this process she would often drag my grandfather all over the country, or shall I say he would chauffeur her from place to place. From courthouses to cemeteries, churches to libraries, they enjoyed the adventure of turning up something new and unknown about the family.

I only wish that I would have started earlier in my pursuit of the past. I would have loved to have the opportunity to sit down and reminisce about the past with my grandparents, great-aunts and uncles, and many of the old timers. It's too late, they are all gone, but not forgotten.

To them, we will always be grateful for helping us to preserve our piece of history.

Homer and Mickey
Picture taken on their 60th
Wedding Anniversary
January 31, 1985

Table of Contents

Dedication iii
Table of Contents v
List of Photos, Illustrations, and Charts.. vii
Foreword ix
Preface... xi
Introduction xiii

Descendents of Paris Patrick Comisford and Rosette Helene Gaffney 1
Descendents of William Taygart and Sarah Eagon 33
Descendents of Sampson and Mary Eagon... 41
Descendents of John Blackburn and Ms. Woods.. 45
Descendents of Hans George and Maria Lantz... 49
Descendents of David Daniel Bonnett and Christine Cousine............................... 53
Descendents of Willheim Waggoner and Anna Elizabeth Wagnerin 63
Descendents of Thomas Davis... 67
Descendents of John Young and Emily B. Mills 75
Descendents of Jacob Mills and Mary Shepherd 81
Descendents of Thomas Shepherd and Catherine Palmer...................................... 91
Descendents of William Wright and Mary DeCoursey 93
Descendents of James Green and Elizabeth Tapp 101
Descendents of William and Elinder Tapptico 111
Descendents of Andrew Bourne and Christian Price.. 119
Descendents of Henry Johnson and Mary Taliaffero.. 123
Descendents of Robert Taliaferro and Katherine Dedman 125
Descendents of Henry Newby and Mary Pollard... 127
Descendents of William McKinley and Tamara Brown 131
Descendents of John Aplin and Hannah Paine 139
Descendents of Stephen Paine, Sr. and Neele Rose Adcocke............................... 149
Descendents of Gregory Belcher and Catherine Allcock 155
Descendents of Edward Rainsford and Elizabeth Dillee 161
Descendents of William Owen and Elizabeth Davies... 167
Descendents of Nicholas Arnold and Alice Gulley 171
Descendents of Edward Smith.. 179
Descendents of James Barker and Barbara Dungan 181
Descendents of Rev. Pardon Elisha Tillinghast and Lydia Masters Taber 183
Descendents of Philip Taber and Lydia Masters 187
Descendents of John Masters and Jane Cox 191
Descendents of Zachariah Rhodes and Joanna Arnold... 193
Descendents of Richard and Mary Carder 197
Descendents of John and Elizabeth Gray.. 199
Descendents of William Turpin and Catharine Jenckes 203
Descendents of Thomas and Grace Arnold... 207
Descendents of George Parkhurst and Phebe Leete.. 211
Descendents of Roger Burlingame and and Mary Elizabeth Barlingstone 215
Descendents of Thomas Angell and Alice Ashton 219

Descendents of Joseph Jenckes and Joan Hearn..225
Descendents of Henry Ballard and Elizabeth Townsend..231
Descendents of Rev. Chaddus Browne and Elizabeth Sharparowe 233
Descendents of Robert Holmes and Katherine Johnson 237

Descendents of James and Barbara Ann Stichter..245
Descendents of James Brumfield and Patience Sutton 253
Descendents of William V. Atkinson and Elizabeth Parker 265
Descendents of Dr. Richard Parker and Mary Perkins 271
Descendents of William Lucas and Ann Scarbouch...275
Descendents of Stephen Bartram and Elizabeth Swearingen...................................279
Descendents of John Jacob and Ana-Eva Stehli, Sr..281
Descendents of Michael Yeasley and Catherine Welsh Norfsenger Entler 287
Descendents of Elias Hinds and Mary Polly Bailey 289

Descendents of George Abel and Elizabeth Rockerfeller West...............................291
Descendents of Richard Adam Steele and Rebecca Jane Makemie........................295

Descendents of Samuel and Esther Harris...303
Descendents of Jacob and Christina Haas 317
Descendents of Thomas Phillips and Mary Philipps 321
Descendents of Johann Gottfried Wilkins and Christina Nonemacher...................327
Descendents of Daniel and Anna Griffith..329
Descendents of Jacob Reily and Sally Tilton 331
Descendents of John Tilton and Mary Pearsall...333
Descendents of Henry Brazier and Susan Spicer..337
Descendents of Charles Carter and Rachel Sharp...339
Descendents of Thomas Wilson and Mary Riley..343
Descendents of Johann Uhrich Kotterman and Agnes Katherine Kuhlewein.........349
Descendents of Enoch and Emetine Miller..353
Descendents of George H. Juniper 355
Descendents of William Rankin and Jane Steen...359
Descendents of John McGee and Mary E. Woods..365

List of Military Service 369

Our Famous American Cousins – Presidents of the United States of America 376
Our Famous American Cousins – Others 378

Robert Taliaferro Relationship to President George Washington...........................381
Robert Taliaferro Relationship to President Thomas Jefferson 382

Sources 383

Index by Names...387

List of Photos, Illustrations, and Charts

Homer and Micky Comisford	iii
History of Hebron, Ohio	3
Streets of Hebron, Ohio in the early 1900's	5
Tin plate photo of Andrew Thomas Comisford	6
Joseph Paris Comisford	8
Charles Brants Comisford	11
Charles Brants Comisford – Inmate #1932, Nevada State Prison Inmate Photo, 1917	13
William Flavia Comisford	15
Sadie Comisford, 1913	17
Perry Paris Comisford	17
Jessie Helen (Davis) Comisford	18
Jessie Helen, Flavia, Charley, Homer, and Perry Comisford	19
Charles Benne Comisford	20
Francis Flavia Comisford	21
Elizabeth, Helen, Flavia, and Tommy Comisford	22
Homer Whitcome Comisford	22
Mildred Ada (McKinley) Comisford	23
Homer and Elizabeth (Binckley) Comisford	26
William Davis and Josephine Theresa (Stichter) Comisford	27
The Comisford Boys	32
The first Old Harmony Church	33
Sarah (Lantz) Tygard	35
Residence of Eagon B. Tygard, 1875	36
Flavius J. Tygard, Leavenworth Penitentiary Photo	38
Sampson Eagon Inn in Staunton, Virginia	44
Jean Bonnet Tavern in Bedford, Pennsylvania	56
Lewis Bonnett, Frontiersman and Indian Fighter	58
Fort Henry	59
Peter Waggoner	65
Marcus Whitcome Davis, 1864	68
Jane Emily (Young) Davis	69
Hebron High School – Class of 1899	72
Orriel (Young) Pugh	76
Homer Comisford and Mary Eleanor House	79
Lemuel Wright and his daughter Sarah, 1897	98
Willie, Josie, Chloe and Loren Smith	99
James Tapp	117
Pearl Navada (Wright) Abel	136
Charles Ellsworth Abel	136
Abel family photo	138
William Henry Aplin	146
Aplin family photo	146
Chart of General Douglas MacArthur	157
Chart of Benedict Arnold	172
Chart of King Edward I	184
Chart of President Franklin Delano Roosevelt	189

Chart of President George Herbert Walker Bush 195
Chart of President George Walker Bush 195
Chart of Clara Barton 212
The "Pine Tree Shilling" 226
Chart of President Abraham Lincoln 238
William Adam Stichter 246
Mary Connors Malone 246
Joseph T. Stichter 247
Margaretta Genevieve Stichter 248
William Joseph Stichter 249
Inez Marie (Broomfield) Stichter 250
Angelene (Brumfield) Carroll 259
Brumfield family photo 263
William Lewis Hinds 290
George Thomas Abel, David Wesley Abel, and Nancy Rozella (Abel) Hodder 293
William Haines Lytle 296
Lydia J. Harris 309
Olaf and Laura E. (Harris) Wetterholm 310
Arthur and Flora C. (Carter) Harris 312
Arthur Eugene Harris 312
Norma Bertene Juniper 313
The Arthur and Norma Harris Family Children 316
Samuel Jones Philipps 325
Bert C. and Mary S. (Wilson) Carter 341
Pearl and Daisy Mae (Rankin) Juniper 357

Pearl Juniper, William J. Stichter, Gary E. Harris, William D. Comisford,
Thomas E. Harris, 3rd Ohio Volunteer Infantry Reunion at Ohio State House 374

Robert Comisford, Bruce Smith, William J. Stichter, Steven C. Comisford,
Thomas P. Comisford, Robert C. Comisford, Arthur Harris,
William J. Stichter, Jr., Mark A. Comisford, Homer P. Comisford,
Arhur E. Harris, William H. Lytle 375

President George Washington 376
President Thomas Jefferson 376
President Abraham Lincoln 376
President William McKinley 376
President Theodore Roosevelt 377
President Franklin Delano Roosevelt 377
President George Herbert Walker Bush 377
President George Walker Bush 377
Governor Benedict Arnold 378
Benedict Arnold 378
Daniel Boone 378
Lewis Wetzel 379
General William H. Lyle 379
Clarissa Harlowe Barton 379
Wyatt Berry Sapp Earp 380
General of the Army Douglas McArthur 380

Foreword

Having been a Certified Public Accountant (a "CPA") and an auditor for over twenty years, I've always enjoyed digging for information. Thus, when I started the project of tracing back my genealogy, it wasn't much different than jumping into someone's accounting records. It just happened to be in this case, there were a lot of different records, and they were spread out all over the country, in county courthouses, public libraries, cemeteries, family bibles and church records, published records, and most recently, the internet (a valuable resource for sharing information.)

When I started the project, I soon realized I knew very little about my family. Like most people, I had in my earlier years the opportunity to ask older members of the family about my forebears but neglected to do so. Fortunately, my grandmother provided me with a good starting point.

It was a real challenge and very rewarding to be able to reconstruct the past. Genealogy can be fascinating and useful when it serves to stimulate the understanding of history. It's not just when was somebody born or when did they die, it's much, much more. It's understanding why one would leave the comforts and security of civilization to start fresh in a new world, or venture into the wilderness, or fight to protect one's rights or the rights of another.

This book attempts to trace the lineage of families back to when the family ventured to the American Colonies and in some cases, why they did so. What they did and how did their labors and their lives contribute in building our American History? There were members of the Massachusetts Bay Company, the Virginia Company, Quakers, Huguenots, Irish Catholics – all trying to escape religious persecution and find religious freedoms in the American Colonies.

It's taken sometime to get to this point (almost twenty years since I started), but I have finally put together the story for others to read now and in the future.

Sunbury, Ohio 2006
William D. Comisford, Jr.

Preface

When I took over this project in the late 1980's, my grandfather had already passed away and my grandmother was in failing health. She and I would often talk for hours, she telling me stories and showing me photo after photo of family members, events and places. She seemed to know just everything about our family, yet there were family lines, secrets, mysteries and stories that she still was unable to uncover or tell.

In my attempt to expand her efforts, I have tried to research as many family lines as possible. Each has added an important element as to who we are. I have also had the benefit of the Internet, which has taken researching genealogy to another level. The ease of access to the researchof others has allowed me to create a more comprehensive record of people, places and events.

Our immigration is one from poverty and religious persecution and a real desire for the American Dream. Life and times in early America was not easy, and to be a pioneer in such times was even more hazardous to one's health. Survival during such times depended on working together and at times, just being lucky.

I want to thank everyone that has assisted me or who has contributed to this history of my family, especially my wife, Susan. She has endured many a visit to old cemeteries, searching for headstones, visits to courthouses, libraries, and just countless hours of researching.

While there may be mistakes, I have attempted to write this book to give a true account of the people, places and events. I hope that you can enjoy the reading of this book as much as I have enjoyed compiling it.

Introduction

History often begins at a point in time when something significant happens. In the case of the Comisford Family this took place over 170 years ago, with the marriage of a young couple and a voyage across a large ocean. A new era began in the life of a new family. The marriage of Paris Patrick Comisford to Rosette Helene Gaffney took on new meaning when the day following their wedding they boarded a ship for a long voyage across the Atlantic Ocean to the new Americas. From Ireland to the new Americas was quite an adventure for anyone, let alone a couple of newly-weds.

During the voyage the family grew by one. With their arrival in New York City and travels up the Hudson River to the fertile farming country of Washington County, New York, their small family began to grow, as that of a young country. With the dream of someday owning and farming their own property, the family pulled up stakes and headed off for the Historic Crossroads of Ohio. Here they acquired farmland in Hebron, Ohio and settled down to raise their family.

While many years have now passed by and several generations have passed on, the Comisford Family has grown, and while some have moved on, most still call Licking County and Central Ohio

HOME

In expanding the search of our ancestors, the story seems the same for all – a journey to America to escape religious persecution, to escape poverty, and/or to open up new opportunities. The need for religious freedom was a strong one and to acquire one's own land was often only a dream.

One could hardly imagine the hardships and the sacrifices they would have to make. Many would not make it because of disease or illness on the voyage to America or due to the tough conditions when they arrived. Others would lose their lives at the hands of the American Indians and/or protecting their new found freedom. Was the risk worth it?

We Hope So!

Across the vast ocean, over the mountains – they still pushed on. They endured the hardships and often the unknown to find a better life, for them and their families.

As proud Americans, ancestors of this Comisford family have helped to blaze the way into the frontier and have helped preserve the American way of life through their participation in the many skirmishes, battles, and even the wars this young country has endured. In the Colonial battles with Indians, the French and Indian War, the American Revolutionary War, the War of 1812, The War with Mexico, the American Civil War, the Spanish American War, World War I, World War II, the Korean War and the Vietnam War our family has taken up arms.

The Comisford family can lay claim to eight (8) United States of America Presidents as cousins.

George Washington
Thomas Jefferson
Abraham Lincoln
William McKinley
Theodore Roosevelt
Franklin Delano Roosevelt
George Herbert Walker Bush
George Walker Bush

We established the "iron-works", the first "foundry and forge" in the American Colonies, along with the first patent and the dies for minting coins.

We were the famous Indian scouts Daniel Boone and Lewis Wetzel, blazing the trail across the Appalachian Mountains into the Ohio River Valley and the Northwest Territory.

We were on a Civil War battlefield fighting to preserve the Union. At the same time, we were attending to the wounded with the "Angel of the Battlefield."

We were at the OK Corral – defending freedom and the law in a rapidly growing country.

Through the recording of this history, we can all look back on our heritage and remember those that ventured forth, their travels through time, their good times and their bad times. We do this so that our grandchildren and their children will understand their heritage and know those that came before.

To those – We'll Always Remember.

Descendents of Paris Patrick Comisford and Rosette Helene Gaffney

First Generation

1. Paris Patrick Comisford (1815 – 1880) - Ireland may well have been the most miserable country on the face of the earth during the early nineteenth century — especially for a Catholic. The Protestants, even though they represented less than a fourth of the total population, controlled both the church and the government. Of the 4.5 million people living in Ireland in 1800, 3.15 million were Catholic, and ninety-nine percent of all Catholics were either peasants or common laborers. Impoverished and illiterate, they received harsh treatment from their Protestant landlords who subjected them to intolerable rents. While they had no political rights whatsoever, the heavy burdens of tithing and taxation fell upon them nevertheless. And with each passing year, the plight of the Catholics steadily worsened. The population of the country was increasing at an alarming rate. In 1700, there were only 1.25 million people on the island. In one-hundred years, that number quadrupled, and by 1830 the population was near 8 million. With such a high population density, the already wretched condition of the Catholic peasant became even more lamentable. What little cultivable land there was, had to be divided. While the aristocratic Protestant enjoyed an estate of several hundred acres, the peasant was forced to eke out a living on three or four acres, usually in a little hut or cabin (often called a "smoking dunghill"). This was all one could ever hope for.

Emigration to the new Americas was only a dream for many a poor Catholic. The fare for the voyage was often between £4 and £10 per person, way to much for a poor Catholic. In 1827 the British government repealed all restrictions on emigration, and fares dropped to £2 to £3 per person. Still a lot, but this was a little easier to save for.

Paris Patrick Comisford was the son of a poor Catholic agricultural laborer growing up during this difficult time in Ireland. Born on August 13, 1815 in County of Clare, Ireland, the future for young Paris was not promising. The dream of reaching the "promised land" became a reality when the day after his wedding to Rosette Helene Gaffney in 1835, he and his new bride, set sail for the New

World - America. They severed the roots of their Irish heritage in order to plant fresh seeds of hope in new soil.

After a long voyage, they arrived in the Bay of New York City, America. During the long voyage, Rosa, as Paris called her, became pregnant for their first child and after arriving in New York City they became the proud parents of Catherine Ann. They lived for a while in New York City, Paris as a laborer.

Soon they were to follow the Hudson River north to a small farming community in Washington County, New York called Argyle. Argyle was settled in the early 1800's by the Highland Scotsmen, Covenanter Presbyterians. The nearby towns of Hebron and Salem were settled by Protestant Irish of Scotch race. The first Catholic Church in the County was established in 1830. As in Ireland, the religious tension in this area was very intense.

While in Argyle, they became the parents of a son, Andrew Thomas on August 19, 1839 and another daughter, Mary in May 1840. In Argyle they participated for the first time in the taking of the US Census during June of 1840. The family was soon to be lured away from Argyle to the "Historic Crossroads of Ohio", a small town at the crossroads of the Ohio and Erie Canal and the National Road, Hebron, Ohio. The Ohio and Erie Canal connected Lake Erie at Cleveland, Ohio to the Ohio River at Portsmouth, Ohio and was constructed through Hebron in 1827 - 1828. The National Road, connecting Cumberland, Maryland with Vandalia, Illinois, just east of St. Louis, was completed in 1834. This was the only crossing of the canal and the road and it gave Hebron the opportunity to become the main center of business and industry for the entire area. Thus, from Argyle, they headed off in covered wagon west towards Buffalo, New York, where they then followed the lake (Lake Erie) towards Cleveland, Ohio. From Cleveland, the family travel along the Ohio and Erie Canal into Licking County and Newark, Ohio. After spending several years in Newark, on October 15, 1849, Paris and Rosa finally acquired their own home, a farm located in Hebron, along Eighth Street, along the Ohio-Erie Canal and the National Road (Cumberland Road). They acquired the property from David and Samuel Groves by deeds of October 4, 1849 and November 22, 1850. Here, they would spend the rest of their lives. The farm consisted of one hundred and fifty-six acres, 86 acres of which were within the corporation limits of Hebron, the farmhouse lying north of the village on the refugee line. The family grew cereals best adapted to the soil and climate and in addition raised some stock, including cattle, sheep

History of Hebron, Ohio
Chartered in 1835

In its beginning, Hebron was one of the most well-known villages in the state because of its connection with two principal canals and a major roadway. Known as the "Historic Crossroads of Ohio," Hebron was founded in 1827, by John W. Smith. The name Hebron means refuge and the early settlers may have hoped it would be just that. In the Bible, the city of Hebron was King David's capital city. People thought John Smith was crazy when he began to stake out lots for the village because most of it was swampland and not really suitable for buildings. But Smith realized its potential as a major canal shipping point. Hebron earned the tag "Historic Crossroads of Ohio" because both the Ohio and the Erie Canals and the National Road crossed within its borders. The Ohio Canal, connecting Lake Erie at Cleveland with the Ohio River at Portsmouth, was constructed through Hebron in 1827 - 1828. The first canal boat which ran on the waters of the Ohio Canal was built in Hebron and was christened on July 4, 1828. It was called the Licking Summit. Unfortunately, the boat was found to be too wide to pass through the locks and had to be returned to the turning basin in Hebron, where it was used for sometime as a saloon and house of ill repute before it eventually rotted away. The National Road, connecting Cumberland, Maryland, with Vandalia, Illinois just east of St. Louis, was completed through Hebron in 1834. This was the only crossing of the canal and road in Ohio and provided Hebron the opportunity to become the main center of business and industry for the entire area. Hebron thus became a major processing and distribution point for meat, grain and in its early days, whiskey. At the height of this industry boom, Hebron had five warehouses, most of which were four or five stories high and two distilleries for making whiskey, a major necessity for the early settlers. also had several taverns, the most famous being the Scab Tavern, named because parts of the plaster on the outside had fallen off, and the Diamond Queen, which was the first to cater to the stagecoaches and Ohio Canal traffic. With its warehouses, slaughterhouses, stagecoach stops, tannery, distilleries and numerous stores, Hebron grew by leaps and bounds and in just eight years, it was incorporated and granted a charter by the State of Ohio in 1835. It had and elected major and village council. Hebron was soon to have four general stores, four grocery stores which also sold drugs and handled the mail, two telegraph operators, two notary publics, and six doctors. In 1870 - 1873 plans were made and completed for a new school building on North High Street. There were three grade school rooms and the high school. School census in 1888 showed that there were 163 pupils registered. The demise of Hebron as a major industrial city came with the advent of the railroad through Hebron in 1880. Connecting the Southern Ohio coal fields with the Great Lakes, the railroad brought faster travel to the area and the decline of the canal.

and hogs.

During this time, Hebron was a thriving town, consisting of four general stores, four grocery stores, which also sold drugs and handled the mail, five warehouses, most of them four or five stories high, two distilleries, making whiskey which was shipped by canal boats, several slaughterhouses, a stagecoach stop, and a tannery.

While in Ohio, the family grew. Ellen July was born on March 5, 1845, Patrick Henry on April 2, 1848, an infant son born in May 1850 who passed away shortly after birth, Joseph and Margaret (twins) in August 1852, and Clara in May 1854.

Paris and the family were part of the founders of the St. Francis de Sales Catholic Church in Newark, Ohio. The family rented a pew for parishioners at the church located in the English, Side of B.V.M. After the death of Rosa a beautiful stained glass window was donated in her memory.

After a long and lingering illness, Paris departed this life on the morning of May 27, 1880 at the age of 63. The following was written in The Newark Advocate on Thursday, May 28, 1880:

> *"P. P. Comisford, Esq., a well-known and highly respected farmer living near Hebron, this county, died on Wednesday morning, after a long and lingering illness. He was one of he oldest citizens of the community in which he lived."*

He was buried in Mt. Calvary Cemetery, south of Newark on State Route 13, within the Comisford family plot. Originally, the plot was enclosed with steel post and a chain fence, but through the years, both have disappeared.

After Paris passed away, Rosa lived on the farm with her son Joseph until she passed away on September 21, 1893. Rosa was also buried in Mt. Calvary Cemetery.

Children of Paris Patrick Comisford and Rosette Helene Gaffney:

+ 2.   i.   Catherine Ann Comisford (1836 – 1869);
+ 3.   ii.   Andrew Thomas Comisford (1839 – 1882);
+ 4.   iii.   Mary M. Comisford (1843 – 1922);
   5.   iv.   Ellen July Comisford (1845 – 1880) - Ellen was born shortly after the family's arrival to Ohio on March 5, 1845 and was one of the early baptismals at St. Francis de Sales Church, Newark, Ohio. She married Truman Herman Haynes, who was born in 1841. Together they lived on South Second Street in Newark, Ohio and had no children. Ellen passed away on December 3, 1880 and is buried in Mt. Calvary Cemetery, Newark, Ohio. Truman died January 28, 1893 of a heart attack;
+ 6.   v.   Patrick Henry Comisford (1848 – 1915);
   7.   vi.   An infant son born in May 1850 who passed away shortly after birth;
+ 8.   vii.   Joseph Paris Comisford (twin) (1853 – 1925);

| + | 9. | viii. | Margaret Comisford (twin) (1853 – 1904); and |
| + | 10. | ix. | Clara Comisford (1854 – 1887). |

Streets of Hebron, Ohio in the early 1900's

Second Generation

2. Catherine Ann Comisford (1836 – 1869) - Catherine Ann Comisford was conceived by Paris and Rosa on board the ship from Ireland to America and born sometime in 1836 while the family was in New York City. Catherine married Joannem 'John' Malay on October 15, 1868. Her sister, Mary was the maid of honor for the wedding, which took place at St. Francis de Sales Church in Newark, Ohio. John came to America around 1851 from Ireland and settled in Mt. Vernon, Knox County, Ohio. He was a section foreman for the B & O Railroad. Catherine passed away shortly after her wedding in 1869 and is buried in Mt. Calvary Cemetery. John would remarry and live at Summit Station, where he would pass away on June 30, 1901. He is buried in St. Joseph's Cemetery in Newark, Ohio.

3. Andrew Thomas Comisford (1839 – 1882) - Andrew Thomas Comisford was born August 19, 1839 in New York, the oldest son of Paris Patrick Comisford and Rosette Helene Gaffney. Andy, as he was known, married Melissa Tygard of Hebron, Ohio on November 6, 1867. They were married by Elder George. N. Tussing, a Primitive Baptist minister who rode the circuit and served many congregations in the Central Ohio area.

Melissa was born May 21, 1837 in Blacksville, in the western portion of Virginia, the daughter of Eagon Blackburn, and Sarah Elizabeth (Lantz) Tygard.

The Tygard family moved to Ohio in 1867 and lived on a farm just east of the Comisford family farm, where the Ohio Canal passed through heading north toward Newark. ndy and Melissa (often called "Lizzie") took up residences north of Hebron and Andy became a farmer, while Lizzie was a housekeeper. Over time, Andy began to acquire various properties: property from Ira Goodwin on August 9, 1873; 117.5 acres from Jacob and Rebecca Beaver on December 23, 1881; and inlots #316 and #317 in the Village of Hebron from William and Jane Priest on January 6, 1882.

Andrew Thomas Comisford

As reported in the Columbus Dispatch on August 1, 1882,

> "A small fire occurred in the north part of the Town of Hebron last Sunday, originating in the dwelling owned by A.T. Comisford. The Fire Department was called out and the flames were quickly extinguished before much damage was done. The fire originated from an imperfect flue."

Both Andy and Lizzie passed away while in their prime, A.T. of typhoid pneumonia at the young age of 43 on December 11, 1882 and Lizzie of typhoid fever and a paralytic stroke at the age of 48 on October 14, 1885. Both are buried in Hebron Cemetery, Hebron, Ohio.

There early deaths forced their boys to be on their own very early in their lives. They lived among relatives and worked wherever they could, till they were old enough to be on their own.

Children of Andrew Thomas Comisford and Melissa Tygard:
- 11. i. an infant daughter born and died on September 11, 1868;
- + 12. ii. Charles Brants Comisford (1870 – Unknown);
- + 13. iii. William Flavia Comisford (1873 – 1951); and
- + 14. iv. Perry Paris Comisford (1875 – 1960).

4. Mary M. Comisford (1843 – 1922) - Mary M. Comisford was born sometime in 1843 in New York, just prior to the family's move to Ohio. She married Isaac Green, the son of Theodore Green and Elizabeth Malone, both born in Maine, in 1876 in Hebron, Ohio. Isaac was born April 15, 1845. Isaac worked for the Post office in Hebron as Postmaster and became a State of Ohio Representative.

Mary was a member of the Roman Catholic Church in Newark. In their later years they moved to Jersey in Licking Township. Mary passed away March 10, 1922 at the age of 79 from cancer of the cervix of uterus and is buried in Mt. Calvary Cemetery.

Children of Isaac Green and Mary M. Comisford:
- + 15. i. Murlie Rosa Green (1877 – Unknown); and
- 16. ii. Joseph 'Josie' Green, born July 22, 1883 and baptized September 20, 1883.

6. Patrick Henry Comisford (1848 – 1915) - Patrick Henry Comisford was born on April 2, 1848 in Newark, Ohio. Henry married Mary O'Day, the daughter of Parker and Julia O'Day, on July 3, 1877. They were married by Probate Judge, George Grass of Newark, Ohio. Eagon B. and Sarah Tygard were the witnesses at their wedding. Mary was born on November 14, 1852 in Fairfield County, Ohio. They settled near Hebron, where Henry was a farmer.

It was reported in the Newark Weekly Advocate on July 16, 1885, *"A disgraceful fight between Jim Richards and Henry Comisford occurred last Saturday night arising from Comisford's hogs playing havoc in Richard's garden and resulting in a banged up countenance for both."*

Several years later it was reported in the Newark Daily Advocate on February 16, 1899, *"Henry Comisford froze his feet last Friday while watching a game of pool at George Smith's room."*

Mary passed away on November 18, 1915, and Henry passed away less than two weeks later on November 29, 1915. They are both buried near Kirkersville, Licking County, Ohio.

Children of Patrick Henry Comisford and Mary O'Day:
- 17. i. Joseph Comisford (twin) (1879 – 1879) – Joseph was born on July 15, 1879 and died as an infant;
- 18. ii. Paris P. Comisford (twin) (1879 – Unknown) – Paris was born on July 15, 1879;
- + 19. iii. Alisha Augusta Comisford (1881 – 1964);
- 20. iv. Julia Rosealie Comisford (1885 – Unknown) - Julia was born on October 6, 1885. Julia was injured and recovered from injuries she sustained in the train wreck that her sister Clara was killed in;
- 21. v. Clara Comisford (twin) (1887 – 1918) - Clara was born on August 25, 1887. Clara married George Solinger. Clara was killed on August 18, 1918, after jumping from their stalled automobile on the railroad tracks on Williams Street in Newark, Ohio, from being struck by a fast moving train; and
- 22. vi. Cora Comisford (twin) (1887 – Unknown) – Cora was born on August 25, 1887.

8. Joseph Paris Comisford (1853 – 1925) - Joseph Paris Comisford, a twin with Margaret, was born in August of 1853 on the family farm in Hebron. Joseph never married and remained on the family farm taking care of his mother Rosa until she died in 1893.

In December of 1886 Joseph was nursed back to health by his mother, Rosa, from a serious bout with typhoid fever. This was the year there was a typhoid epidemic in Licking County.

While never married it was reported in the Newark Daily Advocate on January 3, 1896,

Joseph Paris Comisford

"Our society people were very much surprised to see in the papers, the marriage license of Mr. Joe Comisford and Miss Oldaker, as they are well known here, their many friends join in wishing them a long life of bliss."

Aside from operating the family farm, Joseph was one of the original promoters of the Hebron Banking Company and was an original Director of the Bank.

Joe was the victim of a runaway on his way to town one day as reported in the Newark Daily Advocate on February 10, 1897,

> *"Quite an exciting runaway occurred here Tuesday. Joseph Comisford came to town with two horses attached to a big sled. The horses frightened and started to run, dragging Jos. quite a distance. They finally broke loose and ran west as far as the railroad, where they were captured. Fortunately Jos. escaped with a few scratches."*

In 1909, a biography of Joseph was published in the "1909 Centennial History of the City of Newark and Licking County Ohio" by E.M.P. Brister.

Joseph lived to the age of 71, passing away on March 9, 1925, while living at 126 W. Church Street in Newark, Ohio, the home of his nieces, Marie and Lillian Hickey. He is buried in Mt. Calvary Cemetery. Upon his death, he gave most of his property and possessions to his nieces: Marie, Lillian and Florence Hickey, which included stock in the Hebron Banking Company, stock in the Columbus Chain Company and the original family farm.

9. Margaret Comisford (1853 – 1904) - Margaret 'Maggie' Comisford, a twin with Joseph, was born in August of 1853 on the family farm in Hebron. Maggie remained on the family farm taking care of her mother Rosa until she married Edward Hickey of Clay Lick on March 11, 1886. Edward was a very successful retail merchant in Licking County, born in the County of Clare, Ireland on August 18, 1838, the son of Thomas and Hanoro (Hogan) Hickey.

Several years after her brother, A.T. had died of typhoid pneumonia, it was reported in the Columbus Dispatch on April 8, 1885, *"Maggie Comisford is reported dangerously sick with typhoid fever."* She recovered.

Maggie passed away on October 26, 1904, while Edward passed away on April 2, 1924. Maggie and Edward, along with their son, Karl, are buried in Mt. Calvary Cemetery, south of Newark, Ohio. Marie and Lillian were never married and both are buried in St. Josephs Cemetery, north of Newark, Ohio on State Route 13.

Children of Edward Hickey and Margaret Comisford:
- 23. i. Karl Hickey (Unknown – 1942) – Karl is buried in Mt. Calvary Cemetery;
- 24. ii. Marie Hickey (1894 – 1975) – Marie was born on March 4, 1894. She never married, lived with her sister, Lillian, and passed away on November 18, 1975 at 126 West Church Street, Newark, Ohio. She is buried in St. Joseph's Cemetery; and
- 25. iii. Lillian Hickey (1899 – 1982) – Lillian was born in 1899 and died January 1, 1982. She is buried in St. Joseph's Cemetery.

10. Clara Comisford (1854 – 1887) - Clara Comisford, the last child of Paris and Rosa, was born on May 24, 1854 on the family farm in Hebron. Clara married George C. Davy, a young dry goods clerk on January 29, 1878. George was the son of William C. Davy and Sarah J. Allan. George and Clara took up residence in Shawnee in Perry County where they raised their children.

Clara passed away on April 3, 1887 and is buried in Mt. Calvary Cemetery south of Newark, Ohio. George moved the family to Kirkersville, where his mother, Sarah Davy, moved in with the family. George, Nellie, Clara Mae, and Sarah are all buried in the Kirkersville Cemetery off of the National Trail Road, Route 40.

Children of George C. Davy and Clara Comisford:
- 26. i. Nellie A. Davy (1878 – Unknown) – Nellie was baptized December 30, 1878 at St. Francis de Sales Church, Newark, Ohio, and died Mary 3, 1941 and is buried in Kirkersville Cemetery;
- 27. ii. Clara Mae Davy (1884 – Unknown) – Clara was born on May 24, 1884, baptized July 1, 1884, and died on July 7, 1939 and is buried in Kirkersville Cemetery; and
- 28. iii. Florence Davy (1887 – 1981) – Florence was born March 8, 1887 at Shawnee, Ohio, who passed away in March of 1981.

Third Generation

12. Charles Brants Comisford (1870 – Unknown) - Charles Brants Comisford, 'Uncle Charley' was born July 14, 1870 in Hebron, Ohio. The oldest son of Andrew Thomas and Melissa (Tygard) Comisford, he was forced to help care for his younger brothers when both parents passed away, while the boys were very young.

Charley moved around quite a bit, living in Jersey for awhile, then to Alexandria, until finally he took off for the Wild West. Sometime around 1894, Charley headed out for Texas where he stayed until returning home on January 20, 1896. After a short stay, on March 30, 1896, he and his brother Perry took off for fame and fortune in the goldfields of Cripple Creek, Colorado, where they intended to make their future home. While Charley remained in Colorado, Perry returned to Ohio for good.

Charles Brants Comisford

In 1903, Charley was heard from in Poland, Arizona, County of Yavapal, Territory of Arizona. Several times he wrote home for someone to send him money. When none was sent, he was never heard from again. Last known whereabouts, from a postcard, was in Goldfield, Nevada in 1911.

It was later discovered in a Nevada State newspaper, that Charley had been involved in killing, a hold-up man:

> "Mason, NV, July 7, 1913 – A hold-up man was killed at Ludwig under circumstances that are most peculiar, says the Mason Valley News. It seems that after making a successful hold-up the robber was killed by his victim, yet the fact the authorities have declined to pass up the case is an indication that the survivor's explanation of the fight to death is not satisfactory to them.

> Roy Coats, Paul Arents, B.H. Silverman and others were partial witnesses. They heard cries for help about half way between Ludwig and Morningstar, and on arriving at the scene found "Shorty" Comisford lying on the body of a man chocking him. The cries for help were coming from Comisford, who explained he feared to let go for fear the man would get up and kill him. Upon examination the man was found to be dead, with his skull crushed and cut in a horrible manner.
> Comisford explained that he had been held up and made to deliver by the dead man, that the robber then turned and started down the hill, whereupon, Comisford said he grabbed a heavy rock and smashed the hold-up man's head, afterwards holding him and chocking him while screaming for help.
> The dead man's head showed the effect of numerous blows. He had a pocketbook and watch belonging to Comisford, also a face mask.
> The dead man was unidentified by name at last report.
> Comisford is being held awaiting an examination into the case."

Charley was subsequently released and not charged.

It was later found out, that while a miner in Tonopah, Nevada, Charley was involved in an incident where he killed another man. He was charged and convicted of murder in the second degree. On appeal in the Fifth Judicial District Court, Nye County, Nevada in October of 1917, the conviction was reversed and remanded. In the second trial Charley was found guilty of manslaughter and sentenced to 2 to 10 years in the State penitentiary in Carson City, Nevada.

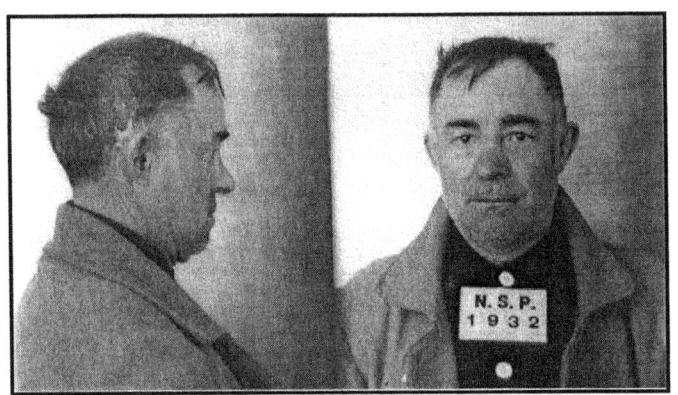

Charles Brants Comisford
Inmate #'s 1932 (1916 NSP-0034) and 2167 (1919 NSP-0041)
Nevada State Prison Inmate Photo, 1917

    According to the story and the testimony as reported by J.A. Sanders, District Attorney of the County of Nye, State of Nevada, *"... that the deceased E.W. Riley on the 12th day of August, 1916, opened and started in the saloon business, in the place known and called the Blue Ribbon Saloon, in the Town of Tonopah, Nye County, Nevada. That the defendant (Charley Comisford) entered the said saloon in the early part of the evening of August 12th, 1916 and had several drinks with the different parties who came into the saloon. Among those who entered were Lilly Turner, Lilly Hayden, Joe Flores and Charles Brickman. They bought some drinks at the bar and the defendant drank with them and about that time the defendant and Lilly Hayden had a short conversation and the defendant then walked to the other end of the bar where a man by the name of Buchanon was standing and defendant stated to Buchanon several times that if Lilly Hayden also known as fighting Bill bawled him out like she did others that he would cut her throat and also cut her guts out.*

    The two women and the two men, Flores and Brickman, and Riley went up stairs where some wine was purchased and the defendant remained down stairs. Harry Grier and some other men came into the saloon while the other bunch were up stairs and Grier bought a drink and then asked to see Riley and one of the bartenders went up stairs and called Riley and he came down, and had a drink at the bar. It appeared that the defendant while not quarrelsome was butting into the conversations that were being held by the different customers of the place and Riley asked him several times to refrain from doing so and to stay at the other end of the bar and drink all that he wanted but not to butt in. Finally Riley walked over to the defendant and gently and quietly let him out of the saloon. About this time the bunch from up stairs came down and some more wine was being served and they were waiting for Riley to return when suddenly Riley fell in the door way and bleeding from a cut in his right groin. The defendant was seen standing at the door with the knife open in his hand, then he turned and ran down the street and Flores and another man followed him. When they got close to the defendant he pulled the knife and told them to stand back or he would cut them also. Jack Grant, the night officer then arrived on the scene and arrested the defendant and took the knife from him. Doctors arrived on the scene in less than two minutes from the time that Riley was cut but the femoral artery was severed and they could not save him on account of the great loss of blood.

Two witnesses Ableman and Mc Biff Wilson testified that they saw Riley and the defendant on the side walk and did not see any trouble but that when the deceased turned to go back into the saloon the defendant rushed after him and pushed Riley into the doorway.

A witness for the defendant by the name of Louie Mantell testified that he was standing across the street and when he first noticed Riley and the defendant they were standing near the edge of the sidewalk about three feet apart. He heard Riley call the defendant some names and then saw Riley hit the defendant, then turn and go towards the saloon and the defendant rushed up in back of him and struck Riley in the back. Riley also had a knife wound in the right hip. The defendant then ran down the street.

All of the testimony except that of the defendant's was to the effect that there was no trouble in the saloon but that of the men went out quietly. The defendant interposed the plea of self defense, saying that he had to use the knife to protect him self stating that the deceased had a hold of him and hitting him but all of the witnesses who saw anything of the trouble outside testified that Riley and defendant were not clinched."

Apparently, Charley wasn't the model inmate while spending time at the state prison. On August 11, 1921, Charley attempted suicide by cutting the veins in the bend of his right elbow.

On August 18, 1921 after being examined by Drs. A. Huffaker and Donald MacDean, Charley was found to be insane and was subsequently committed to the State Insane Asylum, the Nevada Hospital for Mental Diseases, Reno, Nevada. On August 28, 1921, Charley escaped, never to be heard from again.

13. **William Flavia Comisford (1873 – 1951)** - William Flavia Comisford was born August 11, 1873 in Hebron, Ohio, the second son of Andrew Thomas Comisford and Melissa Tygard. After the death of both of his parents, at the young age of 12, William and his brothers lived with family in the Hebron Area. In April of 1886, both he and his brother Charlie were down with the measles. Sometime in 1887, he and Charlie moved to Jersey because of work.

William married Miss Alice B Kirk, the accomplished daughter of Mr. and Mrs. Elijah Kirk of Hebron. They were quietly married at the home of the Rev. Benjamin Green on Sunday evening, October 21, 1894.

William Flavia Comisford

On February 6, 1896 it was reported in the Newark Daily Advocate,

> *"The foundation of the new office to be erected on the Rettkee property is now being laid. Wm. Comisford is hauling the material for the new building with four horses. He reports the roads very bad on top, but solid underneath."*

While living at 493 West Main Street in Newark, Ohio, William was employed as a train dispatcher for the Ohio Electric Railway.

As reported in the Newark Daily Advocate:

> *"William Comisford, boss of a gang of men on the gravel train on the C.B.L. & N. road, met with quite a serious accident Monday. While standing on the pilot of the car he slipped and fell. His foot was caught and he was dragged about 30 feet sustaining very serious injury. Dr. G.N. Brown was summoned and after attending his injuries he accompanied Mr. Comisford to his home in Newark. Mr. Comisford's foot was badly mashed and several toes were amputated."*

Alice died at age 38 on March 19, 1911. After Alice's death, William was remarried in 1927 to Marie Moses. They had no children together. William died on Christmas Day in 1951 and is buried in Hebron Cemetery, along with his son, Benjamin Rue, his daughter-in-law, Esther Comisford, and his daughter, Sadie, in the Comisford Family plot.

Children of William Flavia Comisford and Alice B. Kirk:
29. i. Benjamin Rue 'Bruce' Comisford (1897 - 1923) – Bruce was born April 5, 1897, married Bea Kains October 4, 1916, who died shortly afterwards on October 2, 1917, then married Esther M. Bieber, who passed away March 27, 1971, and he died January 20, 1923; and
30. ii. Sadie Comisford (1906 – 1922) – Sadie was born on March 17, 1906 and died of complication from pneumonia at 16 years of age on April 4, 1922.

Sadie Comisford, 1913

14. Perry Paris Comisford (1875 – 1960) - Perry Paris Comisford was born July 8, 1875, the youngest son of Andrew Thomas and Melissa (Tygard) Comisford, in Hebron, Ohio. At a very early age both his parents passed away. Perry was then raised by his older brothers Charles and William.

On Halloween, October 31, 1897, Perry was married to Jessie Helen Davis, the daughter of Marcus Whitcome and Jane Emily (Young) Davis. They were joined in marriage, by Elder J.J Van horn, V.D.M. in Hebron, Ohio. Jessie was born August 26, 1877 in Hebron, Ohio.

Perry Paris Comisford

Both Perry and Jessie attended the Hebron School, where in 1886 there were 41 students in the Primary Department, 42 in the Grammar School and 25 in High School. That same year they both participated in the closing exercises for the Hebron Public Schools, which took place on Saturday, June 12, 1886. Jessie recited *"Yesterday"*, while Perry recited *"Old Grimes"*. Jessie would go on to be the Valedictorian of her high school class. She had a gift for speaking, an elocutionist.

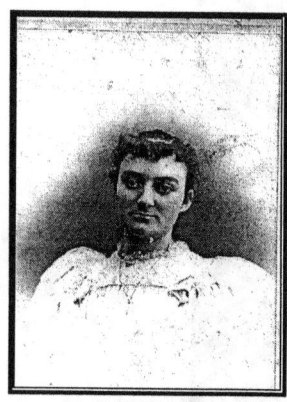

Jessie Helen Davis

During 1900, Perry worked for Spore. Soon though, Perry and Jessie would settle on a farm just east of Hebron, Ohio on the National Pike (old Route 40) just east of the river, where they raised three boys.

Perry became quite a land baron during the 1920's and lost nearly everything during or after the Great Depression of the 1930's. He had farms located at Outville Road, James Road, Burg Street behind Denison University, and Sharon Valley Road.

Short after Perry signed Jessie's name on a mortgage, which ultimately took her life savings, their relationship deteriorated. While they remained together, things were never the same.

Over the years, Jessie developed quite a collection of porcelain dolls and antiques. Perry was always a big teaser, didn't much like tomatoes, but loved his corn flakes. He also loved to grow flowers and did until the day he died.

After leaving the farms they lived on Sharon Valley Road prior to moving to 76 Western Avenue in 1948. Perry was always active. He would do chores for his neighbors and go after groceries for the elderly ones. One thing he didn't like to do was work on his car. He knew how to turn the switch, but any time he had a problem, he would call his youngest son, Homer. He also hated snakes with a passion. He was just plain scared to death of them.

After the mortgage incident, Jessie never trusted Perry. She would hide her money from him. She would pin it here, there and everywhere to hide it from him. Soon, Jessie also got to the point where she would not go anywhere, except to Mansfield to see her son Flavy. She would never leave the house.

Shortly after returning home from the hospital from a fall and broken hip, Jessie died of an apparent heart attach at the ripe old age of 83 on January 6, 1960. It's said that Perry died two weeks later on January 24, 1960 of a broken heart. They are both buried in Cedar Hill Cemetery, Newark, Ohio.

Children of Perry Paris Comisford and Jessie Helen Davis:
+ 31. i. Charles Benne Comisford (1899 – 1980);
+ 32. ii. Francis Flavia Comisford (1901 – 1979); and
+ 33. iii. Homer Whitcome Comisford (1904 – 1988).

Jessie Helen, Flavia, Charley, Homer, and Perry

15. Murlie Rosa Green (1877 – 1940) – Murlie Rosa Green was born September 15, 1877, the daughter of Isaac and Mary (Comisford) Green, and was baptized on October 24, 1877 at St. Francis de Sales Church in Newark, Ohio. She married Samuel Quinn Lecrone, the son of Isaac and Martha (Helson) Lecrone. Murlie passed away on September 2, 1940, while Samuel passed away March 31, 1943.

Children of Samuel Lecrone and Murlie Rosa Green:
34. i. Leo Bruce Lecrone (1899 – 1959) – Leo was born on February 11, 1899 and died in 1959; and
35. ii. Pauline M. Lecrone (1902 – Unknown).

19. Alisha Augusta Comisford (1881 – 1964) – Alisha Augusta 'Gussie' Comisford was born on November 2, 1881, the daughter of Patrick Henry and Mary F. (O'Day) Comisford. Gussie married Wesley Roshon, who was born in 1879. Gussie passed away November 10, 1964 and is buried in Kirkersville Cemetery. Wesley passed away in 1957.

Children of Wesley Roshon and Alisha Augusta Comisford:
36. i. Henry Roshon (1904 -1935); and
37. ii. Francis Austin Roshon (1905 – 1938) – Francis was born on September 1, 1905 and died March 14, 1938.

Fourth Generation

Charles Benne Comisford, 1972

31. Charles Benne Comisford (1899 – 1980) - Charles 'Chick' Benne Comisford was born March 28, 1899 in Hebron, Ohio, the eldest son of Perry Paris and Jessie Helen (Davis) Comisford. At the age of five, his family moved to a farm just east of Hebron on National Pike (old Route 40), where he attended the Ridgely Tract School, a one room school house. The teacher took turns boarding at her pupils homes. When he was eleven, the family moved to a farm on Route 16, just outside of Granville, Ohio, where he then attended Five Point School. In 1919, Charles became Granville's first motorcycle traffic officer. He received one dollar for each speeder he caught.

Charles first married Etta, prior to 1930 and had a daughter Patty. Then on March 23, 1935, Charles married Marcia "Margie" Muyette Abel, daughter of Charles Ellsworth and Pearl Navada (Wright) Abel. Marcia was born July 26, 1915 in Cambridge, Ohio. Orphaned at the age of eleven, Marcia was sent to live with her Aunt Zella and Uncle Ralph in Pomona, California in 1927. On returning to Ohio, she met Charles and together they had six children.

Much of Charles life was spent in road construction for himself and later for the City of Newark, the County and the State of Ohio. In 1948, the family moved to a farm near Alexandria, Ohio. Charles retired in 1964 from Westinghouse where he was employed as a security guard and boiler operator. Charles passed away July 29, 1980 and is buried in Cedar Hill Cemetery in Newark, Ohio. Margie passed away on January 24, 2003 in Pataskala, Ohio and is buried in Cedar Hill Cemetery.

Children of Charles Benne Comisford and Marcia Muyette Abel:

+ 38. i. Charles Bruce Comisford (Living);
+ 39. ii. David Michael Comisford (Living);
+ 40. iii. Gerald Scott Comisford (Living);
+ 41. iv. Richard Anthony Comisford (Living);
+ 42. v. Jon Brent Comisford (Living); and
+ 43. vi. Kathleen Melissa Comisford (Living).

32. Francis Flavia Comisford (1901 – 1979) - Francis Flavia Comisford was born February 22, 1901 in Hebron, Ohio, the middle son of Perry Paris and Jessie Helen (Davis) Comisford. Flavy, as he was called, attended Hebron, Five Point, Granville, and Newark High School.

Flavy enlisted in the United States Marine Corp. and served during World War I. He was discharged after the war and began working for the Weherle Plant in Mansfield, Ohio.

Francis Flavia Comisford

Flavy married Pearl Ethel Hoffman, the daughter of William Hoffman and Luretta Keiser. Pearl was born on January 25, 1897 and died November 10, 1925 giving childbirth. The baby also died. Flavy then married Elizabeth Hubner on April 10, 1926 in Mansfield, Ohio. Elizabeth, born September 26, 1901 in Santana, Rumania, who immigrated to the United States with her sister, Anna in 1919.

With Flavy retiring from Westinghouse in Mansfield, Ohio in 1961 and Elizabeth retiring from the Isley Ice Cream Store, they soon moved to Phoenix, Arizona where they bought a house on Third Avenue and spent their remaining years.

Elizabeth passed away on August 1, 1969. Flavy remarried Rhea Melletti on September 15, 1971 and remained in Arizona. Flavy passed away on May 26, 1979. Flavy and Elizabeth are both buried in Mansfield, Ohio.

Children of Francis Flavia Comisford and Elizabeth Hubner:
+ 44. i. Thomas Perry Comisford (1927 – 1992);
+ 45. ii. Helen Lillian Comisford (Living); and
   46. iii Robert Charles Comisford (1934 – 1956) – Robert was born on March 20, 1934. He was serving in the United States Marine Corp when he was killed on November 25, 1956, in an automobile accident while returning to his base in Norfolk, Virginia, after a Thanksgiving Day leave with his family.

Elizabeth, Helen, Flavia and Tommy

Homer Whitcome Comisford

33. Homer Whitcome Comisford (1904 – 1988) - Homer Whitcome Comisford, the youngest son of Perry Paris and Jessie Helen (Davis) Comisford, was born September 27, 1904. Homer started school at Hebron School and then attended Five Point School in Granville after the family move. Five Point School was a one room schoolhouse with a pot-belly stove in the center of the room used for heat in the winter. His early teachers were Ruby Board and Olive Weber. As he got older, he began to drive a horse and buggy back-and-forth from the Granville School. Not being one for studying, Homer quit school after the eighth grade and began to work.

Homer was too young to join the Arm Forces and fight in World War I, though he tried. His first real jobs, other than farm work on the family farm, was being employed by the Rugg Halter Factory in Newark, Ohio and delivering ice for Lou Nelden in Granville, Ohio. In 1922, Homer went to work for the Weherle Stove Plant in Newark, the largest stove plant in the world. When laid-off from the Weherle Plant, to find work Homer hopped a freight train headed for Detroit, Michigan with friend, Rollie Hommond. Not finding work, they returned back to Newark. During the fall of 1924, Homer met a young girl on the square in Newark, who went by the name of Mickey. She invited him to a wiener roast to be held the next day. He declined as he said he was heading for California or bust. She thought she would never see him again, until one evening there was a knock on the door and he said I told you I would be back if I went bust.

Mildred Ada McKinley

Two months later, after a short courtship, Homer married Mildred "Mickey" Ada McKinley, daughter of Forest McKinley and Pearl Nevada Wright, in Newport, Kentucky on January 31, 1925. They were married by Theodore W. Bertelsman, Justice of the Peace, Campbell County, Kentucky. Mickey, married at age 15, was born January 1, 1910 in Byesville, Ohio near Cambridge.

Homer and Mickey then took up residence in a small house located on Homer's father's farm located on the National Pike, west of Hebron.

In graduating from the horse and buggy to the automobile, Homer while learning to shift gears, accidentally, we hope, drove the family car through the back of the garage.

They lived at 12 Western Avenue for over 50 years.

Homer acquired his first new car, a 1928 Chevy, in 1929 and shortly thereafter with Buddy in the car, he put it over a river bank. When Buddy returned home, he told his mother, *"Daddy had a wreck and I got a bump on my head."*

Automobiles seem to be a thing with the family, as Mickey was learning to drive, somehow the car ended up on the other side of the wood pile.

Homer worked off and on, between lay-offs and retired from the Roper Stove Company, March 1, 1967. Mickey worked at Pharis Tire and Rubber Company for 12 years and retired from the Hub Clothing Store in 1965 after 16 years.

Homer passed away on November 30, 1988 and is buried in Cedar Hill Cemetery in Newark, Ohio. Mickey passed away on October 12, 1998 after nearly a year of bad health and sever memory loss. She is also buried in Cedar Hill Cemetery.

I have a lot of fond memories of my grandparents. My grandmother was the neatest person and she is greatly missed.

Children of Homer Whitcome Comisford and Mildred Ada McKinley:
+   47.   i.   Homer Paris Comisford (1927 – 1972); and
+   48.   ii. William Davis Comisford (1928 - Living).

Fifth Generation

38.   Charles Bruce Comisford (Living) – Charles Bruce Comisford, the oldest son of Charles Benne and Marcia Muyette (Abel) Comisford, married Marie Klein, the daughter of George Klein. After a divorce to Marie, Bruce married Shirley (Roberts) Woods, daughter of Howard and Mable (Samy) Roberts.

Children of Charles Bruce Comisford and Marie Klein:
    49.   i.   Janet Sue Comisford (Living);
    50.   ii.   Sandra Lea Comisford (Living);
    51.   iii. Charles Bruce Comisford (Living); and
    52.   iv.   Jeffery Scott Comisford (Living).

39.   David Michael Comisford (Living) - David Michael Comisford, the son of Charles Benne and Marcia Muyette (Abel) Comisford, married Linda Flowers. After a divorce to Linda, David married Sammie Jean (Fortner) Fitzgerald, daughter of Thurman and Mary (Queme) Fortner.

Children of David Michael Comisford and Linda Flowers:
    53.   i.   Thomas Michael Comisford (Living);
    54.   ii.   Marcia Lynn Comisford (Living); and
    55.   iii. Penny Mechael Comisford (Living).

40. Gerald Scott Comisford (Living) - Gerald Scott Comisford, the son of Charles Benne and Marcia Muyette (Abel) Comisford, married Judith Ann Shumaker, the daughter of Robert and Kathleen (Bebout) Shumaker, at Johnstown Methodist Church.

    Children of Gerald Scott Comisford and Judith Ann Shumaker:
      56.   i.   Tracy Scott Comisford (Living); and
      57.   ii.   Thomas Brent Comisford (Living).

41. Richard Anthony Comisford (Living) - Richard 'Dick' Anthony Comisford, the son of Charles Benne and Marcia Muyette (Abel) Comisford, married Donna Dupler. Dick served in the Army during the Vietnam War (1968-69). After a divorce to Donna, Dick married Sharon Smith, daughter of Fred and Nancy (Denton) Smith.

    Children of Richard Anthony Comisford and Donna Dupler:
      58.   i.   Michael Anthony Comisford (Living);
      59.   ii.   Virginia Comisford (Living);
      60.   iii. Laura Lea Comisford (Living); and
      61.   iv.   Cynthia Comisford (1972 – 1972) – Cynthia, born May 29, 1972, died in a crib death on August 9, 1972. She is buried in Cedar Hill Cemetery.

42. Jon Brent Comisford (Living) - John Brent Comisford, the son of Charles Benne and Marcia Muyette (Abel) Comisford, married M. Cornellia Fortner, the daughter of Thurman and Mary (Queme) Fortner, at the Alexandria Methodist Church.

    Children of Jon Brent Comisford and M. Cornellia Fortner:
      62.   i.   Brent Comisford (Living); and
      63.   ii.   Brian Comisford (Living).

43. Kathleen Melissa Comisford (Living) - Kathleen 'Kathy' Melissa Comisford, the only daughter of Charles Benne and Marcia Muyette (Abel) Comisford, married Wayne D. Hall, the son of Earl Lester and Oma Lea (Moran) Hall. Kathy inherited her great grandmother's leather-bound trunk, brought by Melissa (Tygard) Comisford in a covered wagon from Western Virginia to Hebron, Ohio in 1867.

    Children of Wayne D. Hall and Kathleen Melissa Comisford:
      64.   i.   Bridgett Hall (Living).

44. **Thomas Perry Comisford (1927 – 1992)** – Thomas 'Tommy' Perry Comisford was born June 19, 1927, the oldest son of Francis Flavia and Elizabeth (Hubner) Comisford. Tommy was in the United States Marine Corp during the Korean War. Tommy married Eleanor Jeanne Homeric on December 15, 1950. Tommy passed away from cancer on May 4, 1992 in Mansfield, Ohio.

> Children of Thomas Perry Comisford and Eleanor Jeanne Homeric:
> 65. i. Patricia Comisford (Living);
> 66. ii. Robert Thomas Comisford (Living); and
> 67. iii. Lori Jeanne Comisford (Living).

45. **Helen Lillian Comisford (1929 - Living)** – Helen Lillian Comisford, the daughter of Francis Flavia and Elizabeth (Hubner) Comisford, married John E. Bauer on July 15, 1950.

> Children of John E. Bauer and Helen Lillian Comisford:
> 68. i. Christopher Michael Bauer (Living); and
> 69. ii. Michael Stephen Bauer (Living).

Homer and Elizabeth (Binckley) Comisford

47. **Homer Paris Comisford (1927 – 1972)** - Homer 'Buddy' Paris Comisford the eldest son of Homer Whitcome and Mildred Ada (McKinley) Comisford. Homer was born August 12, 1927 in Newark, Ohio. Homer attended and graduated from Newark High School in 1945, where he was a member of the football team and track squad.

Homer enlisted in the U.S. Navy toward the end of World War II and was trained at the Great Lakes Naval Station Chicago, Illinois, the San Diego Naval Base in California, and Paris Island, South Carolina. He was discharged from Pensacola, Florida an H/2 Corpman, in April 1946.

On returning to Newark, Ohio, Homer became employed at Pharis Tire and Rubber Company, where he met Elizabeth Catherine Binckley, daughter of Robert and Vida Grace (Ridenour) Binckley. They were married November 27, 1947 at St. Paul's Lutheran Church by the Rev. C.M. Danford.

They moved to Mansfield where Homer became employed at the Westinghouse Electric Plant. On January 1, 1949 they moved back to Newark where Homer joined the Newark Police Department.

After 11 years with Newark Police Department and attaining the rank of Sergeant, Homer left to become the Superintendent of the Licking County Home and served there until he passed away from a self-inflicted gun shot wound on April 30, 1972.

Homer was a member of St. Pauls Lutheran Church, Licking County Shrine Club, Aladdin Temple Shrine, ACME 554 Scottish Rite, WWII Veteran, Draft Board for 10 years and, International Brotherhood of Magicians.

Children of Homer Paris Comisford and Elizabeth Catherine Binckley:
+ 71. i. David William Comisford (1949 – 1995);
+ 72. ii. Steven Charles Comisford (Living);
+ 73. iii. Mark Andrew Comisford (Living);
+ 74. iv. Kirk Matthew Comisford (1957 – 1986);
+ 75. v. Anthony Binckley Comisford (Living); and
+ 76. vi. Shirley Ellen Comisford, an adopted daughter (Living).

48. William Davis Comisford (1928 – Living) - William 'Bill' Davis Comisford, the youngest son of Homer Whitcome and Mildred Ada (McKinley) Comisford, was born December 17, 1928 in Newark, Ohio.

From the start, Bill was an accident prone child. At the age of 6, he fell out of a tree and suffered a compound fracture of his right arm, at age 10, he fell while visiting his grandparents, Perry and Helen Comisford, in

William and Josephine (Stichter) Comisford

Granville and again broke his arm. At age 17, Bill ran into a car, yes he ran into a car coming out of an alley and suffered a fractured skull, fractured jaw bone and again, a broken arm. This time he was laid-up for sometime.

Bill attended Central Junior High School where he was a member of the Thespian Club for honor students. He graduated from Newark High School in 1947 and started working at Newark Stove Company, Cussins and Fearn Store in Newark and then moved to Mansfield to work at the Westinghouse Plant.

On June 5, 1949, Bill married his high school sweet-heart, Josephine Theresa Stichter, daughter of William J. and Inez Marie (Brumfield) Stichter, formerly of Cincinnati. They were married at Neal Avenue Methodist Church in Newark, Ohio by Rev. Frederick Brown.

Having trouble finding a good job, Bill enlisted in the United States Air Force on October 17, 1951. He became a part of the 3920th Air Police Squadron and trained at Sampson, New York and Camp Gordon, Georgia. He was then transferred to the 320th Bombardment Wing, 15th Air Force at March Field, Riverside, California. He also served in London, England and the French Morocco, North Africa. He was discharge from the Air Force as a Staff Sergeant on October 17, 1955. While in the service, Bill and Jo had two children.

Upon returning from California after Bill was shipped overseas, Jo and Bill Jr. were caught in the tornado of 1954 in Newark, Ohio. Several trees were up-rooted on the courthouse square. Then back to California when Bill returned from England and the French Morocco.

Upon leaving the service the family moved back to Newark, Ohio, where Bill again became employed by the Westinghouse Plant. In 1957, Bill joined his older brother Homer on the Newark Police Department. Bill would go on to serve 22 years on the Newark Police Department, retiring with a rank of Sergeant of Detectives.

The family moved to 10 Western Avenue, right next door to Bill's parents, Homer and Mickey, where they were caught up in the flood of 1959. The Raccoon Creek flooded and put about 28 inches of water in the house. There house was the only house around to still have good running water after the flood to clean things up.

The family took many vacations, including trips to California, the Dakotas' to visit Jo's Aunt Margie on the Indian Reservation, to Florida, Washington D.C., and to New York City.

Bill was involved with the Boy Scouts and participated on many of the activities and visited Philmont Scout Ranch with both his sons.

Retirement came early on August 7, 1980, as a result of a heart attach and subsequent by-pass surgery at the Cleveland Clinic.

Bill had an active real estate license at one time and was a member of Masons Acme Lodge #554. At various time, Bill attended the Ohio State University, Institute of Applied Science, Central Ohio Technical College, and the Moundbuilders School of Real Estate

Bill and Jo have been very active and long time members of Neal Avenue Methodist Church in Newark, Ohio. They lived at 22 Valley View Drive, east of Newark for several years, then to 265 Gladys Avenue in Newark.

Children of William Davis Comisford and Josephine Theresa Stichter:
+ 77. i. William Davis Comisford, Jr. (Living); and
+ 78. ii. Randy Scott Comisford (Living).

Sixth Generation

49. David William Comisford (1949 – 1995) – David 'Dave' William Comisford was born April 22, 1949 in Newark, Ohio, the son of Homer Paris and Elizabeth Catherine (Binckley) Comisford. David married Carol Houseman Hinger on March 1, 1976 at the Christian Fellowship Church. They were divorced on September 12, 1980. Dave then married Victoria Spring Goodin on April, 29, 1981 and would divorce her. After the death of Dave's brother Kirk, he married Christina (Reckel) Comisford. Dave was killed in an automobile accident on July 26, 1995.

Children of David William Comisford and Victoria Spring Goodin:
79. i. David Paris Comisford (Living);
80. ii Jeremy Patrick Comisford (1976 – 1994) – Jeremy was born on May 10, 1976 and died of cancer on March 17, 1994, adopted by Dave; and
81. iii. Amanda Nichelle Comisford (Living) – adopted by Dave.

50. Steven Charles Comisford (Living) – Steven Charles Comisford, the son of Homer Paris and Elizabeth Catherine (Binckley) Comisford, married and divorced Carol Sue Williamson, the daughter of Wade and Margaret Williamson.

Children of Steven Charles Comisford and Carol Sue Williamson:
    82.   i.   Heather Lea Comisford (Living); and
    83.   ii.   Ryan Steven Comisford (Living).

51. Mark Andrew Comisford (Living) – Mark Andrew Comisford, the son of Homer Paris and Elizabeth Catherine (Binckley) Comisford, married and divorced Lesley Elise Jordan, then married Lynn E. Foster.

Children of Mark Andrew Comisford and Lesley Elise Jordan:
    84.   i.   Katherine Jordan Comisford (Living).

Children of Mark Andrew Comisford and Lynn E. Foster:
    85.   i.   Seth Foster Comisford (Living).

52. Kirk Matthew Comisford (1957 – 1986) – Kirk Matthew Comisford was born April 28, 1957 in Newark, Ohio, the son of Homer Paris and Elizabeth Catherine (Binckley) Comisford. He married Christina Reckel, the daughter of Charles and Rosana Lee (Schenck) Reckel, on September 2, 1978 at St. Johns United Church of Christ. Shortly after they were married, Kirk was involved in an auto accident, where he became paralyzed from the neck down. Prior to the accident, Chris became pregnant for their daughter, Nicole Diane. After several years in a wheelchair, Kirk had another accident, this time in his wheelchair and passed away on November 30, 1986;

Children of Kirk Matthew Comisford and Christina Reckel:
    86.   i.   Nicole Diane Comisford (Living).

53. Anthony Binckley Comisford (Living) – Anthony 'Tony' Binckley Comisford, the son of Homer Paris and Elizabeth Catherine (Binckley) Comisford, married Melissa Irene Able.

Children of Anthony Binckley Comisford and Melissa Irene Able:
    87.   i.   Lacie Dawn Comisford (Living);
    88.   ii.   Patrick Paris Comisford (Living); and
    89.   iii.   Cody Rae Comisford (Living).

54. Shirley Ellen Comisford (Living) – Shirley Ellen Comisford was an adopted daughter of Homer Paris and Elizabeth Catherine (Binckley) Comisford, married and divorced Tracy Lynn McDonald.

Children of Tracy Lynn McDonald and Shirley Ellen Comisford:
90. i. Kirk Mathew McDonald (Living).

55.   William Davis Comisford, Jr. (Living) – William 'Bill' Davis Comisford, Jr., the son of William Davis and Josephine Theresa (Stichter) Comisford. Bill married his high school sweetheart, Susan Annette Harris, the daughter of Arthur E. and Norma B. (Juniper) Harris.

Children of William Davis Comisford, Jr. and Susan Annette Harris:
91. i. Brandon William Comisford (Living);
92. ii. Melissa Brooke Comisford (Living); and
93. iii. Shane Mathew Comisford (Living).

56.   Randy Scott Comisford (Living) – Randy Scott Comisford, the son of William Davis and Josephine Theresa (Stichter) Comisford, married and divorced Rebecca A. Fullen, the daughter of James and Donna Fullen.

Children of Randy Scott Comisford and Rebecca A. Fullen:
94. i. Scott James Comisford (Living); and
95. ii. Dustin Joseph Comisford (Living).

The Comisford Boys, 1963
Front: David William; Steven Charles; William Davis;
Anthony Binckley; and Kirk Matthew
Back: Mark Andrew and Randy Scott

Descendents of William Taygart and Sarah Eagon

First Generation

1. William Taygart/Tygard (1780 – 1846) - William Taygart/Tygard was born about 1780 in Virginia, the son of John Taygart and Rebecca Blackburn. It is thought that John Taygart was the son of Abraham Tygard an early settler in Fayette County in Southwestern Pennsylvania. It was reported that in 1768 that Abraham and about 27 other families that had settled near the Redstone Settlement in the "Tenmile Country" south of Fort Pitt, were warned to get off the land until it could be bought from the Indians.

William married Sarah Eagon of Blacksville, Western Virginia on December 7, 1809. Sarah was born on January 26, 1794 in Greene County, Pennsylvania, the daughter of Solomon Eagon and Mary Blackburn.

It was said, "that William was a Methodist Circuit Rider in Western Virginia and Pennsylvania, primarily in the Redstone Circuit, traveling with a gun for protection and a bottle of whiskey for snake bites." His son, John Rinehart Tygard

The first Old Harmony Church on Berlin Road, Lewis County, Western Virginia

would follow in his footsteps and was a Methodist Circuit Rider and an ordained Methodist Minister.

William passed away in Guernsey County, Ohio in 1846, while Sarah passed away on March 28, 1857 in Blacksville, Monongalia County, Western Virginia.

    Children of William Taygart and Sarah Eagon:
+   2.   i.   Julia Ann Taygart (1810 – 1867);
+   3.   ii.   Eagon Blackburn Tygard (1812 – 1884);

	4.	iii.	Perrigan L. Taygart (1815 – Unknown) - Perrigan was born on July 15, 1815 and married a Ms. Wells;
	5.	iv.	Mary Taygart (1818 – Unknown) – Mary was born on November 17, 1818 and married William Minor;
	6.	v.	Rebecca Taygart (1820 – Unknown) - Rebecca was born on June 13, 1820 and married Elijah James Coleman;
+	7.	vi.	Clementine Taygart (1822 – 1895);
	8.	vii.	William Taygart, Jr. (1825 – 1841) - William was born on June 19, 1825 and died in 1841 in Guernsey County, Ohio;
	9.	viii.	Sarah Ann Taygart (1828 – Unknown) – Sarah Ann was born on February 6, 1828 and married Hiram Lester;
	10.	ix.	Susan Taygart (1830 – 1915) – Susan was born on March 7, 1830, married Enoch Hennan on August 12, 1878 at the home of Clementine, and died July 7, 1915;
+	11.	x.	John Rinehart Tygard (1825 – 1907); and
+	12.	xi.	Elizabeth Taygart (1835 – 1895).

Second Generation

2. Julia Ann Taygart (1810 – 1867) – Julia Ann Taygart was born on December 31, 1810, the daughter of William and Sarah (Eagon) Taygart. Julia married Elijah Chalfant, the son of Robert and Margaret (Henkins) Chalfant. Elijah was born on September 29, 1812 in Pennsylvania. Elijah served as a county commissioner of Greene County, Pennsylvania in 1847. Elijah passed away on August 23, 1866, while Julia would pass away on October 31, 1867.

    Children of Elijah Chalfant and Julia Ann Taygart:
       13.   i.   Margaret Chalfant (1840 – Unknown);
       14.   ii.   Clementine Chalfant (1842 – Unknown);
       15.   iii. William H. Chalfant (1845 – Unknown);
       16.   iv. Robert Chalfant (1849 – Unknown); and
       17.   v.   Mary A. Chalfant (1854 – Unknown).

3. Eagon Blackburn Tygard (1812 – 1884) - Eagon Blackburn Tygard was born December 31, 1812 in Pennsylvania, the oldest son of William and Sarah (Eagon) Taygart. Eagon married Sarah Elizabeth Lantz of Blacksville, Western Virginia on August 15, 1836.

    Sarah was born on July 15, 1812 in Blacksville, Monongalia County, Western Virginia, the daughter of John Lantz, Jr. and Elizabeth Bonnett.

    According to the 1850, US Census for the Monongalia County, Western Virginia, Eagon was an Inn-keeper in the Blacksville Area. Eagon served as Postmaster for Blacksville in 1846.

    Shortly after the Civil War in 1867, the Tygard family moved to Ohio and lived on a small farm just east of the Comisford family farm, where the Ohio Canal passed through Hebron, heading north towards Newark. Eagon became a prosperous farmer and quite a businessman in the Hebron Area. Eagon accumulated over 250 acres of property and owned two lots and the Diamond Queen Hotel building in Hebron. For years, the Diamond Queen was a saloon and hotel in downtown Hebron on the Historic National Road. He also owned property in Humboldt, Kansas, 168 acres granted to him by U.S. President Ulysses S. Grant by a Patent dated December 10, 1869.

Sarah (Lantz) Tygard

Eagon, a heavy cigar smoker, died on February 26, 1884 of throat cancer, while Sarah died of old age on September 7, 1903, at 91 years old The Tygard's are both buried in Fairmont Cemetery just west of Jacksontown, Ohio.

Children of Eagon Blackburn Tygard and Sarah Lantz:
+ 18. i. Melissa Tygard (1837 - 1885);
    19. ii. Flavius Josephus Tygard (1840 – 1911);
+ 20. iii. Mariah Tygard (1842 – 1886);
+ 21. iv. John L. Tygard (1846 – Unknown);
+ 22. v. William F. Tygard (1849 – Unknown);
+ 23. vi. Sarah E. Tygard (1853 – 1932); and
+ 24. vii. Perry Eagon Tygard (1857 – 1932).

**Residence of Eagon B. Tygard
in Union Township, Licking County, Ohio as published in the
"Combination Atlas Map of Licking County, Ohio" by L.H. Everts, 1875**

7.   Clementine Taygart (1822 – 1895) – Clementine Taygart was born on August 4, 1822 in Greene County, Pennsylvania, the daughter of William and Sarah (Eagon) Taygart. Clementine married George Washington Bell, the son of Jason and Sarah (Noll) Bell, on February 8, 1844. George was born on September 30, 1809 in Virginia. George served as a Justice of the Peace, was a member of the school board, and was at one time the assessor for Jackson Township, Greene County, Pennsylvania. The family owned a 500 acre farm in Greene County and also had a 100 acre farm in West Virginia and nearly 7000 at interest. Clementine passed away in 1895 in Kuhntown, Greene County, Pennsylvania;

    Children of George Washington Bell and Clementine Taygart:
- 25.   i.   Sarah J. Bell (1845 – Unknown);
- 26.   ii.   William H. Bell (1847 – Unknown);
- 27.   iii.   Felix 'Alex' Bell (1849 – Unknown);
- 28.   iv.   Julia A. Bell (1851 – Unknown) – Julia married David Stoneking;
- 29.   v.   Margaret Bell (1853 – Unknown);
- 30.   vi.   Maria Bell (1855 – Unknown) – Maria married J. Harvey Stewart;
- 31.   vii.   Mary Bell (1859 – Unknown) – Mary married Eli Pethtell;

32. viii. Josephine Bell (1862 – Unknown) – Josephine married William Cole;
33. ix. Susan Rebecca Bell (1865 – Unknown) – Susan married Jessie Stewart on November 9, 1893; and
34. x. Elizabeth M. Bell.

11. John Rinehart Tygard (1825 – 1907) - John Rinehart Tygard was born on October 25, 1832, the son of William and Sarah (Eagon) Taygart. John married Susan Cassandra Gordon who died shortly after giving childbirth. John then married Mary J. Murray. John was an ordained minister and served as a circuit ride for the Methodist Protestant Church during 1856, was a justice of the Peace 1865 – 1867. He was a keg manufacturer by trade. The family lived in Fayette County, Pennsylvania, before moving to Pittsburgh. John passed away on November 3, 1907 in Pittsburgh, Pennsylvania.

Children of John Rinehart Tygard and Susan Cassandra Gordon:
35. i. Sarah E. Tygard (1856 – Unknown) – Sarah married Abram Wykoff;

Children of John Rinehart Tygard and Mary J. Murray:
36. i. James Wallace Tygard (1860 – 1928);
37. ii. Perry L. Tygard (1862 – 1942);
38. iii. Fred C. Tygard (1865 – Unknown);
39. iv. Marrion M. Tygard (1867 – Unknown); and
40. v. Charles Edwards Tygard (1870 – 1885).

12. Elizabeth Taygart (1835 – 1895) - Elizabeth Taygart was born on February 13, 1835, the daughter of William and Sarah (Eagon) Taygart. Elizabeth married William Longstreth and settled in Pennsylvania, before moving on to McElroy, Tyler County, West Virginia. Elizabeth passed away on April 7, 1895.

Children of William Longstreth and Elizabeth Taygart:
41. i. Daniel Longstreth (1868 – Unknown);
42. ii. Samuel Longstreth (1869 – Unknown);
43. iii. Fanny A. Longstreth (1873 – Unknown);
44. iv. Malinda A. Longstreth (1875 – Unknown);
45. v. Albert P. Longstreth (1876 – Unknown); and
46. vi. John Longstreth (1879 – Unknown)

Third Generation

18. Melissa Tygard (1837 - 1885) – See Andrew Thomas Comisford, page 5.

19. Flavius Josephus Tygard (1840 – 1911) – Flavius Josephus Tygard was born in 1840 in Blacksville, Monongalia County, Western Virginia, the oldest son of Eagon Blackburn and Sarah Elizabeth (Lantz) Tygard. Flavius married Nancy Miranda (Unknown) and soon thereafter headed west. They settled in Butler, Missouri where he became the president of the Bates National Bank. He was very active in the community and served as the Grand Master of Missouri of the Grand Lodge of Missouri Masons from 1897 to 1898. He also served as a Captain in the Missouri militia. In 1907 Josephus was charged with "misappropriation of funds" after the Bates National Bank failed on September 20, 1906. He subsequently was sentenced by Judge McPherson to serve five (5) years in the federal prison (Leavenworth Penitentiary in Kansas City, Missouri.) Being nearly seventy years old at the time, he spent most of his time in prison in the prison hospital. He was pardoned and released on April 17, 1909. Flavius passed away on April 5, 1911.

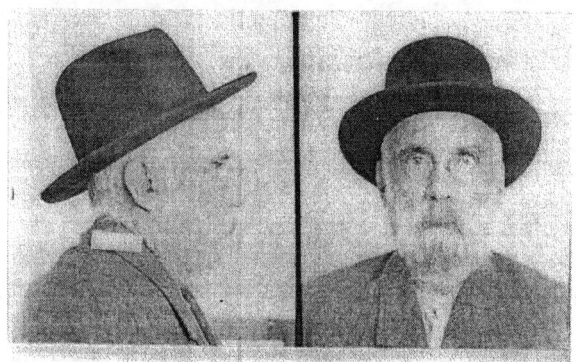

Flavius J. Tygard, Leavenworth Penitentiary Photo

20. Mariah L. Tygard (1842 – 1886) – Mariah 'Hannah' L. Tygard was born on July 8, 1842 in Blacksville, Monongalia County, Virginia, the daughter of Eagon Blackburn and Sarah Elizabeth (Lantz) Tygard. Mariah married John R. McCulloch in Hebron, Ohio. John was born June 11, 1838 in Ohio. His parents were from Ireland. John was a private in the 31st Ohio Volunteer Infantry, Company A, during the Civil War, and served as Justice of the Peace. John served as a school teacher for the Hebron School. Mariah passed away on February 15, 1886 and is buried in Hebron Cemetery, while John died on April 11, 1889 and is buried in Fairmount Cemetery.

Children of John R. McCulloch and Mariah L. Tygard:
- 47. i. Jessie McCulloch (1867 – Unknown);
- 48. ii. William McCulloch (1867 – Unknown); and
- 49. iii. Stillborn infant born and died on September 10, 1879.

21. John L. Tygard (1846 – 1906) – John L. Tygard was born in 1846 in Blacksville, Monongalia, Western Virginia, the son of Eagon Blackburn and Sarah Elizabeth (Lantz) Tygard. John served in the 1st WV Cavalry, Companies A & G as a private, during the American Civil War. Shortly after his family's move to Ohio, John moved on to Arkansas, where he settled in Little Rock. He married Mary.

Children of John L. and Mary Tygard:
- 50. i. Estel Tygard (1876 - Unknown) – Estel Tygard was born in Tennessee in 1876; and
- 51. ii. Gurtrude Ester Tygard (1879 – Unknown) – Ester Tygard was born in Ohio in 1879.

22. William F. Tygard (1849 – Unknown) – William F. Tygard was born in 1849 in Virginia, the son of Eagon Blackburn and Sarah Elizabeth (Lantz) Tygard. William married Minnie Gill, the daughter of Augustus and Fidilia Gill, in Licking County, Ohio. William moved his family west and settled in Rich Hill, Missouri, along with his in-laws.

Children of William F. Tygard and Minnie Gill:
- 52. i. Flavius Tygard (1877 - Unknown).

23. Sarah E. Tygard (1853 – Unknown) – Sarah 'Sadie' E. Tygard was born in 1853 in Virginia, the daughter of Eagon Blackburn and Sarah Elizabeth (Lantz) Tygard. Sadie married Amos Atwood in October 1888. Amos was born in 1854, passed away July 8, 1944. Sadie passed away in Hebron, Ohio on December 14, 1932.

Children of Ammos Atwood and Sarah E. Tygard:
- 53. i. Harry Atwood (1890 - Unknown);
- 54. ii. Wilmer Atwood (1892 – Unknown); and
- 55. iii. Ray Atwood (1894 – Unknown).

24. Perry Eagon Tygard (1857 – 1932) – Perry Eagon Tygard was born in 1857, in Blacksville, Monongalia, Western Virginia, the son of Eagon Blackburn and Sarah Elizabeth (Lantz) Tygard. He first married Emma Alice Deweese, the daughter of Samuel and Maria (Lightly) Deweese, in 1878 in Licking County, Ohio. Emma passed away on December 6, 1889 after a long illness of consumption and was buried in the Kirkersville Cemetery. He then married Ester 'Emma' May Crist in June 1891. He and Emma spent their honeymoon in Pittsburgh. Emma was born October 14, 1865, the daughter of Solomon and Mary (Wiseman) Crist.

Perry was involved in the community, was a charter member and past patron of the Eagon Chapter of Eastern Star, and was a Master of the Hebron Lodge F. & A. M.

Perry passed away following a stroke on September 7, 1932 in Hebron, Ohio, while Emma passed away on January 12, 1959.

Children of Perry Eagon Tygard and Emma Alice Deweese:
56. i. Charles F. Tygard (1881 – 1927) – Charles married Carrie Pearl Cusac and served during the Spanish American War as a private in the Seventh Regiment Ohio Volunteer Infantry, Company K; and
57. ii. Marinda Tygard (1883 – Unknown) – Marinda married William Edwards.

Children of Perry Eagon Tygard and Ester 'Emma' May Crist:
58. i. Vera Tygard (1894 – Unknown) – Vera married Wayne Taylor on July 5, 1911, by the Rev. W.D. Ward in Newark, Ohio and then married a George W. Miller and settled in El Paso, Texas; and
59. ii. Lorie Mildred Tygard (1895 – Unknown) – Lorie married Richard Walter Jarvis on December 21, 1918 in Alexandria, Virginia.

Descendents of Sampson and Mary Eagon

First Generation

1. Sampson Eagon (1740 - BEF 1781) - Sampson Eagon was born about 1740, probably in Ireland, the son of Richard (born about 1709 and died before 1785 in Hartford County, Maryland) and Catherine (born about 1713) Eagon. When Sampson was just a young boy, his parents, along with his brother James set sail for America to start a new adventure. Settling in northeastern Maryland, Sampson married Mary. Mary was also born about 1740.

After the birth of their first son, Solomon, the small family began to move west in search of free and cheap lands. By the early 1770's, they had reached Greene County, Pennsylvania over the Alleghenies on what would later become the National Trail.

Sampson would die sometime after the birth of Susannah in 1781, possibly during the Revolutionary War. Mary would pass away about 1818.

Sampson's and Mary's son, Sampson, would settle in Staunton, Virginia, along the Great Wagon Road.

Children of Sampson and Mary Eagon:
+ 2. i. Solomon Eagon (1766 – 1853);
+ 3. ii. Sampson Eagon (1769 – 1849);
  4. iii. Mary Eagon (1772 – Unknown);
  5. iv. Clementine Eagon (1773 – Unknown);
  6. v. Sarah Eagon (1776 – Unknown); and
+ 7. vi. Susannah Eagon (1781 – 1857).

Second Generation

2. Solomon Eagon (1766 – 1853) - Solomon Eagon was born March 2, 1766 in Maryland, the son of Sampson and Mary Eagon. Solomon married Mary Blackburn on November 11, 1788 in Cecil County, Maryland. Mary was born February 7, 1776 in Maryland, the daughter of John Blackburn and Ms. Woods.

Soon after their marriage, they moved to the Tenmile Country of the Upper Monongahela Valley, settling in Greene County, Pennsylvania. In 1795, Solomon acquired a tract of land situated at the head of Laurel Run from Nathaniel and Leah Hughes, referred to as "Mount Pleasant." Later they would acquire an adjoining tract of land from Abraham Zimmerman.

On August 8, 1806, Solomon was appointed a Trustee for the Methodist Episcopal Church and assisted in acquiring from John Jones, 154 "perches", square rods of land, on which they would build their church. The new church was built on the site of Old Cemetery in East Waynesburg.

In 1829, Solomon was the Tax Collector for Greene County. He also owned a small store in Waynesville with his son William.

Sometime in the 1840's, Solomon and Mary and their daughter Delilah and her family picked up and headed west. After a short stay in Beaver Township, Guernsey County, Ohio where they acquired property and then sold it to William Tygard and his wife, Sarah, they moved on to Oskaloosa, Mahaska County, Iowa.

Here, they would live out the rest of their lives. Solomon passed away on August 29, 1853, while Mary passed away on October 25, 1857. They are both buried in Old White Cemetery, Lincoln Township, Mahaska, Iowa.

Children of Solomon Eagon and Mary Blackburn:
8. i. Mary Polly Eagon (1790 – 1861) – Mary Polly married William Arkron, and died about 1861 in Noble County, Ohio;
9. ii. Elizabeth Eagon (1791 – 1832) – Elizabeth was born on December 28, 1791, married George H. Heisse, and died October 12, 1832;
10. iii. Margaret Eagon (1792 -1878_ - Margaret was born on March 9, 1792 in Greene County, Pennsylvania, married James B. Kent on January 14, 1815, and died March 25, 1878;
+ 11. iv. Sarah Eagon (1794 – 1857);
12. v. Susannah Eagon (1795 – 1859) – Susannah was born on October 22, 1795, married Arthur Inghram, and died November 1, 1859;
13. vi. Clementine Eagon (1799 – 1852) – Clementine married James Greenfield, and died March 26, 1852 in Washington County, Pennsylvania;
14. vii. Thomas I. Eagon (1802 – 1849) - Thomas married Eliza, and died about 1849 in Princeton, Illinois;
15. viii. Lucy Eagon (1803 -1877) - Lucy married Mr. Ankrom;
16. ix. Uriah B. Eagon (1804 - 1850) – Uriah was born on August 21, 1804, married Cassandra Adamson;
17. x. Delilah 'Lilie' Eagon (1805 – 1878) – Lilie was born on December 26, 1805, married Jessee Hook, and died December 7, 1878 in Mahaska County, Iowa; and
18. xi. William Eagon (1811 – 1850) - William married Mary.

3. Sampson Eagon (1769 – 1849) – Sampson Eagon was born on February 6, 1769 in Hagerstown, Maryland, the son of Sampson and Mary Eagon. Sampson married Rebecca Yost, the daughter of Henry and Polly Marie (Waggoner) Yost, on June 22, 1796. Rebecca was born in 1778 in Augusta County, Virginia. Sampson was a wagon-maker in Staunton, Virginia. Sampson would pass-away on May 16, 1849. According to the Annals of Augusta County,

> "...*Sampson Eagon, who lived on the top of the hill, southwest corner of Main and Coalter streets, was a zealous and good man, universally respected, and held religious services at times in his wagon-maker's shop, which stood in the same lot as his dwelling. Hence the eminence on which he lived was called Gospel Hill.*"

Children of Sampson Eagon and Rebecca Yost:
- 19. i. David Eagon;
- 20. ii. Rebecca Eagon;
- 21. iii. Henry Eagon;
- 22. iv. John Eagon;
- 23. v. Sally Eagon;
- 24. vi. Catherine Eagon;
- 25. vii. William Eagon;
- 26. viii. James Eagon; and
- 27. ix. Elizabeth Eagon;

Sampson Eagon Inn in Staunton, Virginia
now a Bed-n-Breakfast,
the home is located next door to the
birthplace of President Woodrow Wilson

7. Susannah Eagon (1781 – 1857) – Susannah Eagon was born on March 3, 1781 in Greene County, Pennsylvania, the daughter of Sampson and Mary Eagon. Susannah married George Kent, the son of Thomas and Ann (Ralston) Kent, on February 10, 1802. Susannah would pass-away on February 16, 1857, while George passed away on March 26, 1862 in Greene County, Pennsylvania..

    Children of George Kent and Susannah Eagon:
- 28.   i.   Ann Kent (1804 - 1830;
- 29.   ii.   Thomas Kent (1806 – Unknown);
- 30.   iii.   William Kent (1810 – 1882);
- 31.   iv.   Solomon Kent (1812 – Unknown);
- 32.   v.   Uriah Kent (1812 – Unknown);
- 33.   vi.   George Layton Kent (1814 – 1850);
- 34.   vii.   Susannah Kent (1815 – 1893);
- 35.   viii.   Sarah Kent (1821 – Unknown);
- 36.   ix.   Ephraim Kent (1827 – Unknown);
- 37.   x.   George Kent (1828 – Unknown); and
- 38.   xi.   Susannah Kent (1815 – 1893).

Third Generation

11.   Sarah Eagon (1794 – 1857) - See William Taygart, page 33

Descendents of John Blackburn and Ms. Woods

First Generation

1. John Blackburn (Unknown – 1801) - John Blackburn married a Ms. Woods (first name unknown) and they settled down in W. Nottingham, Cecil County, Maryland, where they raised five (5) children. It is likely that the family was Quaker, as many of the Blackburn's in W. Nottingham area were. John died sometime before November 10, 1801 in W. Nottingham, Cecil County, Maryland, the date of his will was proven. His children, along with his brother Ephram, were all mentioned in his will.

Will of John Blackburn
Proved November 10, 1801

Be it known to all Christian people whom this may concern that I, John Blackburn, of West Nottingham, Cecil County and State of Maryland, being weak in body, but of sound mind, memory and understanding, do make, ordain and constitute this my last will and testament, thereby disposing of the worldly goods and estate it hath pleased God to bestow me in manner and form as follows, viz. _____ I will and direct that all my just debts and funeral expenses be duly paid and satisfied as soon as possible after my decease and I subject all my estate, both real and personal to the payment of the same.

Item, I give and bequeath unto my daughter Mary Heagen the sum of five shillings, current money of Maryland aforesaid to be paid one year after my decease to her and her heirs forever.

Item, I give unto my son Aphram Blackburn the sum of five shillings current money aforesaid to be paid one year after my decease to him and his heirs forever.

Item, I give and bequeath unto my daughter Susannah Blackburn the sum of five shillings current money as aforesaid one year after my decease to her and her heirs forever.

Item, I give unto my son Jehu Blackburn the sum of fifty pounds current money aforesaid to be paid unto him when he arrives to the age of twenty-one years to and his heirs forever.

Item, All my plantation and house with all my other real and personal estate whatsoever, situate lying of being in Cecil county and State aforesaid or elsewhere, I hereby give, devise, and bequeath subject to the payment of my just debts and the legacy aforesaid unto my son Uriah Blackburn and his heirs forever.

Item, and lastly, I constitute and appoint my brother Aphram Blackburn of the State of Pennsylvania and my son Uriah Blackburn my executors of this my last will and testament and do here by revoke all other wills by me at anytime hereto fore made and declare them void.

his mark

John X Blackburn

Confirming this to be my last will and testament, In witness whereof I, the said John Blackburn, have to this my last will and testament contained in of one sheet of paper to the first whereif left my hand and the second my hand and seal this 15th day of May in the year of our Lord one thousand seven hundred and ninety eight.

his mark

John X Blackburn

Item-it is my will that if my son Jehu should die before he arrives to the age of twenty one years that his legacy left him by this will shall descend and be paid unto my Daughter Susannah Blackburn and her heirs forever.

Signed sealed published and declared by the said John Blackburn as and for his last will of testament in the presence of us who in his presence and at his request have subscribed our names as witnesses thereunto in the presence of each
other---
Jesse Reynolds
John Brown
Nathan Harris

Cecil County November 10, 1801 ---Then came Ephraim Blackburn and Uriah Blackburn and made oath on the holy Evangels of Almighty God that the foregoing is the true and whole last will and testament of John Blackburn late of the said County deceased that hath come to their hand and possession and that they do not know of any other; and also that they have given due notice of their intentions of having probate whereof taken--------Sworn before David Smith Regr
Cecil County November 10th 1801 --- Then came Jesse Reynolds, John Brown, and Nathan Harris, and they being of the People called Quakers and Solemnly,
Sincerely and truly affirm that they did see the said testator sign and seal this will, that they heard him publish pronounce and declare the same to be his last will and testament, that at the time of his so doing he was to the best of their apprehensons of a sound and disposing mind memory and understanding, that they severally subscribed their hands as witnesses to this will in the presence and at the request of the testator and in the presence of each other.----
Affirmed before David Smith, Reqr

Children of John Blackburn and Ms. Woods:
+   2.   i.   Uriah Blackburn (1778 – Unknown);
+   3.   ii. Mary Blackburn (1768 – 1857);
    4.   iii. Ephram Blackburn;
    5.   iv. Susannah Blackburn; and
    6.   v.   Jehu Blackburn.

Second Generation

2. Uriah Blackburn (1778 –Unknown)- Uriah Blackburn was mostly likely born in Baltimore, Maryland, the son of John Blackburn and Ms. Woods. Uriah married Margaret Coulson, the daughter of Thomas Coulson and Martha Wiley. Margaret was born September 1, 1781, at West Nottingham, Cecil County, Maryland. Uriah and Margaret were still alive during the taking of the 1850 US Census, located in Maryland, Baltimore County, 1st District, age 72 and 71.

    Children of Uriah Blackburn and Margaret Coulson:
- 7. i. John Blackburn, who became a layer in Baltimore, Maryland;
- 8. ii. Jehu Blackburn;
- 9. iii. Cassandra Blackburn, who married her cousin;
- 10. iv. Margaret Amelia Blackburn, married Reuben Griffith of Chester County, Pennsylvania
- 11. v. Rachel Blackburn, who followed the Catholic faith and entered the convent at Emmetsburg, Maryland; and
- 12. vi. Mary E. Blackburn, who also followed the Catholic faith and entered the convent at Emmetsburg, Maryland.

3. Mary Blackburn (1768 – 1857) – See Solomon Eagon, page 41

Descendents of Hans George and Maria Lantz

First Generation

1. Hans George Lantz (1725 – 1793) – Hans George Lantz was born in Western Europe about 1725 and died about 1793 and left a will date December 7, 1792. Hans George would marry Maria (unknown) and would be the parents of five children. The family immigrated to the American Colonies through the Port of Philadelphia around 1747. They lived in Frederick County, Maryland before moving to the Shenandoah Valley in Western Virginia, sometime before 1772.

    Children of Hans George and Maria Lantz:
- 2.   i.   George Lantz;
- + 3.   ii.   Johannes Lantz (1749 – 1817);
- 4.   iii.   Andrew Lantz;
- 5.   iv.   Margaretha Lantz; and
- 6.   v.   Jacob Lantz.

Second Generation

3. Johannes Lantz (1749 – 1817) - Johannes Lantz was born June 5, 1749, the son of Hans George and Maria Lantz. Johannes married Clara Fuschain, the daughter of Adam Fuschain on June 23, 1772 according to the Early Records of the Evangelical Lutheran Church of Frederick County, Maryland.

    Johannes would soon take up arms for freedom and joined the Continental Army during the Revolutionary War. Clara would die at an early age during the war or sometime before 1780. After the Revolutionary War, Johannes remarried to Barbara Waggoner, the youngest daughter of Willheim and Agnesa (Fleischer) Waggoner.

    When John died in 1817, he owned over 1,000 acres of farmland lying in Monongalia County, Western Virginia and Greene County, Pennsylvania according to his Will probated on April 5, 1817. Barbara passed away of old age in Wetzel County, Western Virginia in February 1850.

Children of Johannes Lantz and Clara Fuschain:
+ 7. i. John Lantz, Jr. (1773 – 1853);
  8. ii. Andrew Lantz (1775 – Unknown); and
  9. iii. Catherine Lantz (1777 – Unknown).

Children of Johannes Lantz and Barbara Waggoner:
  10. i. Mary Lantz (1782 -1833) – Mary was born on June 10, 1782 in Monongalia County, Western Virginia, married Jonathan Styles, and died in Guernsey County, Ohio September 3, 1833;
  11. ii. William Lantz (1784 – 1825) – William was born on October 29, 1784;
  12. iii. John George Lantz (1787 – 1818) – John was born on January 15, 1787 and died March 13, 1818, George was given, thru his fathers will in 1817, possession of 1 female slave and 2 slave children who he freed and willed his estate to in 1818;
  13. iv. Lewis Lantz (1789 – Unknown);
+ 14. v. Jacob Lantz (1791 – 1858);
  15. vi. Alexander Lantz (1793 – 1873) – Alexander married Margaret Minor on October 30, 1817 in Monongalia County, Western Virginia, and passed away in Wetzel County, West Virginia on January 7, 1873;
  16. vii. Samuel Lantz (1797 – 1809) - Samuel died May 1, 1809; and
  17. viii. Elizabeth Lantz (1800 – 1884) – Elizabeth was born on June 9, 1800 in Greene County, Pennsylvania, married George Fielding Cumberledge on August 14, 1818, and passed away November 23, 1884 in Greene County, Pennsylvania.

Third Generation

7. John Lantz, Jr. (1773 – 1858) - John Lantz, Jr. was born in Shenandoah County, Virginia on August 9, 1773, the son of Johannes and Clara (Fuschain) Lantz. John married Elizabeth Bonnett on Wheeling Creek, Marshall County, Western Virginia, on March 26, 1795. Elizabeth was born September 13, 1773, the eldest daughter of Lewis and Anna Elizabeth (Waggoner) Bonnett.

John farmed the land until his death on September 1, 1858, while Elizabeth lived to be almost 100 years old, passing away on March 11, 1873. After John's death, Elizabeth moved in with her daughter, Sarah and her family. She lived in Hebron, Ohio until her death in 1873. John and Elizabeth are both buried in Lantz Cemetery in Wayne Township, Monongalia County, West Virginia.

Children of John Lantz, Jr. and Elizabeth Bonnett:
- 18. i. Mary Lantz (1796 – Unknown) – Mary was born on February 22, 1796 and married Mr. Chandler on November 12, 1816;
- 19. ii. Margaret 'Peggy' Lantz (1798 – 1890) – Peggy was born on March 9, 1798 and married William Minor on January 9, 1818;
- 20. iii. Elizabeth Lantz (1800 – Unknown) – Elizabeth was born on June 5, 1800 and married Theopylus Minor on October 20, 1823;
- 21. iv. Lewis Lantz (1802 – 1818) – Lewis was born on August 30, 1802 and died July 26, 1818;
- 22. v. John Lantz (1805 -1816) – John was born on April 3, 1805 and died February 27, 1816;
- 23. vi. Nancy Lantz (1807 -1901) – Nancy was born on August 21, 1807, married William Johnson on April 10, 1828, and passed away May 8, 1901;
- \+ 24. vii. William Lantz (1810 – 1881);
- \+ 25. viii. Sarah Elizabeth Lantz (1812 – 1903);
- 26. ix. Jacob Lantz (1814 – Unknown) – Jacob was born on July 22, 1814 and married Minerva Minor on December 8, 1836; and
- 27. x. Alexander Lantz (1817 – Unknown) – Alexander was born on July 8, 1817 and married Nancy Masters.

14. Jacob Lantz (1791 – 1858) – Jacob Lantz was born on October 1, 1791 in Greene County, Pennsylvania, the son of Johannes and Clara (Fuschain) Lantz. Jacob married Delilah Coen. Jacob served during the War of 1812, and passed away October 14, 1858 in Green County, Pennsylvania.

Children of Jacob Lantz and Delilah Coen:
- 28. i. Alexander Lantz;
- 29 ii. Simon Lantz (1815 – Unknown);
- 30. iii. Thomas Lantz (1822 – Unknown);
- 31. iv. John Lantz (1829 – Unknown);
- 32. v. William Lantz (1835 – Unknown) – William was born on April 27, 1835, on the farm where he and his family reside in Wayne Township, he married Minerva Kent, the daughter of William and Elizabeth (Odenbaugh) Kent, on May 22, 1856. Minerva was born on November 24, 1837. They had seven children— Mary, wife of William Wiley; William, who married Belle Phillips; Ulysses; Emma; Harriet; Delilah; and an infant (deceased); and
- 33. vi. Elias Lantz (1837 – Unknown).

Fourth Generation

24. William Lantz (1810 – 1881) – William was born on March 17, 1810, the son of John and Elizabeth (Bonnett) Lantz, Jr. William married Sarah Thomas on September 3, 1831. William served as a Postmaster in Blacksville. *"On April 10, 1855, a fire started in daytime in the residence of William Lantz which stood where the present Lantz residence is located, and 24 houses in the town were destroyed by fire. Mr. Lantz was in Richmond at the time, a member of the Virginia Assemby."* William passed away on January 24, 1881.

   Children of William Lantz and Sarah Thomas:
    34. I. Elizabeth Lantz (1834 – Unknown);
    35. i. John Lantz (1838 – Unknown);
    36. ii. Amelia Lantz (1840 – Unknown);
    37. iii. William Lantz (1843 – Unknown);
    38. iv. Remembrance Lantz (1847 – Unknown);
    39. v. Ellis P. Lantz (1854 – Unknown); and
    40. vi. Emma B. Lantz (1857 – Unknown).

25. Sarah Lantz (1812 – 1903) – See Eagon Blackburn Tygard, page 34.

Descendents of David Daniel Bonnett and Christine Cousine

First Generation

1. David Daniel Bonnett (1658 – 1736) - The Protestant Reformation began by Martin Luther in Germany about 1517 and spread rapidly in France under the leadership of John Calvin. These new Reformers were known as "Huguenots," a phrase meaning "house worshipper" or "house fellowship" and were primarily of French nobility and the social middle class. Many were artisans, craftsmen and professional people. This new "Reform Religion" placed these new French Protestants in direct conflict with both the Catholic Church and the King of France. The followers of this new religion were soon accused of heresy against the Catholic government and the established religion of France, and a General Edict urging extermination of these heretics was issued in 1536. By 1562, over 1200 Huguenots had been slain and the French Wars of Religion would rage on for the next 35 years.

France's King, Henry IV in April of 1598 would sign "The Edict of Nantes," that would allow the French Huguenots some religious freedoms, including the free exercise of their religion in 20 specified towns of France. But then in October of 1685, France's King, Louis XIV signed "The Revocation of the Edict of Nantes," beginning anew persecution of the French Huguenots. Many of the French Huguenots began to flee France for Germany, the Netherlands, and England, while others would find their way to South America and to the American Colonies, especially to the Carolinas, Virginia, Pennsylvania, and New York.

David Daniel Bonnett (aka Louis Bonnett) was born in Fhionque, France about 1658, the son of Jean Pierre Bonnett, who was born about 1630 in Southern France and died sometime after 1699. David married Christine Cousine (aka Christi Causine) about 1692 in Friedrichstal, Germany. Christine was born about 1662. David lived in Thronque, France during the period 1681-87. In 1687, he and his family fled religious persecution, settling in Morlheim, Germany. There was a story that *"Daniel, wife and two children tried to reach coast to escape France for religious freedom. They hid the children, covered with vegetables in baskets on a donkey. A trooper thrust a suffered in the basket and the children suffered flesh wounds but survived. The family escaped to Holland, then to Switzerland from whence Jeanne came to America."* David passed away on September 4, 1736, while Christine had passed away February 21, 1732.

    Children of David Daniel Bonnett and Christine Cousine:
- 2.   i.   Jeanne Coliver Bonnett;
- 3.   ii   Peter 'Pierre' Bonnett (1693 – Unknown) – Pierre was born January of 1693 in France, married Mary Ann Parent, and died 1749-1751;
- 4.   iii.   James Bonnett (1694 – Unknown) - James married Mary Bonticore;
- 5.   iv.   Daniel Bonnett (1695 – 1767) – Daniel was born on January 29, 1695 in France and married Petronella Bouchet;
- 6.   v.   Anna Mary Bonnett (1697 – 1778) – Anna was born on May 6, 1697 in France and married John Soulice; and
- +   7.   vii.   Jean Jacques 'Jacob' Bonnett (1702 - 1755).

Second Generation

7.   Jean Jacques 'Jacob' Bonnett (1702 – 1755) - Jean Jacques 'Jacob' Bonnett was born in 1702 in Friedrichstal, Baden, Germany, the son of David Daniel Bonnett and Christine Cousine. Jacob and Ann Marie (Ancien) Desreux, the daughter of Abram Desreux (born about 1670 and died November 22, 1737 in Friedrichstal, Germany) and Judith Guerit (born about 1680 in Germany and died February 13, 1726), were married on October 19, 1723 and left for America from Rotterdam, Holland via Dover, England, with their three daughters and one son during the summer of 1733. They arrived in the Port of Philadelphia aboard the sailing ship *"Elizabeth"* Edward Lee, Master, on August 27, 1733. On the ship's list, Jacob was listed as "Jaques Bonet". During the voyage their daughters, Susanna and Christina both died.

    The family located in Chester County, Pennsylvania and later to the Upper German settlements of Frederick County, Maryland. During the period in Pennsylvania and Maryland, they would have five more children.

    On May 28, 1743, Daniel Dalany assigned the certificate of survey for his "Wine Garden" to Jacob Bonnett, who on the very same day would reassign the property to his neighbor, Martin Wetzel. Later in 1743, Jacob would also transfer the patent for "Bonnetts Resolution" to Martin Wetzel. Jacob would then move his family to

"Battle ham" located on the west bank of Hunting Creek below the fork of the Creek.

Both Jacob and Ann Marie passed away while in Maryland, sometime between 1752 and 1755. After their deaths, Samuel took over the family and moved the family to Virginia, where they would settle on the South Branch of the Potomac.

Children of Jean Jacques 'Jacob' Bonnett and Ann Marie Desreux:

	8.	i.	Marguerite 'Margaret' Catharine Bonnett (1725 – 1794) – Margaret was born on May 25, 1725 in Friedrichstal, Baden, Germany, married John Conrad Six before 1757, and died in 1794 in Greene County, Pennsylvania;
	9.	ii.	Johann Adam Issak Bonnett (1727 – Unknown) – Johann was born on February 22, 1727 in Friedrichstal, Baden-Wurttemberg, Germany;
	10.	iii.	Susanna Magdeline Bonnett (1729 – 1733) – Susanna died aboard the ship;
	11.	iv.	Christina Bonnett (1731 – 1733) - Christina died aboard the ship;
	12.	v.	Johan Martin Simon Bonnett (1732 – 1793) – Johan was born April 1, 1732 in Friedrichstal, Baden, Germany, married Dorothy Bickley on April 22, 1755, and was killed by Indians in August 1793;
+	13.	vi.	Mary Bonnett (1735 – 1805);
	14.	vii.	Samuel Bonnett (1738 – 1789) – Samuel was born about 1738 in Paoli, Chester County, Pennsylvania, married Mary Elizabeth Lorentz in 1755, and died December 17, 1789 from injuries received from a tree falling on him along Hackers Creek in Western Virginia;
+	15.	viii.	Lewis Bonnett (1737 – 1808);
	16.	ix.	Catherine Bonnett; and
	17.	x.	Elizabeth Bonnett, who married Nicholas Wetzel on April 3, 1749.

The Jean Bonnet Tavern still stands today and is located on the Lincoln Highway near Bedford, Pennsylvania,

The namesake, Jean (John) Bonnet, and his wife purchased the property in 1779. In October 1780, Bonnet was issued a license, allowing that *"Petitioner lives at the Fork of roads leading to Fort Pitt and the Glades with everything necessary for keeping Public House..."*

Third Generation

13. Mary Bonnett (1735 – 1805) – Mary Bonnett was born about 1735 in Paoli, Chester County, Pennsylvania, the daughter of Jacob Bonnett and Ann Marie (Ancien) Desreux. Mary married John Martin Wetzel in Rockingham, Virginia in 1756 and they settled on the South Branch of the Potomac in Virginia.

John was a Captain in the Virginia Rangers, and was with Lewis Bonnett during the French and Indian War. Both families would soon leave the South Branch of the Potomac in search of new opportunities. They settled along Big Wheeling Creek, which is now the Sand Hill District, in Marshall County, Western Virginia. Later Fort Wetzel was built on this location. The wagon train included the Zane's, who would establish Wheeling on the Ohio River, the Bonnett, the Eberly and the Rosecranze families, who all settled in this area. History records show that all these men and their sons were to become notable scouts and Indian fighters in the settlement of the Ohio River Valley Frontier. Captain John Wetzel and his son Martin were in the battle of Point Pleasant in 1774. Martin was one of the soldiers who survived the Foreman Massacre near McMechen and was among the defenders of Fort Henry in 1777. Martin, his brother Lewis, and his dad Captain John Wetzel, were also among the defenders in the second attack on Fort Henry on September 11 - 13, 1782, against the British and the Indians, which is known as the last battle of the Revolutionary War. In 1782, Martin and Lewis were among the defenders of Fort Beeler against the Mohawk and Shawnee Indians.

On June 11, 1786, Captain John Wetzel, along with Captain John Baker, was killed by Indians while crossing the Ohio River at Captiva. There is a monument in their memory, located on Route 7, between Moundsville and Martinsville, West Virginia.

Mary passed away in June of 1805 on Wheeling Creek, in the home owned by her son Jacob Wetzel. She was buried in the McCreary Cemetery.

Children of Captain John Martin Wetzel and Mary Bonnett:
18.   i.   Magdalena Elizabetha Wetzel (1751 – Unknown);
19.   ii.   Martin Wetzel (1757 – Unknown) – Martin was born in 1757 on South Branch of the Potomac River, Shenandoah County, Virginia, married Mary Coffelt in 1784, and died October 18, 1829;
20.   iii.   Eva Christine Wetzel (1759 – Unknown) – Christina was born on the South Branch of the Potomac River, Shenandoah County, Virginia and married John Jacob Wolfe 1774;
21.   iv.   George Wetzel (1761 – 1784) – George was born on the South Branch of the Potomac River, Shenandoah County, Virginia, died in 1784 near Marietta, Ohio;
22.   v.   Lewis Wetzel (1764 – 1808) – Lewis was born in 1764 in South Branch of the Potomac River, Shenandoah County, Virginia, and became a famous Indian fighter;
23.   vi.   Jacob Wetzel (1765 – 1827) – Jacob was born on September 16, 1765 on South Branch of the Potomac River, Shenandoah County, Virginia, married Ruhuma Shepard in 1795, and died in Indiana;

24. vii. Susan Wetzel (1767 – Unknown) – Susan was born on South Branch of the Potomac River, Shenandoah County, Virginia, and married Nathan Goodrich; and
25. viii. John Wetzel, Jr. (1770 – Unknown) - John was born in 1770 on South Branch of the Potomac River, Shenandoah County, Virginia, married Eleanor Williams, and died May 18, 1817.

Lewis Wetzel
Frontiersman and Indian Fighter

Lewis Wetzel (1764 or 1763-1808) was a frontiersman and Indian fighter. Lewis has been featured in several books and was the main character in the first three (3) novels of Zane Grey. Novelist Zane Grey expressed the hope that his treatment of Wetzel "softens a little the ruthless name history accords him." Grey said that "the border needed Wetzel. The settlers would have needed many more years in which to make permanent homes had it not been for him. He was never a pioneer; but always a hunter of Indians." Wetzel County, West Virginia is named for him.

15. Captain Lewis Bonnett (1737 – 1808) - Lewis Bonnet was born in Paoli, Chester County, Pennsylvania in February of 1737, the son of Jacob Bonnett and Ann Marie (Ancien) Desreux. Paoli is situated about 14 miles northwest of the city of Philadelphia. After his parents death around 1752-1755, along with his brother and sisters, he would move to the South Branch of the Potomac in Virginia. While in Virginia, Lewis enlisted into the Virginia Rangers, and was under George Washington command in Braddock's Defeat (1755), a major battle during the French and Indian War.

While on the South Branch, around 1770, Lewis married Anna Elizabeth Waggoner, the daughter of Willheim Waggoner and Anna Elizabeth Wagnerin, in Romney, Virginia. Anna Elizabeth was born March 27, 1749 in White March, Montgomery County, Pennsylvania.

Sometime around 1770 Lewis, along with the Wetzel's, Waggoner's and Six's families moved from the South Branch and settled on Dunkard Creek of the Monongahela. In 1772, Lewis along with John Wetzel and his family would venture to the Wheeling area, stake claims to 400 acres along Wheeling Creek, and preemption rights to another 1,000 acres. They built their cabins and planted corn. Lewis soon sold his property along Wheeling Creek and return to Dunkard Creek.

Lewis was a soldier listed on the payrolls at Pittsburgh during the Dunmore War of 1774. He would fight at the Battle of Point Pleasant. After the campaign he sold his possessions on Dunkard Creek and moved back to Wheeling Creek, where he repurchased his old possession, apparently paying twice what he had sold them for.

Lewis died on March 9, 1808 in Chester County, Virginia, while Anna Elizabeth would pass away around 1816.

> **Fort Henry**
>
> Originally known as Fort Fincastle until 1776, Fort Henry was attacked by the Shawnee in 1774 and almost destroyed. There was no garrison in 1775. The fort enclosed one-half acre, with log barracks, storehouse, cabins, and a well. Fort Henry was attacked in 1777 by Indians under Simon Girty. British and Indians again unsuccessfully attacked in 1782, which was considered the last battle of the American Revolution. It was dismantled after the Indian threat was thought to be over.

Lewis Bonnet Will
(Spelling is as written.)

In the name of God Amen I Lewis Bonnet of the County of Ohio and State of Virginia farmer being very sick and weak in body but of perfect mind and memory thanks be given unto God; calling unto mind the mortality of my body, and knowing that it is appointed for all men once to die, do make and ordain this my last will and testament that is to say principally and first of all I give and recommend my soul into the hand of Almighty God that gave it, and my body I recommend to the earth to be buried in a decent Christian burial at the discretion of my Executors, nothing doubting but at the general Resurrection I shall receive the same again by the mighty power of God. And as touching such worldly estate wherewith it has pleased God to bless me in this life I give, demise and dispose of the same in the following manner and form.

First, I give and bequeath to my beloved wife Elizabeth one of my horse creatures which ever she shall choose, her side saddle and bridle one milch cow of hir own chosing, such choice she my renew yearly out of the stock which I intend to give my son John--Item her bed and bedding table one chest together with the one third of all my personal estate as also her living in the house wherein we now live and a full third of the part of land given to my son John that is the benefits therefrom arising during her natural life time or so long as she shall remain my widow and no longer

2nd. I give and devise unto my son Lewis Bonnet all the upper part of the land that which was laid off to him as will appear by plot bearing date the 26th of November 1807, to have and to hold to him (after my decease) his heirs and assigns forever free & clear of all manner of incumbrance whatsoever.

3d. I give and devise unto my son John Bonnet all the rest or remainder of my plantation for him to have and to hold to him....the said Bonnet his Heirs assigns forever, subject still the third bequeathed to his mother as is herein before mentioned & paying thereout of four hundred & fifteen dollars, to be paid in the manner following that is to say to my daughter Mary who is married to Philip Rodiffer one hundred dollars to be paid as hereinafter directed which with one hundred dollars already received shall be in full of hir portion, To my daughter Barbara who is married to John Rodiffer one hundred dollars one year after my decease. To Elizabeth Launtz one hundred and fifteen dollars which together with eighty five dollars already paid her shall be her full portion. Item to my grand son Lewis Hookis I give and bequeath one horse creature worth fifty dollars to be given him by my son John as soon as the said Lewis shall arrive to the full age of twenty one years.

Further I will and direct that one year after my decease my son John shall pay as follows to Barbarah as is before directed, next fifteen dollars to my daughter Elizabeth Lantz which will make hir equal with the rest--

Then I direct that my son John shall two years after my decease to pay one hundred dollars every year so as to pay up the four hundred & fifteen dollars be equally divided between my daughters Barbarah & Elizabeth & Mary so as their shears be equal.
Further I give and bequeath to my son John Bonnet all the moveable property what is not already heretofore mentioned, further constitute and appoint my two sons Lewis Bonnett and John Bonnett my Executors of this my last will and testament I herby revoke and make null all and every former wills by me heretofore made ratifying and confirming this to be my last will & testament an none other witness my hand and seal the 27th of November A D 1807...

Lewis Bonnet....seal

Signed sealed pronounced as his last will & testament in the presence of us
John Joover
Devald Keefer
Jesse Burch
A copy teste........Moses Chapline...C.O.C.

Children of Lewis Bonnett and Anna Elizabeth Waggoner:
+ 26. i. Elizabeth Bonnett (1773 – 1873);
    27. ii. Barbara Bonnett (1775 – 1860) - Barbara married John Rodeffer around 1800, and passed away on March 21, 1860;
    28. iii. Lewis Bonnett, Jr. (1778 – 1863) – Lewis was born on March 3, 1778 on Dunkard Creek, Virginia, married Jane McClain, and passed away in Marysville, Union County, Ohio on January 10, 1863;
    29. iv. Mary Bonnett (1781 – 1816) – Mary married Philip Rodeffer; and
    30. v. John Bonnett (1785 – 1816) – John was born on August 2, 1785, married Eva Wolf, and died September 2, 1816. John was Captain in the 2nd Virginia Regiment, Norfolk, Virginia, during the War of 1812.

Fourth Generation

26. Elizabeth Bonnett (1773 – 1873) - See John Lantz, Jr., page 50.

Descendents of Willheim Waggoner and Anna Elizabeth Wagnerin

First Generation

1. Willheim Waggoner (1706 - 1763/64) - Willheim Waggoner was born in Dutch Flanders, Germany about 1706. Willheim married Anna Elizabeth Wagnerin in Germany around 1740. While in Germany they started their family with the births of Mary in 1743 and John Peter in 1746. With the prospects of free or cheap land in America the family made plans for a long voyage.

The family set sail for America in the fall of 1748 aboard the ship *"Patience and Margaret"* from Rotterdam, Holland, arriving in the Port of Philadelphia, Pennsylvania on October 25, 1748. They settled in White Marsh, Montgomery County, Pennsylvania where they celebrated the birth of their third child on March 27, 1749, Anna Elizabeth. Anna Elizabeth was baptized in St. Michaels Church on April 24, 1749.

Willheim' wife, Anna passed away shortly after the birth of Anna Elizabeth and he soon remarried to Agnesa Fleischer. A few years after the birth of their first child, Johannes on November 24, 1751 the family traveled on the German Monocacy Road en route to present day Hardy County, Western Virginia (Old Field Virginia) along the South Branch of the Potomac River, where Willheim built a fort-like home for his family. Shortly after arriving hear, Agnesa gave birth to Barbara in 1756

About 1763-64, while Willheim, Mary and John Peter were out working in the fields some distance from the fort, they were attacked by marauding Indians. Willheim was brutally killed and scalped, while Mary and John Peter were taken as captives of the Indians. A rescue party was sent out after the two children, where Mary was shot during the rescue and died. John Peter was carried off to the Indian village where he remained for sometime. He later would escape and find his way back to Philadelphia with a group of French trappers. John Peter was listed in the 1790 US Census in Philadelphia as a shoemaker, with five sons and four daughters.

Children of Willheim Waggoner and Anna Elizabeth Wagnerin:
    2.   i.   Mary Waggoner (1743 – 1763);
    3.   ii.   John Peter Waggoner (1746 – Unknown); and
+   4.   iii.   Anna Elizabeth Waggoner (1749 – 1816).

Children of Willheim Waggoner and Agnesa Fleischer:
+   5.   i.   Johannes Michael Waggoner (1751 – 1843); and
    6.   ii.   Barbara Waggoner.

Second Generation

4.   Anna Elizabeth Waggoner – See Capt. Lewis Bonnett, page 58.

5.   Johannes Michael Waggoner (1751 – 1843) – Johannes 'John' Michael Waggoner was born on November 24, 1751 in White Marsh, Pennsylvania, the son of Willheim and Agnesa Fleischer. Johannes married Margaret Bonnett, the daughter of Samuel and Mary (Lorentz) Bonnett.

According to notes for Johannes Michael Waggoner from the papers in his Revolutionary War Pension Claims File No. 7824: *That while residing near Moorefield, Hardy County, Virginia, John Michael Wagoner, was drafted in 1778 (about the middle of the Revolutionary War), served under Captain John Harness and Colonel Riddel in General McIntosh's campaign, and served as a Ranger under Captain Owen Davy and Colonel Charles Martin. Soon after, he served under Captain Parsons in pursuit of the Tories. In 1781, he was drafted under Captain Thomas Neel and Colonel Lewis. He was at the Battle of Yorktown and the surrender of Cornwallis, with George Washington. In the fall of 1782, he enlisted as an Indian Spy under Edward Freeman (three months). Ordered out by Colonel William Lowther and stationed at West's Fort to guard the frontiers. Johannes served as a spy until the middle of 1792.*

In 1792, Tecumseh, with a party of Indians, went to his house on a branch of Hacker's Creek in Lewis County, Virginia. They raided his house killing one a boy in the front yard. The Indians shot at John Waggoner, but John escaped to a neighbor, the Hardman home. They took his wife and six other children prisoner. About a mile from the house, another boy was found dead and scalped. A short distance further, his wife and two other children were found mangled scalped and dead. His captive son, Peter, in 1812, was recognized among the savages by acquaintance and brought home. Peter married, however, he did have a wife and children among the Indians. John's oldest daughter, Elizabeth was sold into slavery and treated badly. She escaped the Indians by way of Detroit. His other daughter, Mary, remained in captivity until the treaty with the Indians. At that time she was given up by them.

Johannes then married Hannah Kyles about 1793 and settled on a large area of land two miles east of what is now Fort Ashby, West Virginia. He then married Susannah Richards, the daughter of Arnold Richards, on February 16, 1798. Arnold had been killed by Indians and Susannah had become a ward of John Runyan. Johannes would died in 1843 on the family farm, where he was buried a short distance from the house in which he lived.

Children of Johannes Michael Waggoner and Margaret Bonnett:
- 7. i. Elizabeth 'Lizzie' Waggoner (1779 – 1854) – Lizzie was born on November 5, 1779 in Dunkard Bottom, now Preston County, and died on February 1, 1854 in Lewis County, Western Virginia;
- 8. ii. Mary Waggoner (1780 – 1871) – Mary was born on December 9, 1780, married Jacob Wolf, Jr. on April 15, 1800, and died on June 7, 1871; and
- 9. iii. Peter Waggoner (1787 – 1879) – Peter was born on March 13, 1787 in Jesses Run and died March 26, 1879.

Peter Waggoner
(1787-1879)
son of Johannes and Margaret
(Bonnett) Waggoner

Children of Johannes Michael Waggoner and Susannah Richards:
- 10. i. Paul Waggoner (1800 – 1877) - Paul died in 1877 in Colfax, Clinton County, Indiana;
- 11. ii. Henry Waggoner (1802 – 1886) – Henry was born on March 1, 1802 and died on December 8, 1886;
- 12. iii. Elijah Waggoner (1804 – 1899) – Elijah was born on January 10, 1804 and died May 31, 1899;
- 13. iv. John Waggoner (1805 – 1879) – John was born on October 29, 1805, died April 25, 1879, and is buried in Morrison Cemetery;
- 14. v. Catherine Waggoner (1810 – 1879) - Catherine was born in 1810 in Wirt County and died in 1879 in Lewis County, Western Virginia;
- 15. vi. Jacob Waggoner (1810 – 1847) – Jacob was born 1810 and died in 1847 or 1848;
- 16. vii. George Waggoner (1812 – 1877) – George was born on April 4, 1812 in Harrison County, Virginia, died on April 17, 1877 in Roane County, and is buried in Hersman Cemetery;
- 17. viii. William Waggoner (1813 – Unknown) – William was born on July 9, 1813 and married Malinda;
- 18. ix. Susannah Waggoner (1814 – 1905) – Susannah was born on March 16, 1814;
- 19. x. Mariah Waggoner (1818 – 1905) – Mariah was born on November 21, 1818 and died on July 13, 1905; and
- 20. xi. Samuel Waggoner (1821 – Unknown) – Samuel married Nancy Garrison on March 15, 1840.

Descendents of Thomas Davis

First Generation

1. Thomas Davis (1811 - BEF 1860) - Thomas Davis was born in Virginia in 1811 and came to Ohio in the 1820's, along with his mother Elizabeth and a younger brother. The family settled in Bloom Township in Fairfield County. Thomas married Sarah McGinnis on May 28, 1835. They were married in Fairfield County by L. White, M.G. Sarah was born in 1811 or 1812 in Pennsylvania, the daughter of Sam McGinnis and came to Ohio from Pennsylvania with her sister, Julia Ann. Thomas would pass away sometime between 1850 and 1860, while Sarah would pass away some time after 1870.

Children of Thomas Davis and Sarah McGinnis:
+ 2. i. Wesley Perry Davis (1839 – 1923);
+ 3. ii. Marcus Whitcome Davis (1844 – 1910); and
+ 4. iii. Newton Jerod Davis (1847 – 1924).

Second Generation

2. Wesley Perry Davis (1839 – 1923) - Wesley Perry Davis was born on May 1, 1839 in Fairfield County, Ohio, the eldest son of Thomas and Sarah (McGinnis) Davis. The family lived near Carroll, Ohio, where they pursued farming.

According to information obtained from the Civil War Military File of Wesley Perry Davis in the National Archives and Records Administration, Washington, D.C. -- *February 22, 1864, enlisted in Company B, 17th Ohio Volunteer Infantry. Wesley stood 5 feet 8 inches tall, had a light complexion, light hair and gray eyes, when he enlisted in the Union Army on February 23, 1864. Service - Reconnaissance to Dalton, Ga., February 22-27, 1864. Tunnel Hill, Buzzard's Roost Gap and Rocky Face Ridge February 23-25. Atlanta (Ga.) Campaign May 1 to September 8. Demonstrations on Rocky Face Ridge May 8-11. Battle of Resaca May 14-15. At this battle, Wesley incurred an injury resulting in a sprain of his left ankle, he spent time in a hospital in Louisville, Kentucky and later transferred to Columbus, Ohio before he was given a Discharge of Disability and then mustered out of the Army on January 25, 1865. Complications resulting from his injury forced him to walk with the aid of crutches for at least three and a half years.*

Wesley married Elizabeth Hanna on November 17, 1867 in Canal Winchester, Fairfield County, Ohio at the German Reform Church. Elizabeth was the daughter of Joseph Hanna of Fairfield County, Ohio. By 1880, the family had moved to Hebron, Ohio, where they purchased a house on North Street. Wesley continued to work as a farmer, but by 1886, he was deemed a "permanent cripple" and began to receive a disability pension from the government from his Civil War duties.

Wesley passed away from pneumonia at his home in Hebron on December 28, 1923, while Elizabeth would live to be 97 years old, passing away on February 18, 1932. Both are buried in Kirkersville Cemetery.

Children of Wesley Perry Davis and Elizabeth Hanna:
+ 5. i. Charles Joseph Davis (1868 – 1949); and
+ 6. ii. Mary Marie Davis (1874 – 1955).

3. Marcus Whitcome Davis (1844 – 1910) - Marcus Whitcome Davis was born December 1, 1844 in Fairfield County, Ohio, the second son of Thomas and Sarah (McGinnis) Davis. Marcus, along with his two brothers Wesley and Jerod grew up on the family farm in Licking Township, Fairfield County and took care of it after their father passed away. During 1872, Marcus married Jane Emily Young, the daughter of John Young and Emily B. Mills. Jane was born December 12, 1846 in Hebron, Ohio. They moved to Hebron, Ohio where together they raised four daughters.

Marcus Whitcome Davis, 1864

The family grew up in their home on Canal Street (Lot #18) in Hebron, Ohio, where they owned Lots #13-21 and Lots #25-30. The home was a two-story, split level with three or four bedrooms. Here, Marcus worked as a farmer, raising livestock. In 1907, he added another 110 acres to his land holdings by acquiring property on the outskirts of Hebron. While Marcus appears to have been quite a businessman, Jane became one of Hebron's school teachers in 1866 and held that position throughout the 1860's and 1870's. Jane was certified to teach five subjects as seen from the following hand written certification by the Hebron School Board of Examiners:

> "Hebron Oct 2nd 1866
> *We the undersigned, Board of Examiners for the Hebron Union Schools, hereby certify that Emily Jane Young, has been examined in Reading, Writing, Arithmetic, Geography, and English Grammar, and having produced satisfactory evidence of good moral character; she is authorized to teach the above branches in said schools, for the term of one year from the date hereof.*
>   Ira E. Kelsey
>   Board of Examiners"

On Wednesday, August 3, 1910 around 2:00 PM, Marcus while eating lunch by the side of the road on the Buckeye Lake Road, about two miles south of Hebron, dropped dead of a heart attach. Marcus was then buried in the Hebron Cemetery east of Hebron, Ohio.

After Marcus' death, Jane was forced to divide her home in order to take in boarders and had to auction off a good deal of her property. The auction took place on Saturday, September 3rd, 1910 and included such items as 3 head of horses, 10 head of hogs, and various farm machinery and tools.

Jane Emily Davis at near 80, holding Karl Taggart

Here, Jane would live until the early 1920's at which time, due to her failing health. Jane moved in with her eldest daughter Myrtle and her husband and lived to be 79 years old, passing away on May 25, 1926. Marcus' body was then moved from the Hebron Cemetery to the Cedar Hill Cemetery, Newark, Ohio, where both he and Jane are buried.

Children of Marcus Whitcome Davis and Jane Emily Young:

    7.   i.   Myrtle I. Davis (1873 – 1925) – Myrtle was born on March 29, 1873, married Franklin E. Slabaugh, a lawyer, sheriff and judge in Licking County, passed away on December 25, 1925 in Newark, Ohio, and is buried in Cedar Hill Cemetery;

+   8.   ii.   Lillie Belle Davis (1874 – 1960);
+   9.   iii.   Jessie Helen Davis (1877 – 1960); and
+   10.   iv.   Georgia Emma Davis (1881 – 1966).

4.   **Newton Jerod Davis (1847 – 1924)** – Newton Jerod Davis was born on March 25, 1847, the youngest son of Thomas and Sarah (McGinnis) Davis. Newton married Hannah Ann Price, the daughter of Thomas and Catherine Price, sometime before 1874. Newton passed away on April 24, 1924 after a long illness. Hannah passed away on January 28, 1933. Both are buried in the Hebron Cemetery.

Children of Newton Jerod Davis and Hannah Ann Price:

    11.   i.   Lula B. Davis (1874 – 1933) – Lula was born on November 25, 1874 in Fairfield County, Ohio, married Charles Harter, died on January 24, 1933, and is buried in the Hebron Cemetery;
    12.   ii.   Albert Perry Davis (1876 – Unknown) – Albert was born on October 10, 1876 in Fairfield Count, Ohio and married Ada Crawford on November 30, 1896;
    13.   iii.   John William 'Willie' Davis (1880 – 1890) – Willie was born on January 25, 1880 in Fairfield County, Ohio and passed away at the age of 10 on January 25, 1890;
+   14.   iv.   Clarence Clay Davis (1881 – 1946);
    15.   v.   Jesse N. Davis (1884 – Unknown);
    16.   vi.   Raymond Thomas Davis (1890 – Unknown); and
    17.   vii.   Clara May Davis (1893 – Unknown).

Third Generation

5.   **Charles Joseph Davis (1868 – 1949)** – Charles Joseph Davis was born on August 14, 1868, the son of Wesley Perry and Elizabeth (Hanna) Davis. Charles married Nettie May Amspach (1876 – 1963).

Charles was a section foreman for the New York Central Railroad. Charles died on August 21, 1949 in Hebron, Ohio and is buried at the Kirkersville Cemetery.

    Children of Charles Joseph Davis and Nettie May Amspach:
- 18. i. Eliza E. Davis (1894 – 1980); and
- 19. ii. Owen Edward 'Eddie' Davis (1899 – 1923)

6. Mary Marie Davis (1874 – 1955) – Mary Marie Davis was born on May 20, 1874 in Walnut Township, Fairfield County, Ohio, the daughter of Wesley Perry and Elizabeth (Hanna) Davis. Mary married William P. Warner (1871 – 1952) on March 17, 1895 in Licking County, Ohio. She passed away on October 14, 1955.

    Children of William P. Warner and Mary Marie Davis:
- 20. i. Russell William Warner (1895 – 1970);
- 21. ii. Margaret Marie Warner (1898 – 1992); and
- 22. iii. Charles D. Warner (1904 – Unknown).

8. Lillie Belle Davis (1874 – 1960) – Lillie Belle Davis was born on November 21, 1874 in Hebron, Ohio, the daughter of Marcus and Jane Emily (Young) Davis. Lillie married Frank S. Lees on January 11, 1893 in her parent's home. Around 1947, they moved to Canton, Ohio where Lillie died on June 8, 1960. She is buried in the Cedar Hill Cemetery in Newark, Ohio.

    Children of Frank S. Lees and Lillie Belle Davis:
- 23. i. Lillie Lees (1894 – 1898) – Lillie was born on February 7, 1894 in Licking County, Ohio, and died on October 14, 1898 from eating a large quantity of jimson seed, and is buried in the Cedar Hill Cemetery;
- 24. ii. Mildred Lees (1896 – Unknown) – Mildred was born on January 13, 1896; and
- 25. iii. Howard George Lees (1898 – Unknown) – Howard was born on May 3, 1898.

9. Jessie Helen Davis (1877 – 1960) – See Perry Paris Comisford, page 17.

10. Georgia Emma Davis (1881 – 1966) – Georgia Emma Davis was born on October 4, 1881 in Hebron, Ohio, the daughter of Marcus and Jane Emily (Young) Davis. By the time she started attending school, Hebron had built a new four-room brick school building on High Street. She was one of eleven students who graduated from Hebron High School in 1899.

Hebron High School Class of 1899, along with Franklin E. Slabaugh

Emma married Arthur W. Taggart on December 4, 1904, at the home of Emma's parents and was officiated by Elder Adam Dove, pastor of the Primitive Baptist Church. Arthur passed away on July

17, 1965, while Emma passed away at the age of 85 years, on November 10, 1966. They are both buried in Cedar Hill Cemetery.

    Children of Arthur W. Taggart and Georgia Emma Davis:
        26.   i.   Thelma Elmira Taggart (1905 – 1995);
        27.   ii.   Lawrence Taggart (1907 – 1981);
        28.   iii. Frank Taggart (1908 – 1976);
        29.   iv. Karl Arthur Taggart (1917 -1985); and
        30.   v.   Frederick Taggart (Living).

14.   Clarence Clay Davis (1881 – 1946) – Clarence Clay Davis was born on July 10, 1881 in Licking County, Ohio, the son of Newton Jerod and Hannah Ann (Price) Davis. Clarence married Mary R. Mohan. Clarence passed away on July 4, 1946 and is buried in the Hebron Cemetery.

    Children of Clarence Clay Davis and Mary R. Mohan:
        31.   i.   Jessie Ronald 'Ron' Davis (1918 – 1993);
        32.   ii.   Harold J. 'Codge' Davis (1920 – 1990);
        33.   iii. Evelyn M. Davis (1922 – Unknown);
        34.   iv. Robert G. Davis (1924 – Unknown);
        35.   v.   Dolores Ann Davis (1929 – Unknown); and
        36.   vi. Dennis M. Davis, who married Marian E. Fitch.

Descendents of John Young and Emily B. Mills

First Generation

1. John Young (1814 – 1889) - John Young was born December 4, 1814 in Pennsylvania, possibly around Hagerstown, Maryland. John moved to Ohio, settling down in Fairfield County, Ohio where he met his wife to be, Emily B. Mills. Emily was born April 1, 1816 in Perry County, Ohio, the daughter of Jacob and Mary (Shepherd) Mills. They were married in Hebron, Ohio on October 10, 1841.

John was a carpenter and farmhand in the Hebron area, where he and Emily bought their home located at the corner of Third Street and Mound Street (Lot #41) for $650 in January of 1853 from Emily's brother, Warner W. Mills.

John and Emily added to their land holdings the following year by acquiring the property next-door to the house (Lot #42) for $25 from Emily's other brother, Ashford S. Mills. Then, in 1858 they bought outlots #8 and #9 from Ashford for $800.

John became quite a farmer in the area and retired around 1882, at which time he sold the outlots for $2,000. Shortly after this, Emily died of heart disease on December 22, 1882.

In July of 1884, John, along with J.W. Oldaker, David Pierce Burch, William Kirk, and Mary Adela (Young) Burch became the charter members of the Hebron Soap Manufacturing Association.

In November of 1886 John had a stroke and after a long illness, passed away of dropsy on Thursday, May 29, 1889. Both he and Emily are buried in Hebron Cemetery with a large tombstone by the large tree in the northwest corner of the cemetery.

Children of John Young and Emily B. Mills:
+ 2. i. Lavonia Young (1844 – 1886);
+ 3. ii. Jane Emily Young (1846 – 1926);
+ 4. iii. Isabelle T. Young (1849 – 1915);
    5. iv. Orriel Young (1852 – 1920) – Orriel was born on October 1, 1852, married Jim Pugh, and died on November 25, 1920 in Kirkersville, Licking County, Ohio; and
+ 6. v. Mary Adele Young (1856 – 1915).

Orriel (Young) Pugh

Second Generation

2.   Lavonia Young (1844 – 1886) – Lavonia Young was born on November 2, 1844 in Fairfield County, Ohio, the daughter of John and Emily B. (Mills) Young. Lavonia married Jefferson House, the son of John and Mary (Wrolens) House, in 1868. Jefferson was a farmer and served as the Postmaster for Hebron. Lavonia passed away at the age of 41 on May 19, 1886, while Jefferson would pass away on May 20, 1898. Both are buried in the Hebron Cemetery.

Children of Jefferson House and Lavonia Young:
- 7. i. Ada Bell 'Addie' House (1869 – 1953) – Addie never married;
- 8. ii. Gracie House (1874 – 1874);
- \+ 9. iii. Harry Allen House (1875 – 1953);
- \+ 10. iv. Mamie Rachel House (1877 – 1959); and
- \+ 11. v. George R. House (1880 – 1958).

3.   Jane Emily Young (1846 – 1926) - See Marcus Whitcome Davis, page 68.

4.   Isabelle T. Young (1849 – 1915) – Isabelle 'Belle' T. Young was born on November 14, 1849, the daughter of John and Emily B. (Mills) Young. Belle married Jennings R. Hand who died in 1882. She then married Thomas M. White on December 29, 1888 in Jacksontown, Ohio. They settled in Hebron, where T.M. was a butcher. T.M. also would serve as the mayor of Hebron. Belle passed away on October 29, 1922 in Hebron, Ohio and is buried in the Licking Cemetery.

    Children of Jennings Hand and Isabelle T. Young:
    12.   i.   George I. Hand (1875 – 1877).

6.   Mary Adele Young (1856 – 1915) – Mary Adele Young was born on February 14, 1856, the daughter of John and Emily B. (Mills) Young. Adele married David Pierce Burch, a merchant in Hebron on January 22, 1880, at the home of her parents. Adele was very involved in her community and served as the Hebron correspondent to the Newark Advocate. She also served as the Vice President of the National Association of the Christian Church and helped and aided in the work of caring for the orphans, the needy, the sick and the aged poor. She passed away on December 1, 1915 in Hebron, Ohio, after a long illness and confinement to her room for a month with carcinoma of the lungs and is buried in the Hebron Cemetery.

    Children of David Pierce Burch and Mary Adele Young:
    13.   i.   Hazel Burch (1890 – 1890).

Third Generation

9.   Harry Allen House (1875 – 1953) – Harry Allen House was born on September 14, 1875 in Union Township, Licking County, Ohio, the son of Jefferson and Lavonia (Young) House. Harry married Julia Henrietta Smith on April 12, 1908 in Fairfield County, Ohio. Harry was a deputy state fire marshal for sometime. He passed away on February 17, 1953, while Julia would pass away on July 27, 1969. They are buried in Forest Rose Cemetery in Lancaster, Ohio.

Children of Harry Allen House and Julia Henrietta Smith:
    14.   i.   Elizabeth Belle House (1911 – 1916); and
    15.   ii.   Margaret Louise House (1915 – Unknown).

10.   Mamie Rachel House (1877 – 1959) – Mamie Rachel House was born on July 9, 1877 in Union Township, Licking County, Ohio, the daughter of Jefferson and Lavonia (Young) House. Mamie married Francis 'Frank' Marion Good on October 9, 1898 in Fairfield County, Ohio. They lived in Millersport, before moving to Newark, Ohio around 1947. Frank passed away on May 13, 1949, while Mamie passed away in her home on March 13, 1959. They are buried in the Kirkersville Cemetery.

Children of Frank Marion Good and Mamie Rachel House:
    16.   i.   James 'Ervin' Good (1899 – 1980);
    17.   ii.   Harry E. Good (1902 – Unknown); and
    18.   iii.   Carlton Frances Good (1909 – 1975).

11.   George R. House (1880 – 1958) – George R. House was born on May 24, 1880 in Hebron, Ohio, the son of Jefferson and Lavonia (Young) House. He married Maude Williams, who passed away on January 19, 1944. George then married Bessie Crosby. George was a fireman for the City of Newark for 27 years. He passed away on July 5, 1958 and is buried in the Cedar Hill Cemetery.

Children of George R. House and Maude Williams:
    19.   i.   Mary Eleanor House (1911 – 1995).

Homer Comisford and Mary Eleanor House

Descendents of Jacob Mills and Mary Shepherd

First Generation

1. Jacob Mills (Unknown – Unknown) - Jacob Mills was born in Pennsylvania. According to records handed down through the family, records show that Jacob's father or grandfather's name was Thomas Mills, married to Elizabeth. Jacob married Mary Shepherd, the daughter of Thomas and Catherine (Palmer) Shepherd. Mary was born in 1767 in Virginia. It is likely that Jacob and Mary came to Ohio from Frederick County, Virginia, as the record for several of their childrens birth's show Frederick County, Virginia. They came to Ohio early in the 1800's and settled in Hopewell Twp, Perry County (possibly sometime around the time of the War of 1812.) In the 1820 US Census, it shows that Jacob was engaged in commerce in Hopewell Twp of Perry County, Ohio. Jacob must have died sometime between 1820 and 1830, as Mary is listed in the 1830 US Census, Ohio, Perry County, Reading Township. Mary and her family would move to Hebron, Licking County, Ohio some time before 1840, as Mary is then listed in both, the 1840 and 1850 US Census, Ohio, Licking County, Hebron. Mary raised her grandson, Charles C. Marsh, after the death of his parents. Mary passed away in 1857 and is buried in the Hebron Cemetery.

Children of Jacob Mills and Mary Shepherd:
+ 2. i. Rebecca Mills (1798 – 1857);
+ 3. ii. Louisa Mills (1801 – 1901);
+ 4. iii. Mary Ann Mills (1802 – Unknown);
+ 5. iv. Warner W. Mills (1807 – Unknown);
+ 6. v. Adaline Mills (1809 – 1889);
   7. vi. Ashford S. Mills (1810 – 1862) - Ashford was born in 1810 in Virginia. From information obtained from the Civil War Military File of Ashford Mills in the National Archives and Records Administration, Washington, D.C. -- *Born in Frederick County, Virginia around 1819. Ashford had brown eyes, dark hair, a florid complexion, and stood 5 feet 10 inches tall when he enlisted in the Union Army on August 22, 1862. He was actually 51 years old (as substantiated by the 1850 and 1860 US Census). He served for two months as a private in Company H of the 3rd Ohio Volunteer Infantry, before dying from disease on Christmas Day, December 25, 1862 in Louisville, Kentucky;*

+   8.   vii.   Sarah Jane Mills (1813 -1843); and
+   9.   viii. Emily B. Mills (1816 – 1882).

Second Generation

2.   Rebecca Mills (1798 – Unknown) – Rebecca Mills was born in Virginia in 1798, the daughter of Jacob and Mary (Sheperd) Mills. Rebecca married John B. Strawn in 1820 in Perry County, Ohio. John was born on June 13, 1795 in Pennsylvania, the son of Thomas and Hannah (Cooper) Strawn, Jr. John and Rebecca were listed in the 1850 US Census for Hocking County, Ohio. Rebecca passed away on September 30, 1857, while John passed away in April of 1858.

Children of John B. Strawn and Rebecca Mills:
    10.   i.   Elizabeth Strawn (1820 – Unknown) – Elizabeth married Alexander Barclay on March 31, 1840 in Hocking County, Ohio;
+   11.   ii.   George Washington Strawn (1821 – 1902);
+   12.   iii.   Mary Ann Strawn (1823 – 1918);
+   13.   iv.   Isaac Strawn (1825 – 1906);
+   14.   v.   David Oakley Strawn (1827 – Unknown);
+   15.   vi.   Nelson Strawn (1830 – Unknown);
    16.   iii.   Ellen Jane Strawn (1832 – Unknown) – Ellen married Hiram A. Vess on May 25, 1851 in Hocking County, Ohio;
    17.   iv.   Moses Strawn (1837 – Unknown) and
    18.   v.   Amanda Strawn (1840 – Unknown).

3.   Louisa Mills (1801 – 1901) – Louisa Mills was born on January 24, 1801 in Frederick County, Virginia, the daughter of Jacob and Mary (Shepherd) Mills. Louisa married Hiram Cooper on December 7, 1824 in Perry County, Ohio. They were listed on the 1860 US Census for Hancock County, Ohio. Hiram was born in 1803. Hiram died June 19, 1884, while Louisa would pass away on August 9, 1901. Both are buried in Pleasant-McComb Cemetery.

Children of Hiram Cooper and Louisa Mills:
    19.   i.   Caroline Cooper (1830 – Unknown);
    20.   ii.   Jasper F. Cooper (1831 – 1894);
    21.   iii.   Elizabeth Cooper (1834 – Unknown);
    22.   iv.   Louisa Cooper (1836 – Unknown);
    23.   v.   James A. Cooper (1839 – Unknown);
    24.   vi.   Sarah E. Cooper (1842 – Unknown);
    25.   vii.   Allen Cooper (1835 – Unknown); and
    26.   viii. Rebecca A. Cooper (1840 – Unknown).

4. **Mary Ann Mills (1802 – Unknown)** – Mary Ann Mills was born in 1802 in Virginia, the daughter of Jacob and Mary (Shepherd) Mills. Mary Ann married William Sager in 1833 in Perry County, Ohio. William was born in 1802. They were listed in the 1860 US Census for Delaware County, Ohio. Mary Ann passed away on July 22, 1867 and is buried in Liberty Church Cemetery.

    Children of William Sager and Mary Ann Mills:
       27.   i.   Mary E. Sager (1833 – Unknown);
       28.   ii.   Jacob N. Sager (1835 – Unknown)
       29.   iii. Jerome Sager (1837 – Unknown);
       30.   vi. Emily Sager (1839 - Unknown); and
       31.   v.   Thomas Sager (1842 – Unknown).

5. **Warner W. Mills (1807 – Unknown)** – Warner W. Mills was born in 1807 in Virginia, the son of Jacob and Mary (Shepherd) Mills. Warner had two children with Mary Ladley, not sure whether they were ever married or just divorced, but Warner would then marry Elizabeth Griffith around 1837. Around 1851, Warner moved his family to Sperry Mills, three miles south of Newark, where he operated a mill and farmed.

    Children of Warner W. Mills and Mary Ladley:
+   32.   i.   Alcinda Mills (1836 – Unknown); and
+   33.   ii.   Warner Mills (1837 – 1918).

    Children of Warner W. Mills and Elizabeth Griffith:
+   34.   i.   Jacob Thomas Mills (1838 – 1904);
+   35.   ii.   Francis W. Mills (1844 – 1930);
     36.   iii. Dave Mills (1846 – 1846);
     37.   iv. Daniel G. Mills (1846 – 1889) - Daniel was born in 1846 in Ohio, the son of Warner W. and Elizabeth Marie (Griffith) Mills. From information obtained from the Civil War Military File of Daniel G. Mills in the National Archives and Records Administration, Washington, D.C. – *February 23, 1864, enlisted in Company H, Third Ohio Volunteer Infantry. Daniel stood 5 feet 6 inches tall, had a light complexion, dark hair and gray eyes, when he enlisted in the Union Army on February 23, 1864.* He married Edith Binkley on February 26, 1884 in Newport, Kentucky. Daniel passed away on June 9, 1889 and is buried in the Hebron Cemetery;
     38.   v.   Ashford Mills (1850 – 1926) – Ashford Mills was born in April of 1850. He lived in Hebron with his sister, Francis, and was a bridge builder. He died on May 30, 1926 and is buried in the Hebron Cemetery;

       39.   vi.   Sarah E. Mills (1856 – Unknown) – Sarah died sometime before 1870; and
+   40.   vii.   Benjamin Lampton Mills (1860 – 1926).

6.   Adaline Mills (1809 – 1889) – Adaline Mills was born in 1809 in Virginia, the daughter of Jacob and Mary (Shepherd) Mills. Adaline married George W. Binkley on February 17, 1831 in Perry County, Ohio. George was born in 1809. They are listed in the 1850 and 1860 US Census for Perry County, Ohio. George would pass away in 1887, while Adaline passed away in 1889. They are both buried in Binkley Ridge Cemetery in Reading Township, Perry County, Ohio.

    Children of George W. Binkley and Adaline Mills:
    41.   i.   Rebecca Binkley (1833 – Unknown);
    42.   ii.   Homer Binkley (1834 – Unknown);
    43.   iii. Warren Binkley (1838 – Unknown);
    44.   vi.   Louisa Binkley (1841 – Unknown);
    45.   v.   George S. Binkley (1844 – Unknown);
    46.   vi.   Pharsalia Binkley (1846 – Unknown);
    47.   vii. Nancy C. Binkley (1849 – Unknown); and
    48.   viii. Harriet E. Binkley (1854 – Unknown).

8.   Sarah Jane Mills (1813 -1843) – Sarah Jane Mills was born on December 4, 1813, the daughter of Jacob and Mary (Shepherd) Mills. Sarah Jane married Roswell Marsh on August 19, 1841 in Licking County, Ohio. According to the family bible, Roswell was born in Hartland, Windsor County, Vermont on July 28, 1794. A little over a year after their first child, Sarah Jane passed away on July 4, 1843 and is buried in the Hebron Cemetery, Licking County, Ohio. By this time Roswell was now 56 year old and had already lost at least 2 wives -- maybe a couple more -- along with some children, so he simply may not have been able physically and/or mentally to care for his child. Young Charles had gone to live with his maternal grandmother, Mary Mills and during the spring of 1852, Roswell's intestate estate is filed and guardians (including Ashford S. Mills, Sarah's brother) appointed for Charles, who is specifically listed as heir of Roswell.

    Children of Roswell Marsh and Sarah Jane Mills:
+   49   i.   Charles Case Marsh (1842 – 1914).

9.   Emily B. Mills (1816 – 1882) – See John Young, page 75.

Third Generation

11. George Washington Strawn (1821 – 1902) – George Washington Strawn was born on January 15, 1821 in Ohio, the son of John B. and Rebecca (Mills) Strawn. George married Elizabeth Davis on April 16, 1846 in Hocking County, Ohio and died on April 13, 1902.

    Children of George Washington Strawn and Elizabeth Davis:
        50.   i.   Mary A. Strawn (1847 – Unknown);
        51.   ii.   Harriet J. Strawn (1849 – Unknown);
        52.   iii.   Alice Strawn (1853 – Unknown);
        53.   iv.   John Strawn (1856 – Unknown);
        54.   v.   Martha Strawn (1858 – Unknown); and
        55.   vi.   Charles F. Strawn (1863 – Unknown).

12. Mary Ann Strawn (1823 – 1918) – Mary Ann Strawn was born November 13, 1823 in Morgan County, Ohio, the daughter of John B. and Rebecca (Mills) Strawn. Mary Ann married James Hone, the son of Henry and Rebecca (Brown) Hone, on October 4, 1844 in Hocking County, Ohio. James was born in 1822 in Morgan County, Ohio. Mary Ann passed away at the age of 94 on August 31, 1918 in Logan, Benton Twp, Hocking County, Ohio. She is buried in Oak Grove Cemetery.

    Children of James Hone and Mary Ann Strawn:
        56.   i.   John Henry Hone (1845 – Unknown) – John Henry married Lucy Williams;
        57.   ii.   Safety M. Hone (1847 – Unknown) – Safety was born in August 1847 and married Sarah M. Heinlein on September 4, 1872;
        58.   iii.   Rebecca Mae Hone (1848 – 1933) – Rebecca was born on June 15, 1848, married Anthony Wayne Mauk on October 5, 1871, and died on January 6, 1933;
        59.   iv.   Anna E. Hone (1850 – Unknown);
        60.   v.   Mary Ellen Hone (1852 – Unknown);
        61.   vi.   Eliza J Hone (1854 – Unknown);
        62.   vii.   Ruth E. Hone (1855 – Unknown);
        63.   viii.   Elizabeth J. Hone (1856 – Unknown);
        64.   ix.   Mariam C. Hone (1859 – Unknown).
        65.   x.   Harriet A. Hone (1862 – Unknown); and
        66.   xi.   James Brown Hone (1864 – 1923).

13. Isaac Strawn (1825 – 1906) – Isaac Strawn was born in 1825 in Ohio, the son of John B. and Rebecca (Mills) Strawn. Isaac married Mary Schooley on November 3, 1851.

    Children of Isaac Strawn and Mary Schooley:
      67.   i.   Roswell Strawn (1854 – Unknown);
      68.   ii.   George Washington Strawn (1860 – Unknown);
      69.   iii.   Isaac Newton Strawn (1863 – Unknown);
      70.   iv.   Sherman Strawn (1864 – Unknown);
      71.   v.   Clark U. Strawn (1868 – Unknown);
      72.   vi.   Olive Strawn (1870 – Unknown); and
      73.   vii.   Walter C. Strawn (1874 – Unknown).

14. David Oakley Strawn (1827 – Unknown) – David Oakley Strawn was born in 1827 in Ohio, the son of John B. and Rebecca (Mills) Strawn. David married Amy Home on February 11, 1856.

    Children of David Oakley Strawn and Amy Hone:
      74.   i.   Thomas Jefferson Strawn (1857 – Unknown).

15. Nelson Strawn (1830 – Unknown) – Nelson Strawn was born in 1830 in Ohio, the son of John B. and Rebecca (Mills) Strawn. Nelson married Elizabeth Jane Rhoades on October 17, 1852 in Jackson, Ohio. Nelson was a blacksmith. The family would move west into Iowa and then Missouri by 1880.

    Children of Nelson Strawn and Elizabeth Jane Rhoades:
      75.   i.   Mary Catherine Strawn (1853 – Unknown);
      76.   ii.   Susan A. Strawn (1855 – Unknown);
      77.   iii.   Nelson Strawn (1858 – Unknown);
      78.   iv.   Isaac N. Strawn (1860 – Unknown);
      79.   v.   Eliza J. Strawn (1860 – Unknown);
      80.   vi.   George Strawn (1862 – Unknown);
      81.   vii.   Charles Strawn (1864 – Unknown);
      82.   viii.   Ellen Strawn (1866 – Unknown); and
      83.   ix.   Hattie Strawn (1868 – Unknown).

32. Alcinda Mills (1836 – Unknown) – Alcinda Mills was born in 1836, the daughter of Warner W. Mills and Mary Ladley. She lived with her father during the taking of the US Census of 1850, while her brother Warner, lived with his mother's family. Alcinda married Charles Friend and they settled in Fairfield County, Ohio.

Children of Charles Friend and Alcinda Mills:
    84.   i.   Augusta Ellen Friend (1858 – 1934) – Augusta was born in September 1858. She married Stanley Rees on February 2, 1884 in Licking County, Ohio. She passed away on July 26, 1934 in Columbus, Ohio and is buried in Licking Cemetery in Union Township, Licking County, Ohio.

33.   **Warner W. Mills (1837 – 1918)** – Warner W. Mills was born in 1837, the son of Warner W. Mills and Mary Ladley. In the 1850 US Census, Warner was living with his mother's family (shown as Warner Ladley.) Warner became a Captain in the 32nd Ohio Volunteer Infantry, and served as the Secretary and Treasurer of the Regimental Association of the 32nd OVI after the war.

Warner became a dry goods merchant and would spend time in Muskingum County and Gratiot, before moving to Columbus. Warner married Caroline 'Carrie' Matilda Sims around 1865 in Gratiot, the daughter of Simeon Walter Sims, Sr. and Susannah Seagrave. Carrie was born on February 6, 1842 in Gratiot, Ohio. Warner passed away on August 23, 1918 in Columbus, Ohio, while Carrie would pass away on February 26, 1931. Both are buried in Green Lawn Cemetery in Columbus, Ohio.

Children of Warner W. Mills and Caroline Matilda Sims:
    85.   i.   Mahlon Mills (1866 – Unknown);
    86.   ii.   Anna E. Mills (1868 – 1904);
    87.   iii.   Mary Mills (1870 – 1924);
    88.   iv.   Kate Mills (1872 – 1926);
    89.   v.   Earl Mills (1874 – Unknown);
    90.   vi.   Glen Mills (1876 – Unknown);
    91.   vii.   Webb Mills (1878 – 1934); and
    92.   viii.   Isaqueena Mills (1880 – 1896).

34.   **Jacob Thomas Mills (1838 – 1904)** – Jacob Thomas Mills was born on October 9, 1838 in Ohio, the son of Warner W. and Elizabeth Marie (Griffith) Mills. When 13, Jacob moved with his family to the Sperry Mills, three miles south of Newark, where he worked for his father at milling and farming.

From information obtained from the Civil War Military File of Jacob Thomas Mills in the National Archives and Records Administration, Washington, D.C. and the regimental history – *April 21, 1861, enlisted in Company H "Licking Tigers" Newark, Licking County. (Formerly the "Wide Awakes"), Third Ohio Volunteer Infantry, and afterwards re-enlisted. Service - West Virginia Campaign July 6-17, 1861. Action at Middle Fork Bridge, W. Va.,*

July 6-7. Rich Mountain July 10-11. Pursuit to Cheat Mountain Summit July 11-16. Moved to Elkwater Creek August 4. Operations on Cheat Mountain September 11-17. Action at Elkwater September 11. Cheat Mountain Pass September 12. Scout to Marshall October 3. Reconnaissance to Big Springs October 6. Moved to Louisville, Ky., November 26-28. Duty at Elizabethtown and Bacon Creek, Ky., till February, 1862. Advance on Nashville. Tenn., February 10-25. Occupation of Nashville February 25-March 17. Advance on Murfreesboro, Tenn., March 17-19. Reconnaissance to Shelbyville, Tullahoma and McMinnville March 25-28. Moved to Fayetteville April 7. Advance on Huntsville, Ala., April 10-11. Capture of Huntsville April 11. Pursuit to Decatur April 11-14. Action at Bridgeport April 27. West Bridge, near Bridgeport, April 29. Duty at Huntsville till August 23. March to Louisville, Ky., in pursuit of Bragg August 23-September 25. Pursuit of Bragg into Kentucky October 1-15. Battle of Perryville October 8. March to Nashville, Tenn., October 16-November 7, and duty there till December 26. Advance on Murfreesboro December 26-30. Battle of Stone's River December 30-31, 1862, and January 1-3, 1863. At Murfreesboro till April, 1863. Streight's Raid to Rome, Ga., April 26-May 3. Day's Gap, Sand Mountain and Crooked Creek and Hog Mountain, April 30. East Branch Black Warrior Creek May 1. Blount's Farm Gadsden, May 2. Near Centre May 2. Cedar Creek, near Rome, May 3. Regiment captured. Exchanged May, 1863. At Camp Chase, Ohio, reorganizing till August. Quelling Holmes County Ohio Rebellion June 13-18. Pursuit of Morgan July 15-26. Moved to Nashville, Tenn., August 1, thence moved to Bridgeport, Ala., and guard duty there till October. Expedition against Wheeler October 1-8. Duty at Battle Creek, Looney Creek and Kelly's Ford till November 27. Garrison duty at Chattanooga, Tenn., till June, 1864. Ordered to Camp Dennison, Ohio, June 9. Mustered out June 23, 1864.

 Jacob married Caroline 'Carrie or Cora' Green on December 25, 1867 in Granville, Ohio, locating in Jersey, Ohio, where Jacob practiced medicine and farmed. Carrie was the daughter of Henry R. and Caroline (Tight) Green. Jacob applied for a disability pension from the Army in 1882, claiming disability from rheumatism, contracted in camp on the bank of Elk Water River, Virginia, in August 1861. They moved to Columbus, Ohio around 1898 and lived at 461 West Seventh Street. Jacob passed away on January 31, 1904 in Columbus, while Carrie passed away on May 3, 1918. They are both buried in Maple Grove Cemetery in Granville, Ohio.

35. Francis W. Mills (1844 – 1930) – Francis 'Frank' W. Mills was born on August 29, 1944 in Hebron, Ohio, the daughter of Warner W. and Elizabeth Marie (Griffith) Mills. She married Philander R. Hand on September 13, 1864 in Hebron, Ohio. Philander was a farmer and had served during the Civil War in Company H of the 31st Ohio Volunteer Infantry. He died from effects of the war on April 25, 1870. Francis kept a boarding house in Hebron for much of her life and passed away on May 18, 1930 in Hebron, Ohio. She is buried in the Licking Cemetery in Union Township, Licking County, Ohio.

    Children of Philander R. Hand and Francis W. Mills:
    93.   i.   Alberta Hand (1870 – 1871) – Alberta was born on February 16, 1870 and died on April 27, 1871.

40. Benjamin Lampton Mills (1860 – 1926) – Benjamin Lampton Mills was born on March 22, 1860 in Hebron, Ohio, the son of Warner W. and Elizabeth Marie (Griffith) Mills. Benjamin married Nora Janett Beem on October 20, 1904. Nora was born in 1868. Benjamin died from spinal meningitis on March 12, 1926 at his home in Jersey, Ohio and is buried in the Universalist Cemetery in Jersey, Licking County, Ohio. Nora passed away in 1949.

    Children of Benjamin Lampton Mills and Nora Janett Beem:
    94.   i.   Daniel J. Mills (unknown – 1910); and
    95.   ii.   Roger B. Mills (1914 – 1991) – Roger married Hazel L. Cramer and passed away on June 5, 1991 and is buried in the Jersey Universalist Cemetery in Jersey Township, Licking County, Ohio.

49. Charles Case Marsh (1842 -1914) – Charles Case Marsh was born on February 10, 1842 in Hebron, Licking County, Ohio, the son of Roswell and Sarah Jane (Mills) Marsh. Charles served in the Civil War in the 31st Ohio Volunteer Infantry, Companies F & S. After the war, Charles first married Effie Jane, who passed away on September 7, 1870 and is buried in the Hebron Cemetery. Then on March 14, 1876 at Salt Lick Township, Perry County, Ohio, Charles married Sarah Ellen Grant. Sarah was born on November 27, 1852. Together, they had a daughter, Olive Mabel March, born September 15, 1878. Charles passed away on February 13, 1914 in Columbus, Ohio, while Sarah would pass away on September 30, 1945

    Children of Charles Case Marsh and Sarah Ellen Grant:
    96.   i.   Olive Mabel Marsh (1878 – Unknown);

Descendents of Thomas Shepherd and Catherine Palmer

First Generation

1. Thomas Shepherd (1740 – 1805) – Thomas Shepherd was born sometime between 1740 and 1746 in New Jersey. Thomas married Catherine Palmer, the daughter of John and Catherine Palmer, most likely in Frederick County, Virginia. The Shepherd family was Quakers that had moved to Virginia from Maryland. Catherine passed away in 1774. Thomas then married Sarah 'Sally' Castleman, then Martha Humphrey. Thomas would pass away on September 06, 1805 in Frederick County, Virginia (now Clarke County.)

Children of Thomas Shepherd and Catherine Palmer:
- 2. i. Moses Shepherd (1765 – 1845) – Moses married Mary Ross and died September 1, 1845 in Frederick County, Virginia;
- 3. ii. Sarah Shepherd (1766 – 1842) – Sarah was born on April 1, 1766, married John Stephen Castleman by 1787, and died April 14, 1842, with will proven April 25, 1842;
- + 4. iii. Mary Shepherd (1767 – 1857);
- 5. iv. John Shepherd (1769 – Unknown) – John married Polly Odell;
- 6. v. Catherine 'Kitty' Shepherd (Unknown – 1863) – Kitty married Eli Hunt in December 1792 in Frederick County, Virginia, moved to Chester County, Pennsylvania, then married William Clark, and died on June 7, 1863 in Chester County, Pennsylvania; and
- 7. vi. Thomas Shepherd – Thomas married Mary Gold, then Nancy Gold, and then Elizzabeth Buff in October 1823.

Children of Thomas Shepherd and Sarah Castleman:
- 8. i. David Shepherd (1777 – 1841) – David married Phebe Hooper;
- 9. ii. Joseph Henry Shepherd (1781 – 1856) – Joseph was born on November 24, 1781 in Frederick County, Virginia, married Amelia Houston Burchell, and died on December 31, 1856 in Clark County, Virginia;
- 10. iii. Rebecca Shepherd (1782 – Unknown) - Rebecca married John Dare;
- 11. iv. Hannah Shepherd (1785 – Unknown) – Hannah married William Jackson;
- 12. v. James Shepherd (1786 – Unknown) – James married Hannah Hall and then Elizabeth Haines; and

13. vi. Nancy Ann Shepherd (1790 – 1850) – Nancy married George Hanthorn.

Children of Thomas Shepherd and Martha Humphrey:
14. i. Marcy Shepherd (1793 – 1859) – Marcy was born on June 20, 1793 in Wickliffe, Frederick County, Virginia, married William Albert Castleman, and passed away on September 23, 1859:
15. ii. Jonah Hunphreys Shepherd (1795 – 1849) – Jonah married Catherine Ferguson;
16. iii. Humphrey Shepherd (1798 – Unknown) – Humphrey married Catherine Crigler and then married Ellen McIntyre;
17. iv. Tacy Shepherd (1802 – 1849);
18. v. Parkinson Daniel Shepherd (1804 – 1883) - Parkinson married Elias Ann Gnat; and
19. vi. Martha Shepherd (1805 – 1875) – Martha married Richard Osborn.

Second Generation

4. Mary Shepherd (1767 – 1857) - See Jacob Mills, page 81.

Descendents of William Wright and Mary DeCoursey

First Generation

1. William Wright (Unknown – Unknown) - William Wright was the son of Solomon and Mary (DeCoursey) Wright. Both Solomon and Mary were born in England and it is likely that William was born in England prior to the family immigrating to the American Colonies. They arrive in the American Colonies sometime prior to 1760, as William served on a jury of 12 men in 1760 to lay out a road out of Howell's Road, a straight course across Conato to Beaufort's Line & James May. It was also noted in the county records for Edgecombe County, North Carolina, that he and his father, Solomon, worked on the road from Conato to James May in June of 1762. William would marry Mary sometime prior to 1748.

      Children of William and Mary Wright:
+   2.   i.   Francis Wright (1748 – 1838).

Second Generation

2. Francis Wright (1748 – 1838) - Francis Wright is the only son known between William and Mary (DeCoursey) Wright. He was born in 1748 in North Carolina. He married Sarah Winlock, the daughter of Joseph and Margaret (Fielding) Winlock.

Sarah's brother was General Joseph Winlock (1758-1831). He served in the Revolutionary War, rising from a private to captain. He went to Kentucky in 1787, where he became a delegate to the first Kentucky Constitutional Convention in 1792. He was the Kentucky State Senator from 1800 to 1810. He was commissioned a Brigadiar General in the State Militia in 1812. He commanded regiments to aid General William Henry Harrison in the Northwest Territory. He is buried in the family cemetery in Shelby, Kentucky.

Together, Francis and Sarah would have eight children. Sometime prior to 1820, Francis moved his family to Sumner County, Tennessee. Sarah passed away on August 17, 1838, while Francis passed away a couple of months later on October 18, 1838.

Children of Francis Wright and Sarah Winlock:
+ 3. i. Fielding Winlock Wright (1775 – Unknown);
  4. ii. William Wright (1777 – Unknown) - William married Betsy Holt October 30, 1810, in Rockingham County, North Carolina;
  5. iii. Reuben Wright (1782 – Unknown) - Reuben married Philisia McDaniel on July 28, 1809 in Rockingham County, North Carolina;
  6. iv. Charles Wright (1785 – Unknown);
  7. v. Margaret Wright (1790 – Unknown);
  8. vi. Martha Wright (1792 – Unknown);
+ 9. vii. Nancy Wright (1794 – 1876); and
+ 10. viii. Thornton Wright (1795 – Unknown).

Third Generation

3. **Fielding Winlock Wright (1775 – Unknown)** – Fielding Winlock Wright was born in 1775 in Rockingham County, North Carolina, the son of Francis and Sarah (Winlock) Wright. Fielding served during the War of 1812 in the 6th Regiment, 4th Company, detached from Rockingham Regiment. He married Francis McDaniel and sometime prior to 1820, moved his family to Sumner County, Tennessee.

Children of Fielding Winlock Wright and Francis McDaniels:
  11. i. Isaac Newton Wright (1807 – 1880) – Isaac was born on November 15, 1807 in North Carolina and died on November 11, 1880 in Robertson County, Tennessee;
  12. ii. Mary Watson Wright (1812 – Unknown) – Mary married John Wesley Webb on June 2, 1830 in Robertson County, Tennessee; and
  13. iii. Francis DeCoursey Wright (1822 – Unknown) – Francis married Daniel A. Webb.

9. **Nancy Wright (1794 – 1876)** - Nancy was born about 1794 in Rockingham County, North Carolina, the daughter of Francis and Sarah (Winlock) Wright. Nancy married John Swearington Butt on September 15, 1809. John was born on October 5, 1791 in Rockingham County, North Carolina. John and Nancy owned land on Little Rockingham Creek near Wentworth in Rockingham County, North Carolina. About 1830, John and Nancy migrated to Sumner County, Tennessee and settled north of Portland near the Kentucky-Tennessee border. John would pass away on April 2, 1875 in Simpson County, Kentucky and is buried in the Prikle Cemetery. Nancy died on January 28, 1876 in Logan County, Kentucky and is buried in

Stevenson Church Cemetery.

Children of John Swearington Butt and Nancy Wright:
- 14. i. Elizabeth Johnson Butt (1810 - 1895) – Elizabeth was born on August 10, 1810 and married Alexander Prikle;
- 15. ii. William Alfred Butt (1812 - 1882) - William was born on July 20, 1812 and married Emily Boren;
- 16. iii. Hazel Green Butt (1814 - Unknown) – Hazel was born on April 26, 1814 and married Mary Barker;
- 17. iv. Ruebin Pinkney Butt (1817 - 1898) - Ruebin was born on September 9, 1817 and married Susanna Mayes;
- 18. v. Richard Calvin Butt (1820 - 1899) – Richard was born on August 16, 1820 and married Elizabeth Henton;
- 19. vi. John Frances Butt (1822 - 1868) - John was born on October 28, 1822 and married Cyrena Bush;
- 20. vii. Johnson Crofford Butt (b.1824) - Johnson was born on November 5, 1824;
- 21. viii. Elisha Swearington Butt (1828 - 1880) - Elisha was born on January 16, 1828 and married Amelia Groves; and
- 22. ix. Nancy Butt (1831 – 1920) – Nancy was born on August 10, 1831 and married John Hendricks Mayes.

10. Thornton Wright (1795 – Unknown) - Thornton Wright is the youngest son of Francis and Sarah (Winlock) Wright. He was born about 1795 in Rockingham County, North Carolina. He married Polly Webster on May 9, 1814 in Rockingham County, North Carolina. He then married Lucinda in Virginia and would settle in Culpeper County, Virginia. Thornton was a shoemaker. Prior to 1860 the family moved from Culpeper County, Virginia to Belmont County, Ohio.

Children of Thornton and Lucinda Wright:
- + 23. i. Lemuel Wright (1825 – Unknown);
- 24. ii. James Wright (1830 – Unknown) – James was born in 1830 in Virginia;
- 25. iii. Joseph W. Wright (1832 – Unknown) – Joseph was born in 1832 in Virginia;
- 26. iv. Peter W. Wright (1836 – Unknown) – Peter was born in 1836 in Virginia;
- + 27. v. Charles H. Wright (1839 – Unknown);
- + 28. vi. Martha Wright (1842 – Unknown);
- + 29. vii. Emily Jane Wright (1846 – Unknown); and
- + 30. viii. Columbia Jane Wright (1850 – Unknown).

Fourth Generation

23. Lemuel Wright (1825 – AFT 1897) - Lemuel Wright was born in Virginia in 1825, oldest son of Thornton and Lucinda Wright. Lemuel married Elizabeth Green, the daughter of John and Sarah (Newby) Green, in Culpeper County, Virginia in 1847. Elizabeth was born in 1823 in Virginia. Together Lemuel and Elizabeth would have Sarah "Sally" "Sadie" Amanda on October 11, 1848.

During the taking of the 1850 US Census, Lemuel, Elizabeth, and Sarah were living with Elizabeth's father, John Green. Lemuel was employed as a shoemaker. It appears, Elizabeth sometime before or right after the Wright families moved to Ohio. Lemuel was living in 1897.

Children of Lemuel Wright and Elizabeth Green:
+   31.   i.   Sarah 'Sally' 'Sadie' Amanda Wright (1848 – 1926).

27. Charles H. Wright – (1839 – Unknown) – Charles Wright was born in Virginia in 1839, the son of Thornton and Lucinda Wright. Charles married Elizabeth, possibly in Kentucky. Charles was in Franklin, Wright County, Minnesota during the 1870 US Census, along with his brother Peter and his wife, Ann. In 1880, Charles and his family are in Jersey County, Illinois.

Children of Charles H. and Elizabeth Wright:
   32.   i.   Horace Wright (1869 – Unknown) – Horace is not listed with the family in the 1880 US Census;
   33.   ii. James F. Wright (1873 – Unknown);
   34.   iii. Annie M. Wright (1875 – Unknown); and
   35.   iv. Stella G. Wright (1877 – Unknown).

28. Martha Wright (1842 – Unknown) – Martha Wright was born in 1842 in Virginia, the daughter of Thornton and Lucinda Wright. Martha married Charles Stilwell on December 24, 1860 in Ohio. The family is located in Macoupin County, Illinois during the taking of the 1870 US Census.

Children of Charles Stilwell and Martha Wright:
   36.   i.   George Stilwell (1865 – Unknown);
   37.   ii. Joseph Stilwell (1866 – Unknown);
   38.   iii. Everett Stilwell (1869 – Unknown) – Everett is not listed on the 1880 US Census; and
   39.   iv. Flora Stilwell (1874 – Unknown).

29. Emily Jane Wright (1846 – Unknown) – Emily 'Emma' Jane Wright was born in 1846 in Virginia, the daughter of Thornton and Lucinda Wright. Emma married John C. Durham on October 24, 1866 in Macoupin County, Illinois. John was born in Kentucky. The family would settle in Texas by 1880.

    Children of John C. Durham and Emily Jane Wright:
    40.   i.   Nora Durham (1868 – Unknown) – Nora was born in Illinois;

30. Columbia Jane Wright (1850 – Unknown) – Columbia Jane Wright was born in 1850 in Virginia, the daughter of Thornton and Lucinda Wright. Columbia married Jesse Stilwell on October 1, 1872 in Macoupin County, Illinois.

    Children of Jesse Stilwell and Columbia Jane Wright:
    41.   i.   Dellie Stilwell (1875 – Unknown);
    42.   ii.   Myrtle Stilwell (1876 – Unknown);
    43.   iii.   James W. Stilwell (1877 – Unknown); and
    44.   iv.   Jessie T. Stilwell (1879 – Unknown).

Fifth Generation

31. Sarah Amanda Wright (1848 – 1926) - Sarah 'Sally' 'Sadie' Amanda Wright was born on October 11, 1848 in Culpeper County, Virginia, the daughter of Lemuel and Elizabeth (Green) Wright. Sarah was not married when she had her two children. Her daughter, Bernice, was listed as Josephine Williams in the 1880 US Census, Ohio, Guernsey County, Oxford Twp. She later in life married a former Civil War soldier, Nathan Smith, the father of her son-in-law, James Willie Smith, on April 7, 1916. Nathan served as a Sgt. in the 76th OVI, Company H. Sarah passed away on February 4, 1923 in Newark, Ohio. Both Sarah and Nathan are buried in Cedar Hill Cemetery in Newark, where Nathan is buried in the Civil War section of the cemetery.

    Children of Sarah Amanda Wright:
+   45.   i.   Bernice 'Josie' Wright (1875 -1946); and
+   46.   ii.   Pearl Navada Wright (1886 – 1926).

Photo taken of Lemuel Wright and his daughter, Sarah, around 1897 near Byesville, Guernsey County, Ohio

Sixth Generation

45. Bernice "Josie" Wright (1875 -1946) – Bernice 'Josie' Wright was born on July 5, 1875, the daughter of Sarah Amanda Wright (her father is possibly a "Williams".) Josie married James 'Willie' Smith on September 20, 1893 in Robins, Guernsey County, Ohio, and died May 26, 1946 in North Canton, Ohio.

    Children of James Smith and Bernice Wright:
+   47.   i.   Chloe Opal Smith (1896 -1980); and
+   48.   ii.   Loren Wilson Smith (1907 – Unknown).

Willie, Josie, Chloe and Loren Smith

46. Pearl Navada Wright (1886 – 1926) - See Forest E. McKinley, page 135.

Seventh Generation

47. Chloe Opal Smith (1896 -1980) – Chloe Opal Smith was born on October 16, 1896 in Robins, Guernsey County, Ohio, the daughter of James and Bernice (Wright) Smith. Chloe married Ralph Willis on December 24, 1919 in Columbus, Ohio. Chloe passed away on September 7, 1980 and is buried in North Canton, Ohio.

    Children of Ralph Willis and Chloe Opal Smith:
      49.   i.   Virginia Evelyn Willis (1921 - 1971); and
      50.   ii. William Ralph Willis (1924 – Unknown).

48. Loren Wilson Smith (1907 – Unknown) - Loren Wilson Smith was born on October 16, 1896 in Byesville, Guernsey County, Ohio, the son of James and Bernice (Wright) Smith. Loren married Dorothy Arlene Hartong, the daughter of Madison and Effie Hartong, on October 31, 1933 in Wheeling, West Virginia. They would settle in California.

    Children of Loren Wilson Smith and Dorothy Arlene Hartong:
      51.   i.   Sandra Josephine Smith (1948 - Unknown).

Descendents of James Green and Elizabeth Tapp

First Generation

1. James Green (Unknown – 1766) - James Green married Elizabeth Tapp sometime before 1748. Elizabeth Tapp was born about 1734 in Virginia, the daughter of William and Christian (Bourne) Tapp. Together James and Elizabeth had a son, William, born about 1750 in Culpeper County, Virginia, who married Mary, and died about 1831 in Culpeper County, Virginia.

James was a farmer and acquired 200 acres through the Northern Neck Warrant Land dated February 5, 1748 in Orange County, Virginia (later Culpeper County.)

On July 20, 1758, as recorded in the Culpeper County, VA Deeds, pg 146-149:

> *William Tapp of Culpeper County and Christian Tapp his wife to James Green of same, planter. For £50 lawful money. 190 acres, part of a greater tract conveyed to William Tapp by James Pendleton, Gent., in Culpeper County... formerly granted to Colonel Henry Williss by patent remaining in the Secretaries Office of this Colony which said land was conveyed to James Pendleton, 270 acres of which was transferred by deed to William Tapp...190 acres bounded as by survey made by Richard Young, surveyor...on the north side of Indian Run...to the mouth of Willis's Run ...corner to a tract of land belonging to Henry Huffman...up a small branch...line of William Tapp...*
>   *Signed William Tapp*
>   *Christian (X) Tapp*
> *Wit: Richard Young, Survr.*
> *20 July 1758. Acknowledged by them.*

James died sometime prior to May 13, 1766, as his estate was appraised as of that date in Culpeper, Culpeper County, Virginia. The appraisal was as follows:

> *James Spilman, John Barbee, John Read appraisers of the estate of James Green, dec'd*
> *negro Jack, Charles, Bowain?, Phillis, one featherbed and furniture, one do, one do, one desk, 9 chairs, one chest, 1 square table, 1 case and botels, 2 linen wheals, 1 bedsted & cord, 11 bottles, 1 pr of hillards?, 1 slate, a parcel of books, 4 belts, a parcel of shoe tools & lasts, 1 saddle 7 2 bridle, 2 pair cotton cards, 1 woolong wheal, a parcel of old lumber, 1 gun caganet & catharage box, 1 gun and moulds, 4 jugs, 1 lume & gear, a parcel of pots & hooks, 2 pad locks, 1 tea cittle, a parcel of Puter and old sumt?, water vessels, 2 griddles, 1 sack bag, 1 frying pan, 4 grubbing hoes, 4 hilling hoes, 8 broad hoes, 1 whip san, 1 crobent san?, 3 narrow axes, 3 broad axes, 2 hand saws, 1 gouge augers & chipels, 2 wedges, parcel of plains, a parcel of old coopers tools, two hamers 7 awls, 5 reaping hock, one sythe, one front foot adds and branding iron, six plows, one cart, 3 pr of chains 3 pr harnis and cart saddle, 7 tubs and other lumber, one sorral mare, one bay mare, one sorrel mare, 1 bay mare, one grey horse, 20 head of cattle, 28 head of hogs, 4 cow hides, 10 head of sheap, a parcel of phyals 1 hone and punch bole one fidle 3 judgs*
> *total; £ 311.5.6*

James oldest son, William, inherited his father's estate under the rules of primogeniture.

Children of James Green and Elizabeth Tapp:
+ 2. i. William Green (1750 – 1831).

Second Generation

2. William Green (1750 - 1831) - William Green was born about 1750 in Culpeper County, Virginia, the oldest son of James and Elizabeth (Tapp) Green. William married Mary and together they had thirteen (13) children.

It's likely, that William was one of the signers of Culpeper County legislative petitions in the 1770's on record in the Virginia State Library, presumed to the Minutemen of Culpeper County. Many of the members of the Minute Battalion would join the regular Continental Arny during the American Revolution, enlisting in Colonel Daniel Morgan's 11th Virginia Continental Regiment.

Mary died before William and he passed away about 1831. The Will of William Green was filed as an exhibit in the suit of James Bowen, administrator with the will annexed of Sally Green, deceased, plaintiff against Elizabeth Green, Nancy Green and others, defendants, Filed in the Circuit Superior Court of Law and Chancery of Culpeper County with will, October 1, 1844. The original will book M in which this will was filed was lost in the 1860's during the American Civil War.

I William Green Senr of Culpeper County being of sound & perfect mind & wishing to dispose of such worldly goods as I may die possessed of, do make & ordain this my last will & testament in manner & form following, that is to say:

1st It is my will & desire that my executor hereafter named first pay my funeral expenses and all my just debts.
2ndly. I give to my daughters Elizabeth, Nancy, Rebecca, Polly, Sally, Margaret & my granddaughter Julia Ann Green daughter of my son Aaron Green & to the heirs of their body lawfully begotten, one hundred & twelve acres of land including the house in which I now reside, and all the cleared land on the north side of Indian run and east side of the road and seven thirteenths of the whole of my timberland; but if that should prove insufficient to make 112 acres, then the balance to be laid off on the west side of the road running parallel with the run, but if either of my last mentioned daughters or granddaughter should die without lawful heirs of their bodies then at their deaths their share or shares to revert to the survivor or survivors of my last mentioned daughters or granddaughter.
3rd. I give to my daughters Elizabeth, Nancy, Rebecca,

Polly, Sally, Margaret and my granddaughter Julia Ann Green Negroes Betty, Frank, Mary, George, Maria, Henry and Aggy and their future increase from this date and all my personal estate of every description, but if either or all of my last mentioned daughters or granddaughter should die without lawful heirs of their bodies, then her or their share or shares of all my real and personal estate to revert to the survivor or survivors of my last mentioned daughters or granddaughter.

4th. I give to my son James W Green one thirteenth part of the whole of my woodland and a sufficient quantity of cleared land running parallel with and adjoining the land of my above named daughters and granddaughters on the west side of the road to make Sixteen acres.

5th. I give to my sons John, William, Moses, Thomas and my daughter Susan Hawkins all the balance of my land to be equally divided amongst them.

My son Moses Green has in his possession a bill of sale for my said Negro woman Betty, but has no right to her as he bought her for me and the purchase money was paid by me. Now if my son Moses should contend for the said Negro, it is my will that all the real and personal estate which I have hereinbefore bequeathed to him shall be immediately given to my daughters and granddaughter Elizabeth, Nancy, Rebecca, Polly, Sally, Margaret and Julia Ann Green to hold in like manner as the other property which I have given them.

And lastly I do hereby constitute and appoint my two friends Conway Spilman and John F Latham executors of this my last will and testament hereby revoking all other or former wills or testaments by me heretofore made, In witness whereof I have hereunto set my hand and affixed my seal this 11th day of July in the year one thousand, eight hundred and twentynine.

Signed, sealed, published and his

Declared as and for the last will and William X Green (Seal)
Testament of the above named William mark
Green in the presence of

Martin Fishback
Fred Fishback
William H Mason

At Court held for Culpeper County the 11th day of May, 1831
This last will and testament of William Green, deceased, was exhibited to the court & proved by the oaths of Fred Fishback and William H Mason witnesses thereto and ordered to be recorded. And at a court held for Culpeper County the 20th day of June 1831 this said last will and testament was again exhibited to the court, and on the motion of John F Latham and Conway Spilman the executors therein named Certificate is granted them for obtaining a probate thereof in due form they having made oath thereto, and given bond with security according to law.

Teste
F P Lightfoot

Children of William and Mary Green:
	3.	i.	Mary Polly Green (Unknown – 1850) - Mary Polly died about 1850 in Culpeper County, Virginia;
	4.	ii.	Sarah "Sally" Green (Unknown – 1840) - Sally died about 1840 in Culpeper County, Virginia;
	5.	iii.	Margaret S. Green (Unknown – Unknown) - Margaret married Hiram B. Crump on May 17, 1836 in Culpeper County, Virginia;
	6.	iv.	Aaron Green (Unknown – 1815) – Aaron died about 1815 in Culpeper County, Virginia leaving two children Julia Ann and James W;
	7.	v.	James Green (Unknown – Unknown) - James died before 1831;
+	8.	vi.	William Green (Unknown – 1843);
	9.	vii.	Elizabeth Green (1774 – 1857) – Elizabeth was born in 1774 in Culpeper County, Virginia, never married and died in 1857 in Culpeper County, Virginia;
	10.	viii.	Nancy Ann Green (1778 – 1854) – Nancy was born in 1778 in Culpeper County, Virginia, never married and died in 1854 in Culpeper County, Virginia;
	11.	ix.	Rebecca Green (1780 – 1852) – Rebecca was born in 1780 in Culpeper County, Virginia, never married and died in 1852 in Culpeper County, Virginia;
+	12.	x.	John Green (1782 – Unknown);
+	13.	xi.	Thomas Green (1789 – 1844);

+   14.   xii.   Moses Green (1790 – 1846); and
+   15.   xiii. Susan Smith Green (1800 – Unknown).

Third Generation

8.   William Green (Unknown – 1843) – William Green, the son of William and Mary Green, married Matilda Hardin and died in December of 1843 in Culpeper County, Virginia.

Children of William Green and Matilda Hardin:
16.   i.   Robert W. Green;
17.   ii.   Richard A. Green;
18.   iii.   Eliza Ann Green;
19.   iv.   Lucy E. Green (1824 – Unknown);
20.   v.   William Andrew Jackson Green (1829 – Unknown);
21.   vi.   Bird Green (1832 – Unknown);
22.   vii.   Boargenes Green (1833 – Unknown);
23.   viii. Selina Frances Green (1837 – Unknown);
24.   ix.   Felix Green (1836 – Unknown);
25.   x.   Thomas W. Green (1841 – Unknown); and
26.   xi.   George T. W. Green (1842 – Unknown).

12.   John Green (1782 – Unknown) - John Green was born about 1782 in Culpeper County, Virginia, the son of William and Mary Green. John married Sarah Newby, the daughter of Edward and Mary Newby, in Culpeper County, Virginia. Sarah passed away sometime before 1850.

John was listed in the 1850 US Census, Virginia, Culpeper County and died sometime after that and prior to the 1860 US Census. At the time, his daughter Elizabeth and her family was living with him.

Children of John Green and Sarah Newby:
+   27.   i.   Amanda Green (1817 – Unknown);
+   28.   ii.   Hiram Green (1817 – 1877);
+   29.   iii.   Elizabeth Green (1823 – Unknown);
    30.   iv.   Mary Green; and
    31.   v.   Augustine Green.

13.   Thomas Green (1789 – 1844) – Thomas Green was born in 1789 in Culpeper County, Virginia, the son of William and Mary Green. Thomas married Mary Hawkins on January 20, 1812 in Culpeper County, Virginia. Thomas passed away in 1844 in Barren, Kentucky.

Children of Thomas Green and Mary Hawkins:
- 32. i. Rebecca Catherine Green;
- 33. ii. Harriet Green;
- 34. iii. George W. Green;
- 35. iv. James W. Green (1813 – Unknown);
- 36. v. Andrew Jackson Green (1814 – Unknown);
- 37. vi. Robert William Green (1817 – Unknown);
- 38. vii. Susan Elizabeth Green (1823 – Unknown);
- 39. viii. Edward Churchman Green (1827 – Unknown);
- 40. ix. Sarah Ann Green (1829 – Unknown);
- 41. x. Mary Jane Green (1831 – Unknown);
- 42. xi. Louisa Green (1833 – Unknown); and
- 43. xii. Virginia Felix Green (1837 – Unknown).

14. **Moses Green (1790 – 1846)** – Moses Green was born about 1790 in Culpeper County, Virginia, the son of William and Mary Green. He married Harriet Bayse on February 12, 1818. Moses died July 6, 1846 in Rappahannock County, Virginia.

Children of Moses Green and Harriet Bayse:
- 44. i. James Bayse Green (1818 – Unknown) – James was born on December 22, 1818 in Culpeper County, Virginia;
- 35. ii. Thilbert Green (1820 – 1832) – Thilbert was born on February 19, 1920 in Culpeper County, Virginia;
- 36. iii. Mary L. Green (1821 – 1891) – Mary was born on June 12, 1820 in Culpeper County, Virginia, married William Andrew Jackson Green on November 13, 1850 in Culpeper County, Virginia, and died on April 17, 1891 in Newark, Ohio;
- 37. iv. Aylette F. Green (1822 – 1909) – Aylette was born on September 15, 1822 in Rappahannock County, Virginia, married Emily Bayse on August 5, 1844, then married Lizzie Cunningham on September 22, 1897 in Fauquier, Virginia, and died in Rappahannock County, Virginia on March 3, 1909;
- 38. v. Cassander E. Green (1824 – 1840) – Cassander was born on February 12, 1825 in Culpeper County, Virginia;
- 39. vi. Elmira Fermande Green (1825 – 1905) – Elmira was born on July 11, 1825 in Culpeper County, Virginia, married George W. Taylor on December 8, 1842 and died on December 23, 1905 in Pataskala, Ohio;
- 40. vii. Ferdinand E. Green (1827 – 1881) – Ferdinand was born on March 31, 1827 in Culpeper County, Virginia, married Mary Mildred Butler on September 14, 1854, and died on September 16, 1881 in Newark, Ohio;
- 41. viii. Taylor Bayse Green (1828 – 1903) – Taylor was born on December 25, 1828 in Culpeper County, Virginia, married Elizabeth Jerusha Smith on February 18, 1855, and died March 15, 1903 in Hurricane, Lincoln, Missouri;

42. ix. Selucas G. Green (1830 – 1832) – Selucas was born on June 14, 1830 in Culpeper County, Virginia;
43. x. Brunetta Taylor Green (1832 – 1869) – Brunetta was born on February 14, 1832 in Culpeper County, Virginia, married John Robert Riley on November 2, 1857 and died about 1869 in Fetterman, Taylor, West Virginia;
44. xi. Philadelphius Green (1834 – 1924) – Philadelphius was born on July 22, 1834 in Culpeper County, Virginia, married Maria L. Green on November 29, 1858, then married Anna J. Lemly in 1866, and died on June 27, 1924 in Newark, Ohio;
45. xii. Edward Augustus Green (1836 – 1918) – Edward was born on October 22, 1836 in Rappahannock, Virginia, married Elizabeth T. Leary on May 9, 1860, then Frances Bennett on April 7, 1887, and died November 12, 1918 in Warren, Virginia;
46. xiii. Amelia Frances Green (1838 – 1907) – Amelia was born on March 5, 1838 in Rappahannock, Virginia. married David K. Platto on December 25, 1859 in Newark, Ohio, and died on July 16, 1905 in Newark, Ohio;
47. xiv. Sophia Ball Green (1839 – Unknown) – Sophia was born on December 5, 1839 in Rappahannock, Virginia and married William Mala, then married William H. Jones on September 5, 1866 in Appling, Columbus, Georgia;
48. xv. Elizabeth Valentine Green (1842 – Unknown) – Elizabeth was born on October 24, 1842 in Rappahannock, Virginia and married Benjamin F. Miller; and
49. xvi. Joseph Thomas Green (1844 – 1922) – Joseph was born on September 24, 1844 in Rappahannock, Virginia, married Melvina Ann Swick on March 8 1867, and died on September 20, 1922 in Union County, Ohio.

15. Susan Smith Green (1800 – Unknown) – Susan Smith Green was born in Culpeper County, Virginia, the daughter of William and Mary Green. She married Benjamin Hawkins.

Children of Benjamin Hawkins and Susan Smith Green:
50. i. Winfield Scott Hawkins;
51. ii. John William Hawkins (1816 – Unknown) – John married Margaret N.;
52. iii. James Alexander Hawkins (1824 – Unknown);
53. iv. Henry Clinton Hawkins (1830 – Unknown);
54. v. Mary Jane Hawkins (1821 – Unknown);
55. vi. Sarah Martha Hawkins (1826 – Unknown);
56. vii. Susan Frances Hawkins (1828 – Unknown); and
57. viii. Margaret Ann Hawkins (1832 – Unknown) - Margaret married Edward Churchman Green on July 25, 1850 in Culpeper County, Virginia.

Fourth Generation

27. Amanda Green (1817 – Unknown) – Amanda was born in 1817 in Culpeper County, Virginia, the daughter of John and Sarah (Newby) Green. Amanda married John Wright on December 22, 1838 in Culpeper County, Virginia. Prior to 1850, the family moved to Brown County, Illinois to be close to Amanda's brother Hiram.

    Children of John Wright and Amanda Green:
       58.   i.   Collumbia Wright (1842 – Unknown);
       59.   ii.   John G. Wright (1845 – Unknown); and
       60.   iii. Robert Wright (1848 – Unknown).

28. Hiram Green (1817 – 1877) - Hiram Green was born in Culpeper County, Virginia, on December 25, 1817, the son of John and Sarah (Newby) Green. Hiram came to Illinois about 1838, with some of his relatives, and worked by the month for some time, but was a cooper at the time of his marriage to Nancy Tolle on January 18, 1843. Nancy was born in Ohio, November 30, 1824, the daughter of James and Lovey (Tolle) Tolle. She lived there until two or three years of age, and then went to Kentucky with her parents. In 1836 they continued to move West and sold every thing except some household goods, and with a two-horse wagon came overland and first settled in Schuyler County for two months. Hiram and Nancy settled on a farm of 160 acres in the Brown County, Illinois, where Hiram built a log house and there they lived for about six years, then bought another eighty acres and built a better house. There the family lived until 1873, when they sold it and bought a farm of 240 acres in Brown County, Illinois. They were faithful members of the Union Baptist Church. Hiram died on August 2, 1877.

    Children of Hiram Green and Nancy Tolle:
       61.   i.   Mary Jane Green (1843 – Unknown);
       62.   ii.   Sarah Green (1844 – Unknown);
       63.   iii. Lovey Mariah Green (1846 – Unknown);
       64.   iv. Ann G. Green (1848 – Unknown);
       65.   v.   Juliet Green (1851 – Unknown);
       66.   vi. William F. Green (1853 – Unknown);
       67.   vii. Celinda E. Green (1856 – Unknown);
       68.   viii. Angeline Green (1857 – Unknown);
       69.   ix. George W. Green (1859 – Unknown);
       70.   x.   Purlina Green (1862 – Unknown);
       71.   xi. Olive Green (1864 – Unknown);
       72.   xii. Almira Green (1867 – Unknown); and

73. xiii. Infant (1868 – Unknown) – passed away as an infant.

29. Elizabeth Green (1823 – Unknown) - See Lemuel Wright, page 96.

Descendents of William and Elinder Tapptico

First Generation

1. William Tapptico I 'Great Man' (1655/58 – 1710) - William Tapptico I (known as the "Great Man") was born around the period 1655 to 1658 in Virginia a member of the Wicocomico Indian Nation of the Powhatan Empire. This Native American Tribe was encountered by Captain John Smith of the Virginia Company when the English first came to Virginia around 1608, as mentioned in Capt. Smith's journals. There is no certainty as to who William's parents were. Although, it is known that during this time frame, Machywap was Chief of the Chicacoan. He very well could be the father of William. William married Elinor (possibly Jones) and together they had two (2) children.

William and Elinor sold their lands in Dorchester County, Maryland and moved to Northumberland County, Virginia around 1695. The following is taken from Early Virginia Records:

> *Att a Councill held att James Citty y'e 29'th Apr'll 1693*
> *Present*
> *His Excell'y, Ralph Wormely Sec'r, William Byrd, Chr: Wormely, Edward Hill, Hen:Whiteing, Hen: Hartwell, Richard Lee Esq'rs*
> *On reading the Peticon of Taptico and other of the Wickocomoco Indians about their Lands, and the order of the Gen'll Court dates June the 17th 1678 and an order of Councill dates May the 22'd 1683 relateing thereto. It is the opinion and Advice of the Councill and Ordred in Councill that Cap't John Smithe one of the Persons Complained of by the said Indians, have regard that they be not disturbed, to the Infringement of the aforesaid Orders.*

It's likely that William died sometime prior to 1710, as his son, William is referred to as the "King of the Wicocomico Indians." Elinor would pass away on September 16, 1719 in Northumberland County, Virginia.

Children of William and Elinder Tapptico:
+ 2. i. William Tapptico II (1690 – 1719); and
   3. ii. Elizabeth Tapptico.

Second Generation

2. King William Tapptico II (1690 – 1719) - William Tapptico II was born around 1690 in Northumberland County, Virginia, the son of William and Elinor Tapptico. William (known as "King William Taptico") would be the last recognized colonial Tribal Chief of the Wicocomico Indians. William was referred to in the "Executive Journals of the Council of Colonial Virginia" as follows:

April the 19th 1710.

Present: The Honorable Edmund Jenings Esqs. President, Dudley Digges, Robert Carter Esqrs., James Blair Com'ry, Phillip Ludwell, Henry Duke, William Churchill   Esqrs.

***WILLIAM TAPTICO KING OF THE WICOCOMICO INDIANS** came before the President and Council and presented three Indian arrows as an acknowledgment for their land **HE AND HIS NATION** holds in Northumberland County which at the desire of the sd. King is ordered to be noted in the Council books to perpetuate the claim of the said Nation of Indians to this land.*

    William married Elizabeth (possibly "Elizabeth Barrick") and together they would have three (3) children. When William died in 1719 in Northumberland County, Virginia, his wife Elizabeth settled the estate. At the onset of settling the estate, she began the process by signing the documentation as "Elizabeth Taptico" and in finalizing the process by signing "Elizabeth Tapp".
    With the land in Northumberland County passing to Captain John Smith or his heirs in 1719, according to the land agreement dated 1696, the family was left with no land on which to live. The loss of land and home forced a move to Spotsylvania County, Virginia by 1722.

    Elizabeth would pass away October 31, 1724 in Spotsylvania

County, Virginia.

The following is the will of William Tapptico as it was written:

Know all men by these presents that I, William Tapptico, of the County of Northumberland in the Colony of Virginia and King of the Wiccocomoco Indians am holden and firmly bound unto Phillip Smith of the aforesaid County and Colony in the full and perfect sum of 1,000 pounds current money of Virginia to be paid unto he said Phillip Smith, his heirs, executors, administrators or assignees which payment well and truly to be made. I do hereby bind myself, my heirs, executors and administrators firmly by these presents as witness my hand and seal this 31st day of December, 1718. Whereas the above bound William Tapptico's father died in the 1695 or 6 obtaining liberty of John Smith of Purton in Gloucester County to seat, tend, and occupy a certain nect (sic) of land commonlY Old Town Neck and as much lands and land at the mouth of the neck of the said William Tapptico, Elinder his wife. William Taptico, Jr. and the heirs male begotten could tend and after their decease to return to the said John Smith and his heirs forever. Now know ye that the season (illegible) request of him the said Phillip Smith, his heirs, etc.: make over to the said Smith all his right, title and interest in and to the above said neck and all the right and property of the said Taptico and his heirs both without the said neck and shall and with at all times forever exhonerate, acquit, and disclaim and forever defend the same from all manner of persons claiming from, by, or under him the said William Taptico or his heirs: male of his body then the above obligation to be void and of none effect. In witness whereof I set my hand and seal this day and year above written.

Witnesses: Capt. Maurice Jones William {drawing of seal} Tapptico Bridgett Ward

Children of William and Elizabeth Tapptico II:
+ 4. i. William Tapp III (1707 – 1791);
  5. ii. Charity Tapp (1709 – Unknown) - Charity died in Spotsylvania County, Virginia; and
  6. iii. Vincent Tapp (1714 – Unknown) – Vincent married Elizabeth Bourne in Spotsylvania County, Virginia.

Third Generation

4. William Tapp III (1707 – 1791) - William Tapp III was born about 1707 in Richmond, Essex County, Virginia, the son of William and Elizabeth Tapptico. William married Christian Bourne, the daughter of John and Elizabeth (Johnson) Bourne in 1725.

William received a Northern Neck Grant from Lord Fairfax dated March 5, 1747 for 587 acres. This land would be the home of William and his family for the rest of his life, with many of his children and grandchildren living in the area. The homestead dating to at least 1750 still stands in part today. Upon William's death, the land passed to his son, Lewis and his widow and to her step-children who eventually sold the land out of the family. Christian was given 57 acres of land by her father in 1765.

Christian passed away about 1780, after the drafting of William's will, as she is mentioned in his will. William passed away sometime prior to the recording of his will on January 17, 1791.

The Will of William Tapp was dated June 27, 1780 and was recorded January 17, 1791 in Culpeper County, Virginia in Will Book C, 1783-1791, page 406 and is as follows:

> *In the name of God Amen I William Tapp of Culpeper County being sick & weak in body but of sound mind & memory calling to mind the mortality of my body and that it appointed for all men once to die, I recommend my soul into hands of God that gave it me; & as touching such worldly goods as God in his mercy hath been pleased to bestow upon me I dispose of the same in the following manner.... Imprimis, I lend unto my loving wife Christian all my Estate Real & personal during her life the same peaceably to possess & enjoy. Item I give unto my son Vincent Tapp & his heirs after my said wife's decease the land & manor Plantation whereon I now live... containing one hundred & ninety-five acres, more or less. Item I give unto my Grandson William*

Tapp, son of my said son Vincent a Tract or parcel of Land adjoining the land & Plantation whereon I now live Containing Forty three acres more or less to him & his Heirs...Item I give unto my Daughter Ann Cunningham wife of John Cunningham and to her Heirs, after my wifes decease a negro wench named agy (?)... Item I give unto my Daughter Alice Graham wife of John Graham & to her Heirs, after my wife's decease a negro man named Peter. .. Item I give unto my Daughters Ann Cunningham and Alice Graham above said after my wife's decease all my Stock of Cattle, to them & their Heirs to be equally divided between them.... Item I give unto my Daughter Elizabeth Green & to her heirs after my wife's decease my Horse Bridle & Saddle.... Item I give unto my Daughter Sarah Jett wife of John Jett & to her Heirs after my wife's decease all my Stock of Hogs & Sheep... Item I give unto my sons William Tapp & Lewis Tapp and their Heirs the sum of one Shilling Sterling money each....Item I give unto William Yates son of Mary Yates Dec'd, & to his heirs the sum of one hundred pounds in Continental Bills of Credit of the Congress of this State as is now Current.... Item my will is that all the remainder of my Estate of every kind whatsoever, be sold and the Money thance arising be equally divided between my Children, Vincent Tapp, Elizabeth Green, Sarah Jett, Ann Cunningham & Alice Graham & them & their heirs... Item I constitute & appoint my son Vincent Tapp, & my Friend James Jett Executors of this my last will and Testament, hereby revoking all Former wills, Legacies by me made Ratifying & Confirming this and no other to be my last will and Testament. In witness I have set my hand & seal this 27th day of June 1780. Signed Sealed & Declared to be the last will & Testament of Will'm Tapp

Wm Tapp [signature]
In the presence of us
Thomas Hopper
Jacob Wall
Ann (X) Wall September 10th 1789 the within last will & testament of William Tapp acknowledged before us, under an exception as mentioned to the annexed Codicil

Moses Tapp Sias Tapp Be it known unto all persons that it is now my intent & meaning that the within Bequest of one hundred pounds of continental bills of Credit of Congress or of this State unto William Yates is not to be Considered as any part of my last will and Testament as therein mentioned and I do hereby disannull the same accordingly, As Witness my hand & Seal this 10th day of September 1789. Moses Tapp Sias Tapp Wm [his mark] Tapp (L. S.) At a Court held for Culpeper County this 7th Day of January 1791 (not clear) This last will & Testament of William Tapp dec'd , was exhibited to the Court together with the Codicil thereto annexed & was proved by the oaths of Moses Tapp & Sias Tapp two of the witnesses thereto I ordered to be Recorded James Jett the only Executor therein named came into Court & refused to take upon himself the burthen of the Execution thereof. John James CC

Children of William Tapp III and Christian Bourne:

	7.	i.	Vincent Tapp (1727 – 1791) – Vincent was born about 1727 in Culpeper County, Virginia, married Mary Mollie Jett about 1754, and died in Culpeper County, Virginia on January 17, 1791;
	8.	ii.	Sarah Tapp (1729 – Unknown) – Sarah was born about 1729 in Culpeper County, Virginia and married John Jett;
	9.	iii.	Ann Tapp (1731 – Unknown) – Ann was born about 1731 in Culpeper County, Virginia and married John Cunningham;
	10	iv.	William Tapp (1732 – Unknown) – William was born about 1732 in Culpeper County, Virginia;
	11.	v.	Mary Tapp (1732 – Unknown) – Mary was born about 1732 in Virginia;
+	12.	vi.	Elizabeth Tapp (1736 – Unknown);
	13.	vii.	Alice Tapp (1736 – Unknown) – Alice was born about 1736 in Culpeper County, Virginia and married John Graham; and
	14.	viii.	Lewis Tapp (1745 – Unknown) – Lewis was born about 1745 in Virginia.

**James Tapp, son of Vince Tapp and
Mary Mollie Jett**

Fourth Generation

12. Elizabeth Tapp (1736 – Unknown) - See James Green, page 101.

Descendents of Andrew Bourne and Christian Price

First Generation

+ 1.i. Andrew Bourne (1650 – Unknown); and
   2.ii. John Bourne (1654 – Unknown).

1. Andrew Bourne (1650 – 1695) - Andrew Bourne was born about 1650 in England, the son of Ann. Ann was born in 1635 in Plymouth, Devonshire, England and died in 1695 in Virginia.

In 1689, Andrew and his brother, John, made an agreement with the London Merchant, George Luke to serve him for a full term of four years in consideration for him paying their passage to the American Colonies, with their mother and one other child, being the sum of five thousand pounds of tobacco.

After arriving in the American Colonies, George Luke brought suit against the brothers:

> *Stafford Co., VA Orders 1689-1690 Item 570 court held 10 March 1689-90, where "George Luke make suit that he had made an agreement on the fourteenth of October last with Andrew and John Bourne late of Plymouth, Devon in England to serve him for the full term of four years from April next ensuing in considering of paying their passage with their mother and one child more being the sum of five thousand pounds of tobacco---and forasmuch as the said Andrew and John Bourne did then at the time of drawing their indenture clandestinely steal away. George Luke--prays that an order for the said Andrew and John Bourne to serve according to the time profixed--."*

Andrew married Christian Price about 1672 in Rappahannock County, Virginia and they settled about six miles from the town of Fredericksburg in Virginia, where Andrew would die in July 1695. Christian then married Henry Johnson on October 2, 1700. Christian would pass away on August 13, 1713 in Essex County, Virginia, leaving the family home to her son, John.

Children of Andrew Bourne and Christian Price:
+   3.   i.   John Bourne (1673 - 1721);
    4.   ii.   Peter Bourne (1681 – 1720) – Peter was born about 1681 in Rappahannock County, Virginia and died in 1720 in Essex County, Virginia; and
    5.   iii.   Robert Bourne (Unknown – 1727) – Robert was born in Rappahannock County, Virginia and died on May 2, 1727 in St. George, Spotsylvania County, Virginia.

Second Generation

3.   John Bourne (1673 – 1721) - John Bourne was born about 1673 in Rappahannock County, Virginia, the son of Andrew and Christian (Price) Bourne. John married Elizabeth Johnson, the daughter of Henry Johnson and Mary Taliaferro, on October 30, 1702 in Essex County, Virginia. Elizabeth was born about 1676 in Rappahannock County, Virginia.

John and his family lived on 87 acres in St. Mary's Parish, Essex County, Virginia, formerly owned by Richard Johnson. John passed away about 1721 in Essex County, Virginia, while Elizabeth would pass away around 1760 in Fredericksburg, Spotsylvania County, Virginia.

Children of John Bourne and Elizabeth Johnson:
    6.   i.   John Bourne (1707 – Unknown) – John was born about 1707 in Essex County, Virginia and married Ellen Eleanor Davis in 1774 Culpeper County, Virginia;
+   7.   ii.   Christian Bourne (1708 – 1780);
    8.   iii.   Andrew Bourne (1711 – 1790) – Andrew was born about 1711 in Essex County, Virginia, married Jane Morton about 1735, and died on January 18, 1790 in Culpeper County, Virginia;
    9.   iv.   Sarah Bourne (1713 – Unknown) – Sarah was born about 1713 in Essex County, Virginia;
    10.   v.   Robert Bourne (1715 – 1757) – Robert was born about 1715 in Essex County, Virginia, married Elizabeth, and died on June 23, 1757 in Orange County, Virginia;
    11.   vii.   Francis Bourne (1717 – Unknown) – Francis was born about 1717 in Essex County, Virginia;
    12.   viii.   James Bourne (1719 – Unknown) – James was born about 1719 in Essex County, Virginia; and
    13.   ix.   Henry Bourne (1719 – 1787) – Henry was born about 1719 in St. Mary's, Essex County, Virginia, married Ann Morton on July 3, 1745, and died on October 15, 1787 in Fayette County, Kentucky.

Third Generation

7. Christian Bourne (1708 – 1780) -See William Tapp III, page 116.

Descendents of Henry Johnson and Mary Taliaferro

First Generation

1. Henry Johnson (1648 – 1703) - Henry Johnson was born in England about 1648 and left for the American Colonies in 1666. He was part of the group of the individuals brought to the American Colonies by Robert Taliaferro (the "Immigrant".) Henry married one of Robert's daughters, Mary Catherine about 1675 in Essex County, Virginia. Mary Catherine was born about 1658 in Rappahannock County, Virginia.

Mary Catherine died in February of 1695. Shortly after her death Henry made a *"Deed of Gift, 25 Jul 1695. Henry Johnson is intended to marry "gives his four daus, all under 21, personal property, Elizabeth the eldest, Sarah the second, Catherine the third, Ann the fourth and youngest dau."* Henry then married Christian Bourne, the widow of Andrew Bourne. Henry would pass away on June 10, 1703. Henry's will, divided his personal estate among four of his children: Richard, Sarah, Catherine and Ann, his oldest daughter Elizabeth "having had her part."

Children of Henry Johnson and Mary Taliaferro:
- + 2. i. Elizabeth Johnson (1676 – 1760);
- 3. ii. Richard Johnson (Unknown – 1770) – Richard was a Colonel in the Virginia Militia and died on October 10, 1770 in Newcastle, Spotsylvania County, Virginia;
- 4. iii. Sarah Johnson;
- 5. iv. Catherine Johnson; and
- 6. v. Anne Johnson, was born in Rappahannock County, Virginia and married Edward Myhill on October 5, 1701 in Essex County, Virginia.

Second Generation

2. Elizabeth Johnson - See John Bourne, page 120.

Descendents of Robert Taliaferro and Katherine Dedman

First Generation

1. Robert Taliaferro "Tolliver" (1626 – 1687) - Robert Taliaferro "Tolliver" (known as the "Immigrant") was born in Stepney, Middlesex, England on November 11, 1626, the son of Francis and Marion Bennett (Haie) Talliaferro. His mother Marion Bennett died shortly after giving birth to Robert on November 13, 1626.

Robert emigrated from England to the American Colonies about 1645, settling in York County, Virginia. He received Land Patent in Gloucester County, Virginia in 1655 which included 6,500 acres, jointly owned with Major Lawrence Smith. By 1660, Robert had received 6,300 acres by head rights alone, having transported 126 people to Virginia.

Robert married Katherine (aka Sarah Grimes) Dedman, the daughter of Henry and Katherine Dedman, and the step-daughter of Rev. Charles Grymes, in 1653 in Essex County, Virginia. Katherine was born in 1626 in Igtham, Kent, England, and it is likely that she and her family were among those transported by Robert to Virginia.

Robert was referred to as the Immigrant in the literature of the time, probably to distinguish him from his son Robert. He and all his sons were protestant's, and in the York County, Virginia records, where the name first appears about 1645, the spelling is sometimes "Toliver."

Robert passed away about 1687 in York, Gloucester County, Virginia, while Katherine passed away in 1687 in Rappahannock County, Virginia.

Children of Robert Talliaferro and Katherine Dedman:

    2.   i. Francis Taliaferro (1654 – 1710) – Francis was born about 1654 in Essex County, Virginia, married Elizabeth Catlett, and died before August 10, 1710 in Virginia;

+   3.   ii. Christian Taliaferro (1654 – 1713);

	4.	iii.	John 'The Ranger' Talliaferro (1656 – 1720) – John was born about 1656 in Powhatan, Essex County, Virginia, married Sarah Smith in 1682, and died June 21, 1720. John was a Lieutenant of the York County Rangers in 1692. He was a Justice of Essex County in 1695 and later the sheriff. He served in the House of Burgesses in 1699;
+	5.	iv.	Mary Catherine Taliaferro (1658 – 1695);
	6.	v.	Sara Taliaferro (1660 – 1734) – Sara was born about 1660 in Gloucester County, Virginia;
	7.	vi.	Catherine Taliaferro (1660 – 1682) – Catherine was born about 1660 in Gloucester County, Virginia and married John Battale;
	8.	vii.	Charles Taliaferro (1663 – 1734) – Charles was born about 1663 in Essex County, Virginia, married Mary Carter, and died about 1734 in Essex County, Virginia;
	9.	viii.	Richard 'the Pirate' Taliaferro (1665 - 1715) – Richard was born about 1665 in Richmond, Virginia, married Elizabeth Eggleston, then Martha Sarah Wingfield, and died in 1715, Richard was a ship captain; and
	10.	ix.	Robert Taliaferro (1667 – 1726) – Robert was born about 1667 in Richmond, Virginia, married Sarah Catlett, then Margaret Buckner, and died June, 6, 1726 in St. Paul's, King George County, Virginia.

Second Generation

3.   Christian Taliaferro (1654 – 1713) – See Andrew Bourne, page 119.

5.   Mary Catherine Talliaferro (1658 – 1695) - See Henry Johnson, page 123.

Descendents of Henry Newby and Mary Pollard

First Generation

1. Henry Newby (1695 – 1741) – Henry Newby was born in 1695 North Neckor, York County, Virginia, the son of Henry and Mary (Pollard) Newby. Henry married Mary Whaley, the daughter of Oswald Whaley, in 1717 in Lancaster County, Virginia. Mary was born in Scotland in 1695. Henry was a farmer and was listed on the *"Lancaster Co. – Saint Maryes White Chappel Parish List of Tithables – 1716."* Henry passed away on October 14, 1741 in Lancaster County, Virginia. Mary, along with her son, Henry, was listed *"March 1756, Lancaster County Tobacco Proprietors – Lancaster Co, Virginia."* Mary passed away on January 15, 1762 in White Chapel Parish, Lancaster County, Virginia.

  Children of Henry Newby and Mary Whaley:
+ 2. i. Oswald Newby (1715 - 1786);
  3. ii. Henry Newby (1720 – 1764);
  4. iii. James Newby (1724 – 1791) – James was listed on the 1783 Tax List for Lancaster County, Virginia, with 6 whites and 11 blacks in the household;
  5. iv. Sarah Newby (1726 – 1795);
  6. v. Hannah Newby (1728 – Unknown) – Hannah married Joseph Bailey;
  7. vi. Whaley Newby (1730 – 1796) – Whaley severed during the Revolutionary War, married Elizabeth Thomson, and died in Simpson County, Kentucky; and
  8. vii. William Newby (1732 – 1815) – William married Ann Miller on December 21, 1781 in Lancaster County, Virginia, also listed on the 1783 Tax List for Lancaster County, Virginia, with 3 whites and 4 blacks in the household.

Second Generation

2. Oswald Newby (1715 – 1786) – Oswald Newby was born in Lancaster County, Virginia in 1715, the son of Henry and Mary (Whaley) Newby. Oswald married Sarah Ann Davis, the daughter of John and Margaret Davis. Oswald would pass away on April 9, 1786, while Sarah would pass away on November 21, 1808.

Children of Oswald Newby and Sarah Ann Davis:
- 9. i. Irene Newby (1737 - Unknown);
- 10. ii. Robert Newby (1738 – 1772);
- 11. iii. Prichard 'Pritchett' Newby (1740 – Unknown) – Pritchett was a postmaster in Culpeper County, Virginia;
- + 12. iv. Edward Newby (1742 – 1791);
- 13. v. Oswald Newby (1744 – 1800);
- 14. vi. William P. Newby (1746 – Unknown) – William married Betty Hutton on April 22, 1791, then Elizabeth Pemberton in 1809;
- 15. vii. Mary Newby (1750 – Unknown) – Mary married Larkin Pemberton on October 7, 1788 in Lancaster County, Virginia;
- 16. viii. Esther Newby (1752 – 1813) – Esther married Joseph Ficklin on February 3, 1785 in Lancaster County, Virginia, and died in April 1813;
- 17. ix. Peggy Newby (1754 – Unknown) – Peggy married John Shackelford on August 2, 1794 in Culpeper County, Virginia;
- 18. x. Sarah Ann Newby (1768 – Unknown) – Sarah married Richard Norris on January 11, 1791 in Lancaster County, Virginia; and
- 19. xi. Priscilla Newby (1781 – Unknown) – Priscilla married Thomas Flint on September 7, 1797 in Lancaster County, Virginia.

Third Generation

12. Edward Newby (1742 – 1791) – Edward Newby was born in Lancaster County, Virginia in 1742, the son of Oswald and Sarah Ann (Davis) Newby. Edward married Mary and they settled in Culpeper County, Virginia. Edward passed away on July 17, 1826 in Culpeper County, while Mary passed away before him.

Culpeper Will Book K, page 292
Edward Newby's will

> *In the name of God Amen I Edward Newby of the County of Culpeper and State of Virginia do make my will in the manner & form following to wit*
> *I give and bequeath to my sons Armistead, Elsey, Henry & Pollard my tracts of land whereon I now reside containing two hundred and eighty-eight acres more or less to be equally divided between the above named Armistead, Elsey, Henry & Pollard Newby.*

I also give & bequeath to Armistead Newby two Negroes named Eliza & Samuel.

To Elsey I give two Negroes named John & Harriet

To Henry Newby I give & bequeath two Negroes named Lewis & Marcil?

To my son Pollard Newby I give & bequeath two Negroes named Tabitha & her child Summerfield

I also give & bequeath to my son William Newby a Negro woman named Susanna

I also give & bequeath to my daughter Lucy Bailey a Negro woman called Charlotte & her increase to the heirs of her body forever after my said daughter Lucy's decease

I also give & bequeath to the infant children of John Green, Day?, Amanda, Hiram, Mary & Augustine Green a Negro man named Emanuel after the above mentioned infant children of John Green shall have arrived at the years of maturity they then shall have the liberty to sell said Negro Emanuel & divide the money arising from sale of said negro equally

and after my just debts are paid the balance of my stock, furniture, etc., taking out two beds, one for Armistead Newby, one for Henry Newby, to be sold and equally divided among my four sons Armistead, Elsey, Henry & Pollard after defraying all necessary charges

I constitute & appoint my sons Armistead & Pollard Newby executors of this my last Will & Testament given under my hand & seal this 29th day of March Anno Domini one thousand eight hundred & twenty five

Edward Newby

Atteste
Benjamin Lillard
Theophelus Hoff
Jacob H. (X) Hoff

At a Court held for Culpeper County the 17th day of July 1826

This last Will and Testament of Edward Newby dec'd was exhibited to the court and proved by the oaths of Benjamin Lillard and Theophelus Hoff two of the witnesses thereof and ordered to be recorded and at a

court held for said county the 21st day of August 1826 on the motion of Pollard Newby one of the executors therein named certificate was granted him for obtaining a probaet thereof in due form he having made oath thereto & given and security according to law

            Teste H. W.
Lightfoot CC

Children of Edward and Mary Newby:
- 20. i. Armistead Newby (1772 – Unknown);
- 21. ii. Elsey Newby (1805 – Unknown);
- 22. iii. Henry Newby (1783 – Unknown);
- 23. iv. Pollard Newby (1785 – 1856) – Pollard married Catherine F. Washington on October 25, 1813 in Fauquier County, Virginia and died on September 2, 1856;
- 24. v. William P. Newby (1789 – Unknown);
- 25. vi. Lucy Newby, married a Mr. Bailey; and
- + 26. vii. Sarah Newby.

Fourth Generation

26. Sarah Newby - See John Green, page 106.

Descendents of William McKinley and Tamara Brown

First Generation

+ 1. William McKinley (1775 – 1758); and
+ 2. Andrew McKinley (1780 – 1860).

1. William McKinley (1775 – 1858) – William McKinley was born in Loudoun County, Virginia in 1775, came to Ohio with his brother Andrew and owned property in Belmont County, Ohio prior to acquiring about two hundred and eighty (280) acres of land in Guernsey County, Ohio, where he established a good home and became influential among the early settlers. William married Tamara Brown on February 12, 1812. Tamara was also born in Loudoun County, Virginia. Tamara passed away in 1845, while William lived to be eighty three years old, passing away in 1858. It was said, "that William's great-great-grandfather was an ancestor of the 25th President of the United States of America, William McKinley.

Children of William McKinley and Tamara Brown:
- 3.   i.   Sarah McKinley (1812 - 1854) – Sarah married Evan Cowgill;
+ 4.   ii.   Ebenezer McKinley (1815 – 1857);
- 5.   iii.   Israel McKinley (1816 – Unknown);
- 6.   iv.   A son known only as 'Uncle Piedmond' McKinley, thought to have gone west to find fame and fortune;
- 7.   v.   Mary McKinley (1819 – 1840) – Mary married John Groves in 1836;
+ 8.   vi.   Willoughby McKinley (1820 – 1896); and
- 9.   vii.   Aaron McKinley, who lived on the home place, married Sarah Collin in 1850, and died childless.

2. Andrew McKinley (1780 – 1860) – Andrew McKinley was born in Loudoun County, Virginia in 1780, came to Ohio with his brother William. Andrew married Elizabeth Millison in 1815. Andrew died in 1860 in Belmont County, Ohio.

Children of Andrew McKinley and Elizabeth Millison:
- 10. i. Ruth McKinley (1816 – Unknown) – Ruth married Joseph P. McGeath in 1834;
- 11. ii. William McKinley (1817 – Unknown) – William married Tamson Burns in 1845;
- 12. iii. John McKinley (1820 – Unknown);
- 13. iv. Elza McKinley (1822 – Unknown) – Elza married Eleanor McGeath in 1849;
- 14. v. Lucinda McKinley (1824 – Unknown) – Lucinda married Jesse Tracy in 1842;
- 15. vi. Elizabeth McKinley (1826 – Unknown) – Elizabeth married Asa T. French in 1844; and
- 16. vii. Jane McKinley (1828 – Unknown) – Jane married Van Leer Drummond in 1848.

Second Generation

4. Ebenezer McKinley (1815 – 1857) - Ebenezer McKinley was born June 21, 1815, the son of William and Tamara (Brown) McKinley, who came from Virginia between 1806 and 1810 to Belmont County, Ohio and then on to Guernsey County, locating in the northwestern part of Valley Township.

Ebenezer grew up on the family farm and married Lucinda Russell, the daughter of Thomas Russell, a soldier during the War of 1812 with England, in Guernsey County, Ohio. Lucinda was born April 3, 1814 in Belmont County, Ohio and was brought to Guernsey County by her parents at an early age.

Ebenezer died at the early age of forty-two on October 30, 1857, while Lucinda out-lived him by thirty-seven years, passing away on November 12, 1894.

Children of Ebenezer McKinley and Lucinda Russell:
- 17. i. Thamer E. McKinley (1841 – Unknown) – Thamer married Landon Starr and lived near Claysville and had five children;
- + 18. ii. Sarah A. McKinley (1843 – Unknown);
- 19. iii. Rachel McKinley (1843 – 1844) - Rachel died on August 30, 1844, one year of age;
- + 20. iv. William A. McKinley (1845 – 1875);
- + 21. v. Thomas W. McKinley (1847 – 1924);
- + 22. vi. Aaron W. McKinley (1850 – 1921);
- 23. vii. Clarinda J. McKinley (1855 – Unknown) - Clarinda married John Bristol and lived near Byesville; and
- 24. viii. Ebenezer Hayden McKinley (1857 – Unknown) - Ebenezer married Alice Clark and moved to Columbus, Kansas and had two children.

8. Willoughby McKinley (1820 – 1896) – Willoughby McKinley was born April 23, 1821 in Virginia, the son of William and Tamara (Brown) McKinley. Willoughby married Elizabeth Carter, the daughter of Richard and Rachel Carter, in 1845 and lived at Cumberland for a number of years before moving to Humeston, Wayne County, Iowa during the fall of 1863. He first acquired 320 acres from the Rev. Kyle of Guernsey County, Ohio, then another 720 acres in Richman Township, and then 40 acres of timberland in Clay Township. Willoughby raised sheep and it was said *"....he was often annoyed and suffered losses by the wolves killing his sheep."* Willoughby was a charter member of Garden Grove Lodge, F&A.M. and was a member of the Christian Church at Humeston. Elizabeth passed away on July 12, 1885, while Willoughby would pass away on August 19, 1896.

Children of Willoughby McKinley and Elizabeth Carter:
+ 25. i. John R. McKinley (1846 – Unknown);
   26. ii. Rachel A. McKinley (1849 – Unknown) – Rachel married Augustus Taylor of Humeston, Iowa; and
   27. iii. George W. McKinley (1853 – Unknown).

Third Generation

18. Sarah A. McKinley (1843 – Unknown) – Sarah A. McKinley, the daughter of Ebenezer and Lucinda (Russell) McKinley, married Stephen V. Hickle. Stephen was born in 1839 in Ohio. The family would live near Cumberland, Ohio.

Children of Stephen Hickle and Sarah A. McKinley:
   28. i. Walter C. Hinkle (1876 – Unknown).

20. William A. McKinley (1845 – 1875) – William A. McKinley, the son of Ebenezer and Lucinda (Russell), married Elizabeth Hammontree. William died young in 1875.

Children of William McKinley and Elizabeth Hammontree:
   29. i. Irena B. McKinley, died as an infant; and
   30. ii. Celte McKinley, died as an infant.

21. Thomas W. McKinley (1847 – 1924) – Thomas W. McKinley was born on August 12, 1847, the son of Ebenezer and Lucinda (Russell) McKinley. Thomas married Mary J. Heskett in 1869.

Thomas and his children were in Guernsey County for the 1880 US Census. Mary died sometime before 1880, while Thomas would pass away on June 18, 1924.

    Children of Thomas W. McKinley and Mary J. Heskett:
+   31.   i.   Walter Ray McKinley (1873 – Unknown); and
     32.   ii.   Mary McKinley (1877 – Unknown).

22.   Aaron W. McKinley (1850 – 1921) - Aaron W. McKinley was born March 22, 1850 the son of Ebenezer and Lucinda (Russell) McKinley. Aaron married Mahala 'Nellie' Ellen Aplin, the daughter of Welcome Gray Aplin and Mahala (Collins) Moore. Mahala Ellen was born on February 7, 1854 in Ohio.

Aaron farmed in Jackson Township of Guernsey County, Ohio until he passed away on October 28, 1921, from paralysis and hardening of the arteries. Mahala Ellen would spend the rest of her days living with her son, Forest and passed away almost 20 years later on June 17, 1941. Both Aaron and Mahala Ellen are buried in Harmony Cemetery in Guernsey County, Ohio.

    Children of Aaron W. McKinley and Mahala Ellen Aplin:
     33.   i.   Charles McKinley (1887 – Unknown);
+   34.   ii.   Forest E. McKinley (1889 – 1961); and
     35.   iii. Fern.

25.   John R. McKinley (1846 – Unknown) – John R. McKinley was born on February 23, 1846 in Cumberland, Guernsey County, Ohio, the son of Willoughby and Elizabeth (Carter) McKinley. John married Hannah J. Davis, the daughter of Thomas and Mary (Barry) Davis, of Noble County, Ohio, on September 1, 1869. Hannah was born in Ohio in 1852. They moved to Richmond, Wayne County, Iowa where they were listed in the 1880 US Census. John was a practical and enterprising agriculturist, where he raised a drove of sheep and farmed. John was a member of the Hueston Lodge, No.61, K.P. of which he was a chancellor commander, a member of the Chappaqua Lodge, No. 121, I.O.O.F., a member of the Christian Church, and also served his township as a clerk and justice of the peace. Hannah passed away in 1895.

Children of John R. McKinley and Hannah J. Davis:
- 36. i. Oliver Willis McKinley (1870 – Unknown) - Oliver was born on October 28, 1870;
- 37. ii. Alice Orpha McKinley (1871 – Unknown) – Alice was born on December 8, 1871;
- 38. iii. Willoughby McKinley (1875 – Unknown) - Willoughby was born on November 30, 1875; and
- 39. iv. Grace McKinley (1882 – Unknown) – Grace was born on February 6, 1882.

Fourth Generation

31. Walter Ray McKinley (1873 – Unknown) – Walter Ray McKinley, the son of Thomas W. and Mary J. (Heskett) McKinley and married Claudia.

Children of Walter Ray and Claudia McKinley:
- 40. i. Byron McKinley (1902 – Unknown);
- 41. ii. Fred L. McKinley (1904 – Unknown);
- 42. iii. Walter M. McKinley (1908 – Unknown);
- 43. iv. Claro G. McKinley (1910 – Unknown); and
- 44. v. Thomas L. McKinley (1912 – Unknown).

34. Forest E. McKinley (1889 – 1961) - Forest McKinley was born the middle child of Aaron W. and Mahala Ellen (Aplin) McKinley.

Forest grew up on the family farm in the southwestern part of Jackson Township of Guernsey County, Ohio and spent most of his time assisting with the general chores of the farm and attended the neighboring schools.

Forest was never married to Pearl Navada Wright, the youngest daughter of Sarah Amanda Wright of Byesville, Ohio. Pearl was born July 23, 1886 in Robins, Ohio. Pearl grew up in Byesville where she lived with her mother in a boarding house. Together Forest and Pearl had one daughter, Mildred Ada, born on New Years Day, 1910 in Byesville, Ohio.

Forest would go on to marry Margaret Belle Dunning on June 11, 1913. Margaret was born on October 7, 1886, the daughter of John David and Sarah C. (Mercer) Dunning. Margaret passed away on August 15, 1958, while Forest would pass away on July 16, 1961.

Pearl, soon after the birth of Mildred, would marry Charles Ellsworth Abel, the son of David Wesley Abel and Elma Steele, on May 11, 1912 in Cambridge, Ohio. They were married by the Rev. Jay Goodrich. They soon moved to Newark, Ohio where they raised their children.

Charles Ellsworth Abel **Pearl Navada Wright**

While living at 155 Essex Street in Newark, Ohio, three (3) years after the death of her son, William, Pearl died on March 21, 1926 of enteritis. She is buried in Cedar Hill Cemetery, as were Austin and William. Charles died on the morning of March 21, 1927, when struck by an eastbound Pennsylvania freight train while walking along the tracks at the bottom of Buena Vista Street, Newark, Ohio. He was walking to work at the Holophane Plant. He is also buried in Cedar Hill Cemetery.

Children of Forest E. McKinley and Pearl Navada Wright:
+ 45. i. Mildred Ada McKinley (1910 – 1998).

Children of Forest E. McKinley and Margaret Dunning:
46. i. Jenevieve McKinley (1915 – Unknown) – Genevieve married Howard Miller on July 31, 1938;
47. ii. Byron Arthur McKinley (1921 – 1922); and
48. iii. Majestic Eileen McKinley (1926 – Unknown) – Majestic married Willard Albright on August 2. 1944.

Children of Charles Ellsworth Abel and Pearl Navada Wright:
+ 49. i. Bernadine Madge Abel (1913 - 1998);
+ 50. ii. Marcia Muyetta Abel (1915 - 2003);
  51. iii. Austin Charles Abel (1918 – 1921) – Austin was born May 26, 1918 and died at the age of three on August 24, 1921;
+ 52. iv. Sarah Delores Abel (1921 - 2003); and,
  53. v. William Mead Abel (1923 – 1923) – William was born January 23, 1923 and died in a crib death January 28, 1923.

Fifth Generation

45. Mildred Ada McKinley (1910 – 1998) - See Homer Whitcome Comisford, page 22.

49. Bernadine Madge Abel (1913 - 1998) – Bernadine 'Deenie' Madge Abel was born on May 26, 1913, the daughter of Charles Ellsworth and Pearl Navada (Wright) Abel. Deenie married Fredrick Allen Cayton on June 26, 1926 in Mt. Vernon, Ohio. Fred, the son of James and Clara (Parker) Cayton, was born on April 9, 1902 in Adams County, Indiana. Fred passed away on June 24, 1968, while Deenie passed away on February 4, 1998.

Children of Frederick Allen Cayton and Bernadene Madge Abel:
  54. i. Frederick 'Fredie' Allen Cayton (1947 – 1951); and
  55. ii. Lois Lynn Cayton (Living)

50. Marcia Muyetta Abel (1915 - 2003) - See Charles Benne Comisford, page 20.

52. Sarah Delores Abel (1921 - 2003) – Sarah Delores Abel was born on February 1, 1921, the daughter of Charles Ellsworth and Pearl Navada (Wright) Abel. Sarah married Joseph William 'Bill' Boyer on June 30, 1939 at United Brethren Church. Bill served in the Navy during World War II. Sarah passed away on March 20, 2003, while Bill would pass away on September 10, 2004.

Children of Joseph William Boyer and Sarah Delores Abel:
  56. i. Judith Eileen Boyer (Living)
  57. ii. Joseph William Boyer, Jr. (Living);
  58. iii. James Edward Boyer (Living);
  59. iv. Margaret Ellen Boyer (Living);
  60. v. Anita Louise Boyer (Living);
  61. vi. Thomas Allen Boyer (Living); and
  62. vii. John Steven Boyer (Living).

Bernadene (Abel) Cayton, Mildred (McKinley) Comisford,
Marcia (Abel) Comisford, Helen Comisford, Elizabeth Comisford,
Sarah (Abel) Bover

Descendents of John Aplin and Hannah Paine

First Generation

1.　John Aplin (1710 – 1772) - John Aplin was born in 1710 in Taunton, England, the son of John Aplin, where he attended the Taunton Grammar School from June 5, 1716 to January 25, 1720. He came to the American Colonies sometime between 1725 and 1734, likely on business for a London law firm, fully expecting to return to England. He tried to return to England three times, but became shipwrecked each time. On his third and final trip, he barely escaped with his life. At this point, he decided that the Lord had ordained that he should remain in the American Colonies. Sometime before 1734 he would marry Hannah Paine, the daughter of Solomon Paine and Abigail Owen. Hannah was born in 1719.

John, educated at Oxford, became a prominent lawyer in Providence, Rhode Island where he and Hannah would raise their family. John, who could read Latin, was often called upon to translate official church and government document which came from England written in Latin. John became a freeman on May 1, 1744

Hannah died at the early age of 40 on October 21, 1758. She was buried in the Old North Burial Grounds in Providence, where her tombstone reads as follows:

> "In Memory of Mrs. Hannah Aplin, the wife of Mr. John Aplin, who died October the 21st 1758 at the age of 40 years. She was a prudent wife, a tender mother and faithful friend."

John would then marry Sarah Bowen on April 24, 1760 in Providence, Rhode Island.

Late in life John would move to Plainfield, Windham County, Connecticut, where he would pass away on July 22, 1772. John's gravestone reads as follows:

> "This Stone covers the Remains of
> JOHN APLIN
> A Lawyer of such happy Talents
> that he shone

the distinguished Ornament of his Profession in the Colony of Rhode Island
where he chiefly practised.
His Genius was not confined to the Science of Law.
For his great Knowledge in History
supported by an extensive and ready Memory
gave him always Opportunity
in Conversation with his many Friends
to afford them such rational Entertainment
that he delighted
at the same time that he instructed.
He abounded with native Humor,
in the Application of which he was singularly successful.
He was born in Taunton in the County of Somerset
In Great Britain
to whose Constitution in Church and State
he was a Zealous Friend
and which he constantly and Strenuously Affected.
After making a decent Provision for a numerous Progeny
he retired to Plainfield
where he had lived but a few years
when he submitted to the Doom inevitable to Mortals
On the 22d Day of July 1772
in the 63d Year of his Age"

Children of John Aplin and Hannah Paine:

+ 2.   i.   John, Aplin, Jr. (1734 – 1806);
  3.   ii. Benjamin Aplin (1736 – 1799) – Benjamin was born in 1736 or 1737, never married, and died in August 1799. He hired Daniel Knower on September 30, 1777 to take his place in the Revolutionary War;
  4.   iii. Rebecca Aplin (1739 – 1790) – Rebecca was born in November 15, 1739, married John Nash on December 2, 1759, and died on August 6, 1790;
  5.   iv. Hannah Aplin (1743 – 1808) – Hannah was born in 1743 or 1744, never married, and died on July 17, 1808;
  6.   v.   James Aplin (1745 – 1809) – James was born in 1745 or 1746, first married Rachel, then Thankful Gary, and died in 1809;
+ 7.   vi. William Aplin (1737 – Unknown);
  8.   vii. Joseph Aplin (1737 – 1804) – Joseph was born between 1737 and 1749 and died in April 1804. Joseph settled in Canada, where he became the Attorney General of Prince Edward Island;

9. viii. Samuel Aplin (1750 – 1750) – Samuel was born in June 1750 and died as an infant on July 18, 1750;
10. ix. Thomas Aplin (1752 – 1819) – Thomas was born in 1752 or 1753, married Mary Fuller, and died on April 10, 1819; and
11. x. Robert Aplin (1757 – 1821) – Robert was born in 1757, married Damaris Howe, and died on April 10, 1821.

Children of John Aplin and Sarah Bowen:
12. i. Sarah Aplin (1761 – 1853) – Sarah was born February 6, 1761, married Charles Waterman on April 22, 1790 in Cornish, Cheshire County, New Hampshire, and died February 4, 1853 in Oxford, Butler County, Ohio;
13. ii. Oliver Aplin (1760 – 1833) – Oliver was born between 1760 and 1765, married Elizabeth Gilbert on February 24, 1793, and died in 1833;
14. iii. Mary Aplin (1762 – 1777) – Mary was born between 1762 and 1772 and died July 8, 1777

Second Generation

2. John Aplin, Jr. (1734 – 1806) - John Aplin, Jr. was born in 1734 or 1735, the oldest son of John Aplin and Hannah Paine. John married Elizabeth Arnold, the daughter of Stephen Arnold and Marcie Tillinghast. Elizabeth was born on January 23, 1738 in Providence, Rhode Island. Together they would raise four children.

John died in 1806, while Elizabeth died on January 15, 1795. They are both buried in the Old North Burial Grounds of Providence, Rhode Island.

Children of John Aplin, Jr. and Elizabeth Arnold:
15. i. Stephen Arnold Aplin (1762 – 1836) – Stephen died November 24, 1836 in Providence, Rhode Island and buried in the Old North Burial Grounds;
16. ii. Henrietta Aplin (1764 – 1848) – Henrietta married Jonathan Ellis Simmons on August 11, 1796 in Providence, Rhode Island, and died May 27, 1848 in Providence, Rhode Island and is buried in the Old North Burial Grounds;
17. iii. William Aplin; and
+ 18. iv. Benjamin Aplin (1769 – 1843).

7. William Aplin (1737 – Unknown) – William was born in 1737 and 1749, the son of John Aplin and Hannah Paine. William married Ruth Nichols. William participated in the Revolutionary War and was listed in 1840 US Census, Revolutionary War Pensioners.

Children of William Aplin and Ruth Nichols:
  19.   i.   Hannah Aplin (1779 – Unknown).

Third Generation

18. Benjamin Aplin (1769 – 1843) - Benjamin Aplin was born on November 26, 1769 in Providence, Rhode Island, the son of John and Elizabeth (Arnold) Aplin, Jr. Benjamin married Lydia Gray, the daughter of Amasa and Sarah Lydia (Turpin) Gray on December 16, 1792 in Providence, Rhode Island. Lydia was born on August 14, 1777 in Providence, Rhode Island. Benjamin own paper mills and made paper in Providence.

Sometime between 1830 and 1840, Benjamin and his family would leave Rhode Island and settle in Norwich, Muskingum County, Ohio, where Benjamin was a farmer and the town Postmaster. He passed away on December 23, 1843 and was buried in the Norwich Presbyterian Cemetery in Norwich, Ohio. Lydia would pass away soon after Benjamin on September 19, 1845 and was also buried in the Norwich Presbyterian Cemetery.

Children of Benjamin Aplin and Lydia Gray:
  20.   i.   John Turpin Aplin (1793 – 1811) –John was born on September 4, 1793 and died January 28, 1811;
  21.   ii.   Edward Allen Aplin (1794 – Unknown) – Edward was born on December 7, 1794 and married Edna A. Hardesty on July 12, 1849 in Providence;
+ 22.   iii. Elizabeth Gray Aplin (1796 – 1849);
  23.   iv.   Lydia Gray Aplin (1798 – 1803) – Lydia was born on February 3, 1798 and died January 21, 1803;
  24.   v.   Henry Seymore Aplin (1800 – 1811) – Henry was born on August 13, 1800 and died October 28, 1811;
  25.   vi.   Lydia Gray Aplin (1803 – 1873) – Lydia was born on February 27, 1803, married William Pierce on April 30, 1822 in Providence, died on February 3, 1873 in Guernsey County, Ohio, and is buried in the Old Buffalo Cemetery;
  26.   vii. Benjamin Baker Aplin (1805 – Unknown) - Benjamin was born October 14, 1805 and married Esther Mercy on December 29, 1833 in Woodstock, Connecticut. Benjamin's son, Albert M., was an Orderly in Company B of the 31st Ohio Volunteer Infantry during the Civil War;
+ 27.   viii. Welcome Gray Aplin (1807 – 1884);
  28.   ix.   Sarah Cook Aplin (1809 – 1860) – Sarah was born on October 30, 1809, married Elizah Wortman on May 30, 1840 and died in 1860 in Muskingum County, Ohio;
  29.   x.   Ann Russel Aplin (1810 – 1811) – Ann was born on June 8, 1810 and died on October 8, 1811;

	30.	xi.	Henry Seymore Aplin (1811 – Unknown) – Henry was born on October 28, 1811;
+	31.	xii.	William Henry Aplin (1813 – 1907);
+	32.	xiii.	John Turpin Aplin (1815 – 1883);
+	33.	xiv.	Albert C. Aplin (1817 – Unknown);
	34.	xvi.	A daughter born April 21, 1818; and
+	35.	xvii.	Charles Joseph Aplin (1821 – 1899).

Fourth Generation

22. Elizabeth Gray Aplin (1796 – 1849) – Elizabeth Gray Aplin was born on June 26, 1796, in Providence, Rhode Island, the daughter of Benjamin and Lydia (Gray) Aplin. Elizabeth married Elisha Lincoln on May 22, 1816 in Woodstock, Connecticut. She died on February 23, 1849, while Elisha died on August 7, 1850, in Hocking County, Ohio, and both are buried in the Morris Chapel Cemetery.

Children of Elisha Lincoln and Elizabeth Gray Aplin:
36.	i.	Albert Aplin Lincoln (1818 – Unknown);
37.	ii.	Lydia Ann Lincoln (1820 – Unknown);
38.	iii.	Benjamin Aplin Lincoln (1821 – Unknown);
39.	iv.	Edward Henry Lincoln, died an infant;
40.	v.	Elizabeth Pray Lincoln (1824 – Unknown);
41.	vi.	Edward Henry Lincoln (1828 – Unknown);
42.	vii.	William Stowell Lincoln (1828 – 1848);
43.	viii.	Julian Welcome Lincoln (1830 – Unknown);
44.	ix.	Charles James Lincoln (1832 – Unknown);
45.	x.	Marea Marie Lincoln (1834 – Unknown);
46.	xi.	Sarah Adeline Lincoln (1836 – 1857);
47.	xii.	Lucy Webb Lincoln (1839 – Unknown); and
48.	xiii.	Sanford Elisha Lincoln (1841 – Unknown).

27. Welcome Gray Aplin (1807 – 1884) - Welcome Gray Aplin was born on September 4, 1807 in Providence, Rhode Island, the son of Benjamin and Lydia (Gray) Aplin. He left with his parents for the Ohio River Valley during the 1830's. He, along with his brother Benjamin, bought large tracts of land on Billy's Run, at the head of Elk Fork, Jackson County, Western Virginia, at delinquent tax and commissioner's sales. Sometimes they paid as low as five cents per acre. These lands passed by inheritance to their brother, William, who owned several thousand acres of land, and was, at one time, reported to be the wealthiest man in the county.

Welcome, first married Maria Browning in 1838. She died soon after and he then married Mahala (Collins) Moore, the widow of Joseph W. Moore, sometime around 1850.

Welcome was a farmer and owned a farm in Buffalo Township of Guernsey County, Ohio. Welcome would pass away on April 15, 1884, while Mahala would pass away on November 4, 1903. They are both buried in the Old Hartford Cemetery in Guernsey County, Ohio.

Children of Joseph W. Moore and Mahala Collins:
- 49. i. Elizabeth Moore (1833 – Unknown);
- + 50. ii. Rhoda A. Moore (1835 – Unknown);
- 51. iii. Jemina Moore (1843 – 1873) – Jemina died on September 19, 1873 in Valley Twp., Guernsey County, Ohio of typhoid fever; and
- 52. iv. Joseph Moore (1848 – Unknown).

Children of Welcome Aplin and Mahala Collins:
- 53. i. Charles F. Aplin (1851 – 1924) - Charles died on February 23, 1924 in Hocking County, Ohio;
- 54. ii. Ira E. Aplin (1852 – 1928) – Ira died on July 13, 1928 in Guernsey County, Ohio;
- + 55. iii. Mahala 'Nellie' Ellen Aplin (1854 – 1941); and
- 56. iv. Maria Aplin (1857 – Unknown) – Maria was born in 1857 and died before 1880.

31. **William Henry Aplin (1813 – 1907)** – William Henry 'Billy' Aplin was born on August 2, 1813, the son of Benjamin and Lydia (Gray) Aplin. Billy married Mary Francis Lett on August 29, 1847 in Ripley, Western Virginia, the daughter of Lemuel C. Lett. Mary was born on March 14, 1833. Billy and Mary had received three slaves as a wedding present from Mary's father. Billy would eventually set them free (Samp, Jim, and Judy). The one, known as "Nigger Jim" stayed with the Alpins. Billy paid him for working on the farm and Jim would teach school for the young slaves. One night, Jim was beaten and hung from a tree on the Rader farm at Gay West Virginia, it was never known who did it or why. Billy loved to read. He was a farmer, a shoemaker, an astronomer, a surveyor, and at times, an attorney. He moved to a farm between Red Knob and Gay, Western Virginia in 1841, then to Ohio in early 1863 due to the Civil War. He inherited from his brothers, Benjamin and Welcome, thousands of acres, making him one of the wealthiest men in the county. Billy deeded each of his surviving girls about 290 acres, and built a two-story white house on each plot. Mary passed away on July 7, 1882,

while Billy passed away on July 29, 1907 in Gay, West Virginia. Both are buried in Halbert Cemetery.

Children of William Henry Aplin and Mary Francis Lett:

57. i. John Aplin (1848 – 1864) – John was born on February 24, 1838 in Ripley, Western Virginia. He enlisted during the Civil War in Company A of the 129th Ohio Volunteer Infantry. He died on January 27, 1864 in a hospital in Cumberland Gap, Tennessee, unknown cause and burial site;
58. ii. Lydia Aplin (1851 – 1928) - Lydia married Venson Tibbles on December 23, 1871 in Ripley, West Virginia, then married Benjamin T. Hudson on September 19/20, 1877 in Ripley;
59. iii. Emily Aplin (1853 – 1856) - Emily got caught in the belt of the family grist mill and was killed on May 31, 1856;
60. iv. Sarah Aplin (1855 – 1912) – Sarah married David Megary 'Doc' Archer on June 29, 1877 in Ripley, West Virginia and died February 26, 1912;
61. v. Alice Aplin (1858 – 1920) – Alice married Rev. James Alfred Rogers on October 28, 1877 in Ripley, West Virginia and died on April 20, 1920;
62. vi. Eliza Jane Aplin (1860 - 1919) – Eliza married George Anderson March 21, 1901 in Ripley, West Virginia, then married William Henderson 'Sank' Westfall on November 28, 1903 in Ripley, and died on October 24, 1919;
63. vii. Everet Aplin (1862 – 1864) – Everet was born on April 6, 1862 in Gay, West Virginia and died on September 18, 1864 in Athens, Ohio;
64. viii. Esther Aplin (1864 – 1947) – Esther married Thomas Waybright on March 7, 1884 in Ripley, West Virginia and died on July 9, 1947; and
65. ix. Walter Aplin (1867 – 1868).

William Henry Aplin

32. John Turpin Aplin (1815 – 1883) – John Turpin Aplin was born on June 18, 1815, the son of Benjamin and Lydia (Gray) Aplin. John married Mariah.

    Children of John Turpin and Mariah Aplin:
        66.   i.   Ida Aplin (1850 – Unknown);
        67.   ii.   Alice E. Aplin (1853 – Unknown);
        68.   iii. Infant son, who died on May 31, 1856; and
        69.   iv. Laura H. Aplin (1859 – Unknown).

33. Albert C. Aplin (1817 – 1904) – Albert C. Aplin was born on March 25, 1817, in Providence, Rhode Island, the son of Benjamin and Lydia (Gray) Aplin. Albert married Elizabeth Ann Miller on December 3, 1839. Elizabeth was born in 1820 in Rushville, Ohio. Albert passed away on June 29, 1904 in Cambridge, Story County, Iowa and is buried in the Cambridge Cemetery.

    Children of Albert C. and Elizabeth A. Aplin:
        70.   i.   Emily Aplin (1841 – 1847) – Emily died on September 28, 1847 and is buried in Norwich Presbyterian Cemetery;
        71.   ii.   Mary Miller Aplin (1842 – Unknown) - Mary married John Rudolph Smith on August 3, 1886 in Story County, Iowa;
        72.   iii. Lydia Aplin (1842 – Unknown) – Lydia married E. Smith;
        73.   iv. Benjamin Aplin (1844 – Unknown) Benjamin served during the Civil War in the 31st Ohio Volunteer Infantry, Company E;
        74.   v.   Charles J. Aplin (1846 – Unknown) – Charles became a physician, married Aldie Reed on May 8, 1884;
        75.   vi. William Aplin (1848 – Unknown) – William became a physician, married Mariah Ann Earp on October 15, 1873 in Marion County, Iowa (Mariah was a 1st cousin of the famous lawman, Wyatt Earp), then married Laura 'Lana' Belle Eggleston on June 4, 1890 in Hamilton, Caldwell County, Missouri, and died after 1910;
        76.   vii. Alice Aplin (1851 – Unknown) – Alice married Clark McCoy;
        77.   viii. Arthur S. Aplin (1852 – 1900) – Arthur was born on September 6, 1852 in Hocking County, Ohio, became a physician, married Sylvia Boitnott on December 13, 1888 in Cambridge, Story County, Iowa, and died on February 19, 1900 in Story County, Iowa;
        78.   ix. Emma Aplin (1855 – Unknown) – Emma married Joseph C. Mather;
        79.   x.   Clarance Aplin (1857 – Unknown) – Clarance became a school teacher in Iowa;
        80.   xi. Clara J. Aplin (1859 – Unknown) – Clara became a school teacher in Iowa;

81.   xii.   Anna Olivia H. Aplin (1862 – Unknown) – Olivia became a school teacher in Iowa and married E.L. Meek on September 9, 1888 in Story County, Iowa; and
82.   xiii.   Maurice H. Aplin (1868 – Unknown) – Maurice became a farmer in Iowa.

35.   Charles Joseph Aplin (1821 – 1899) – Charles Joseph Aplin was born on February 12, 1821 in Woodstock, Connecticut, the youngest son of Benjamin and Lydia (Gray) Aplin. Charles was a physician. Charles passed away on December 7, 1899 in Vinton County, Ohio and is buried in the New Plymouth Cemetery in Washington, Hocking County, Ohio.

Children of Charles and Elizabeth Aplin:
83.   i.   John M. Aplin (1857 – Unknown);
84.   ii.   Welcome C. Aplin (1859 – Unknown);
85.   iii.   Brenda Aplin (1861 – Unknown);
86.   iv.   Mahala C. Aplin (1864 – Unknown); and
87.   v.   Charles B. Aplin (1867 – Unknown).

Fifth Generation

50.   Rhoda A. Moore (1835 – Unknown) – Rhoda Moore was the daughter of Joseph W. Moore and Mahala Collins. Rhoda married John Frye, a farmer in Guernsey County, Ohio.

Children of John Frye and Rhoda A. Moore:
88.   i.   Charles W. Frye (1858 – Unknown).

55.   Mahala 'Nellie' Ellen Aplin (1854 – 1941) - See Aaron McKinley, page 133.

Descendents of Stephen Paine, Sr. and Neele Rose Adcocke

First Generation

1. Stephen Paine, Sr. (1602 – 1679) - Stephen Paine, Sr. was born in 1602 in Great Ellingham, Norfolk, England, the son of Dann and Margaret Payne. Dann was born about 1581 in Great Ellingham, England and died about 1612 and left a will dated October 12, 1612. Margaret survived Dann and later married Francis Stacye. Dann and Margaret were the parents of two children: Edward, born about 1600 and Stephen.

Stephen married Neele Rose Adcocke, the daughter of John Adcocke and Elizabeth Eldred, sometime before 1624 in England. Neele Rose was born February 20, 1602 or 1603.

Stephen, a miller by trade, along with his family and four (4) servants, left England aboard the ship *"Dilligent of Ipswick"*, John Martin, Master, for the American Colonies. He financed this move to the American Colonies by selling his home, "Heynons", in Great Ellingham to his father-in-law, John Adcocke, and seven rods of land and other property to his mother and step-father. He was also one of eleven shippers of wheat and malt, listed aboard the ship *"Blessing"*, bound from Yarmouth to New England on May 2, 1638.

The family arrived in Boston Harbor on August 10, 1638, along with several other families from Hingham, England, including the Reverend Robert Peck and a good part of his congregation. They were bound for Hingham, Plymouth County, Massachusetts, about 14 miles southeast of Boston. Hingham had been settled by many of their friends and neighbors from old Hingham in England. Stephen became a freeman in 1639 and was elected a Deputy in 1641.

In 1643, Stephen again moved his family, to start the small town of Seekonk, later named Rehobeth, and now known as New Bedford, Massachusetts. In 1644, he was elected as one of the "townsmen", a position responsible for deciding controversies in town affairs. In 1645, he was elected as a Deputy to the Court at Plymouth and held this position of office until 1660.

In 1661, Stephen, along with his two sons, Stephen and Nathaniel, and Captain Thomas Willet (latter to become the first English Mayor of New York), acquired from Warmsitter, a Sachem

Indian, a tract of land adjoining Rehobeth, where the present town of Attleboro now sits.

Neele Rose passed away sometime before 1662, at which time Stephen married Alice Parker, the widow of William Parker of Taunton. Stephen would pass away on August 16, 1679, outliving his children. Alice passed away on December 5, 1682.

Stephen's will, dated July 18, 1679, was proven at Plymouth on October 30, 1679, where his estate was valued at £6733, 15s, 10d, a man of prominence.

Children of Stephen Paine, Sr. and Neele Rose Adcocke:
2.   i.   John Paine (1624 – Unknown) – John was born in 1624 in Great Ellingham, Norfolk, England and died at a young age in Hingham, Massachusetts;
+ 3.   ii. Stephen Paine, Jr. (1629 – 1677);
4.   iii. Nathaniel Paine (1631 – 1676) – Nathaniel was born in 1631 in Great Ellingham, Norfolk, England, who married Elizabeth about 1660, and died about March 1676 or 1677; and
5.   iv. Rebecca Paine (1638 – 1638) – Rebecca was born about 1638 in England and died during the voyage to the American Colonies prior to August 10, 1638.

Second Generation

3.   Stephen Paine, Jr. (1629 - 1677) - Stephen Paine, Jr. was born September 20, 1629 in Great Ellingham, Norfolk, England, the son of Stephen Paine, Sr. and Neele Rose Adcocke. Stephen, along with his parents, two brothers, a sister, and four (4) servants, left England aboard the ship *"Dilligent of Ipswick"*, John Martin, Master, set sail for the American Colonies. The family arrived in Boston Harbor on August 10, 1638, where they settled in Hingham, Plymouth County, Massachusetts, about 14 miles southeast of Boston.

In 1643, Stephen again moved with his family, to start the small town of Seekonk, later named Rehoboth, and now known as New Bedford, Massachusetts.

Stephen married Anne Chickering, the daughter of Francis Chickering and Ann Fiske, on November 3, 1652. Anne was born in St. James, England. Together Stephen and Anne would have nine children.

Stephen took the Oath of Fidelity in 1657 and would become a prominent citizen and landowner of the towns of Rehoboth, Swansey, and Attleboro, Massachusetts. He became a tanner and was active in the affairs of Rehoboth.

Stephen acquired the home of Edward Inman, including eleven acres of land on the northern edge of Providence, Rhode Island, along the Moshassuck River in September of 1666.

Stephen served under Major Bradford in the First Plymouth Colony Company during the King Phillip's War in 1675. He participated in the Narraganset Expedition. He also gave generously, contributing a sizeable amount of money to the cause.

Stephen passed away, shortly after the King Phillip's War and before his father and was buried in Rehoboth on January 24, 1677 or 1678.

Children of Stephen Paine, Jr. and Anne Chickering:

   6.   i.   Stephen Paine (1654 – 1710) – Stephen was born on November 23, 1654 in Rehoboth, Bristol, Massachusetts, who married Elizabeth Williams in 1703, then Mary Brintnall on August 12, 1707, and died in 1710 in Rehoboth, Massachusetts;

   7.   ii.   Rebecca Paine (1656 – Unknown) – Rebecca was born on December 20, 1656, who married Peter Hunt on December 24, 1673, and then married Samuel Peck on November 21, 1677;

+   8.   iii.   John Paine (1658 – 1718);

   9.   iv.   Mary Paine (1660 – 1709) – Mary was born on July 11, 1660 in Rehoboth, Massachusetts, who married Enoch Hunt on October 29, 1679, and died March 12, 1709 or 1710;

   10.   v.   Samuel Paine (1662 – 1735) – Samuel was born on May 12, 1662 in Rehoboth, Massachusetts, who married Anne Peck on December 16, 1685 in Rehoboth, Massachusetts, then married Abigail Bartholomew on January 18, 1708 or 1709 in Woodstock, Connecticut, and died May 11, 1735 in Woodstock, Windham County, Connecticut;

   11.   vi.   Elizabeth Paine (1664 – 1736) – Elizabeth was born on October 27, 1664 in Rehoboth, Massachusetts, who married Jacob Pepper on February 10, 1683 or 1684 in Rehoboth, Massachusetts, and died before May 24, 1736 in Roxbury, Suffolk County, Massachusetts;

   12.   vii.   Sarah Paine (1666 – 1711) – Sarah was born on October 12, 1666 in Rehoboth, Massachusetts, who married Daniel Aldis on November 23, 1688, and died April 17, 1711;

   13.   viii.   Nathaniel Paine (1667 – 1717) – Nathaniel was born on September 20, 1667 in Rehoboth, Massachusetts, who married Dorothy Chaffee on May 4, 1694, and died March 18, 1717 or 1718 in Rehoboth, Bristol County, Massachusetts; and

14. ix. Benjamin Paine (1673 – 1698) – Benjamin was born on March 9, 1673 or 1674 in Rehoboth, Massachusetts, who was unmarried, and died in April 1698 in Rehoboth, Massachusetts.

8. John Paine (1658 – 1718) - John Paine was born on April 3, 1658 in Rehoboth, Bristol County, Massachusetts, the son of Stephen Paine, Jr. and Anne Chickering. John married Elizabeth Belcher on February 3, 1679 in Rehoboth, Massachusetts. Elizabeth was the daughter of Josiah Belcher and Urania Rainsford. Elizabeth was born July 10, 1663 in Boston, Suffolk County, Massachusetts.

John became a surveyor by trade and was a surveyor of highways in 1686. He would own property in Swansea and Bristol Massachusetts and in Providence, Rhode Island. On the death of John's grandfather, Stephen Paine, John received a 10 acre lot in Swansea on the east side of the Swansey River, between the property of Captain Thomas Willet and Chafee's Meadow. From his father, Stephen Paine, he inherited land in Bristol.

While living in Swansea, John was active in the community and served as a representative.

Elizabeth passed away in 1709 in Rehoboth, Bristol County, Massachusetts. John then married Martha Smith in 1709 and soon moved to Providence, Rhode Island, where he acquired the farm of Richard Phillips, located near the Mashapauge Pond. He sold the family home in Swansea to Josiah Turner on April 11, 1711.

John died on September 26, 1718 in Providence, Providence County, Rhode Island. After John's death Martha married Abel Potter, her step-daughter, Rebecca's husband.

Children of John Paine and Elizabeth Belcher:
15. i. Elizabeth Paine (1682 – 1756) – Elizabeth was born on July 12, 1682 in Rehoboth, Bristol County, Massachusetts, married Thomas Wait on September 25, 1711 in Rehoboth, Massachusetts, and died before December 22, 1756;
16. ii. John Paine (1682 – 1723) – John was born in February 1682 or 1683 in Rehoboth, Massachusetts, married Mary Davis, and died July 19, 1723;
17. iii. Stephen Paine (1686 – Unknown) – Stephen was born on June 5, 1686, first married Martha Smith, and then Sarah Vallet on October 13, 1715;
18. iv. Josiah Paine (1686 – 1763) – Josiah was born on March 17, 1686 or 1687 and died January 16, 1763;
19. v. Joseph Paine (1693 -1718) – Joseph was born on May 3, 1693;

20.	vi.	Rebecca, Paine (1694 – 1719) – Rebecca was born on May 1, 1694 and married Abel Potter;
+ 21.	vii.	Solomon Paine (1696 – 1752);
22.	viii.	Benjamin Paine (1699 – 1784) – Benjamin was born in 1699 in Providence Rhode Island, first married Jemina Esten, then Amey Mowry on November 2, 1734, then Elizabeth Owen on August 14, 1719, then Anne Arnold on December 24, 1731, and died on January 1, 1784 in Smithfield, Providence County, Rhode Island;
23.	ix.	Nathan Paine (1701 – 1756) – Nathan married Elizabeth Angell;
24.	x.	Gideon Paine (1703 – 1756) – Gideon was born in 1703 in Swansea, Bristol County, Massachusetts, married Rebecca Corp on November 14, 1756 in Smithfield, Providence County, Rhode Island, and died on January 7, 1756 in Smithfield, Rhode Island; and
25.	xi.	Urania Paine (1706 – Unknown) – Urania was born July 4, 1706 in Rehoboth, Massachusetts, married Uriah Mowry, and died sometime before 1773.

Children of John Paine and Martha Smith:

26.	i.	William Paine (1711 – Unknown) – William was born on November 11, 1711 in Providence, Rhode Island;
27.	ii.	Abigail Paine (1713 – Unknown) – Abigail was born on October 13, 1713 in Providence, Rhode Island;
28.	iii.	Ezekial Paine (1715 – Unknown) – Ezekial was born on August 26, 1715 in Providence, Rhode Island and married Ruth Seely; and
29.	iv.	Samuel Paine (1717 – Unknown) – Samuel was born on November 22, 1717 in Providence, Rhode Island.

21. Solomon Paine (1696 – 1752) - Solomon Paine was on born June 21, 1696 in Rehoboth, Massachusetts, the son of John Paine and Elizabeth Belcher. Solomon married Abigail Owen on March 13, 1718 in Providence, Rhode Island, the daughter of Ebenezer Owen and Hannah Belcher. Abigail was born about 1689 in Braintree, Massachusetts.

Solomon, along with his brother-in-law Josiah Cleaveland, *"...a man of wealth and of prominence in both town and church at Canterbury"* participated together in the formation of a new separatist Church. They were followers of Rev. George Whitefield (Calvinistic-Methodist). This new Church was at odds with the established Church at Canterbury (Congregational) over theological matters, enough, that the two sons of Josiah, Ebenezer and John, were temporarily expelled from Yale College for attending its services.

Solomon passed away on September 26, 1718 in Providence, Rhode Island.

Children of Solomon Paine and Abigail Owen:
+   30.   i.   Hannah Paine (1719 – 1758); and
     31.   ii.   Ebenezer Paine (1720 – Unknown) – Ebenezer was born February 16, 1720.

30.   Hannah Paine (1719 – 1758) - See John Aplin, page 139.

Descendents of Gregory Belcher and Catherine Allcock

1. Gregory Belcher (1606 – 1674) - Gregory Belcher was born March 30, 1606 in Ashton Parish, Warwick, England, the son of Thomas Belcher and Deborah Hunt. Thomas was born about 1578 in Wardend Parish of Aston County, Warwicks, England, while Deborah was born about 1582 in Wardend Parish of Aston County, Warwicks, England. Thomas and Deborah were the parents of three children: John, born August 24, 1604 in Wardend, Ashton, Warwickshire, England; Gregory; and Margery, born July 9, 1615 Wardend, Ashton, Warwickshire, England.

Gregory Belcher would marry Catherine Allcock on December 11, 1627 in Manchester, Lancashire (Greater Manchester), England. Catherine was born in 1610 in Wilmslow, Cheshire, England. It's not certain whether Gregory and his young wife were among those that arrived in the American Colonies in the Winthrop Fleet, but they did join the Massachusetts Bay Colony and would be in the Colonies sometime before 1631.

A farmer by trade, Gregory was granted a lot of 52 acres at Mount Wollaston (Braintree) on December 30, 1639. He paid 3 shillings an acre. He settled here and would farm the land. He became a freeman on May 13, 1640 and was made a selectman in 1646, an office in which he served until June, 1665.

Gregory, along with his son-in-law Alexander March, acquired the iron works of Braintree. This property included 200 acres of land with it. The iron works had gone bankrupt in 1653 and was subsequently acquired by Thomas Wiggin.

Gregory, along with seven others, on September 16, 1639 drafted and signed the covenant of the First Church of Braintree, founding the first church in Braintree.

When Gregory died on November 25, 1674, he owned interest in several farms, along with his ownership of the iron works. He was buried in Hancock Cemetery in Norfolk, Massachusetts. Catherine would pass away on July 20, 1680.

Children of Gregory Belcher and Catharine Allcock:
+ 2. i. Josiah Belcher (1631 – 1682);
  3. ii. Elizabeth Belcher (1632 – Unknown) – Elizabeth was born on June 24, 1632 in Of Wetherfield, Hartford County, Connecticut and married Thomas Gilbert about 1651;
  4. iii. John Belcher (1633 – 1693) – John was born in 1633 in Braintree, Suffolk County, Massachusetts and died in 1693;
  5. iv. Moses Belcher (1635 – 1691) – Moses was born about 1635 in Braintree, Suffolk County, Massachusetts, married Mary Nash on May 23, 1666 in Braintree, Massachusetts, and died on July 15, 1691;
  6. v. Samuel Belcher (1637 – 1697) – Samuel was born on August 24, 1637 in Braintree, Suffolk County, Massachusetts, married Mary Billings on December 15, 1663 in Braintree, Massachusetts, and died on June 17, 1697;
  7. vi. Mary Belcher (1639 – 1669) – Mary was born on July 8, 1639 in Braintree, Suffolk County, Massachusetts, married Alexander Marsh and died on June 17, 1669;
  8. vii. Joseph Belcher (1641 – 1678) – Joseph was born on December 25, 1641 in Braintree, Suffolk County, Massachusetts, married Rebecca Gill about 1664 and died in 1678. Joseph was a soldier and quartermaster during the King Philip War (1675-1676) where he was wounded in the knee during an attack on Swansey at Mile's garrison; and
  9. viii. Gregory Belcher (1643 – Unknown) – Gregory was born in 1643 in Braintree, Suffolk County, Massachusetts and married Elizabeth Ruggles on March 25, 1690 in Braintree, Massachusetts.

Gregory Belcher
To
General Douglas MacArthur

The direct line from Gregory Belcher to General Douglas MacArthur World War II hero, was prepared by Rhonda R. McClure.

General MacArthur will long be remembered as a hero to many Americans for his part in World War II. The son of a general in the Civil War, he and his father are the only father and son to be awarded the Congressional Medal of Honor. During his career, he was the youngest army chief of staff ever appointed, presided over the Japanese surrender on September 2, 1945, was a Congressional Metal of Honor Recipient, and toyed with the idea of running for president. The following is the direct line:

Gregory Belcher—Catherine Allcock
(3/30/1606-11/25/1674) - (1610-7/20/1680)
|
Samuel Belcher—Mary Billings
(8/24/1637-6/17/1679) - (Unknown-Unknown)
|
Gregory Belcher—Elizabeth Ruggles
(2/28/1664/1665-7/4/1727) - (12/26/1669-11/1748)
|
Joseph Belcher—Deborah Hunt
(8/19/1704-Unknown) - (3/8/1710/1711-3/21/1753)
|
Gregory Belcher—Deborah Williams
(1/26/1738/1739-Unknown) - (1737-5/2/1774)
|
Benjamin Belcher—Sarah Barney
(9/17/1765-12/17/1833) - (6/26/1771-10/14/1867)
|
Benjamin Barney Belcher—Olive Unknown
(1793/1794-9/5/1859) - (Unknown-9/13/1845)
|
Arthur MacArthur—Aurelia Belcher
(1/26/1815-8/24/1896) - (Unknown-Unknown)
|
Arthur MacArthur—Mary Pinkney Hardy
(6/2/1845-9/5/1912) - (1852-Unknown)
|
General Douglas MacArthur
(1/26/1880—1964)

Second Generation

2. Josiah Belcher (1631 – 1682) - Josiah Belcher was born in 1631 in Braintree, Suffolk County, Massachusetts, the son of Gregory Belcher and Catherine Allcock. Josiah married Urania Rainsford on March 3, 1655, the daughter of Edward Rainsford and Elizabeth Dillee. Urania or "Ranis" as she was known was born on April 4, 1638 in Boston, Suffolk County, Massachusetts.

Josiah became a wheelwright and they settled in Boston, where they acquired an estate located on what is now the southeasterly corner of Essex Street and Harrison Street.

Josiah became one of the founders of the Third or Old South Church of Boston. He died on October 17, 1682 at the age of 52 and was buried in the Granary Burying Ground, where his gravestone sill remains. Ranis would pass away on October 2, 1691.

Children of Josiah Belcher and Urania Rainsford:
- 10. i. Josiah Belcher (1655 – 1682) – Josiah was born on December 23, 1655, remained unmarried, and died in the autumn of 1682. Josiah served during the Narraganset Campaign in King Phillip's War, and took part in the Great Swamp Fight on December 16, 1675. He drowned at Weymouth in 1682, as mentioned in Judge Sewall's Diary;
- 11. ii. John Belcher (1657 – Unknown) – John was born on October 9, 1657 and died in infancy;
- 12. iii. John Belcher (1659 – Unknown) – John was born on December 23, 1659;
- 13. iv. Jonathan Belcher (1661 – Unknown) – Jonathan was born on September 1, 1661 and was unmarried. Jonathan was a goldsmith in Boston;
- + 14. v. Elizabeth Belcher (1663 – 1709);
- 15. vi. Joseph Belcher (1665 – Unknown) – Joseph was born on October 4, 1665, was unmarried, and died sometime between 1700 and 1708. Joseph was a shipwright;
- 16. vii. Rebecca Belcher (1657 – Unknown) – Rebecca was born on December 31, 1657 and married Joseph Fuller on November 30, 1687 in Lynn, Massachusetts;
- 17. viii. Edward Belcher (1669 – 1700) – Edward was born on January 19, 1669 or 1670, who was unmarried, and died before May 14, 1700;
- 18. ix. Anna Belcher (1671 – Unknown) – Anna was born on February 18, 1671 or 1672 and married Joseph Johnson, a coppersmith of Boston;

19.	x.	Dorothy Belcher (1673 – Unknown) – Dorothy was born on October 28, 1673 and married Edmund Gross of Boston;
20.	xi.	Abigail Belcher (1675 – 1717) – Abigail was born on March 10, 1675 and died after June 8, 1717;
21.	xii.	Nathan Belcher (1677 – 1699) – Nathan was born in 1677 and died July 3, 1699;
22.	xiii.	Ruth Belcher (1678 – 1731) – Ruth was born on December 21, 1678, married Benjamin Tolman on December 28, 1703 in Boston, and died on January 1731 or 1732; and
23.	xiv.	Benjamin Belcher (1680 – 1716) – Benjamin was born on March 20, 1680 and died on April 19, 1716 in Newport, Rhode Island.

Third Generation

14. Elizabeth Belcher (1663 – 1709) - See John Paine, page 152.

Descendents of Edward Rainsford and Elizabeth Dillee

First Generation

1. Edward Rainsford (1607 – 1680) - England during the 17th century was a land beset by religious strife. Intertwined in politics, this strife led to a rebellion and the ultimate beheading of King Charles I.

The Puritans, in an effort to worship in a way of their own choosing, elected to become a part of the Massachusetts Bay Company.

The Massachusetts Bay Company was formed, and approved by King Charles I, to settle and exploit the American Colonies. The Puritans, by gaining control of the Massachusetts Bay Company, would be able to rule the new colony from the New World, rather than from England. Thus, they would be able to avoid the politics and external influences exercised by England.

The Puritans soon gained control of the Massachusetts Bay Company and began to plan for their religious colony in the Americas. As their leader for this new settlement, they chose, John Winthrop.

Then, on April 7, 1630 the first four ships left London for the New World. These ships were followed by a number of others over the next few months. These ships included the flagship *"Arbella"*, the *"Ambrose"*, the *"Talbot"*, the *"Jewel"*, the *"Charles"*, the *"Mayflower"*, the *"William and Francis"*, the *"Hopewell"*, the *"Whale"*, the *"John and Dorothy"*, the *"Rose"*, and the *"Success and Trial"*. Abandoning their homes and farms, they would take on a perilous voyage across the Atlantic Ocean to settle in an unknown wilderness. There were about one thousand settlers who left England, of which about one-third would perish during or soon after the voyage. The first ships arrived in Boston Harbor on June 8, 1630.

The winter of 1630/1631 proved to be exceedingly harsh, with about two hundred of the new settlers dying, while another two hundred opted to return to England in the spring. The colony would only survive due to the leadership of John Winthrop.

Edward Rainsford and his young wife were members of the Massachusetts Bay Colony and would travel to the American Colonies in the Winthrop Fleet. Edward was christened on September 10, 1607 in Staverton, Northamptonshire, the son of Robert Rainsford and Mary Kirton.

While listed as a cooper merchant, Edward became a fisherman and merchant in the Colonies. Together, they settled in Boston, where they became members of the Boston Church. Edward's young wife died in June 1632, while giving child birth to twins.

Edward married Elizabeth Dillee on December 15 1633. Elizabeth was born about 1616 in England. Edward went back to England and then returned to the Massachusetts Colony aboard the ship *"Abigail"* in 1635.

Edward became a freeman on April 17, 1637. He became a deacon in the church in 1666/1667. He, along with Jacob Eliot were dismissed as deacons on February 12, 1669 *"for setting their hands with other brethren to desire their dismission from the church because the church had chosen Mr. Davenport for their pastor."* Edward then became the ruling elder of the Third Church of Boston at its formation in May, 1669.

Over the years, Edward would become the owner in several ships, a lighter and a warehouse *"with privileges,"* the right to trade with ships entering the Boston Harbor. He would then resell the merchandise.

When Edward passed away at the age of 71 years, on August 16, 1680 in Boston, Massachusetts, his estate amounted to £1638 7s. 11d. His estate included the following:

- *dwelling house, barn, with the land valued at £260;*
- *house and land late belonging to Nathan Raynsford deceased valued at £300;*
- *land upon Raynsford's Island valued at £10;*
- *land upon LongIsland valued at £10;*
- *a warehouse with privileges bought from John Phillips valued at £230. The warehouse shop had fish and dry goods, such as thread, gloves, buttons and cloth;*
- *three-sixteenth part of the a ship, Jeremy Cushen, Commander valued at £150;*
- *one-fourth of the ketch Mary, Jno. Gardner, Commander valued at £100;*
- *one-fourth of the ketch Swallow, Benjamin Pickman,*

Commander valued at £100;
- one-sixteenth of ship Sarah, Thomas Tuck, Commander valued at £30;
- a lighter and canoe valued at £12; and
- 1 negro boy Nat and 1 negro girl Nancee valued at £40

Elizabeth would pass-away on November 16, 1688 in Boston at the age of 81 years.

Last Will and Testament of
Edward Rainsford

Edward Raynsford Senior of Boston in New England, merchant, being sick and weak of body, bequeathed to "my loving and dear wife Elizabeth Raynsford" the use of all real and personal estate during her life; "my said dear wife shall have liberty" to give away by will the full sum of £100; "my dear wife may if she see cause before her decease give some part of my estate to such of my children that shall be in necessity for their present relief, which shall be deducted out of that child or children's portion";
"I hereby forgive my daughter Mary Parcyfull the debt of £10 more or less that her husband now oweth unto me, and also I give unto my said daughter Mary Parcyfull the sum of £10 to be paid unto her in goods";
to "my grandchildren, namely Jonathan, Dorothy and Mary, all children of my son Jonathan Raynsford deceased, the sum of £50 apiece to be paid unto them" at twenty-one, but if "my said grandchildren Dorothy & Mary do not carry themselves dutifully to their grandmother and take her and their Aunt Gording's advice in disposing of themselves in marriage that then such of them that so refuseth to do shall forfeit their legacy";
to "my son Solomon Raynsford ... all the land that I formerly laid out to him for an house lot"; to "my son David Raynsford ... all that piece of land which I formerly laid out to him";
"my son Edward Raynsford shall have that house that was my son Nathan Raynsford's, with all the land that

belongs to it, he paying to my executrix £350";
after "my said wife's decease the full remainder of all my real and personal estate ...shall be equally divided amongst my children hereafter named, viz., John Raynsford, David Raynsford, Solomon Raynsford, Edward Raynsford, and Ramus Belchar, Elizabeth Greenough, & Anna Hough, and that if any of my children die before my said wife then my will is that their children shall enjoy the legacy hereby bequeathed to such child or children";
"if any of my said children die before my executrix childless, then the legacy hereby bequeathed unto them shall be equally divided amongst my grandchildren, that is to say the children of the children that have been born to me by my now wife";
"my said dear wife Elizabeth Raynsford the sole executrix"; "my loving friends Mr. Edward Willis and Mr. John Hayward both of said Boston" overseers.

In his will, dated 3 August 1680 and proved 28 August 1680,

Children of Edward Rainsford and his first wife:
    2.   i.   Josiah Rainsford, and
    3.   ii.   Mary Rainsford.

Children of Edward Rainsford and Elizabeth Dillee:
    4.   i.   John Rainsford (1634 – Unknown) – John was born on June 30, 1634 in Boston, Suffolk County, Massachusetts and married Susanna Vergoose;
    5.   ii.   Jonathan Rainsford (1636 – Unknown) – Jonathan was born before October 23, 1636 in Boston, Suffolk County, Massachusetts and married Mary Sunderland;
+   6.   iii. Urania 'Ranis' Rainsford (1638 – Unknown);
    7.   iv. Nathan Rainsford (1641 – 1676) – Nathan was born about September 27, 1641 in Boston, Suffolk County, Massachusetts, married Mary "Marie" Allen, and died before April 29, 1676 in Boston, Massachusetts;
    8.   v.   David Rainsford (1644 – Unknown) – David was born about August 30, 1644 in Boston, Suffolk County, Massachusetts and married Abigail;
    9.   vi. Solomon Rainsford (1646 – Unknown) – Solomon was born about October 17, 1646 in Boston, Suffolk County, Massachusetts and married Pricilla Getchell;

10.	vii.	Elizabeth Rainsford (1648 – 1689) – Elizabeth was born about February 19, 1648 or 1649 in Boston, Suffolk County, Massachusetts, married Mr. Freenough, and died about 1689 in Boston, Massachusetts;
11.	viii.	Hannah Rainsford (1650 – Unknown) – Hannah was born before January 12, 1650 or 1651 in Boston, Suffolk County, Massachusetts;
12.	ix.	Anna Rainsford (1651 – Unknown) – Anna was born on February 1, 1651 or 1652 in Boston, Suffolk County, Massachusetts and married Samuel Hough; and
13.	x.	Edward Rainsford, born before October 1, 1654 in Boston, Suffolk County, Massachusetts and married Huldah Davis.

Second Generation

6. Urania 'Ranis' Rainsford (1638 – Unknown) - See Josiah Belcher, page 158.

Descendents of William Owen and Elizabeth Davies

First Generation

1. William Owen (1611 – 1702) - William Owen was born about 1611 in England. At the age of 23, William left London, England on February 17, 1634, headed for Barbados aboard the ship *"Hopewell"* Captain Thomas Wood, Master. William was among 150 passengers, which included a John Owen, age 20, and an Owen Williams, age 21, possibly relatives.

William would arrive in the American colonies sometime before 1650. On July 29, 1650, William married Elizabeth Davies, the daughter of Margaret Davies. Margaret, at the age of 32, along with her three children, the youngest being Elizabeth, sailed from London, England on April 17, 1635 aboard the ship *"Elizabeth"*, Captain William Stagg, Master. This ship carried 28 passengers, primarily women and children. They would settle in Braintree, Massachusetts, where Margaret would marry Charles Grice. Elizabeth was born in 1634 in Kent, England.

William became a freeman on May 7, 1651. William and Elizabeth were members of the Braintree Church where in January 1691 the Reverend Moses Fiske made mention that *"William and Elizabeth are mentioned as having been long in full communion."* William passed away on January 17, 1702 at Braintree, Massachusetts. Elizabeth would pass away soon after on June 3, 1702, also in Braintree, Massachusetts.

Children of William Owen and Elizabeth Davies:
- 2. i. Daniel Owen (1651 – 1651) – Daniel died as an infant in August, 1651 in Braintree, Norfolk, Massachusetts;
- 3. ii. Deliverance Owen (1654 – 1726) – Deliverance was born on February 15, 1654, who married John Eddy May 1, 1672 at Taunton, Massachusetts, then John Paddock after 1715, then Mr. Smith, and died on May 3, 1726 in Norton, Massachusetts;
- + 4. iii. Ebenezer Owen (1657 – 1690);
- 5. iv. Daniel Owen (1659 – Unknown) – Daniel was born November 23, 1659 in Braintree, Norfolk County, Massachusetts;
- 6. v. Nathaniel Owen (1660 – 1733) – Nathaniel was born after 1660, and died November 30, 1733 in Braintree, Norfolk County, Massachusetts;

7.	vi.	An unknown child, born August 1, 1667;
8.	vii.	Obadiah Owen (1670 – Unknown) – Obadiah was born on February 1, 1670 or 1671;
9.	viii.	Thomas Owen (1670 – Unknown) – Thomas was born on February 1, 1670 or 1671; and
10.	ix.	Josiah Owen (1672 – 1746) – Josiah was born after 1672, married his brother Ebenezer's widow, Hannah in 1691, and died in Providence, Rhode Island on April 27, 1746.

Second Generation

4. Ebenezer Owen (1657 – 1690) - Ebenezer Owen was born March 1, 1657 in Braintree, Massachusetts, the son of William Owen and Elizabeth Davies. Ebenezer married Hannah Belcher, the daughter of John and Sarah Belcher. Hannah was born April on 6, 1664 in Braintree, Massachusetts. Together, Ebenezer and Hannah would have four children.

Ebenezer was one of twelve militiamen who served in the Massachusetts Regiment, Fourth Company, under Captain Isaac Johnson and participated in the taking of the Narragansett stronghold at Kingston, Rhode Island during the King Phillip's War.

In 1690, Ebenezer would again take up arms, when he joined Sir William Phipps of Maine, who commanded the naval forces that captured Port Royal in Nova Scotia, during King William's War. There were more than thirty vessels and two thousand men under Sir William's command. The fleet was successfully repelled by the French at Quebec, Canada and soon would return to Boston. On the return to Boston, several of the crew would die of smallpox, of which Ebenezer was one. The following was reported:

> *"Upon the 9th day of Agust ther went ont a fleet Souldiers to Canadee in the year 1690, and the small pox was abord and they died, sixe of it; four thrown overbord at Capan, Corporall John Parmtr, Isaak Thayr, Ephraim Copeland and Ebenezer Owin, Thes and Samuell Bas, and John Cheny was thrown overbord at Nantaskett."*

In 1691, after the death of Ebenezer, Hannah would marry Ebenezer's brother Josiah. Then on Christmas Day, 1691, she was summoned before the Court of Assistants at Boston:

"On the charge 'for that by indirect meanes and by the connivance of some Josiah OWEN and said Hannah OWEN procured a marriage by the Word of God and the Statutes of England.' Hannah pleaded guilty by acknowledging that 'she was said Josiah Owen's Brother's Relict.' The court thereupon directed that the relation should be broken off forthwith and that Hannah should on the following Sunday appear before the Braintree congregation and make public confession of her transgression. At the same time the court by letter advised the Braintree pastor of its action.

In the disciplinary record kept by the Braintree pastors, Rev. Moses Fiske set down that on receipt of this message, he, with Major Quincy and Deacon Thompson, went to discourse with Hannah. Unexpectedly they found with her at their cottage Josiah who had eluded the civil authorities. The good pastor and his retinue undertook to bring Josiah to a suitable state of repentance, but finding him 'obstinate and reflecting,' charged him to be present in the congregation the following Sunday to hear what should be said to him there. The clergyman also records that Josiah was urged by his father to be compliant. Instead, Josiah and Hannah fled the jurisdiction before Sunday arrived. Josiah was solemnly excommunicated at the service which he thus missed."

Hannah and Josiah fled, taking their family to Providence, Rhode Island, where they would remain.

Children of Ebenezer Owen and Hannah Belcher:
	11.	i.	Mary Owen;
	12.	ii.	Josiah Owen (1687 – 1725) – Josiah was born May 15, 1687 in Braintree, Massachusetts and died before 1725 in Providence, Rhode Island;
+	13.	iii.	Abigail Owen; and
	14.	iv.	Unknown daughter, who married John Woodward.

Third Generation

13. Abigail Owen - See Solomon Paine, page 153.

Descendents of Nicholas Arnold and Alice Gulley

First Generation

1. Nicholas Arnold (1550 – Unknown) - Nicholas Arnold was born about 1550 in England. A tailor, Nicholas married Alice Gulley, the daughter of John and Alice Gulley, in 1570 in Ilchester, England. Alice was born on September 26, 1553 in England. Together Nicholas and Alice would have five children. Alice died a sudden death in 1596 (possibly giving childbirth to Elizabeth), leaving Nicholas desolate.

    Children of Nicholas Arnold and Alice Gulley:
+   2.   i.   William Arnold (1587 – 1685);
     3.   ii.   Tamzen Arnold (1570 – Unknown) – Tamzen was born on January 4, 1570 or 1571 in England;
     4.   iii. Joanna Arnold (1577 – 1620) – Joanna was born on November 30, 1577 in Ilchester, Somerset, England, married William Hopkins, and died March 10, 1620 or 1621 in Yeovilton, Somerset, England;
     5.   iv. Margery Arnold (1581 – Unknown) – Margery was born on August 30, 1581 in England; and
     6.   v.   Elizabeth Arnold (1596 – Unknown) – Elizabeth was born on April 9, 1596 in England.

Second Generation

2. William Arnold (1587 – 1676) - William Arnold was born on June 24, 1587 in Ilchester, Somerset, England, the son of Nicholas and Alice (Gulley) Arnold. While still young, William would join his father in the tailor's guild. In 1614, William married Christian Peake, the daughter of Thomas Peake. Christian was born February 15, 1582 or 1583 in Muchelney, Dorset, England.

    William was elected a church warden in 1622. Then on May 1, 1635, William, along with his wife, their four children, two of his sister Joanne's children, and several neighbors, set sail for the American Colonies. They left England from Dartmouth (probably on the sailing ship *"Mary and John"*) and landed in the Massachusetts Bay, the American Colonies, on June 24, 1635.

    They first settled in Hingham, Massachusetts. Then in 1636, they joined Roger Williams and ten other families to found the

Providence Plantation in Rhode Island. William had a town lot in the first settlement there. William was an original member of the first Baptist Church in the American Colonies. Two years later in 1638, he built a home in the wilderness about a mile north of the Pawtuxet Falls, establishing a hamlet around the falls and cove where the Pawtuxet River flows into the upper Narragansett Bay. This area was attractive as it had a sheltered harbor, as well as readily available water power (the Native American term "pawtuxet" means "little falls").

In 1661, William served as a commissioner to the colonial assembly from Providence. In 1673, he deeded all the rights to his first allotment in the Providence Plantation to John Sheldon. Being an educated man, William learned the Indian language and would often act as an interpreter.

William died in 1675 (during the "King Philip War") at the age of 88 in Providence, Rhode Island. Christian would pass away several years later in 1699 in Pawtuxet, Providence County, Rhode Island.

**William Arnold
To
Major General Benedict Arnold
Continental Army and
Traitor at West Point**

The direct line from William Arnold to Benedict Arnold. The following is the

William Arnold - Christian Peake
(6/24/1587-9/7/1685) - (2/15/1582/83-1659)
|
Benedict Arnold - Damaria Westcott
(12/21/1615-6/20/1678) - (1/27/1621-Unknown)
|
Benedict Arnold - Mary Turner
(2/10/1642-7/4/1727) - (BET 1630/1657-12/16/1690)
|
Benedict Arnold - Patience Coggleshall
(8/28/1683-2/2/1718/19) - (12/6/1685-12/21/1721)
|
Benedict Arnold - Hannah Lathrop (Waterman) King
(ABT 1715-1761) - (1717-ABT 1758)
|
Benedict Arnold
(1/14/1741—6/14/1801)

Children of William Arnold and Christian Peake:
7. i. Elizabeth Peake Arnold (1611 – 1685) – Elizabeth was born on November 23, 1611 in England, married William Carpenter on November 1, 1635 in Amesbury, Wiltshire, England, then Thomas Hopkins in 1645, and died on September 7, 1685 in Providence, Providence County, Rhode Island;

	8.	ii.	Benedict Arnold (1615 – 1678) – Benedict was born on December 21, 1615 in Bighere, Ilchester, Somerset, England, married Damaria Westcott on December 17, 1640, then Mary Turner on March 9, 1671, and died on June 19, 1678 in Newport, Newport County, Rhode Island. Benedict became the first Governor of Rhode Island in 1663;
+	9.	iii.	Joanna Arnold (1617 – Unknown) – Joanna was born on February 27, 1617 in Ilchester, Somerset, England, married Zachariah Rhodes on January 2, 1646 in Newport, Newport County, Rhode Island, then Samuel Reape on January 11, 1666 or 1667, and died in Pawtuxet, Providence County, Rhode Island;
+	10.	iv.	Stephen Arnold (1622 – 1699); and
	11.	v.	Nicholas Arnold (1627 – 1635) – Nicholas was born on January 15, 1627 in Lemington, Dorset, England and died prior to 1635.

Third Generation

9. Joanna Arnold (1617 – Unknown) – See Zachariah Rhodes, page 193.

10. Stephen Arnold (1622 – 1699) - Stephen Arnold was born on December 22, 1622 in Bighere, Ilchester, Somerset, England, the son of William and Christian (Peake) Arnold. Stephen immigrated to the American Colonies with his parents in 1635 and first settled at Hingham, Massachusetts, then on to Providence and Pawtuxet in Rhode Island. Stephen married Sarah Smith, the daughter of Edward Smith, on November 24, 1846 in Providence, Rhode Island. Sarah was born in 1629 in England.

Stephen bought land from both John Sayles and his father, William Arnold. He also bought land from Quonontholt, son of Miantonimi in 1678 (a Native American.) He built a gristmill near the falls and laid out the "Arnold Road" northward to join the Pequot Trail that led south to Connecticut. He served as assistant Governor in May 1680. He held this office several times under several different governors, one being his brother Benedict Arnold.

Stephen passed away on November 15, 1699 in Pawtuxet, Providence County, Rhode Island, while Sarah didn't pass away until April 15, 1713 in Pawtuxet, Rhode Island.

Children of Stephen Arnold and Sarah Smith:

12.   i.   Ester Arnold (1647 – Unknown) – Ester was born on September 22, 1647 in Pawtuxet, Providence County, Rhode Island, married James Dexter about 1670, then William Andrews on October 30, 1680, then Edward Hawkins about 1684, and then James Dexter;

+ 13.   ii.   Israel Arnold (1649 – 1716);

14.   iii.   Stephen Arnold (1654 – 1720) – Stephen was born on November 27, 1654 in Pawtuxet, Providence County, Rhode Island, married Mary Sheldon on January 12, 1688 in Providence, Rhode Island, and died March 1, 1720 in Cranston, Rhode Island;

15.   iv.   Elizabeth Arnold (1659 – 1728) – Elizabeth was born on November 2, 1659 in Pawtuxet, Providence County, Rhode Island, married Peter Greene on December 16, 1680 in Pawtuxet, Providence County, Rhode Island, and died June 5, 1728 in Rhode Island;

16.   v.   Sarah Arnold (1665 – 1727) – Sarah was born on June 26, 1665 in Pawtuxet, Providence County, Rhode Island, married Silas Carpenter about 1685, and died on November 26, 1727; and

17.   vi.   Phebe Arnold (1670 – 1730) – Phebe was born on November 9, 1670 or 1671 in Pawtuxet, Providence County, Rhode Island and married Benjamin Smith on December 25, 1691.

Fourth Generation

13.   Israel Arnold (1649 – 1716) - Israel Arnold was born on October 30, 1649 in Pawtuxet, Rhode Island, the son of Stephen and Sarah (Smith) Arnold. He married Mary Barker, the daughter of James and Barbara (Dungan) Barker, on April 16, 1677. Mary was born about 1655 in Newport, Rhode Island. Israel and his family resided in the south part of the Arnold Purchase in Pawtuxet on the Providence River, north of John Greene. Like his father, he served as a Deputy Governor of the Rhode Island Colony.

Israel passed away on September 15, 1716 in Warwick, Rhode Island and left a will that was proven on March 23, 1717. Mary passed away on September 19, 1723.

The "Israel Arnold House" located along the Great Road in Lincoln, Providence County, Rhode Island, built around 1695 is the oldest privately owned house in Rhode Island today.

Children of Israel Arnold and Mary Barker:
+ 18. i. Israel Arnold (1678 – 1753);
   19. ii. William Arnold (1681 – 1759) – William was born in 1681 in Warwick, Kent County, Rhode Island, married Deliverance Whipple in 1705, and died on June 15, 1759 in Coweset, Kent County, Rhode Island;
   20. iii. Elisha Arnold (1683 – 1748) – Elisha was born about 1683 in Warwick, Kent County, Rhode Island, married Hannah Carpenter on December 9, 1709 in Kent County, Rhode Island, then Patience Hyde in 1711, then Jane Blount on December 28, 1727, and died on December 23, 1748 in Warwick, Kent County, Rhode Island;
   21. iv. Stephen Arnold (1685 – 1724) – Stephen was born about 1685 in Warwick, Kent County, Rhode Island, married Sarah Greene on November 28, 1706 in Rhode Island, and died on December 5, 1724 in Warwick, Kent County, Rhode Island;
   22. v. James Arnold (1689 – 1777) – James was born in 1689 in Warwick, Kent County, Rhode Island, married Elizabeth Rhodes on October 25, 1711, and died on February 1, 1777 in Warwick, Kent County, Rhode Island;
   23. vi. Mary Arnold (1690 – 1746) – Mary was born about 1690 in Warwick, Kent County, Rhode Island and married Anthony Low on October 8, 1702;
   24. vii. Sarah Arnold (1690 – 1726) – Sarah was born about 1690 in Warwick, Kent County, Rhode Island, married Silas Carpenter on December 21, 1708, and died on November 26, 1726;
   25. viii. Joseph Arnold (1692 – 1718) – Joseph was born about 1692 in Warwick, Kent County, Rhode Island and died on March 9, 1718 in Warwick, Kent County, Rhode Island;
   26. ix. Josiah Arnold (1694 – 1758) – Josiah was born in 1694 in Warwick, Kent County, Rhode Island, married Elizabeth Arnold on December 27, 1716 in Rhode Island, and died in 1758 in Warwick, Kent County, Rhode Island; and
   27. x. Barbara Arnold (1696 – Unknown) – Barbara was born about 1696 in Warwick, Kent County, Rhode Island and married Benjamin Carpenter.

Fifth Generation

18. Israel Arnold (1678 – 1753) - Israel Arnold was born on January 16, 1678 in Warwick, Kent County, Rhode Island, the son of Israel and Mary (Barker) Arnold. He married Elizabeth Smith, the daughter of Benjamin and Lydia (Carpenter) Smith, on February 28, 1698 or 1699 in Warwick, Kent County, Rhode Island. Elizabeth was born about 1672 in Warwick, Kent County, Rhode Island.

Elizabeth died on February 7, 1718 in Warwick, Kent County, Rhode Island, possibly from complications of child birth, as she had just given birth to twins, Phebe and Simon on December 25, 1717. Israel would then marry Dorothy Whipple Rhodes on December 24, 1719 and then Elizabeth Stafford Case after 1723. Israel would pass away on August 3, 1753 in Warwick, Kent County, Rhode Island.

Children of Israel Arnold and Elizabeth Smith:
- 28. i. Elizabeth Arnold (1699 – 1753) – Elizabeth was born on January 19, 1699 or 1700 in Warwick, Kent County, Rhode Island, married a Mr. Mason, and died after 1753;
- 29. ii. Israel Arnold (1701 – 1743) – Israel was born on July 19, 1701 in Warwick, Kent County, Rhode Island, married Mary Rhodes on January 14, 1724, then Mary Remington, and died on August 17, 1743;
- 30. iii. Lydia Arnold (1702 – 1772) – Lydia was born on January 8, 1702 or 1703 in Warwick, Kent County, Rhode Island, married Joseph Sheldon on January 15, 1724 in Providence, Providence County, Rhode Island, and died July 18, 1772 in Warwick, Kent County, Rhode Island;
- 31. iv. Benjamin Arnold (1707 – 1739) – Benjamin was born on January 18, 1707 or 1708 in Warwick, Kent County, Rhode Island and died on April 19, 1739;
- 32. v. Christopher Arnold (1710 – 1791) – Christopher was born on November 7, 1710 in Warwick, Kent County, Rhode Island, married Lydia Tillinghast on November 17, 1735 in Providence, Providence County, Rhode Island, and died on January 6, 1791;
- + 33. vi. Stephen Arnold (1710 – 1743);
- 34. vii. Sion Arnold (1713 – Unknown) – Sion was born on October 13, 1713 in Warwick, Kent County, Rhode Island;
- 35. viii. Mary Arnold (1716 – 1753) – Mary was born on February 25, 1716 in Warwick, Kent County, Rhode Island, married Mr. Carpenter, and died after 1753;
- 36. ix. Phebe Arnold (1717 – 1789) – Phebe was born on December 25, 1717 in Warwick, Kent County, Rhode Island, married John Potter about 1738 in Mashantatuck, Providence County, Rhode Island, and died about 1789 in Pownel, Bennington County, Vermont; and
- 37. x. Simon Arnold (1717 – 1774) – Simon was born on December 25, 1717 in Warwick, Kent County, Rhode Island, married Lydia Green on March 1, 1738 or 1739, and died on March 14, 1774.

Sixth Generation

33. Stephen Arnold (1710 – 1743) - Israel Arnold was born on November 7, 1710 in Warwick, Kent County, Rhode Island, the son of Israel Arnold and Elizabeth Smith. He married Mercy Tillinghast, the daughter of Benjamin Tillinghast and Sarah Rhodes. Mercy was born in 1710 in Warwick, Kent County, Rhode Island.

Stephen died in 1743, while Mercy would pass away almost 40 years later on January 14, 1782 in Providence, Providence County, Rhode Island.

    Children of Stephen Arnold and Mercy Tillinghast:
+   38.   i.   Elizabeth Arnold (1738 – Unknown);
    39   ii.   Mary Arnold (1741 – Unknown) – Mary was born on May 27, 1741 in Providence, Providence County, Rhode Island and married Otis Whipple on December 27, 1767 in Providence, Providence County, Rhode Island;
    40.   iii.   Stephen Arnold (1742 – Unknown) – Stephen was born on December 9, 1742 in Providence, Providence County, Rhode Island.

Seventh Generation

38. Elizabeth Arnold (1738 – Unknown) - See John Aplin, Jr., page 141.

Descendents of Edward Smith

First Generation

1. Edward Smith (1600/1607 – AFT 1675) - Edward Smith was born between 1600 and 1607 in Castle, Lincolnshire, England, the son of Edward Smith and Frances Harper. Edward married in England and they had a child, Sarah. It's likely that shortly after the birth of Sarah, Edward and his young family would be members of the Massachusetts Bay Colony and travel to the American Colonies in the Winthrop Fleet.

Known as "Mr. Edward, Weymouth", he was the town clerk of Rehoboth and became a freeman on June 4, 1645. Edward and his wife were called before the Plymouth Court in 1650, where they were indicted for not going to church to worship on Sunday and for *"attending private meetings."* Shortly thereafter, they would depart for Providence, Rhode Island. While in Providence, Edward would hold several civic offices.

Edward moved to Newport, Rhode Island around 1655, where he was listed as a freeman. In Newport, Edward would serve as Assistant to Court of Commissioner in 1654-55, 1658-59, and 1665-1666, and Deputy in 1665-66 and 1669

Edward died sometime after 1675 in Providence, Providence, Rhode Island.

Children of Edward Smith:
+ 2. i. Sarah Smith (1629 – 1713);
  3. ii. Philip Smith (1634 – 1700) – Philip was born in 1634 in Rehoboth, Bristol, Massachusetts, married Mary about 1665 in Newport, Newport, Rhode Island, and died on December 6, 1700 in Newport, Newport, Rhode Island;
  4. iii. Phebe Smith (1642 – Unknown) – Phebe was born in 1642 in Weymouth, Norfolk, Massachusetts;
  5. iv. Elisha Smith (1644 – 1676) – Elisha was born after 1644 in Rehoboth, Bristol, Massachusetts, married Mary Barker about 1670 in Newport, Newport, Rhode Island, and died after 1676 in Newport, Newport, Rhode Island; and
  6. v. Edward Smith (1650 – 1704) – Edward was born about 1650 in Rehoboth, Bristol, Massachusetts and died in 1704 in Middletown, Monmouth, New Jersey.

Second Generation

2. Sarah Smith (1629 – 1713) - See Stephen Arnold, page 173.

Descendents of James Barker and Barbara Dungan

First Generation

1. James Barker (1617 – 1702) - James Barker was born in 1617 in Essex County, England. His sister, Christiana, married a second husband, a Captain Thomas Beecher, and sailed with him to the America Colonies in 1630, settling in Charlestown, Massachusetts. On March 24, 1634, James and his father, a widower also named James, sailed from Southampton, England on the ship *"Mary & John,"* Robert Sayres, Master. James, Sr. died on the voyage and James, Jr. was taken in charge by a passenger, Nicholas Easton, who later would marry James' sister, Christiana.

In 1644, James married Barbara Dungan, the daughter of William and Francis (Latham) Dungan. Barbara was born in 1628. Barbara was the granddaughter of Lewis Latham, Falconer to King Charles I.

James served as a corporal in 1644 for Newport, Rhode Island, an ensign in 1648, and a member of the General Court of Elections in 1648. His name is on a list called *"Ye Rule of Freeman of Ye Colonies of every Towne"* in 1655 for Newport. In 1655, 1661, and 1663, he was a member of the Court of Commissioners. In 1661, he and 40 others petitioned for a tract of land, now Westerly, Rhode Island, dividing it into 18 shares, James receiving one half share. He was also a trustee at Westerly, and a teacher among the Baptists.

On April 4, 1676, it was voted *"that in troublesome times and straits in this colony, [King Philip's War] the assembly desiring the advise and concurrence of the most judicious inhabitants of it may be had for the whole, we desire at their next sittynge, the company and counsel of Mr. Benedict Arnold, John Clarke, James Barker and 13 others and the General Sergeants, to inform the several persons, the assembly's desire thereon."*

James became Deputy Governor of Rhode Island after Gov. Coddington's death in 1678. James would pass away about 1702, probably in Newport, Rhode Island.

Children of James Barker and Barbara Dungan (all born in Newport, Rhode Island):

	2.	i.	Elizabeth Barker (1646 – 1676) – Elizabeth was born in 1646, married Nicholas Easton on November 30, 1666, and died on July 5, 1676;
	3.	ii.	James Barker (1648 – 1722) – James died on December 1, 1722;
	4.	iii.	Joseph Barker (1650 – Unknown);
+	5.	iv.	Mary Barker (1650 – 1723);
	6.	v.	Sarah Barker, never married;
	7.	vi.	Peter Barker (Unknown – 1725);
	8.	vii.	Christiana Barker, married William Phillips; and.
	9.	viii.	William Barker (1662 – 1741) – William died on November 3, 1741.

Second Generation

5. Mary Barker (1650 – 1723) - See Israel Arnold, page 174.

Descendents of Rev. Pardon Elisha Tillinghast and Lydia Masters Taber

First Generation

1. Rev. Pardon Elisha Tillinghast (1622 – 1718) - Pardon Tillinghast was born January 2, 1622 in Seven Cliffs, near Beachy Head (now Eastborn), Sussex County, England, the son of Pardon and Sarah (Browne) Tillinghast.

Pardon was a soldier of the Allied Army of Parliamentary and served under Oliver Cromwell during the British Civil War. He participated in the Battle of Marston Moor on July 3, 1644, where they defeated the Royalist Cavalry. Shortly after this, Pardon would leave for the American Colonies, where on November 19, 1645, he was admitted a resident of Providence, Rhode Island, with a one quarter interest of the original proprietors.

In 1654, Pardon married Sarah Butterworth in Swansea, Massachusetts. Sarah was born in 1633 in Rehoboth, Massachusetts, the daughter of Henry Butterworth and Mary Lambotham.

Sarah would pass-away shortly after the birth of their daughter Mary in 1661. Pardon would then marry Lydia Masters Taber, the daughter of Philip and Lydia (Masters) Taber, on April 16, 1664 in Providence, Rhode Island. Lydia was born in 1648 in Barnstable, Massachusetts.

In 1678, Pardon became the pastor of the First Baptist Church in Providence and served there until his death. He preached and officiated without any remuneration. He built the first meeting-house of this religious society, the oldest in America of its denomination, at his own expense. On April 14, 1711, he deeded his house called the Baptist Meeting House, *"situated between the Town Street and salt water, together with the lot whereon said meeting house standeth, to the Church and their successors, for the Christian love, good will and affection which I bear to the Church of Christ in said Providence, the which I am in fellowship with, and have the care of as being elder of said Church."*

King Edward I (Longshanks) Plantegenet
(King of England)
to
Pardon Tillinghast

Edward I, born on June 17, 1239, died on July 7, 1307, King of England (1272-1307) completed the conquest of Wales and temporarily subdued Scotland. He was the eldest son of HENRY III. In 1254 he was made duke of Gascony and married Eleanor of Castile (d. 1290).

After 1294, wars in Scotland and France dominated Edward's reign. The death (1290) of Margaret, Maid of Norway, heiress to the Scottish crown, allowed Edward as suzerain to choose a successor, John de BALIOL, and then to claim direct rule over Scotland, which he subdued in 1296. In France the conflict concerned the French king's overlordship over Edward's duchy of Gascony. In 1297, Edward attacked France to assert his rights, but the expedition was cut short by the rebellion in Scotland of Sir William WALLACE. He failed, to quell the risings of Wallace and Robert the Bruce (later ROBERT I), and Scotland remained only half- conquered at his death. He was succeeded by his son Edward II.

King Edward I - Princess Eleanor of Castile, dau. of King Ferdinand III of Spain
(1239-1307)
|
Thomas de Brotherton, Earl of Norfolk - Alice
de Halles, dau. of Sir Roger de Halles
(1301-1338)
|
John, 4th Baron Seagrave - Margaret Plantegenet, Duchess of Norfolk
|
John, 4th Baron Mowbray - Elizabeth Seagrave, dau.& heir.
|
John, 5th Baron de Welles - Eleanor Mowbray
|
Edo de Welles - Maude de Greystock, dau. of Ralph, 5th /Baron de Greystock
|
Sir Lionel de Welles; 6th Baron de Welles, K. G. (Knight of the Garter) - Cecilia (or Joan) dau. of Robert Waterton of
Methley
|
Thomas, Lord Hoo, K.G./ Chancellor to France - Eleanor de Welles
|
Sir Roger de Copley, (15th in descent from King Athelred II) - Anna de Hoo, dau. & co-heir
|
William Lusher, Lord of Rodsell Manor - Ann Copley
|
George Lusher, Gentleman, - Alice Unknown
|
Sir Richard Leachford, Knight, of Shellwood Manor in Leigh, Surrey County - Anne Lusher
|
Rev. Benjamin Browne, Vicar of Ifiel County, Sussex - Sarah Leachford
|
Sarah Browne – Pardon Tillinghast, yeoman and cooper of Streat, Sussez County
(1600 – 1653) – (1601 – 1665)

In addition to his pastoral duties, he was the wealthiest man in Providence, a merchant, served as a member of the House of Deputies, and various post of honor and trust for the town of Providence.

Pardon died on January 29, 1718 in Providence, Rhode Island, while Lydia passed away shortly thereafter in 1720 in Swansea, Massachusetts. They are both buried in the Tillinghast Lot in Providence, Rhode Island.

Children of Rev. Pardon Elisha Tillinghast and Sarah Butterworth:
2.   i.   Sarah Tillinghast (1654 – 1671) – Sarah was born on November 17, 1654 in Newport, Rhode Island and died in 1671 in Providence, Rhode Island;
3.   ii.   John Tillinghast (1657 – 1690) – John was born on July 1, 1657 in Newport, Rhode Island, married Isabelle Sayles in 1678, and died on December 16, 1690 in Providence, Rhode Island; and
4.   iii.   Mary Tillinghast (1661 – 1711) – Mary was born in 1661 in Providence, Rhode Island, married Benjamin Carpenter, and died in 1711.

Children of Rev. Pardon Elisha Tillinghast and Lydia Masters Taber:
5.   i.   Lydia Tillinghast (1665 – 1707) – Lydia was born on April 18, 1665 in Newport, Rhode Island, married John "Hon" Audrey in 1687, and died on June 30, 1707 in Newport, Rhode Island;
6.   ii.   Pardon Tillinghast, III (1667 – 1743) – Pardon was born on February 16, 1667 or 1668 in Providence, Rhode Island, married Sarah Ayers, then married Mary Keech in 1688, and died October 15, 1743 in West Greenwich, Rhode Island;
7.   iii.   Philip Tillinghast (1669 – 1731) – Philip was born on August 15, 1669 in Providence, Rhode Island, married Martha Holmes on May 23, 1692 in Providence, Rhode Island, and died March 14, 1731 or 1732 in Providence, Rhode Island. Philip became a wealthy merchant in Providence and took part actively in public life. He joined Captain Gallup's expedition against Canada in 1690, was a Deputy for twelve terms, Assistant to the Governor in 1714, and a member of the Town Council for eleven years;

+ 8.   iv.   Benjamin Tillinghast (1672 – 1726);
9.   v.   Abigail Tillinghast (1673 – 1744) – Abigail was born on January 30, 1673-74 in Providence, Rhode Island, married Nicholas Tanner Sheldon in 1691, and died in 1744 in Providence, Rhode Island;

10. vi. Joseph Tillinghast (1677 – 1763) – Joseph was born on August 11, 1677 in Providence, Rhode Island, married Freelove Stafford in 1703 in Rhode Island, then married Mary Paris in 1720, and died on December 1, 1763 in Newport, Rhode Island;
11. vii. Mercy Tillinghast (1680 – 1769) – Mercy was born in September 1680, married Nicholas Power III in 1700, and died on November 13, 1769;
12. viii. Hannah Tillinghast (1682 – 1717) – Hannah was born in 1682 in Providence, Rhode Island, married John Hale in 1702, and died on February 19, 1717 or 1718 in Swansea, Massachusetts; and
13. ix. Elizabeth Tillinghast (1685 – 1750) – Elizabeth was born in 1685 in Providence, Rhode Island, married Philip Taber in 1709 and died in 1750 in New London, Connecticut.

Second Generation

8. Benjamin Tillinghast (1672 – 1726) - Benjamin Tillinghast was born on February 2, 1672 in Providence, Rhode Island, the son of Pardon Elisha Tillinghast and Lydia Masters Taber. Benjamin married Sarah Rhodes, the daughter of Malachi and Mary (Carder) Rhodes, in Sussex, England, in 1692. Sarah was born 1679 in Warwick, Rhode Island.

Benjamin was a merchant in Providence. Benjamin would pass away on September 4, 1726 in Providence, Rhode Island, while Sarah would pass away on January 5, 1734 in Providence. Both are buried in the Old North Burial Grounds of Providence.

    Children of Benjamin Tillinghast and Sarah Rhodes:
14. i. Sarah Tillinghast (1702 – Unknown) – Sarah was born on May 20, 1702;
15. ii. Benjamin Tillinghast (1703 – Unknown);
16. iii. James Tillinghast (1705 – 1739) - James married Elizabeth T. Mawney before 1739;
17. iv. Mary Tillinghast (1707 – Unknown);
+ 18. v. Mercy Tillinghast (1710 – Unknown);
19. vi. Abigail Tillinghast (1711 – 1778) – Abigail married Elisha Clarke in December 1734 in Newport, Rhode Island;
20. vii. Elisha Tillinghast (1712 – Unknown); and
21. viii. Lydia Tillinghast (1714 – Unknown).

Third Generation

18. Mercy Tillinghast (1710 – Unknown) – See Stephen Arnold, page 177.

Descendents of Philip Taber and Lydia Masters

First Generation

1. Philip Taber (1604 – 1669) - Philip Taber was born on September 1, 1604 in the County of Essex, England. It is likely that Philip came to the American Colonies as a member of the Winthrop Fleet which arrived during 1630, as he was admitted as a freeman of the Massachusetts Bay Colony on October 19, 1630.

As a carpenter and builder, Philip not only brought a trade to the new world, he brought substantial wealth with him. The Court in Boston asked *"....Upon consideration of the usefulness of a moving fort to be built forty feet long and twenty –one wide, for the defense of this colony, and upon the free offer of some gentlemen lately come over to us of some large sums of money to be employed that way."* Philip was one of the original contributors to this project in 1633-34, by supplying 200 foot of 4" planks, a substantial and useful donation.

Soon, Philip moved on to Watertown, where he was admitted as a freeman on May 14, 1634. Here, he would marry Lydia Masters, the daughter of John and Jane (Cox) Masters of Watertown, on December 21, 1634. As a builder, it's likely that Philip moved with his jobs, as he soon would be in Yarmouth, Massachusetts. Here, Philip was propounded as a freeman of Plymouth Colony on January 7, 1638/39 and was admitted on June 4, 1639. That same year, he served as a Deputy to the first General Court at Plymouth. In 1639, he was also on the committee to make division of the planting lands at Yarmouth. In 1640, he again represented Yarmouth at the General Court at Plymouth.

Sometime before 1647, Philip moved his family to Great Harbor, a new settlement on the island of Martha's Vineyard. The family lived at Pease's Point. Philip was one of the proprietors of the island, as he shared in all the divisions of lands as long as he was a resident of the island. During this time frame, Philip's wife, Lydia, passed away. In 1651, Philip, along with his brother-in-law, Nathaniel Masters, was assisting in the construction of the Mill Dam in New London. In 1653, he served as Selectmen on the Island. Also in 1653, Philip, along with Thomas Mayhew and Thomas Burchard were chosen *"to divide to the inhabitants out of all the Necks so much land as they in the best judgment shall see meet."* "The neck called

Ashakomaksett from the bridge that is the East side of the head of the swamp" was set off to Philip.

On January 3, 1655, the town records of Portsmouth, Rhode Island say *"Philip Tabor is received an inhabitant and taken his ingagment to the State of England and government of this place and bath equal right of commonage with the rest of this towne."* Apparently, Philip had been involved in a scandal on the Island, which made it necessary for him to leave. The town records for Edgartown on May 15, 1655 stated the following, *"It is agreed by ye 5 men yt Philip Tabor is proved to be a man that hath been an attempter of women's chastities in a high degree. This is proved by Mary Butler and Mary Foulger, as divers more remote testimonies by others, and words testified from his own mouth with an horrible abuse of scripture to accomplish his wicked end."*

The above indiscretions did not prevent Philip from taking an active role in his new community, as in 1656 he acted on the jury at the Court of Newport. Then in 1660, 1661 and 1663, he represented Portsmouth as a commissioner to the General Court of the Union of the Rhode Island Colony. He would also serve the town as Rater, Tax Collector and Constable. Then in 1664 or 1665, he sold everything in Portsmouth and move to Providence, Rhode Island, where his daughter, Lydia, would marry Pardon Tillinghast, the leading minister and wealthiest merchant of Providence.

Philip married Jane Lathum sometime after 1649, as in 1671, he and Jane gave evidence against one William Harris, at his Majestie's Court of Justice sitting at Newport for the Colony of Rhode Island and Providence Plantation, for *"...speaking and writing against his Majestie's gracious Charter to his Colony,"* which treasonable conduct was evidently regarded very seriously by the Court. He probably died soon after in Providence or Tiverton, Rhode Island, possibly in 1672.

Children of Philip Taber and Lydia Masters:
2. i. John Taber (1640 – Unknown) – John was born in 1640 in Yarmouth, Massachusetts;
3. ii. Joseph Taber;
4. iii. Philip Taber (1642 – Unknown);
5. iv. Thomas Taber (1645 – 1730) – Thomas was born in February 1645/46 in Dartmouth, Massachusetts, married Esther Cooke, the daughter of John Cooke, a Mayflower passenger, and died on November 11, 1730;
+ 6. v. Lydia Masters Taber (1648 -1720); and
7. vi. Esther Taber.

Philip Taber
to
32nd President of the United States of America
Franklin Delano Roosevelt

Philip Taber and Lydia Masters lend another link to an American President through their son Captain Thomas Taber – Franklin Delano Roosevelt.

Franklin Delano Roosevelt, nicknamed "FDR" was our 32nd President of the Untied States. While in office, he was faced with the Great Depression and World War II. His four terms in office are unparalleled, not only in length but in scope. The following is the direct link:

Philip Taber—Lydia Masters
(9/1/1604-12/11/1669) - (ABT 1616-BEF 1669)
|
Capt. Thomas Taber—Esther Cooke
(2/1645/46-11/11/1730) - (8/16/1650-4/10/1671)
|
Samuel Perry—Esther Cooke
(3/15/1666/67-Unknown) - (4/7/1671-1/14/1748/49)
|
Ebenezer Perry — Abigail Presbury
(3/5/1704/05-AFT 1775) - (ABT 1703-1749)
|
Samuel Perry—Susannah Swift
(6/27/1731-4/15/1805) - (ABT 1734-6/8/1806)
|
Joseph Church—Deborah Perry
(12/14/1752-ABT 1839) - (10/14/1754-ABT 1808)
|
Warren Delano—Deborah Church
(10/28/1779-9/28/1866) - (3/21/1783-8/7/1827)
|
Warren Delano—Catherine Robbins Lyman
(7/13/1809-1/17/1898) - (1/12/1825-2/10/1896)
|
James Roosevelt—Sarah Delano
(1828-1900) - (9/21/1854-9/7/1941)
|
32nd President of the United States of America
Franklin Delano Roosevelt
(1882—1945)

Second Generation

6. Lydia Masters Taber (1648 -1720) – See Pardon Tillinghast, page 183.

Descendents of John Masters and Jane Cox

First Generation

1.   John Masters (1581 – 1639) - John Masters was born before March 8, 1581 in Tiverton, Devonshire, England, the son of John Masters and Elizabeth Thompson. John married Jane Cox in England during the year of 1606. Jane was born in 1586 in Aldenham, Hertsfordshire, England.

John and his young family arrived in the American Colonies as a party in the Winthrop Fleet, the *"Great Emigration."* They likely arrived aboard the flagship *"Arbella"* on June 22, 1630. John and his family accompanied Sir Richard Salton-stall, when they paddled up the Charles River to a green place whose Indian name sounded to some like "Pigs-go-suck." Here they would found the settlement of Watertown, Massachusetts. In 1631, when Sir Richard was force to return to England due to the illness of his two daughters, John was placed in charge of all his interests in Watertown.

John was admitted a freeman in Watertown on May 18, 1631 and became a member of the church at Watertown by July of 1632. In 1631, John was engaged to construct a canal from the river, through the marsh, to the upland, near the foot of Dunster Street. The canal was to be *"12 foot broad and 7 foot deep, for which the Court promiseth him satisfaction, according as the charges thereof shall amount unto."* The cost to build the canal was £30.

In 1632, John and a Mr. Oldham were chosen by Watertown to advise the Governor and Assistants about raising a Public Stock, etc. He would soon after move his family again, where they became early inhabitants of the town of Cambridge, Massachusetts. On September 3, 1635, he owned a house and seven acres of land on the westerly side of Ash Street, near Brattle Street.

John would die in Cambridge, Massachusetts on December 21, 1639, while Jane would pass away 5 days later on December 26, 1639.

Children of John Masters and Jane Cox:
```
     2.    i.   Sarah Masters;
     3.    ii.  Elizabeth Masters;
     4.    iii. Nathaniel Masters;
+    5.    iv.  Lydia Masters (1619 – 1649);
```

6.	v.	Jane Masters;
7.	vi.	Abraham Masters;
8.	vii.	Jane Masters; and
9.	viii.	Nathaniel Masters, who married Ruth Pickworth sometime before 1654.

Second Generation

5. Lydia Masters (1619 – 1649) – See Philip Taber, page 187.

Descendents of Zachariah Rhodes and Joanna Arnold

First Generation

1. Zachariah Rhodes (1603 – 1665) - Zachariah Rhodes, born in 1603 in Leamington Hastings, Rugby (Warwickshire) England, arrived in the American Colonies around 1643, settling in Rehoboth, Massachusetts. Around 1646, on account of difficulty about compulsory payment for preaching, he along with several others removed from Massachusetts to Rhode Island. He would settle at Pawtuxet, where he became a large land proprietor and was a Deputy.

Zachariah married Joanna Arnold, the daughter of William and Christian (Peake) Arnold, on March 7, 1646 in Newport Village, Rhode Island. Joanna was born on February 27, 1616 or 1617 in Leamington Hastings, Rugby (Warwickshire) England.

Zachariah was a commissioner in Providence for several years and in 1663 was appointed to treat with the Indians, regarding a consideration for their lands. He was on the committee who ran the boundary line between Rhode Island and Plymouth Colony. He was also a deputy and town Counselor. He was imprisoned for a short time in a jail in Boston for openly remarking, *"The court has naught to do in maters of Religion."*

Zachariah's "Last Will and Testament" was dated April 28, 1662 and was recorded May 29, 1666.

It was reported in "An Account of the English Homes of the Three Early Proprietors of Providence" by Fred A. Arnold:

1665: Zachary Rhodes was drowned "off Pawtuxtt Shore" late in 1665.

Joanna then married Samuel Reape on January 11, 1666 or 1667. Joanne would pass away on February 11, 1691 or 1692 in Pawtucket, Providence Settlement, Providence Plantations, Rhode Island.

Children of Zachariah Rhodes and Joanna Arnold:
- 2. i. Jeremiah Rhodes (1647 – Unknown) – Jeremiah was born on July 24, 1647 in Providence, Providence County, Rhode Island and married Madeline Hawkins before 1676;
+ 3. ii. Malachi Rhodes (Unknown – 1682);
- 4. iii. Zachariah Rhodes;
- 5. iv. Elizabeth Rhodes;
- 6. v. Mary Rhodes, married John Low on March 3, 1674 or 1675 in Warwick, Kent County, Rhode Island;
- 7. vi. Rebecca Rhodes (Unknown – 1727) – Rebecca married Nicholas Power on February 2, 1672 in Providence, Providence County, Rhode Island, then married Daniel Williams on December 2, 1676 in Providence, Providence County, Rhode Island, and died before January 1, 1727 or 1728 in Providence, Providence County, Rhode Island;
- 8. vii. John Rhodes (1658 – 1716) – John was born in 1658 in Pawtuxet, Kent County, Rhode Island, married Waite Waterman on February 12, 1684 or 1685 in Warwick, Kent County, Rhode Island; and died on August 14, 1716 in Warwick, Kent County, Rhode Island; and
- 9. viii. Peleg Rhodes (1660 – 1724) – Peleg married Sarah between 1690 and 1695, and died on October 6, 1724 in Providence, Providence County, Rhode Island.

**Zachariah Rhodes
To
41st President of the United States of America
George Herbert Walker Bush
43rd President of the United States of America
George Walker Bush**

Zachariah Rhodes—Joanna Arnold
(ABT 1603-10/11/1665) - (2/27/1617-AFT 1692)
|
John Low—Mary Rhodes
(1651-10/30/1695) - (1655-AFT 1692)
|
Ephraim Pierce—Mary Low
(10/1674-10/18/1768) - (ABT 1674-4/29/1709)
|
Dea. Mial Pierce — Judith (Ellis) Round
(4/24/1693-10/18/1786) - (ABT 1694-10/6/1744)
|
Rev. Nathan Pierce—Lydia Martin
(2/21/1715/16-4/14/1793) - (7/1/1718-12/21/1798)
|
Isaac Pierce—Anna Fitch
(9/22/1763-11/26/1849) - (3/1/1763-11/15/1809)
|
Levi Pierce—Betsy Slade Wheeler
(6/8/1797-1838) - (5/30/1800-2/23/1881)
|
Courtland Philip L. Butler—Elizabeth Slade Pierce
(1813-1891) - (1822-1901)
|
Robert Emmet Sheldon—Mary Elizabeth Butler
(1845-1917) - (1850-1897)
|
Samuel Prescott Bush—Flora Sheldon
(10/4/1863-2/8/1948) - (1872-1920)
|
Prescott Samuel Bush—Dorothy Walker
(1895-1972) - (1901-1992)
|
**41st President of the United States of America
George Herbert Walker Bush—Barbara Pierce
(1924-Living) - (1925-Living)**
|
**43rd President of the United States of America
George Walker Bush
(1946—Living)**

Second Generation

3. Malachi Rhodes (Unknown – 1682) - Malachi Rhodes was born in Rhode Island, the son of Zachariah Rhodes and Joanne Arnold. Malachi married Mary Carder, the daughter of Richard and Mary Carder, on May 27, 1675 in Warwick, Kent County, Rhode Island. They were married by Benjamin Smith, Jr., Justice. Together they would have three children. Malachi died in 1862, while Mary died on January 22, 1693.

    Children of Malachi Rhodes and Mary Carder:
        10.   i.   Malachi Rhodes (Unknown – 1714) – Malachi married Dorothy Whipple on March 8, 1699 or 1700 in Providence, Providence County, Rhode Island and died on August 17, 1714 in Warwick, Kent County, Rhode Island;
+   11.   ii.   Sarah Rhodes (1677 – 1742); and
        12.   iii. Mary Rhodes.

Third Generation

11. Sarah Rhodes (1677 – 1742) – See Benjamin Tillinghast, page 186.

Descendents of Richard and Mary Carder

First Generation

1. Richard Carder (1612 – Unknown) - Richard Carder was born in England sometime before 1612 and came to the American Colonies before 1636. He became a Freeman in Boston on May 25, 1636, yet he was not a member of the Church of Boston. In 1637, as a supporter of Wheelwright and Hutchinson *"accused of pestilent heresies"*, he was disfranchised from Boston. He left for Rhode Island, where he was among the eighteen original purchasers of the beautiful Island of Aquedneck and a partner in the civil compact.

He then married Hannah and had a daughter, Susanna. Susanna was born in 1640. She would marry Nathaniel Waterman, and died about 1712.

In 1643 Richard was engaged in the purchase of Warwick, with Gorton and others, and for sustaining his and their rights, he was made a prisoner with all the rest and taken to Boston, where he was sentenced to be incarcerated at Roxbury, in irons. The opinion of the reverend elders overruled the original sentence, that their offence deserved death. Glad enough was the government to discharge him and his fellow-sufferers the following year, with the sentence of banishment on pain of forfeiture of life for coming back.

Richard returned to Warwick, where he married Mary and started their family. Richard and his family remained in Warwick and he died at Newport, Rhode Island during the King Philip War in 1675 or 1676. His will was dated November 29, 1676. Mary would pass away in Newport, Rhode Island in 1691

Children of Richard and Hannah Carder:
    2.   i.   Susanna, married Nathaniel Waterman.

Children of Richard and Mary Carder:
+   3.   i.   Mary Carder (1651 -1698);
    4.   ii.   Sarah Carder (1652 – 1724) - Sarah married Benjamin Gorton and died on August 1, 1724;
    5.   iii. Joseph Carder (1659 – 1694) – Joseph was born in 1659 in Warwick, Rhode Island, married Bethia, and died on March 12, 1694;

6.   iv.   John Carder (Unknown – 1700) – John was born in Warwick, Rhode Island, married Mary Holden, and died on October 27, 1700; and

7.   v.   James Carder (1665 – 1714) – James was born on May 2, 1665 in Warwick, Rhode Island, married Mary Whipple on January 1, 1686 or 1687 in Warwick, Rhode Island, and died on April 25, 1714. A Captain during the King William's War.

Second Generation

3.   Mary Carder (1651 -1698) – See Malachi Rhodes, page 196.

Descendents of John and Elizabeth Gray

First Generation

1. John Gray (1660 – 1739) - John Gray was born about 1660 in Londonderry, Northern Ireland. John's ancestors were Scotch (often called "Scotch-Irish") and came from Argyshire, Scotland in 1612 and settled near Londonderry, England. John married Elizabeth sometime before 1692 in Agedowey, Ireland and began to start a family. Together John and Elizabeth had eight children, all born in Ireland. John and his family would leave Ireland in 1718 for the American Colonies. Upon arriving, they settled in Worcester, Massachusetts.

Elizabeth passed away on July 1, 1730 in Worcester, Worcester County, Massachusetts, while John died sometime before 1739 in Worcester, Massachusetts.

Children of John and Elizabeth Gray:
- 2. i. Matthew Gray (1692 – 1758) – Matthew married Margaret, and died on September 21, 1758 in Pelham, Hampshire, Massachusetts, buried at the Second Burying Grounds on the Common;
- 3. ii. Mary Gray (1694 – Unknown) - Mary married William Blair about 1715, then married Matthew Barbour on January 31, 1727 in Shrewsbury, Worcester County, Massachusetts;
- 4. iii. William Gray (1696 – 1759) - William married Jean Clark about 1718, and died January 17, 1759 in Pelham, Hampshire County, Massachusetts;
- 5. iv. Robert Gray (1697 – Unknown) - Robert married Sarah Wiley about 1728 or 1729;
- 6. v. John Gray (1700 – 1782) - John married Isabel about 1726 in Worcester, Massachusetts, and died June 7, 1782 in Pelham, Hampshire County, Massachusetts;
- 7. vi. Samuel Gray (1702 – Unknown) - Samuel married Elemor McFarland;
- + 8. vii. James Gray (1703 – Unknown); and
- 9. viii. Sarah Gray (1705 – 1790) - Sarah married Robert Barbour on February 26, 1725 or 1726 in Weston, Middlesex County, Massachusetts, and died on June 9, 1790 in Worcester, Worcester County, Massachusetts.

Second Generation

8.   James Gray (1703 – Unknown) - James was born in 1703 in Northern Ireland, the son of John and Elizabeth Gray. James, along with his parents left Ireland in 1718 to immigrate to the American Colonies, where they settled in Worcester, Massachusetts. James married Elizabeth (possibly Elizabeth Church, the daughter of Richard Church and Elizabeth Noble) sometime before 1732.

Elizabeth would pass away on February 18, 1788 in Westfield, Hampden County, Massachusetts.

Children of James and Elizabeth Gray:

	10.	i.	Jonas Gray (1732 – 1804) – Jonas was born on April 8, 1732 in Worcester, Worcester County, Massachusetts, married Susanna Gray, the daughter of Matthew Gray and Joan Kelso, on November 27, 1759 in Worcester, Massachusetts, and died November 13, 1804 in Townshend, Windham County, Vermont;
	11.	ii.	Catherine Gray (1734 – 1799) – Catherine was born on April 14, 1734 in Worcester, Massachusetts, married John Gray, her cousin, the son of Robert Gray and Sarah Wiley, on October 14, 1762 in Holden, Massachusetts, and died April 11, 1799 in Westfield, Hampden County, Massachusetts;
	12.	iii.	Hannah Gray (1735 – Unknown) – Hannah was born on January 9, 1735 or 1736 in Worcester, Massachusetts;
	13.	iv.	Elizabeth Gray (1738 – Unknown) – Elizabeth was born on November 11, 1738 in Worcester, Massachusetts;
	14.	v.	James Gray (1744 – 1822) – James was born on December 31, 1744 in Holden, Massachusetts, first married Molly Lamson on January 24, 1765 in Oxford, Worcester County, Massachusetts, then married Ruth, then Anne, and died on October 8, 1822 in Bridport, Addison, Vermont;
	15.	vi.	Joseph Gray (Unknown – 1804) - Joseph married Sarah Flagg on October 9, 1771 in Fitchburg, Worcester County, Massachusetts and died in 1804 in Fitchburg, Massachusetts; and
+	16.	vii.	Amasa Gray (1751 – 1798).

Third Generation

16.   Amasa Gray (1751 – 1798) - Amasa Gray was born July 25, 1751 in Holden, Worcester County, Massachusetts, the son of James and Elizabeth Gray. Amasa married Sarah Lydia Turpin, the daughter of John Turpin and Sarah Arnold. Amasa and Sarah were the parents of six children.

Amasa and Sarah owned and operated the "Amasa Gray Tavern" on the Pawtucket turnpike. Amasa represented the town and city of Providence in the general assembly during 1789 and 1790.

Amasa would pass away on August 18, 1798 in Providence, Rhode Island and is buried in the Old North Burial Grounds of Providence, Rhode Island.

Children of Amasa Gray and Sarah Lydia Turpin:
+ 17. i. Lydia Gray (1777 – 1792);
- 18. ii. Sarah Gray (1782 – Unknown) – Sarah was born on January 9, 1782 in Providence, Rhode Island;
- 19. iii. Elizabeth Gray (1783 – Unknown) – Elizabeth was born on February 6, 1783 in Providence, Rhode Island;
- 20. iv. Welcome Gray (1785 – Unknown) – Welcome was born on May 16, 1785 in Providence, Rhode Island;
- 21. v. John Gray (1787 – Unknown) – John was born on October 31, 1787 in Providence, Rhode Island, married Betsey Chedell on April 22, 1810 in Providence, Rhode Island; and
- 22. vi. Amasa Gray (1789 – Unknown) – Amasa was born on January 9, 1789 in Providence, Rhode Island.

Fourth Generation

17. Lydia Gray (1777 – 1792) – See Benjamin Aplin, page 142.

Descendents of William Turpin and Catharine Jenckes

First Generation

1. William Turpin (1690 – 1744) - William Turpin was born in 1690 in Providence, Rhode Island, the son of William Turpin and Ann Pratt. The senior William was the first schoolmaster at Providence, Rhode Island in 1694. William passed away on July 18, 1709 in Providence, Rhode Island, while Ann passed away in 1716. William and Ann were the parents of three children: William; Ann; and Persis.

William married Catharine Jenckes, the daughter of Governor Joseph Jenckes and Martha Browne. Catharine was born in 1694 in Pawtucket, Rhode Island.

William was an innkeeper in the town of Providence. He was licensed August 9, 1711, to keep a house of entertainment at his residence located on Towne Street. The Inn was the largest structure in Providence until the completion of building the Rhode Island State House on Smith Hill in 1901. The Inn was built by William's father about 1695. It was described as follows:

> *The Turpin House -- the 'Old Turpin House' -- was situated in the rear of the house now No. 626 North Main street, the 'town street', the site occupied by the late William G. Angell, directly opposite the Fourth Baptist church. William Turpin, who, it is recorded, was a schoolmaster, turned inn-keeper, and seems to have proved himself a most agreeable and successful host. The house which bore his name was built in 1695, and it soon became the state house of the colony, where, too, the probate court, as well as the general assembly, were wont to meet. Turpin's son, also William, succeed him at his death, July 18th, 1709, until his own death in 1744; and the house seems to have gained and maintained a constantly widening influence, and became the largest in the town, and of a political importance which only ended when the present state house was built in 1762. And it still retained its popularity until the town drifted away*

from it and its fellows in the North End.

In 1727, William was appointed by the town of Providence to repair the pound, stocks and whipping post. He represented the town and City of Providence in the general assembly during 1722 and 1729. He would serve as the town treasurer from 1737 to 1744.

William would pass away on March 15, 1744 in Providence, Rhode Island and is buried in the Old North Burial Grounds, while Catharine would die of old age, at the age of 98, in 1792.

Children of William Turpin and Catharine Jenckes:

+ 2. i. John Turpin (Unknown – 1770);
 3. ii. Elizabeth Turpin (1715 – 1791) – Elizabeth married a Mr. Allen, died January 13, 1791, buried in Old North Burial Grounds of Providence, Rhode Island;
 4. iii. William Turpin (1716 – 1736) – William married a Miss Smith, and died April 27, 1736, buried in Old North Burial Grounds of Providence, Rhode Island;
 5. iv. Martha Turpin (1718 – 1785) – Martha was born in 1718 in Providence, Rhode Island, married Haphet Bicknell, the son of Thomas Bicknell and Ann Turner, on December 8, 1746, and died August 30, 1785;
 6. v. Catharine Turpin (1719 – 1749) Catharine married a Mr. Hawkings, and died December 20, 1749, buried in Old North Burial Grounds of Providence, Rhode Island;
 7. vi. Joseph Turpin;
 8. vii. Anne Turpin (1726 – 1753) – Anne married a Mr. Brown, and died January 25, 1753, buried in Old North Burial Grounds of Providence, Rhode Island;
 9. viii. Esther Turpin;
 10. ix. Lydia Turpin; and
 11. x. Mary Turpin..

Second Generation

2. John Turpin (Unknown – 1770) – John Turpin was the son of William Turpin and Catharine Jenckes. John married Sarah Arnold, the daughter of Thomas and Elizabeth (Burlingame) Arnold. Sarah was born on April 10, 1722.

"A sale was made May 14, 1752, by Job Arnold, of Smithfield, by authority of the General Assembly of Rhode Island, to Amos Hopkins, of Scituate, of 92 acres of land situated in Providence, it "being the property of John Turpin, Lunatick," sold "on petition of Turpin's wife for the support of herself and family." This estate comprised the homestead farm of John Turpin that was given to him by his father, William Turpin, by his will made March 12, 1744."

Children of John Turpin and Sarah Arnold:
    12   i. Elizabeth Turpin (1742 – Unknown); and
+   13. ii. Sarah Lydia Turpin (1753 - Unknown).

Third Generation

13. Sarah Lydia Turpin (1753 – Unknown) - See Amasa Gray, page 200.

Descendents of Thomas and Grace Arnold

First Generation

1. Thomas Arnold (1599 – 1674) - Thomas Arnold was born on April 11, 1599 in Cheselbourne, Dorset, England, the son of Thomas and Grace Arnold. Thomas was baptized on April 18, 1599. He first married in England and had three children. Thomas and his family departed from Dorsetshire England for the American Colonies aboard the sailing ship *"Plain Joan"* on May 15, 1635. They settled in Watertown, Massachusetts where they would remain until 1657. His first wife passed away while in Watertown, and Thomas would marry Phebe Parkhurst, the daughter of George Parkhurst and Phebe Leete, in 1639. The family would move to Smithfield, Providence County, Rhode Island in 1658.

Thomas was fined on several occasions: 20 shillings for offense against the law concerning baptism; £5 for neglecting worship 20 days; and £10 for neglecting public worship 40 days (where his land was levied on to pay it.)

Thomas died in September 1674 in Providence, Providence County, Rhode Island, while Phebe would pass away after 1688 in Watertown, Massachusetts. At the time of Thomas death, he owned nearly 10,000 acres of land.

Children of Thomas Arnold:
- 2. i. Thomas Arnold;
- 3. ii. Nicholas Arnold;
- 4. iii. Susanna Arnold.

Children of Thomas Arnold and Phebe Parkhurst:
- 5. i. Ichabod Arnold (1640 – Unknown) – Ichabod was born in Watertown, Massachusetts;
- + 6. ii. Richard Arnold (1641 – Unknown);
- 7. iii. Elizabeth Arnold (1645 – 1747) – Elizabeth was born in 1645 in Watertown, Massachusetts, married Samuel Comstock on November 23, 1678 in Smithfield, Rhode Island, and died on October 20, 1747 in Smithfield, Providence County, Rhode Island;
- 8. iv. Thomas Arnold (1645 – 1693) – Thomas was born on May 3, 1645 in Watertown, Massachusetts and died after 1693;
- 9. v. Nicholas Arnold (1647 – Unknown);

10. vi. John Arnold (1647 – 1722) – John was born on February 19, 1647 or 1648 in Watertown, Massachusetts, married Hannah, and died on January 5, 1722 or 1723;
11. vii. Joanne Arnold (1650 – Unknown) – Joanne was born in 1650 in Watertown, Massachusetts; and
12. viii. Eleazer Arnold (1651 – Unknown) – Eleazer was born on June 17, 1651 in Watertown, Massachusetts, married Eleanor Smith in 1672 in Smithfield, Providence County, Rhode Island

Second Generation

6. Richard Arnold (1641 – 1710) - Richard Arnold was born March 22, 1640 or 1641 Middlesex, Massachusetts, the son of Thomas Arnold and Phebe Parkhurst. He married Mary Angell, the daughter of Thomas Angell and Alice Ashton, in 1666 in Providence, Rhode Island. Mary was born on March 22, 1642 in Watertown, Middlesex, Massachusetts. Richard served during the King William's War of 1697. Richard and Mary were fined 40 shillings for fornication at one time. Together they had the four children. Richard would pass away on April 22, 1710.

Children of Richard Arnold and Mary Angell:
13. i. Richard Arnold Jr. (1666 – Unknown) – Richard was born in 1666 in Smithfield, Providence County, Rhode Island, married Mary Woodward, then Dinah Thorton on November 14, 1715 in Providence, Rhode Island;
14. ii. Mary Arnold (1666 – Unknown) – Mary married Thomas Steere;
15. iii. John Arnold (1670 – 1756) – John was born on November 1, 1670 in Smithfield, Providence County, Rhode Island, married Mary Mowry in 1695, then Hannah Hayward on October 31, 1742, and died October 27, 1756; and
+ 16. iv. Thomas Arnold (1673 – 1725).

Third Generation

16. Thomas Arnold (1673 – 1725) – Thomas Arnold was born on March 24, 1673 or 1674 in Smithfield, Providence County, Rhode Island. Being a Quaker, Thomas refused to go on the expedition against Canada, during the King William's War. Thomas married Elizabeth Burlingame, the daughter of Roger and Mary (Lippitt) Burlingame, on December 5, 1706. Elizabeth was born on January 9, 1683 in Mashantatack, Providence County, Rhode Island. Thomas passed away on February 3, 1725 or 1726. Elizabeth would then

marry William Spencer on April 11, 1734 in Providence. Rhode Island. She would pass away on May 5, 1752 in Providence.

Children of Thomas Arnold and Elizabeth Burlingame:
	17.	i.	Job Arnold (1707 – 1776) – Job married Keisah Hawkins, then Freelove Arnold;
	18.	ii.	Jonathan Arnold (1708 – 1801) – Jonathan married Abigail Smith on June 10, 1714;
	19.	iii.	Mary Arnold (1710 – Unknown) – Mary married Joseph Newell about 1734;
	20.	iv.	Thomas Arnold (1713 – Unknown) – Thomas married Amey Smith on November 9, 1737;
	21.	v.	Elizabeth Arnold (1717 – 1727); and
+	22.	vi.	Sarah Arnold (1722 – Unknown).

Fourth Generation

22. Sarah Arnold (1722 – Unknown) - See John Turpin, page 204

Descendents of George Parkhurst and Phebe Leete

First Generation

1. George Parkhurst (1588 – 1695) - George Parkhurst was born about 1588, probably in Ipswich, Suffolk, England, the son of John Parkhurst. He married Phebe Leete, the daughter of Robert Leete and Alice Grundy. Phebe was born about 1590 in Ipswich, Suffolk, England. For sometime, they resided at Parkhurst Manor, Guiflord, Surrey, England.

George and his family came to the American Colonies around 1634 and settled in Primrose. The family would move to Watertown and then to Boston. Phebe died about 1643 probably in Watertown, Middlesex County, Massachusetts. George then married Susanna Gaylord Simpson in November of 1643.

George died on June 18, 1695 and was buried in St. Lawrence, Ipswich, Suffolk, England.

Children of George Parkhurst and Phebe Leete:
+ 2. i. Phebe Parkhurst (1612 – 1688);
  3. ii. Mary Parkhurst (1614 – 1687) – Mary was baptized on August 28, 1614 in Ipswich, Suffolk County, England, married Rev. Thomas Carter in Hinderclay, Suffolk County, England, and died March 28, 1687 in Woburn, Massachusetts;
  4. iii. Samuel Parkhurst (1616 – Unknown) – Samuel was baptized on February 2, 1616 or 1617;
  5. iv. Deborah Parkhurst (1619 – Unknown) – Deborah was baptized on August 1, 1619 and married John Smith;
  6 v. George Parkhurst (1621 -1698) – George was born in June 1621 in Ipswich, Suffolk Co., England, married Sarah Browne, and died March 1698 in Watertown, Middlesex County, Massachusetts;
  7. vi. John Parkhurst (1623 – Unknown) – John was baptized on October 19, 1623;
  8. vii. Abigail Parkhurst (1625 – Unknown) – Abigail was baptized on January 1, 1625 or 1626;
  9. viii. Elisabeth Parkhurst (1628 – Unknown) – Elizabeth was baptized on May 18, 1628 and married Joseph Merry; and
  10 ix. Joseph Parkhurst (1629 – Unknown) – Joseph was baptized on December 21, 1629.

Children of George Parkhurst and Susanna Gaylord Simpson:
- 11. i. Daniel Parkhurst (1649 – Unknown) – Daniel was born about 1649 in Boston, Suffolk County, Massachusetts;
- 12. ii. Joshua Parkhurst (1653 – Unknown) – Joshua was born about 1653 in Boston, Suffolk County, Massachusetts; and
- 13. iii. Caleb Parkhurst (1653 – Unknown) – Caleb was born about 1653 in Boston, Suffolk County, Massachusetts.

**George Parkhurst
To
Clara Barton
"The Angel of the Battlefield"**

Clara Barton, known as "The Angel of the Battlefield" during the Civil War, founded the American Red Cross in 1881. Before this, Clara worked as a teacher for 10 years (a career she began in an attempt to overcome her shyness) and would establish one of the first free public schools in New Jersey.

The following is the direct line:

George Parkhurst—Phebe Leet(e)
(1587-1655) - (Unknown-BEF 1643)
|
George Parkhurst—Sarah Browne
(6/5/1621-3/16/1697/98) - (1628-10/6/1691)
|
John Parkhurst—Abigail Gearffield
(6/10/1644-9/12/1725) - (6/29/1646-10/18/1726)
|
Abraham Gale, Jr.—Rachael Parkhurst
(1674-9/15/1718) - (12/30/1678-1/30/1767)
|
Samuel Gale—Rebecca Unknown
(1/31/1704/05-1/31/1746/47) - (Unknown-Unknown)
|
Unknown Stone—Esther Gale
(Unknown-Unknown) - (1730-Unknown)
|
David Haven Stone—Sarah Treadwell
(12/6/1750-12/9/1827) - (3/5/1749-Unknown)
|
Captain Stephen Barton—Sarah Stone
(8/18/1774-3/21/1862) - (1/13/1783-7/18/1851)
|
Clarissa "Clara" Harlowe Barton
(12/21/1821—4/12/1912)

Second Generation

2. Phebe Parkhurst (1612 – 1688) – See Thomas Arnold, page 207.

Descendents of Roger Burlingame and Mary Elizabeth Barlingstone

First Generation

1. Roger Burlingame (1620 – 1718) - Roger Burlingame was born on January 24, 1620 in Kent, England the son of Thomas and Elizabeth (Howard) Burlingame. Roger married Jacolyn Huntingdon around 1647 and they had one son, Roger. Roger had enlisted in the British Army at age 16, serving in his Uncle Roger Burlingham's regiment, where he eventually attained the rank of Captain. His company was sent to the American Colonies, where they landed in Boston, Massachusetts on May 10, 1650. Soon thereafter he resigned his commission. He went on to Connecticut, intending to buy a farm and send for his wife and son in England, not knowing that his wife had died.

On February 16, 1656 he purchased a farm near Pequiot, Connecticut, which he would later sell on March 1, 1659. Shortly after that he was living in Warwick, Rhode Island.

In 1662, Roger along with Thomas Ralph and John Hared, purchased from the Cooweeseete Indians 4000 acres at Patuexet (at a place called Mashantack or by some, Paquabuck.) The grant or deed was dated June 6, 1662 and the section was called the Mashantack Purchase (included what is now Cranston, Rhode Island.)

Roger married Mary Elizabeth Barlingstone on October 3, 1663 in Warwick, Kent County, Rhode Island. Mary was born on March 3, 1643, in Providence, Providence County, Rhode Island, the daughter of William Barlingstone.

> *On 7 Mar 1663, Tollarton Harris testified in court that on 12 Jul 1662 he saw Samuel Gorton, George Goff, Roger Burlingame, and Ebenezer Moone mowing the grass on the property of W. Field and W. Harris, near a place called Toskeonke on the north side of the Pawtuxet River. Similar testimony was given by Andrew Harris. Roger Burlingame, along with Thomas Ralph and John Harrud, claimed that they had been granted the property, totaling 4000 acres, by the Cooweeseette*

Indians on 6 Jun 1662. Field and Harris claimed that they had been granted the property by the King. The court found in favor of Field and Harris and ordered Burlingame and the others to leave the land, and pay 10 shillings damages. They did not leave, however. The Town Sergeant put off enforcing the verdict, knowing that the community favored Burlingame and the others. On 1 May 1670, T. Harris testified that on 21 Apr 1670 he and the General Sergeant went to John Harrud's home to execute the verdict, and were turned away at gunpoint. Harrud was supported by about 15 men, including John Weeks Sr. and Jr., Edmund Calvery, Roger Burlingame and Benjamin Barton. Eventually, Burlingame, Harrud, and Ralph won out, partly due to Harris' death.

Roger would become a large landowner in both the Mashantack and Warwick, Rhode Island areas. He and his family were of the Quaker Faith and attended the Oaklawn Baptist Church of Providence, Rhode Island. For many years or at least until 1711, it was said that *"the Friends held their meetings in Roger Burlingame's Mansion House."*

During the King William's War, on April 24, 1697, in Providence, Providence, Rhode Island, Roger was one of 21 men who were ordered by a Council of War *"to take ten men each, to search for the Indian enemies, and if possible to expel or kill them. If they were too strong however, he was to warn the inhabitants."*

Roger was elected constable in Providence on June 7, 1697. He was elected to the town council of Providence on July 6, 1698. He and his family were Quakers, and up until about 1711, they held their meetings at his *"Mansion House"* (a 2 1/2 story house Roger built on the land he bought from the Cooweeseette Indians on June 23, 1662 and May 13, 1663.)

Roger would pass away in Providence, Rhode Island on September 1, 1718. Mary died sometime prior to Roger. Roger's will was dated November 28, 1715 and was proven on September 13, 1718. At his death, Roger's estate was valued at 199 pounds, 13 shillings, 8 pence, and included a mare, three cows, three yearlings, a calf, two sheep, two swine, an old sword, clothing, scales, cash, etc.

Children of Roger Burlingame and Jacolyn Huntingdon:
2. i. Roger Burlingame (1648 – 1765) – Roger married Sarah Eleanor Sweet on December 21, 1699 in Warwick, Rhode Island, and passed away on December 13, 1765 in Cranston, Rhode Island.

Children of Roger Burlingame and Mary Elizabeth Barlingstone:
3. i. John Burlingame (1664 – 1719) – John was born on August 1, 1664 in Kingston, Rhode Island, married Mary Knowles Lippitt on November 19, 1688 in Warwick, Rhode Island, and died on June 24, 1719 in Cranston, Providence County, Rhode Island;
4. ii. Thomas Burlingame (1666 – 1758) – Thomas was born on February 6, 1666 or 1667, married Martha Lippitt on October 5, 1686 in Warwick, Rhode Island, and died on July 9, 1758 in Cranston, Providence County, Rhode Island;
5. iii. Jane Burlingame (1668 – Unknown) – Jane was born on November 21, 1668 in Mashantatack, Providence County, Rhode Island, married John Potter in 1691 in Warwick, Kent County, Rhode Island, and died in Warwick, Rhode Island;
6. iv. Mary Burlingame (1668 – 1760) – Mary was born on January 14, 1668 or 1669 in Stonington, Connecticut, married Amos Stafford on December 19, 1689 in Warwick, Kent County, Rhode Island, and died on October 14, 1760 in West Greenwich, Rhode Island;
7. v. Alice Burlingame (1673 – Unknown) – Alice was born about 1673 in Providence, Providence County, Rhode Island;
8. vi. Mercy Burlingame (1675 – Unknown) – Mercy was born on August 3, 1675 in Providence, Providence County, Rhode Island;
9. vii. Roger Burlingame (1678 – 1765) – Roger was born on May 30, 1678 in Mashantatack, Providence County, Rhode Island and died on December 13, 1765 in Coventry, Kent County, Rhode Island;
10. viii. Peter Burlingame (1680 – 1712) – Peter was born on September 7, 1680 in Providence, Providence County, Rhode Island and died unmarried on December 23, 1712 in Providence, Providence County, Rhode Island;
+ 11. ix. Elizabeth Burlingame (1684 – 1752); and
12. x. Patience Burlingame (1685 – 1746) – Patience was born on May 8, 1685 in North Providence, Providence County, Rhode Island and died on August 8, 1746 in Providence, Providence County, Rhode Island.

Second Generation

11. Elizabeth Burlingame (1684 – 1752) – See Thomas Arnold, page 208.

Descendents of Thomas Angell and Alice Ashton

First Generation

1.   Thomas Angell (1618 – 1694) - Thomas Angell was born on May 1, 1618 in St. Albans, Hertsfordshire, England, the son of James "Henry" Angell and Mary Honeychurch. Thomas came from London to the American Colonies as a servant or apprentice to Roger Williams. He first settled in Salem and then moved to Providence, Rhode Island in 1636, with Roger Williams. He served as the Town Clerk of Providence between 1658 and 1675. He took the oath of allegiance in June of 1668. Thomas married Alice Ashton, the daughter of John Ashton, and together they would have seven children.

Thomas passed away on September 2, 1694 in Providence, Providence County, Rhode Island and Alice passed away shortly after Thomas.

Will of Thomas Angell dated May 23, 1685

Here followeth the Record of the last will & Testamt: of Thomas Angell of Providence, deceased,
Be it knowne unto all People by these presents That I Thomas Angell of Providence in the Colloney of Rhoad Island & Providence Plantations in New England being now very Aged & not knoweing how soone it may please God to Remove me out of this world, and least any discontent or discord should arise after my departure conserning what Estate I shall leave behind; & being desireous that what I do leave may be Enjoyed according as my mind is it should be, Do now whilst I am in some measure of strength and whilst I am of sound & Perfect memory, make ordaine & appoynt this to be my last will & Testament: first I do make voyd & null all & Every other will by me made at any time formerly either by word or writing & this will & Testament only to stand in force.
Item I do give & bequeth unto my son John Angell my si×ty acres of land lieing within the Towneshipp of

Providen|ce| aforesaid in my Right of the first devision, And also my si×ty acres of land in the fifty acre or second devision adjoyneing to the same, & lieing & being neere the place Caled Cauncaunjawatchuck to be unto him, his Heirs & Assignes forever. As also the one halfe of my Right of Commoning within the said Providence Towneshipp so farr west as the seven mile line, that is to say for Commoning or feeding of Cattell Cutting of Timber or firewood or any other vse wch Commoning is Considered in, saveing onely makeing Claime to any devision of land thereby; that shall not be; As also together with the said halfe Righ of Common, the one halfe of my Right of Lands & Commoning I do give & bequeath which lieth on the west side of the seven mile line, unto my said son John Angell to be unto him and his Heirs & Assignes for[]ver together with all & every their Appurtenances.

Item, I Do give & bequeath unto my son James Angell my dwelling house which standeth in the aforesaid Providence Towne ne×t unto the streete, and my house lott or home share of land whereon the said house standeth, together with my other house lott or home share of land to it adjoyneing, as also all my meaddowes, & my Twenty acres of land lieing on Wayboysett side of the water neere the Cove Called Hawkins his Cove; And my si× acres of land lieing in that Tract of land Called the neck where the Cove or salt Creeke called Bailies Cove lieth neere unto | the | said si× acres of Land; As also my Tenn acres of land, lieing in the valley bordering upon the Northerne side of the River Called Wanasquatuckett, And not farr from Thomas Olney of Providence aforesaid his orchard & meaddowes lieing upon the said River; And also halfe my Right of Comoning within the Plantation of Providence aforesd so farr West as the seven mile line, with all the lands which are yet devideable, or may yet, or hereafter be devided or laid out on the East side of the seven mile line unto a whole Purchase Right of Common: As also the one halfe of all my lands & Common within the Towneshipp of Providence aforesaid lieing on the west side of the seven mile line: All which said lands meaddowes & Common, with my aforesd dwelling house together with my Barne, & all other my houseing (the house which I now dwell in only E×cepted) to be unto my said son James Angell, to him his Heirs & Assignes forever, together with all & every their Appurtenances.

Item I do give & bequeath unto my daughter Anphillis Smith & unto my daughter Mary Arnold, & unto my daughter Deborah sabeere, & unto my daughter Alice whipple, & unto my daughter Margery whipple unto Each of them two shillings in silver Money to be paid unto them by my E×ecutor hereafter & E×ecutri× hereafter Named:

Item I do give & bequeath unto my loveing wife Alice Angell my now dwelling house wherein I now dwell to be unto her for her vse duiring the time of her Widdowhood; and in Case shee Marrey not, then for the sd house to be unto her duiring the terme of her naturall life with a small plot of land adjoyneing to the said house for a little Garden; As also before the said house Conveniency of yard Room As also free Egresse & Regress for her to pass & repass as shee may have Ocation through any of the afore devised lands: But in Case my said wife |do| Marrey then at the day of her marriage shall the said house & small Plot of land come into the hands of my said son James Angell with all ye Privelidges aforesaid to be unto him his Heirs & Assignes forever; but in case shee marrey not, then shall the said house & sd small Plot of land with the said Privelidges Come into the hands of my said son James Angell after the decease of his mother to be unto him & his Heirs & Assignes forever; And that my sd son James Angell shall keepe the said house in such Repare as may be Comfortable for his said mother to dwell in duiring the time of her makeing use thereof as aforesaid. I do also give unto my wife one milch Cow to be her owne, & that the said Cow shall be by my sd two sons (viz) John Angell & James Angell constantly, both summer|ed| & wintered for the vse of my said wife, & when the said Cow by Reason of Age or other thing which may make her unfit for milke doth faile, then shall my said son

James take that said Cow himselfe & put another in its Roome, & so in Case any Causalty befalls at any time what cow is so for my sd wife her vse as afore E×prest then shall my said son James still put another Milch Cow in its Roome; the which sd Cow shall be at my sd wife her dispose, Either if shee marrey or at her death; And that my said two sons John Angell & James Angell their Heirs E×ecutors Administrators & Assignes shall yearely pay unto my said wife (their mother) si×teene shillings in money untill shee marrey, & in case shee marrey not, then duiring the terme of her naturall life; the which said si×teene shillings shall yearely be the one halfe paid by my said son John & the other halfe by my said son James. And that my said | two | sons John Angell & James Angell their Heirs, E×ecutors, Administrators & Assignes shall take Care & shall provide for the Comfortable maintenance of my said wife duiring the terme of her Widdowhood, & if she marrey not, then duiring the terme of her naturall life; And that such Care shall by them be taken & such Provision by them be made that my said wife may sufficiently, suteably & Comfortably be kept & maintained both in health & in sickness with sutable tendance & all other Nessesareys as her Condition shall Constantly Require; the which Charge shall be Equally borne by my said two sons; But in Case my sd two sons shall neglect or faile, or Either of them their Heirs E×ecutors Administrators or Assignes shall Neglect or faile of the performance thereof, Then shall a third part of the defective party their lands afore devised be unto my said wife for her vse & Proffitt duiring the terme of her widdowhood, & if shee marrey not, then duiring the terme of her naturall life; The which Third part of the said lands shall be the third part of ye same which may be most Advantag|e|ous to my said wife. I do also give & bequeth unto my said wife all my household goods to be her owne & at her owne dispose; That is to say all my Bedds bedding, Cloathing both woollen & linnen, & all sorts of vessells both Iron, Brass, Pewter, wood & all other things to the house belonging which are Nessesary for house keepeing which may be Counted household goods: Table linnen as well as other is included; as also if any moneys be left at my decease, the same I do give unto my said wife.

Item I do give & bequeth unto my son James Angell all my Cattell of all sorts only E×cepting one Cow which I have before disposed of to my wife; As also unto my said son James Angell I do give all my Tooles of what sort soever & all other my Estate both Moveable goods and Chattells not before dispossed of: And unto my said son James I do give to him his Heirs & Assignes forever all other my lands Rights Interests & Titles whatsoever not before disposed of. And I do make ordaine Constitute & appoynt my loveing wife Alice Angell my lawfull E×ecutri× & my son James Angell my lawfull E×ecutor, both Joyntly, unto whome I do give all my debts unto me from any Person due, & they to pay all debts from me to any person due; & to see that my body be decently buried & to E×ecute & performe this my will according My true meaneing & intent therein, And I do desire and appoynt my loveing friends & neighbours Nathaniell Waterman & Thomas Olney to be the overseers of this my Will./

In witness of the Premisses I do here unto set my hand | & seale |

the Twenty & third day of may in the yeare one Thousand si× hundred Eighty & five.

Signed & Sealed in the
The marke of X Thomas Angell
presence of us Thomas Olney,
Nathaniell Waterman,
Epenetus Olney

Be it knowne unto all People by these presents that I the aforesd Thomas Angell do Add this as a Coddicill to my aforesaid will; That is, I do also give & bequeth unto my said son John Angell, unto him his Heirs & Assignes for ever my Ten acres of land which was unto me laid out in luie of my Right of my share of Meaddow in the second or fifty acre devision, it lieing & Adjoyneing to my afore specified lands neere Cauncaunjawatchuck; The which sd Ten acres of land was forgotten before before when

the other lands was disposed of; In witness whereof I do hereunto set my hand the Twenty & third day of May in the yeare one Thousand si× hundred Eighty & five.
Signed in th presence of us,
The marke of X Thomas Angell
Thomas Olney, Nathaniell Waterman, Epenetus Olney/

James Angell E×ecutor to the abovesd will appeared this day before the Towne Towne Councill of Providence being the 18th day of September 1694 & made oath unto the said will: Thomas Olney; Nathaniell waterman & Epenetus Olney, the 18th of September 1694 appeared before the Towne Councill of Providence & attested upon Engagement unto the abovesd will as Witnesses./
The 18th of September 1694 the Towne Councill of Providence have E×amined & do approve the aforesd will; Attests Joseph Jencks Assistant
Steven Arnold Assistant, Joseph Williams Assistant

Recorded August ye 15th 1711 Tho: Olney Clerk.

Children of Thomas Angell and Alice Ashton:

	2.	i.	Amphillis Angell (1635 – Unknown) – Amphillis was born about 1635 and married Edward Smith on May 9, 1663 in Rhode Island;
	3.	ii.	John Angell (1646 – Unknown) – John married Ruth Field;
+	4.	iii.	Mary Angell (1642 – Unknown);
	5.	iv.	James Angell;
	6.	v.	Deborah Angell, who married a Mr. Sabeere;
	7.	vi.	Alice Angell (1649 – Unknown) – Alice was born about 1649 and married a Elzear Whipple; and
	8.	vii.	Margery Angell (1666 – Unknown) – Margery married a Jonathan Whipple.

Second Generation

4. Mary Angell (1642 – Unknown) – See Richard Arnold, page 208.

Descendents of Joseph Jenckes and Joan Hearn

First Generation

1. Joseph Jenckes (1599 – 1683) - Joseph Jenckes was born in Blackfriars, London, England on August 26, 1599, the son of John Jenckes and Sarah Fulwater. Joseph was educated at Hammersmith, England. He was a master mechanic in an iron foundry in Colebrook, Buckinghamshire, England. Joseph married Joan Hearn, the daughter of George Hearn, in Blackfriars, London, England on November 5, 1627.

Together Joseph and Joan would have three children before Joan would pass away at an early age. In 1643, Joseph was persuaded to leave Hammersmith to establish the first smelting and foundry ("iron works") in the American Colonies. It was by his hands and his direction, that the first furnaces were erected and he personally cast the first article, an iron pot holding about a quart. This pot has survived time and is now located in the Essex Institute, Salem, Massachusetts. The foundry was located along the Sangus River in Lynn, Essex County, Massachusetts.

Joseph's sons joined him in America in 1645 and he remarried sometime before 1650. He married Elizabeth Darling, who was born about 1604 in England.

In 1646, Joseph was granted the first exclusive right for the use of an invention by the Massachusetts Colony. Joseph had invented a speedier engine for water-mills and also for the manufacturing of scythes and other edged tools. The General Court of Massachusetts allowed him fourteen years of exclusive rights and protection of others for the engine. In 1655, he was granted a second exclusive right for seven years to manufacture an improved grass scythe. This grass scythe remained substantially unchanged and in use for over 300 years.

In 1652, at the request of the Massachusetts Colony, Joseph made the dies for striking the first coins manufactured in the Colonies. The "Pine Tree Shilling" was produced in a threepenny piece, a sixpenny piece and a shilling. The coin had "Masatusets," with a pine tree, on one side and "New England, Ammo 1652," and the number of pence in Roman numeral on the other.

The "Pine Tree Shilling"

In 1654, Joseph built the first fire-engine in the Colonies for the city of Boston. At the time, there were few such engines in the world. Over the years, Joseph would be instrumental in the development of many improvements to tools and machinery and would receive patents on many of his most useful inventions.

Joseph passed away in his early eighties on March 16, 1683 in Lynn, Essex County, Massachusetts.

Children of Joseph Jenckes and Joan Hearn:
+ 2. i.   Joseph Jenckes (1628 – 1717);
  3. ii. Elizabeth Jenckes (Unknown – 1638) - Elizabeth died about 1638 in Hounslow, England; and
  4. iii. George Jenckes.

Children of Joseph Jenckes and Elizabeth Darling:
  5. i.   Sarah Jenckes (1650 – Unknown);
  6. ii. Samuel Jenckes (1654 – 1738) – Samuel was born about 1654 in Lynn, Essex County, Massachusetts and died March 13, 1738 in Lynn, Massachusetts;
  7. iii. Deborah Jenckes (1658 – Unknown) – Deborah was born on June 11, 1658;
  8. iv. John Jenckes (1660 – Unknown) – John was born on July 27, 1660; and
  9. v.   Daniel Jenckes (1663 – Unknown) – Daniel was born on April 19, 1663.

Second Generation

2.   Joseph Jenckes (1628 – 1717) - Joseph Jenckes was born in Coinbrook, London, Buckinghamshire, England on October 12, 1628, the son of Joseph Jenckes and Joan Hearn. Joseph's mother passed away sometime before 1643, when Joseph's father left for the American Colonies to establish the first smelting and foundry ("iron works") in the Colonies. Joseph and his brother, George, joined their father in the American Colonies in 1645. Joseph followed in his

father's trade as an iron founder. Around 1655, with the rapid destruction of the forest about Lynn, Massachusetts, he followed Roger Williams to the Rhode Island Colony. He acquired from the Indians a tract of woodland along the Blackstone River in the Territory of Providence, which included the Pawtucket Falls. Here, he would build a foundry and forge. He married Hester Ballard, the daughter of William and Elizabeth (Lee) Ballard, in 1656 in Lynn, Essex County, Massachusetts. Hester was born in 1633 in England. Together Joseph and Hester would have ten children.

In 1675, during the King Phillip's War with the Indians, Joseph's foundry was destroyed. The foundry was rebuilt and would provide the foundation by which Providence would become the "iron workshop" for the Colonies at the beginning of the Revolutionary War.

In 1661, Joseph became a member of the Governor's Council and also would serve as a member of the House of Deputies.

Joseph passed away on January 14, 1717 in Pawtucket, Providence County, Rhode Island, in the town he founded.

Children of Joseph Jenckes and Hester Ballard:
+ 10. i. Joseph Jenckes, Jr. (1656 -1740);
   11. ii. Elizabeth Jenckes (1658 – 1740) – Elizabeth married Samuel Teft in South Kingstown, Washington County, Rhode Island, and died in 1740;
   12. iii. Sarah Jenckes (1660 – 1708) – Sarah was born in 1660 in Lynn, Essex County, Massachusetts, married Nathaniel Brown, and died in 1708;
   13. iv. Nathaniel Jenckes (1662 – 1723) – Nathaniel was born on January 29, 1662 in Lynn, Essex County, Massachusetts, married Hannah Bosworth on November 4, 1686 in Hingham, Massachusetts, and died August 11, 1723. Nathaniel was a blacksmith by trade and served as a Major in the Massachusetts Militia;
   14. v. Ester Jenckes (1664 – 1720) – Ester was born in 1664 in Rhode Island, married Samuel Willard, and died in 1720;
   15. vi. Mary Jenckes (1666 – Unknown) – Mary was born about 1666 in Rhode Island and married Daniel Jenks;
   16. vii. Ebenezer Jenckes (1669 – 1726) – Ebenezer was born on September 17, 1669 in Providence, Providence County, Rhode Island, who married Mary Butterworth on March 4, 1695, and died August 14, 1726;
   17. viii. Joanna Jenckes (1672 – 1756) – Joanna was born in 1672 in Providence, Providence County, Rhode Island, married Sylvanus Scott about 1692, and died March 12, 1756 in Smithfield, Rhode Island;

18. ix. William Jenckes (1674 – 1765) – William was born about 1674 or 1675, married Patience Sprague about 1696 in Providence, Rhode Island, and died July 19, 1765 in Smithfield, Rhode Island. William was the Chief Justice of the County Court; and
19. x. Abigail Jenckes (1676 – Unknown) – Abigail was born in 1676 in Rhode Island, married Thomas Whipple.

Third Generation

10. Joseph Jenckes, Jr. (1656 – 1740) - Joseph Jenckes was born in Pawtucket, Providence County, Rhode Island in 1656, the son of Joseph Jenckes and Hester Ballard. Joseph became a land surveyor and was instrumental in helping to establish the boundaries for the Rhode Island Colony, with its neighboring colonies. Joseph married Martha Browne, the daughter of John and Mary (Holmes) Browne, in 1680 in Pawtucket, Providence County, Rhode Island. Martha was born in 1665 in Pawtucket, Providence County, Rhode Island. Together Joseph and Martha would have nine children.

Joseph became a member of the General Assembly in 1679, where he served as clerk and speaker. He served as a commissioner of the Rhode Island Colony, settling the boundary disputes that arose with Massachusetts and Connecticut, and later, between New Hampshire and Maine. During this period, he wrote a reply to the King of England, as to the *"condition of affairs of Rhode Island,"* and answering twenty-seven questions propounded by the Lords of the Privy Council. He would also serve as Councilor for most of the years from 1680 to 1712. He became a freeman in 1681. In 1697 he became the Rhode Island State Auditor and served in this capacity until 1704. In 1717, he became the chairman of a commission to compile and publish the laws of the Colonies, and to make a map of the Colonies for the English government.

Joseph became the deputy governor in 1715 and served in this position until he became the Governor of Rhode Island in 1727. After serving five years, he declined to run for re-election.

Martha passed away sometime before 1727, as Joseph became married to Alice Dexter, the widow of John Dexter, and daughter of John Smith and Sarah Whipple, on February 3, 1727. Joseph passed away on June 14, 1740 in Pawtucket, Providence County, Rhode Island, at the age of 84. After lying in state at Providence, his body was buried in the North Burial Grounds of Providence. In addition to being the Royal Governor of Rhode Island, he was also known for standing seven feet two inches in his stocking feet.

Children of Joseph Jenckes, Jr. and Martha Browne:
- 20. i. Joseph Jenckes (1682 – Unknown) – Joseph was born in 1682 in Pawtucket, Providence County, Rhode Island and died young;
- 21. ii. Mary Jenckes (1682 – Unknown) – Mary was born about 1682 in Pawtucket, Providence County, Rhode;
- 22. iii. Obadiah Jenckes (1684 – Unknown) – Obadiah was born in 1684 in Pawtucket, Providence County, Rhode Island;
- 23. iv. Nathaniel Jenckes (1686 – Unknown) – Nathaniel was born 1686-1687 in Pawtucket, Providence County, Rhode Island and married Catherine Scott;
- 24. v. Martha Jenckes (1692 – Unknown) – Martha was born in 1692 in Pawtucket, Providence County, Rhode Island and married John Andrews;
- + 25. vi. Catharine Jenckes (1694 – 1792);
- 26. vii. Ester Jenckes (1695 – Unknown) – Ester was born in 1695 in Pawtucket, Providence County, Rhode Island and married Benjamin Bucklin;
- 27. viii. John Jenckes (1696 – 1726) – John was born June 9, 1696 in Pawtucket, Providence County, Rhode, became a doctor and died of smallpox in London, England in 1726; and
- 28. ix. Lydia Jenckes (1705 – Unknown) – Lydia was born about 1705 in Providence, Providence County, Rhode Island and married Christopher Mason.

Fourth Generation

25. Catharine Jenckes (1694 – 1792) – See William Turpin, page 203.

Descendents of Henry Ballard and Elizabeth Townsend

First Generation

1. Henry Ballard (1575 – 1642) - Henry Ballard was born in 1575 in St. Mary, Southwell, Nottingham, England. Henry married Elizabeth Townsend in 1599. Elizabeth was born in 1577 in Tenterton, Kent, England. Henry passed away sometime after 1642 in Warwick, England.

    Children of Henry Ballard and Elizabeth Townsend:
      2.   i.   Phillip Ballard (1597 – Unknown) – Phillip was born in 1597 in Nottinghamshire, England;
      3.   ii.   Elizabeth Ballard (1599 – Unknown) – Elizabeth was born in 1599 in Nottinghamshire, England;
      4.   iii.   Thomas Ballard (1600 – Unknown) - Thomas was born in 1600 Southwell, Nottinghamshire, England;
      5.   iv.   Catharine Ballard (1602 – Unknown) – Catharine was born in 1602 in Southwell, Nottinghamshire, England;
+   6.   v.   William Ballard (1603 – 1639);
      7.   vi.   Ann Ballard (1604 – Unknown) – Ann was born in 1604 in Southwell, Nottinghamshire, England;
      8.   vii.   Phillip Ballard (1609 – Unknown) – Phillip was born in 1609 in Southwell, Nottinghamshire, England; and
      9.   viii.   Anne Ballard (1610 – Unknown) – Anne was born about 1610 in Southwell, Nottingham, England.

Second Generation

6. William Ballard (1603 – 1639) - William Ballard was born August 12, 1603 in Sanford Priors, Warwickshire, England, the son of Henry Ballard and Elizabeth Townsend. William married Elizabeth Lee in 1632 in England. Elizabeth was born about 1609 in Suffolk, England.

    William and Elizabeth left for the American Colonies from London, England, with their two children during late July of 1635. They arrived safely in the Massachusetts Bay aboard the sailing ship *"James"* John May, Master. On the ship's roll of passengers, William was listed as a *"Husbanman"*.

They settled in the Town of Saugust (which latter changed its name in 1637 to Lynn, when the first official minister, Samuel Whiting, arrived from King's Lynn, England). The community was mostly an agricultural community and also became a major shoe center for the colonies with several tanneries.

William became very involved in the community of Lynn. He served as Magistrate, Salem Quarterly Court from June 26, 1638 through July 27, 1638. He was appointed a member of the committee to lay out land granted by the colony and as the Lynn representative on the committee to levy colony rate on September 6, 1638. He would latter serve on the committee to determine the boundary between Salem and Lynn. He was admitted to the *"Ancient and Honorable Artillery Company,"* in 1638.

William passed away sometime before June 6, 1639, as he was replace by Timothy Tomlins on the committee to determine the boundary between Salem and Lynn.

Elizabeth would remarry in 1640, William Knight, and latter Allen Bread on March 28, 1656. She would pass away on March 15, 1687 in Lynn, Massachusetts.

Children of William Ballard and Elizabeth Lee:
+ 10. i. Hester Ballard (1633 – Unknown);
 11. ii. John Ballard (1634 – 1725) – John was born 1634 in England, married Susan Story on June 29, 1655 in Lynn, Essex County, Massachusetts, then Elizabeth Phelps and Rebecca Stevens, and died June 11, 1725 in Lynn, Massachusetts.
 12. iii. William Ballard (1635 – 1686) – William was born shortly after their arrival in Massachusetts in 1635, married Rebecca, and died on March 15, 1686 or 1687 in Lynn, Essex County, Massachusetts; and
 13. iv. Nathaniel Ballard (1636 – 1721) – Nathaniel was born in 1636 in Lynn, Essex County, Massachusetts, married Rebecca Hudson on December 16, 1662 in Lynn, Massachusetts, and died January 1, 1721 or 1722 in Lynn, Massachusetts.

Third Generation

10. Hester Ballard (1633 – Unknown) - See Joseph Jenckes, page 226.

Descendents of Rev. Chaddus Browne and Elizabeth Sharparowe

First Generation

1. Rev. Chaddus Browne (1600 – 1650) - Chaddus "Chad" Browne was born about 1600 in High Wycombe, Buckinghamshire, England, the son of Arthur Brown (born in 1574 in High Wycombe, Buckinghamshire, England) and mother unknown (born in 1579 in High Wycombe, Buckinghamshire, England.) Chad married Elizabeth Sharparowe on September 11, 1626 in High Wycombe, Buckinghamshire, England. Together in England they would have their first son, John born about 1629.

The family soon emigrated from England aboard the ship *"Martin"* where they arrived in Boston, Massachusetts in July of 1638. While on the ship, Chad witnessed a nuncupative will of a passenger who died on the voyage to the new colonies. The family first settled in Salem, Massachusetts, staying there but a short time. Unable to endure the intolerance of the first church, the Puritans, during the autumn of 1938, they joined the Roger Williams Colony. Roger Williams and twelve others from Salem had executed what is known as the "initial deed", assigning the Providence Plantations (which he named for God's guidance and care) acquired by purchase from the Narragansett Indians. Chad acquired a home lot located at the corner of the present Market Square and College Street in the new colony of Providence, Rhode Island (land now occupied by Brown University).

Chad was a surveyor by profession and served as the town surveyor. He along with two others compiled a list of the original divisions or grants of land for the town of Providence. In 1642, he was ordained as the first elder of the oldest Baptist church in America. He was known as the "Peacemaker" for his success in adjusting the quarrels of his flock.

Chad passed away on September 2, 1650 in Providence, Rhode Island and was buried on his own ground (a spot now occupied by the Court House), whence his remains were removed in 1792 to the North Burial Ground in Providence, where his gravestone with the following inscription can be seen today:

"In Memory of Chad Brown Elder of the Baptist church in this town. He was one of the original Proprietors of the Providence Purchase having been exiled from Massachusetts for Conscience Sake. He had five sons John, James, Jeremiah, Chad and Daniel who have left a numerous Posterity. He died about A.D. 1665. This Monument was erected by the Town of Providence."

Elizabeth would pass away in 1672 in Providence, Rhode and is buried in North Burial Ground in Providence.

Children of Chaddus Browne and Elizabeth Sharparowe:
+ 2. i. John Browne (1629 – 1677);
3. ii. Daniel Browne (1638 – 1729) – Daniel was born about 1638 in Providence, Rhode Island, married Alice Hearndon (Harrington), and died September 29, 1729;
4. iii. James Browne (1639 – 1683) – James was born about 1639 In Newport, Rhode Island, married Elizabeth Carr in 1670 in Newport, and died sometime before 1683;
5. iv. Jeremiah Browne (1640 – 1690) – Jeremiah was born about 1640 in Providence, Rhode Island, married Mary Slocum about 1680, and died about September 16, 1690 in Newport, Rhode Island;
6. v. Judah Chad Browne (1642 – 1663) – Judah was born about 1642 in Providence, Rhode Island, never married, and died May 10, 1663 in Newport, Rhode Island; and
7. vi. Deborah Browne (1645 – Unknown) – Deborah was born about 1645 in Providence, Rhode Island.

Second Generation

2. John Browne (1629 – 1677) - John Browne was born about 1629 in St Albans, England the son of Chaddus and Elizabeth (Sharparowe) Browne. John, eight years old at the time, emigrated from England with his parents on the ship *"Martin"* to Boston, Massachusetts, landing in July, 1636. The family first settled in Salem, Massachusetts, but shortly moved on to Providence, Rhode Island.

John married Mary Holmes, the daughter of Obadiah and Catherine (Hyde) Holmes in 1654 in Providence, Rhode Island. Mary was born in 1635 in Stockport, Lancashire, England.

John, like his father became a surveyor by profession. He was a respected and honored man in early Providence. He was one of the commissioners from Providence to meet with commissioners from other towns, within the colony of Warwick, on August 31, 1654, for the purpose of adjusting certain difficulties which threatened to disturb the peace and harmony of the colony.

John became a freeman in 1655 and served as surveyor of highways in 1659. He was subsequently a moderator, a deputy to the Rhode Island General Assembly, and assistant for Providence. He was appointed in 1662, along with Roger Williams and Thomas Harris, Jr., to the Town Council of Providence. In 1672 he sold the home lot of his father to his brother, James, of Newport, who resold it the same day to Daniel Abbott. Nearly one hundred years later a part of it was repurchased by his great-grandsons, John and Moses Brown, and by them presented to the College of Rhode Island, at the time of its removal from Warren to Providence. The cornerstone of University Hall, for many years the only building, was laid by John Brown, May 31, 1770.

John passed away on September 13, 1677 in Providence, Rhode Island and was buried in the North Burial Ground in Providence. Mary would pass away in 1690 in Providence, Rhode and most likely buried in North Burial Ground in Providence.

Children of John Browne and Mary Holmes:
- 8. i. Mary Browne (1654 – 1662) – Mary was born on February 10, 1654-55 in Lynn, Massachusetts, married Thomas Pierson and then Arthur Aylesworth, and died May 18, 1662 in Quidnessett, East Greenwich, Rhode Island;
- 9. ii. Hannah Browne (1658 – Unknown) – Hannah was born on May 2, 1658 in Milford, Connecticut, married Joseph Riggs in 1671 in Newark, New Jersey and then married Aaron Thompson;
- 10. iii. Phebe Browne, who married Daniel Dod about 1671 in Essex County, New Jersey and then married Samuel Ward;
- 11. iv. Sarah Browne (1661 – 1678) – Sarah was born March 18, 1661 in Providence, Rhode Island, married Thomas Jacobs in Ipswich, Massachusetts and then married John Pray, and died January 29, 1678 or 1679 in Ipswich, Massachusetts;
- 12. v. John 'James' Browne (1662 – 1732) – John was born on May 18, 1662 in Providence, Rhode Island, and died October 28, 1732 in Providence, Rhode Island. John served under Capt. John Whipple of Ipswich, during the King Phillip's War;
- + 13. vi. Martha Browne (1665 – 1727);

14.	vii.	Obadiah Browne (1668 – 1716) – Obadiah was born about 1668 in Providence, Rhode Island, married Mary about 1685, and died August 24, 1716 in Providence, Rhode Island
15.	viii.	Deborah Browne (1670 – Unknown) – Deborah was born about 1670 in Providence, Rhode Island; and
16.	ix.	Mary Browne (1672 – 1740) – Mary was born about 1672 in Newport, Rhode Island and died June 15, 1740.

Third Generation

13. Martha Browne (1665 – 1727) – See Joseph Jenckes, Jr., page 228.

Descendents of Robert Holmes and Katherine Johnson

First Generation

1. Robert Holmes was born August 18, 1578 in Stockport, Manchester, Lancaster, England. A farmer, Robert married Katherine Johnson on October 8, 1605 at Stockport, England. Katherine was born in 1584 in Stockport. Together Robert and Katherine had nine children.

Katherine passed away and was buried at Stockport on September 8, 1630, while Robert died and was buried in Stockport on November 12, 1640.

Children of Robert Holmes and Katherine Johnson:

	2.	i.	John Holmes (1607 – Unknown) – John was baptized at Stockport, England on May 3, 1607 and died before 1640;
+	3.	ii.	Obadiah Holmes (1607 – 1682);
	4.	iii.	Joan Holmes (1610 – Unknown) – Joan was baptized at Didsbury, England on February 2, 1610/11;
	5.	iv.	Samuel Holmes (Unknown – 1613) - Samuel died and was buried at Stockport, England on November 2, 1613;
	6.	v.	Samuel Holmes (1616 – Unknown) – Samuel was baptized at Didsbury on February 23, 1616/17, a graduate of Oxford University;
	7.	vi.	Nathaniel Holmes (1618 – 1631) - Nathaniel was baptized at Didsbury on July 12, 1618 and died and buried at Stockport, England on September 25, 1631;
	8.	vii.	Robert Holmes (1621 – Unknown) – Robert was baptized at Stockport, England on March 21, 1621. He inherited his father's holdings at Reddish;
	9.	viii.	Joseph Holmes (Unknown – 1623) – Joseph died and buried at Stockport on June 13, 1623; and
	10	ix.	Joseph Holmes (Unknown – Unknown).

Obadiah Holmes
to
16th President of the United States of America Abraham Lincoln

The discovery of the direct line from Obadiah Holmes to the 16th President of the United States of America was made by Wilbur Nelsen, who published a small booklet on the subject: Obadiah Holmes, Ancestor and Prototype of Abraham Lincoln (Newport, 1932). The following is the

Obadiah Holmes—Catharine Hyde
(1607-1682) - (1608-1684)
|
Lydia Holmes—Major John Bowne
(1637-AFT 1693) - (ABT 1630-1683/84)
|
Sarah Bowne—Richard Salter
(1669-AFT 1714) - (Unknown-AFT1728)
|
Hannah Salter—Mordecai Lincoln, Jr.
(Unknown-ABT 1727) - (1686-1736)
|
John Lincoln—Rebecca Flowers
(1716-1743) - (1720-1806)
|
Abraham Lincoln—Bathsheba Herring
(1744-1786) - (ABT 1750-ABT 1836)
|
Thomas Lincoln—Nancy Hanks
(1778-1851) - (1784-1818)
|
16th President of the United States of America Abraham Lincoln
(2/12/1809—4/15/1865)

Second Generation

3.   Obadiah Holmes (1607 – 1682) - Obadiah Holmes (Hulmes) was born March 8, 1607 in the rural area of Reddish, five miles southeast of the center of Manchester, England, the son of Robert Holmes and Katherine Johnson. Obadiah was baptized in Didsbury Chapel on March 18, 1610. With two of his brothers, John and Samuel. It is said that he was educated at Oxford University, while he never graduated. He would later say, *"...that he had been neglectful and strayed from his religious duties and responsibilities for a period of five years."* Upon the illness of his mother, Obadiah would say, *"It struck me that my disobedient acts caused her death, which forced me to confess the same to her—my evil ways."*

Two months after his mother's death, Obadiah took Catharine Hyde as his wife on November 20, 1630. They were married at Manchester's Collegiate College Church. Catharine was born on October 27, 1608 in Manchester, Lancaster, England, the daughter of Gilbert Hyde. Their first child, John was born in 1631 in Reddish, Parish of Manchester, Lancashire, England and would died at an early age on June 27, 1633. He was buried at Stockport with *"infant of Obadiah Hulmes of Redich"* on his grave.

With the persecution of the Puritans in England, Obadiah and Catharine, along with their son Jonathan, joined the Great Migration to the American Colonies. They set sail in 1638 from Preston, down the River Ribble, across the Irish Sea, and out into the Atlantic Ocean. After a very stormy voyage they entered Boston Harbor, the American Colonies, nearly six weeks later. By January, 1639, they had made their way up the coast to settle in Salem, Massachusetts Colony. On the 23rd of January, they received one acre of land for a house and a promise of ten more acres *"to be laid out by the town."*

Obadiah, along with several other citizens of Salem, started the first glass factory in the Colonies, producing common window glass.

After several years of living in Salem and being a member of the First Church of Salem, Obadiah would become disturbed by the rigidity of the established church. Being somewhat vocal of his dislike for the doctrines and the practices of the church, he would soon leave Salem, excommunicated by the church. By 1645, he and his family had removed to the newly created community of Rehoboth, approximately 40 miles south of Boston. Here he became a freeman in 1648.

Again, being dissatisfied by the established church, Obadiah, became the leader of the Schismatists, a movement towards the Baptists views. Being harassed by the local authorities and church, he along with his followers, left the Massachusetts Colony and moved to Newport, Rhode Island.

In July, 1651, Obadiah, along with 2 others, would return to Massachusetts, only to be placed under arrest and tried on charges of *(1) conducting a private worship service at the same time as the town's public worship; (2) "offensively disturbing" the public meeting in Lynn; (3) "seducing and drawing aside others after their erroneous judgment and practices"; and (4) "neglecting or refusing to give in sufficient security for their appearance" at the next meeting of the county court.* Without producing either, an accuser, a witness, a jury, law of God or man, they were found guilty (prejudged). Obadiah, rather than pay his fine, on September 5, 1651 was taken to the whipping-post on Boston Common, where he received thirty strokes, with a three-cord whip. Throughout the whipping, he let out not a groan or a murmur. The first sounds from his lips were the words to the magistrates, who stood witness to the whipping, *"You have struck me as with roses."*

Obadiah returned to Newport, where in 1652, he became the second minister of the first Baptist Church in the American Colonies. He would be the minister of the church in Newport until his death on October 15, 1682. He was buried in his own field on the Middleton Plantation. Catharine would pass away during the spring of 1684.

Last Will and Testament of Reverend Obadiah Holmes

These are to signify that I, Obadiah Holmes of Newport on Rhode Island, being at present through the goodness and mercy of my God of sound memory; and, being by daily intimations put in mind of the frailty and uncertainty of this present life, do therefore - for settling my estate in this world which it has pleased the Lord to bestow upon me - make and ordain this my Last Will and Testament in manner following, committing my spirit unto the Lord that gave it to me and my body to the earth from whence it was taken, in hope and expectation that it shall thence be raised at the resurrection of the just.
Imprimis, I will that all my just debts which I owe unto any person be paid by my Executor, hereafter named, in

convenient time after my decease.

Item. I give and bequeath unto my daughter, Mary Brown, five pounds in money or equivalent to money.

Item. I give and bequeath unto my daughter, Martha Odlin, ten pounds in the like pay.

Item. I give and bequeath unto my daughter, Lydia Bowne, ten pounds.

Item. I give and bequeath unto my two grandchildren, the children of my daughter, Hopestill Taylor, five pounds each; and if either of them decease, the survivor to have ten pounds.

Item. I give and bequeath unto my son, John Holmes, ten pounds.

Item. I give and bequeath unto my son, Obadiah Holmes, ten pounds.

Item. I give and bequeath unto my grandchildren, the children of my son Samuel Holmes, ten pounds to be paid unto them in equal portions.

All these portions by me bequeathed, my will is, shall be paid by my Executor in money or equivalent to money.

Item. I give and bequeath unto all my grandchildren now living ten pounds; and ten shillings in the like pay to be laid out to each of them - a bible.

Item. I give and bequeath unto my grandchild, Martha Brown, ten pounds in the like pay.

All [of] which aforesaid legacies are to be paid by my Executor, hereafter named in manner here expressed: that is to say, the first payment to [be] paid within one year after the decease of my wife, Catherine Holmes, and twenty pounds a year until all the legacies be paid, and each to be paid according to the degree of age.

My will is and I do hereby appoint my son Jonathan Holmes my sole Executor, unto whom I have sold my land, housing, and stock for the performance of the same legacies above. And my will is that my Executor shall pay unto his mother, Catherine Holmes, if she survives and lives, the sum of twenty pounds in money or money pay for her to dispose of as she shall see cause.

Lastly, I do desire my loving friends, Mr. James Barker, Sr., Mr. Joseph Clarke, and Mr. Philip Smith, all of Newport, to be my overseers to see this my will truly *performed. In witness whereof, I have hereunto set my hand and seal, this ninth day of April, 1681.*

Obadiah Hullme [Holmes][Seal]

Signed, sealed and delivered in the presence of
Edward Thurston
Weston Clarke

(Edward Thurston, Sr., and Weston Clark appeared before the Council [of Newport], December 4, 1682, and did upon their engagements [pledges] declare and own that they saw Obadiah Holmes, deceased, sign seal and deliver the above written will as his act and deed; and, at the time of his sealing hereof, he was in his perfect memory, according to the best of our understandings. Taken before the Council, as attested. Weston Clarke, Town Clerk.)

Children of Obadiah Holmes and Catharine Hyde:

11. i. John Holmes (1631 – 1633) - John was born in 1631 in Reddish, Parish of Manchester, Lancashire, England and would died at an early age on June 27, 1633;
12. ii. Jonathan Holmes (1634 – 1713) – Jonathan was born in 1634 in Stockport, Lancashire, England, married Sarah Borden on December 20, 1667 in Portsmouth, Rhode Island, and died in 1713 in Newport, Rhode Island;
+ 13. iii. Mary Holmes (1635 – 1690);
14. iv. Lydia Holmes (1637 – Unknown) – Lydia was born in 1637 in Stockport, Lancashire, England and married Major John Bowne in 1662.
15. v. Martha Holmes (1640 – 1682) – Martha was christened on May 3, 1640 in Salem, Essex County, Massachusetts, married John Odlin about 1660 in Boston, Massachusetts, and died about 1682;
16. vi. Samuel Holmes (1641 – 1679) – Samuel was christened on March 20, 1641/42 in Salem, Essex County, Massachusetts, married Alice Stillwell on October 26, 1665, and died in 1679;
17. vii. Obadiah Holmes (1644 – Unknown) – Obadiah was christened on June 9, 1644 in Salem, Essex County, Massachusetts and married Elizabeth Cooke;
18. viii. Joseph Holmes (1646 – Unknown) – Joseph was born in January, 1646 in Salem, Essex County, Massachusetts;

19.	ix.	Hopestill Holmes (1648 – Unknown) – Hopewell was born in 1648 in Salem, Essex County, Massachusetts, married a Mr. Taylor and died sometime before April 1681;
20.	x.	John Holmes (1649 – 1712) – John was born 1649 in Salem, Essex County, Massachusetts, married Francis Holden on December 1, 1671, then married Mary Sayles on October 12, 1680, and died October 12, 1712; and
21.	xi.	Sarah Holmes (1651 – Unknown) – Sarah was born 1651 in Newport, Newport County, Rhode Island.

Third Generation

13. Mary Holmes (1635 – 1690) – See John Browne, page 234.

Descendents of James and Barbara Ann Stichter

First Generation

1. James Adam Stichter (1830 – Unknown) – James Adam Stichter and Ann Marie were both born in Germany around 1830 and married in Bavaria/Germany (possibly Stetten, Germany.) They arrived in New York City, along with James' sister Barbara Ann (born about 1839 in Germany) during the mid-1850's. They located in Brooklyn, where James was employed as a barber. James and Ann Marie would pass away sometime after 1880 and before 1891. Barbara Ann married the widower, George Schlosser, where they lived at 266 Bridge Street in Brooklyn and attended St. Boniface's Church. Barbara passed away on March 3, 1891.

Children of James and Ann Marie Stichter:
+ 2. i. William Adam Stichter (1857 – Unknown);
   3. ii. Barbara K. Stichter (1858 – Unknown);
   4. iii. Anna Maria Stichter (1860 – Unknown) - Anna was born in June 1860, never married. She along with her sister Elizabeth would raise their brother William's children:
   5. iv. Phillip John F. Stichter (1861 – Unknown) – Philip became a barber;
+ 6. v. George A. Stichter (1865 – Unknown);
   7. vi. Elizabeth M. Stichter (1868 – Unknown) – Elizabeth was born in January 1868, never married; and
   8. vii. Barbara K. Stichter (1873 – Unknown).

Second Generation

2. William Adam Stichter (1857 – Unknown) - William Adam Stichter was born in 1857 in Brooklyn, New York, the son of James and Ann Marie Stichter. William married Johanna 'Josie' Kratzenburg, the daughter of Stephen and Gertrude Ann Kratzenburg, about 1879. Josie was born about 1861 in New York City. They had a son, William A., Jr., born March 1880. During the US Census of 1880 they lived at 110 Tillery Street in Brooklyn, New York. Josie died on Wednesday, September 1, 1880 in Brooklyn at the home of her parents at 183 Park Avenue, Brooklyn. It is unknown as to what happened to young William. It is thought that he may have died as an infant in a highchair accident.

William Adam Stichter married Mary Connors Malone, the daughter of Joseph Malone and Margaret Connors, who was born in 1869 in the County of Armagh, Ireland, and came to America in 1884. Together, they would settle in Brooklyn and raise a family. William followed in his father's trade and became a barber. In 1897, William was listed in the Lain Directory for Brooklyn as a machinist, living at 661 Hicks.

On January 28, 1901 at their home at 245 36th Street in Brooklyn, Mary became deathly ill from an appendicitis attack and died. She was buried in Calvary Cemetery on January 30, 1901. It was said that William could not handle the death of Mary and took to drinking. It's thought that he may have died in the Bowery (an area of flophouses, brothels and bars – America's best known skid row), as his children were then raised by his two sisters, Anna Marie and Elizabeth.

Children of William Adam Stichter and Johanna Kratzenburg:
    9.   i.   William A. Stichter, Jr. (1880 – Unknown);

Children of William Adam Stichter and Mary Connors Malone:
+   10.   i.   Joseph T. Stichter (1894 – 1963);
+   11.   ii.   Margaretta Genevieve 'Margie' Stichter (1895 – 1991); and
+   12.   iii. William Benjamin Stichter.

William Adam Stichter   **Mary Connors Malone**

6. George A. Stichter (1865 – Unknown) – George A. Stichter was born in June of 1865 in Brooklyn, New York, the son of James Adam and Ann Marie Stichter. George married Catherine V. (Unknown) around 1895. Catherine was born in 1875. In 1900, George and Catherine lived at 523 Lexington Avenue in Brooklyn. George was a clerk in a store according to the 1880 US Census.

Children of George A. and Catherine V. Stichter:
- 13. i. George A. Stichter, Jr. (1896 – Unknown) – George was born in June, 1896;
- 14. ii. William Stichter (1902 – Unknown);
- 15. iii. Serovica Stichter (1907 – Unknown);
- 16. iv. Frank Stichter (1907 – Unknown);
- 17. v. Agnes Stichter (1908 – Unknown);
- 18. vi. Lillian Stichter (1910 – Unknown);
- 19. vii. Alfred Stichter (1911 – Unknown);
- 20 viii. Catherine Stichter (1915 – Unknown); and
- 21. ix. Delores Stichter (1917 – Unknown).

Third Generation

10. Joseph T. Stichter (1894 – 1963) – Joseph 'Joe' T. Stichter was born in 1894 in Brooklyn, New York, the oldest son of William Adam and Mary Connors (Malone) Stichter. Joseph attended St. James School in Brooklyn, graduated from Manhattan College and later received his Master of Arts degree from Columbia University. He became Brother Baden William and devoted the rest of his life to Manhattan College, where he taught four years in high school and joined the college faculty in 1927. In 1932, he left to teach at De La Salle Academy, Newport, Rhode Island. Later he also taught at La Salle Institute, Troy, New York, and St. Joseph's Collegiate Institute in Buffalo, New York. From 1937 to 1939 he was exchange professor of Spanish at the University of Alberta in Canada. Returning to Manhattan in 1939, he taught in the

BROTHER ABDON WILLIAM, F.S.C.
Born April 13, 1894
Entered Brothers of the Christian Schools
March 18, 1910
Died November 20, 1963

Army Specialized Training Program during World War II. He was made a full professor of Spanish in 1946 and headed the department from then until June of 1963. A heavy pipe and cigar smoker, Joseph contract cancer of the throat and would required several surgeries. He would later die on November 20, 1963, the day before the assassination of President John F. Kennedy, in St. Joseph's Hospital in Yonkers.

11. Margaretta Genevieve Stichter (1895 – 1991) - Margaretta Genevieve Stichter was born August 20, 1895 in Brooklyn, New York and was baptized September 1, 1895 at St. Mary Star of the Sea in Brooklyn. She attended St. James Academy in Brooklyn. She lacked five days of attaining the age of sixteen before entering the Sisters of the Blessed Sacrament on August 15, 1911 in Philadelphia. She took her first vows on February 17, 1914 and final vows on July 25, 1919 at Xavier Prep in New Orleans, Louisiana and became Sister Mary William.

Her missionary journey began in Philadelphia and continued through New Orleans, Rock Castle, St. Louis, Chicago and St. Paul Mission in Marty, South Dakota. Sister taught in the elementary, high and university levels and reached into both the apostolates. Eventually Sister came to specialize in Science - especially Chemistry. She spent thirty-six years in this field at Xavier Prep and Xavier University. She was a firm teacher who was deeply loved. She challenged her students to their full potential, accepting nothing but their best and usually getting it.

Sister's career in the formal classroom came to an end in 1943 when she was given an assignment at St. Paul Mission in counseling. Sister remained at St. Paul for ten years and was then assigned to the same role at Xavier Prep where she achieved like success with her grandmotherly, experienced practical wisdom. In 1970 Sister returned to the Motherhouse in Philadelphia and began a new apostolate, that of the pen. In January 1981, with failing health, Sister was assigned to St. Michael's Hall to receive the care then needed.

Sister passed away on March 5, 1991.

Sister was known to her fellow Sisters as Sister "Bill" and to her older alumni members as "Peaches and Cream", for her lovely skin and honey colored hair.

12. William Joseph (Benjamin) Stichter (1899 – 1967) - William 'Bill' Benjamin Stichter was born January 27, 1899 in Brooklyn, New York the youngest child of William Adam and Mary Connors (Malone) Stichter. Bill, with his brother Joe and his sister Margie were raised by their two aunts, Anna 'Ma' and Elizabeth Stichter at 91 Second Street in Brooklyn, New York. Ma and Elizabeth owned and operated a small grocery store in Brooklyn.

Bill received his employment certificate from the City of New York on June 3, 1914 (height 5'4", weight 132 lbs., gray eyes.) In 1917, he was employed as a telephone operator.

William Joseph Stichter

Bill enlisted in the United States Navy during the World War on May 3, 1917. He was assigned to the Aragon Barracks, No. 614. Reporting for duty at the Navy Yard in Brooklyn, New York, he was soon transferred to Fort Lafayette Section Base #6 where he became an electrician 3rd class. On September 29, 1917, he was transferred to Pelham Base. From there, he spent time at Montauk Naval Air Station in Rhode Island, the US Naval Air Station at Morehead City in North Carolina, the Naval Mine Station at Yorktown, Virginia, and then back to New York City where he was released on May 2, 1921. He was released from active duty with an Honorable Discharge and awarded the Victory Button.

Inez Marie Brumfield

Shortly after his discharge, Bill met Ina while working for the railroad in the city of Cincinnati, Ohio. Inez Marie Brumfield was born February 18, 1901 in Huntington, Wayne County, West Virginia, the daughter of James Cephas and Narcissus (Harvey) Brumfield. Bill and Ina were married on January 18, 1923, by Priest of the Catholic Church, Jas L. Goney, across the Ohio River from Cincinnati, in Newport, Kentucky.

In 1939 the family moved from Cincinnati to Newark, Ohio, where Bill became employed as a salesman.

Bill re-enlisted in the United States Navy during World War II as an Electrician's Mate, Second Class, United States Navy Reserve on March 17, 1944. During his service, Bill went from the Naval Recruiting Station in Cincinnati, Ohio to the U.S. Navy Training Station, Great Lakes, Illinois to U.S. Naval Advance Base, Personnel Depot, San Bruno, California in the LION EIGHT FLIGHT UNIT G-2, to Advance Base, Receiving Barracks, U.S. Naval Base, Port Huenene, California to the U.S. Naval Hospital at San Diego, California where he received a medical discharge on April 20, 1945.

Bill was again, issued an Honorable Discharge and received an Honorable Service Button for his service and an Honorable Discharge Button.

On Bill's return from the Navy, things were not always good at home. While Bill tried to provide for his family, he picked up a drinking problem that would take its effect on all.

Things finally took a turn for the worst, when Ina died from an overdose of sleeping pills on June 27, 1946.

Upon retiring, Bill moved to Hollywood, Florida, where he would become heavily involved in the Catholic Church. This became a favorite vacation site for many of his children and grand-children.

While Bill's youngest daughter and her family were visiting him in Florida over a spring break, Bill passed away of a heart attack in his big chair on April 5, 1967. After a memorial service held in his church in Florida, he was brought back to Ohio and was buried next to Ina in Cedar Hill Cemetery in Newark.

    Children of William Joseph and Inez Marie (Brumfield) Stichter:
+   22.   i.   Anna Marie Stichter (1924 – Living);
+   23.   ii.   Marjorie Elizabeth Stichter (1926 – Living);
     24.   iii.   Josephine Teresa Stichter (1928 – Living); and
+   25.   iv.   William Joseph Stichter, Jr. (1930 – Living).

Fourth Generation

22. Anna Marie Stichter (1924 – Living) - Anna 'Ann' Marie Stichter was born on May 14, 1924 in Newport, Campbell County, Kentucky, the daughter of William Joseph and Inez Marie (Brumfield) Stichter. Ann married Ivan F. Carter, the son of Truman F. and Rebecca Ann (Mitchell) Carter, in Newark, Ohio.

    Children of Ivan F. Carter and Anna Marie Stichter:
     26.   i.   Patricia Ann Carter (Living);
     27.   ii.   Ronald I. Carter (1947 – 1994);
     28.   iii.   Scott D. Carter (1953 – 1997); and
     29.   iv.   Michael Carter (Living).

23. Marjorie Elizabeth Stichter (1926 – Living) - Marjorie 'Margie' Elizabeth Stichter was born on July 5, 1926, the daughter of William Joseph and Inez Marie (Brumfield) Stichter, in Newport, Campbell County, Kentucky. Margie married Wallace 'Wally' C. Lappen, the son of Charles and Frieda Lappen, in September 1947 in Newark, Ohio. Wally was born on August 12, 1923 in Hocking County, Ohio. Wally served in the Navy during World War II. After living in Columbus, Ohio for several years, the family would move to Florida, where Wally would die in February 1973 from a mosquito bite. Margie then married Ernie Fouts. Ernie had also served during World War II in the Navy.

    Children of Wallace Lappen and Marjorie Elizabeth Stichter:
     30.   i.   Mark Lappen (Living);
     31.   ii.   Larry Lappen (Living); and
     32.   iii.   Nancy Lappen (Living).

24. Josephine 'Joy' Teresa Stichter (1928 – Living) - See William Davis Comisford, page 27.

25. William Joseph Stichter, Jr. (1930 – Living) – William 'Bill' Joseph Stichter was born on February 9, 1930 in Cincinnati, Ohio. Bill married and divorced Jeri Trout and Mary Wickersham, and then married Ruth Novak.

    Children of William Joseph Stichter and Jeri Trout:
        33.   i.   William Stichter (Living);
        34.   ii. Michelle Stichter (Living); and
        35.   iii. Jeffery Stichter (Living).

    Children of William Joseph Stichter and Mary Wickersham:
        36.   i.   Sean Stichter (Living).

Descendents of James Brumfield and Patience Sutton

First Generation

1. James Brumfield (1647 – Unknown) - James 'Jake' Brumfield was born about 1647 in England, the son of Thomas Brumfield. Jake arrived in the American Colonies around 1672 as follows:

> "Robert Taliafero,...Rappahonnock Company (VA) ,March 17, 1672/3..grant 639 acres for transport of 14 persons:.... Pestee Sutton, James Bromfield,...Thomas Brumfield, ...etc."

Shortly after arriving in the American Colonies, Jake would marry Patience 'Peshee' Sutton (born about 1651 in England) in Rappahannock County, Virginia. Together, they would settle in Mathews County, Virginia, a small county northeast of Jamestown and Williamsburg.

Children of James Brumfield and Patience Sutton:
- 2. i. Robert Brumfield (1677 – Unknown) - Robert was born in January 1677 in Gloucester, Virginia;
- 3. ii. Martha Brumfield (1680 – Unknown) – Martha was born on September 27, 1680 in Gloucester, Virginia;
- 4. iii. Isabel Brumfield (1682 – Unknown) - Isabel was born on December 20, 1682 in Gloucester, Virginia;
- + 5. iv. James Brumfield II (1685 – 1755);
- 6. v. Ann Brumfield (1687 – Unknown) - Ann was born on June 12, 1687 in Gloucester, Virginia; and
- 7. vi. William Brumfield (1689 – Unknown) – William was born about July 21, 1689 in Gloucester, Virginia.

Second Generation

5. James Brumfield II - (1685 – 1755) - James Brumfield II was born on March 29, 1685 in Gloucester, Virginia, the son of James 'Jake' Brumfield and Patience Sutton. James married Elizabeth Francis Watson about 1716 in Virginia. Elizabeth was born about 1704.

James received 100 acres of patented land in King William County in 1719. He bought 200 acres of land in Amelia County, Virginia in 1739 and also received a patent for an additional 380 acres in 1743. In 1745, he sold 190 acres of this patent land on which his son, William, lived to a Charlie Johnson of Hanover County, Virginia. On December 28, 1749, he sold 190 acres on Saylor Creek in Amelia County, Nottaway Parish between the branches of Dawson Creek on both sided of the road and bounded by Dawson's line to Thomas Tenolds.

Shortly after this in 1749, James and his family moved to Lunenburg County, where he and his son, William, were on the "tithe list."

James would died sometime after 1755.

Children of James Brumfield and Elizabeth Francis Watson:
- 8. i. William Brumfield (1718 – 1799) – William was born in 1718, married Mary about 1744 in Amellia County, Virginia, and died on November 30, 1799 in Charlotte County, Virginia;
- + 9. ii. James Brumfield III (1772 – 1803);
- 10. iii. Robert Brumfield (1724 – 1794) – Robert was born in 1724, married Susannah, then Joannah Berry, and died in October 1794 in Kentucky. Robert was an American Revolutionary War soldier;
- 11. iv. John "John Watson" Brumfield; and
- 12. v. Major Brumfield (1730 – 1815) – Major was born in 1730 in Amelia County, Virginia, married Ann Cobbs on September 25, 1755, and died in 1815.

Third Generation

9. James Brumfield III (1722 – 1803) - James Brumfield III was born around 1722 in Fincastle, Virginia, the son of James Brumfield II and Elizabeth Francis Watson. James married Mary Polly sometime before 1752 in Virginia. Mary Polly was born about 1730 in Fincastle, Virginia.

In 1776, he settled at the mouth of Big Stoney Creek on the David J.L. Snidow place. The following is from *"A History of The Middle New River Settlements and Contiguous Territory, by David E. Johnston (1906)."*

> *Settlements were made by the Bromfields on New River about the mouth of Big Stony Creek, in 1776, and the same year by the Hatfields on said Creek, on what is*

now known as the David J. L. Snidow place, where the Hatfields erected a fort. On Lick Branch, flowing into Big Stony Creek from the north. In the early days, there was a deer lick, and on an occasion it happened that a Bromfield and Hatfield went the same night to watch this lick, neither knowing that the other was there, or to be there. One took the other for a bear moving around in the brush and shot and killed him.

"Outrages and murders were committed by the Indians upon the white settlers in many places, and the people found it necessary to flee to the forts for safety. Along the middle settlements on New River from Barger's Fort on Tom's Creek to Donnally's Fort on Rader's Run, and Cook's Fort on Indian Creek the settlers were kept huddled in the forts during almost the whole summer. At Barger's Fort Captain John Floyd was in command of the military, Christian Snidow at the Snidow and Lybrook Fort at the mouth of Sinking Creek, Captain Thomas Burke at Hatfield's Fort on Big Stony Creek, Captain Michael Woods at Woods' Fort, Captain John Lucas at Fort Field on Culbertson's Bottom. In these Forts or some of them were John Lybrook, John Chapman, Isaac Chapman and others and some of these people were with Captain John Lucas scouting along the New River about Culbertson's Bottom, and stationed at Farley's Fort and Fort Field."

James served during the American Revolutionary War and would pass away in 1803 in Giles County, Virginia.

Children of James and Mary Polly Brumfield:
- 13. i. Humphrey 'Umphrey' Brumfield (1752 – 1846) – Umphrey was born June 22, 1752, married Sarah Sartin, and died in 1846. Participated in the American Revolutionary War, was wounded in the breast from a musket ball. Fought at the Battle of Point Pleasant, October 10, 1774;
- 14. ii. Sarah Brumfield (1757 – Unknown) – Sarah married John Hurt, then Murdock McKenzie;
- 15. iii. Levinia 'Louisa' Brumfield (1759 – 1822) – Louisa married Garland Burgess on March 21, 1787 in Montgomery County, Virginia, and died before July 30, 1822;
- + 16. iv. James Brumfield IV (1760 – 1825);

17. v. Joel Brumfield (1762 – 1822);
18. vi. Celly Brumfield (1764 – Unknown) - Celly married Joseph Tomblin;
19. vii. Micajah Brumfield (1766 – Unknown) – Micajah married Eleanor Hartwell on November 4, 1793 in Montgomery County, Virginia;
20. viii. Fanny Brumfield (1768 – Unknown) - Fanny married Patrick Napier on June 11, 1788 in Montgomery County, Virginia; and
21. ix. Mary Brumfield (1770 – Unknown) - Mary married Thomas Hugh Napier, Jr.

Fourth Generation

16. James Brumfield IV (1760 – 1825) - James Brumfield IV was born around 1760 in Virginia (possibly "Northfork of Bulls Creek, South District of Lunenburg now, Halifax County"), the son of James and Mary Polly Brumfield III. He moved to the mouth of Big Stoney Creek with his parents in 1776 near the Hatfield Fort. James married Susannah and together they had nine children.

James participated in the American Revolutionary War and died about 1825.

Children of James and Susannah Brumfield:
22. i. Susannah Brumfield, married Linsy Crimeans;
23. ii. George Brumfield (1764 – 1815) – George married Anna;
+ 24. iii. William Wirt Brumfield (1786 – 1837);
25. iv. Mary Polly Brumfield (Unknown – 1850) – Mary Polly married Andrew Johnson;
26. v. Sina 'Cincy' Brumfield, married John Jordan;
27. vi. Byrd Brumfield (1789 – 1840) - Byrd married Elenor Stith, then Elizabeth Hatton;
28. vii. Dicy Brumfield (Unknown – 1838) - Dicy married Roland Bias in 1813 in Cabell County, Western Virginia;
29. viii. Sarah 'Sally' Brumfield, married Walker J. L. Sanford; and
30. ix. Ann Brumfield, married William Hatfield on April 2, 1793 in Montgomery County, Virginia.

Fifth Generation

24. William Wirt Brumfield (1785 – 1833) - William Wirt Brumfield was born on about 1785 on Stoney Creek, Montgomery County, Virginia, the son of James and Susannah Brumfield IV. William married Eleanor Hoover, the daughter of Thomas Hoover and Peggy O'Byran. Eleanor was born about 1786.

In the *"History of Buffalo Creek Community"* prepared in 1925, *"...The fertility of the soil and abundance of game soon attracted the attention of settlers. So far as is known the first settler was James McKeand. Then came the Dukes, the Isaacs, the Haneys, the Plymales, the Maloneys, the Brumfields, and Staleys. They built their houses of logs, covered them with boards split from the trunks of trees. A short chimney built of sticks and clay took up the greater portion of one end of the one room. The bare ground in some cases formed the floor. The furniture was crude and rough..."*

By 1809, William had moved his family to a farm on Wolf Creek in Cabell County, Western Virginia. It was said that during the War of 1812, *"Captain William Brumfield raised a Cavalry Company in this county. We had to raise men and supplies, and besides we were assessed $1,540.00. This Company had a hard time, as many of these brave volunteers died in a plague in Norfolk."*

William served as a Justice of the Peace in 1828. William passed away in November 1833 on Wolf Creek, Cabell County, Western Virginia.

Children of William Wirt Brumfield and Eleanor Hoover:
- 31. i. John Humphrey Brumfield (1803 – 1854) – John was born on September 25, 1803 in Rockingham County, Virginia, married Rachel Haskins on July 28, 1823 in Lawrence County, Ohio, and died on October 8, 1854 in District 32, Lincoln County, Western Virginia;
- 32. ii. Susan Brumfield (1809 – Unknown) – Susan was born on January 3, 1809, married John Hatfield on February 27, 1823 in Cabell County, Western Virginia, and died in Kanawha County, Western Virginia;
- 33. iii. Henderson P. Brumfield (1808 – 1844) – Henderson married Malinda Hatton;
- + 34. iv. Allen Trig Brumfield (1812 – 1873);
- 35. v. Bostic Brumfield (1814 – Unknown) - Bostic married Ann Brumfield;
- + 36. vi. Jordan (or Gordon) P. Brumfield (1816 – Unknown);
- + 37. vii. Margaret Ann 'Peggy' Brumfield (1818 – Unknown);
- + 38. viii. Milton D. Brumfield (1821 – Unknown);

39. ix. Catherine Ann Brumfield (1824 – 1869) – Catherine was born on October 22, 1824, married William Hinds on March 8, 1842, died on January 14, 1869 in Lincoln County, Missouri, and is buried in Bryant's Creek Cemetery; and
+ 40. x. William Wirt Brumfield, Jr. (1828 – Unknown).

Sixth Generation

34. Allen Trig Brumfield (1812 – 1873) - Allen Trig Brumfield was born on January 8, 1812 on Wolf Creek, Cabell County, Virginia, the son of William Wirt Brumfield and Eleanor Hoover. William first married Elizabeth Nester on April 25, 1843 in Lawrence County, Kentucky. She died shortly after they were married and William then married Nancy Hanks Adkins, the daughter of Edward Adkins and Nancy Jane Bartram, about 1846. Nancy was born on September 30, 1823 in Cabell County, Western Virginia. She had been married to John Hansford Watts, son of James Watts, about 1837 Catlettsburg, Greenup County (now Boyd County), Kentucky. A farmer, Allen acquired 75 acres of land on Guyandotte River, beginning and continuing on the river bank on the southeast side about 120 poles below Big Ugly Creek, Grant No. 68, on October 30, 1819. He acquired 50 acres of land on Laurel Creek on the left-hand fork of Twelve Pole, Grant No. 98, on March 1, 1847, and another 30 acres (Grant No. 100) on March 31 1848.

Allen would pass away on January 28, 1873, while Nancy did not pass away until May, 13, 1904. They are both buried in Brumfield Cemetery in Shoals, Wayne County, West Virginia, located off Lower Newcomb Creek Road.

Children of Allen Trig Brumfield and Elizabeth Nestor:
41. i. Catherine Ann Brumfield (1845 – Unknown) – Catherine was born on February 17, 1845 in Wayne County, Western Virginia. She married Abraham Johnson. Abraham was in the Union Army, and would die at an early age. Catherine then married James S. Ward on November 10, 1866 in Wayne County, and later passed away on August 8, 1890 and buried in Mt. Vernon Cemetery;

Children of Allen Trig Brumfield and Nancy Hanks Adkins:
+ 42. i. Milton D. Brumfield (1847 – 1888);
43. ii. Bostic 'Uncle Boss' C. Brumfield (1848 – 1932) – Bostic was born on August 13, 1848 in Wayne County, Western Virginia, married Scintha Paralee Davis, then Martha Johnson, and died on August 12, 1932;

44. iii. Christopher Columbus Brumfield (1850 – 1920) – Columbus was born in July 1850 in Wayne County, Western Virginia, married Adeline Luther, then Frances Selena F. Shingleton on June 18, 1881, and died on March 18, 1920 in Wayne County, West Virginia;

45. iv. Lydia Brumfield (1851 – Unknown) – Lydia married Charles Staten;

46. v. Commodore P. Brumfield (1852 – 1926) – Commodore was born about 1852 in Wayne County, Western Virginia, married Polly Ann Adkins on March 11, 1875, and died in 1926;

47. vi. Margaret Ellen Brumfield (1854 – Unknown) – Margaret was born on April 3, 1854 in Wayne County, Western Virginia. She married Stephen Rowe on May 13, 1883 in Wayne County;

48. vii. Henry Clay Brumfield (1856 – 1926) Henry was born on March 3, 1856 in Wayne County, Western Virginia, married Ceres Bowen, then married Sarah Virginia Rowe on October 13, 1887, and died on May 12, 1926 in Wayne County, West Virginia;

49. viii. Louisa Brumfield (1862 – Unknown) – Louisa was born in August 1862 in Cabell County, Western Virginia and married Wiley Hale on March 19, 1882 in Wayne County;

50. ix. George B. Brumfield (1864 – 1946) – George was born about 1864 in Wayne County, West Virginia, married Sarah Roya Thacker on November 20, 1884 in Wayne County, West Virginia, and died on December 16, 1946; and

51. x. Angeline Brumfield (1868 – Unknown) – Angeline was born on June 24, 1868 in West Virginia. She married James T. Birdie Carroll on December 5, 1889 in Wayne County. She passed away on December 2, 1963 and is buried in the Brumfield Cemetery.

MRS. ANGELINE BRUMFIELD CARROLL
Her Grandparents Were Early Settlers Here

36. Jordan (or Gordon) P. Brumfield (1816 – Unknown) – Gordon P. Brumfield was born in 1816, the son of William Wirt Brumfield and Eleanor Hoover. Gordon married Emily Isabee about 1836. Gordan was on the Muster Roll of Captain Elisha McComas, Company C, which participated in the Mexican War in 1847. Gordon headed west to Cooper County, Missouri.

Children of Gordon P. Brumfield and Emily Isabee:
- 52. i. Caroline Brumfield (1836 – Unknown);
- 53. ii. Elenor Brumfield (1837 – Unknown);
- 54. iii. Mary Ann Brumfield (1839 – Unknown);
- 55. iv. William H. Brumfield (1840 – Unknown); and
- 56. v. Susan M. Brumfield (1842 – Unknown);

37. Margaret Ann Brumfield (1818 – Unknown) – Margaret was born in 1818, the daughter of William Wirt Brumfield and Eleanor Hoover. Margaret married Eli Ferinand Harmon on March 16, 1837 and they settled in Cabell and later Putnam County, Western Virginia. Margaret died sometime between 1845 and 1850;

Children of Eli Ferinand Harmon and Margaret Ann Brumfield:
- 57. i. Elizabeth Harmon (1840 – Unknown) – Elizabeth married James W. Burgess on May 1, 1860 in Wayne County, Western Virginia; and
- 58. ii. William H. Harmon (1842 – Unknown) – William married Mary Holstein in 1863 in Wayne County, Western Virginia.

38. Milton D. Brumfield (1821 – Unknown) – Milton D. Brumfield was born in 1821, the son of William Wirt Brumfield and Eleanor Hoover. Milton married Clarissa Hinds, the daughter of Elias and Mary Polly (Bailey) Hinds, on September 20, 1849. Clarissa passed away on August 18, 1866, and then Milton would marry Mary Etta Thacker, the daughter of Joseph and Jane (Rutherford) Thacker. Mary Etta was born about 1843 in Virginia.

Children of Milton D. Brumfield and Clarissa Hinds:
- 59. i. Anthony Brumfield (1846 – Unknown);
- 60. ii. Emaline Brumfield (1848 – Unknown);
- 61. iii. Malinda Brumfield (1851 – Unknown);
- 62. iv. Theadore Brumfield (1853 – Unknown);
- 63. v. Lucinda Brumfield (1855 – Unknown);
- 64. vi. William Brumfield (1859 – Unknown);
- 65. i. Milton J. Brumfield (1861 – Unknown); and
- 66. ii. Euella Brumfield (1865 – Unknown)

Children of Milton D. Brumfield and Mary Etta Thacker:
- 67. i. John J. Brumfield (1867 – Unknown) – John was born on October 10, 1867 and would marry Catherine Hutchinson;
- 68. ii. Joanna Brumfield (1868 – Unknown);
- 69. iii. Nathanel Brumfield (1871 – Unknown); and
- 70. iv. Morgan G. Brumfield (1873 – Unknown).

40.   William Wirt Brumfield, Jr. (1828 – Unknown) – William Wirt Brumfield, Jr. was born in 1828 in Virginia, the son of William Wirt Brumfield and Eleanor Hoover. William married Clerissa, and then Lucinda Brumfield.

    Children of William Wirt Brumfield, Jr. and Lucinda Brumfield:
      71.   i.   Mary E. Brumfield (1856 – Unknown);
      72.   ii.   Maggie E. Brumfield (1861 – Unknown);
      73.   iii. Peneton H. Brumfield (1864 – Unknown);
      74.   iv. Oliver C. Brumfield (1869 – Unknown); and
      75.   v.   Latimer R. Brumfield (1872 – Unknown).

Seventh Generation

42.   Milton D. Brumfield (1847 – 1888) - Milton D. Brumfield was born on January 1, 1847 in Wayne County, Western Virginia, the son of Allen T. Brumfield and Nancy Hanks Adkins.   Milton married Clarissa A. Staley on March 9, 1876 in Wayne County, West Virginia, the daughter of Joseph and Harriett (Hinds) Staley. Clarissa was born about 1858 in Western Virginia. Together Milton and Clarissa would have a son.

Milton was a farmer in Wayne County and would pass away on July 10, 1888 in Wayne County, West Virginia.   Clarissa then married William Napier, the son of Walter Napier and Vienna Watts, on September 14, 1889 in Wayne County, West Virginia

    Children of Milton D. Brumfield and Clarissa Staley:
 +   76.   i.   James Cephas Brumfield (1878 – Unknown).

Eighth Generation

76.   James Cephas Brumfield (1878 – Unknown) - James (called "Joecephas") Cephas Brumfield was born in April 1878 in Union Twp, Wayne County, West Virginia, the son of Milton D. Brumfield and Clarissa Staley. Joecephas married Cora Napier on February 24, 1897 in Wayne County, West Virginia. Cora may have died shortly after they were married, as Joecephas would marry Narcissus Harvey sometime around 1898. Narcissus (called "Sissie") was born June 6, 1877 in Ohio, the daughter of Thomas and Mary Harvey.

The family moved to Indiana and then to Ohio, where they settled in Cincinnati. Joecephas was a big man, standing over six feet tall, while Sissie was less than five feet tall. Joecephas worked as a night watchman. Sometime before 1920, Joecephas wanted a divorce, but Sissie would not give it to him. Joecephas then lived with Julia Staley (b. 1872) in Cincinnati, Ohio. He would use her last name – Joecephas Staley.

Sissie was living at Avon Rest Home when she passed away on April 18, 1959 in Cincinnati, Hamilton County, Ohio and was buried in Greenlawn Cemetery in Milford, Ohio.

Children of James Cephas Brumfield and Narcissus Harvey:
- 77. i. Mary Brumfield (1898 – Unknown) - Mary was born in January 1898 in Huntington, Cabell County, West Virginia and died before 1910;
+ 78. ii. Inez Marie Brumfield (1901 – 1946) - Inez 'Ina" was born February 18, 1901 in Wayne County, West Virginia, married William J. Stichter on January 18, 1923 in Newport, Campbell County, Kentucky, and died on June 27, 1946 in Newark, Licking County, Ohio;
- 79. iii. Ona Brumfield (1903 – 1952) - Ona was born February 4, 1903 in Huntington, Cabell County, West Virginia, died on April 7, 1952, and buried in Greenlawn Cemetery in Milford, Ohio;
- 80. iv. Charles Brumfield (1905 – Unknown) – Charles was born about 1905 in Huntington, Cabell County, Ohio, died sometime before 1920, supposedly in a house fire in Indiana;
- 81. v. Clyde Brumfield (1908 – 1971) – Clyde was born on July 23, 1908 in Huntington, Cabell County, West Virginia, died on June 6, 1971 in Cincinnati, Hamilton County, Ohio, and buried in Greenlawn Cemetery, Milford, Ohio;
- 82. vi. Herman Brumfield, a twin (1911 - 1956) – Herman was born on March 7, 1911 in Huntington, Cabell County, West Virginia, married Nana, and died on November 21, 1956 in Cincinnati, Hamilton County, Ohio, and buried in Greenlawn Cemetery, Milford, Ohio;
- 83. vii. Thurman A. Brumfield, twin (1911 - 2000) – Thurman was born on March 7, 1911 in Huntington, Cabell County, West Virginia, married Joyce Cook, and died on December 9, 2000 in Batavia, Clermont County, Ohio, and buried in Greenlawn Cemetery, Milford, Ohio;

Back Row: Nan Brumfield, Dovalee Brumfield, Herman Brumfield, Nan Brumfield, Ina Brumfield, Narcissus Broomfield, William Stichter, and Inez Stichter; Front Row: Billy Stichter, Milton Brumfield, Marjorie Stichter, Ann Stichter, Georgie Brumfield, and Josephine Stichter.

Eight Generation

78.   Inez Marie Brumfield (1901 – 1946) – See William Joseph Stichter, page 249.

Descendents of William V. Atkinson and Elizabeth Parker

First Generation

1. William V. Atkinson/Adkins (1689-1774) - William V. Atkinson/Adkins was born on March 28, 1689 in Charles City, Henrico County, Virginia. William married Elizabeth Parker, the daughter of Richard and Elizabeth Parker, Jr., on January 17, 1716 in St. James Episcopal Church outside of Richmond in Henrico County, Virginia. Elizabeth was born about 1695 in Charles City, Henrico County, Virginia. In the first year of their marriage, Elizabeth's father gave her 150 acres in Henrico Parrish, stating in the deed *"for love and affection to my daughter Elizabeth, wife of William Atkinson"*.

William and Elizabeth lived on Machumps Creek on the Savannah River. Elizabeth passed away about 1735 in Goochland County, Virginia, possibly during giving child birth. In 1740, William moved westward over the Blue Ridge Mountains (on the very edge of the frontier) where he would live in the Snow Creek District on the Harping and Story Creeks on the Pigg River. Here, William became a land owner and farmer, then changed occupations by becoming a mill operator. Mill operating became a family business.

William passed away around 1774.

Children of William V. Atkinson and Elizabeth Parker:
- 2. i. Richard Adkins (1717 – Unknown) – Richard was born in 1717 in Henrico County, Virginia and married Mary Polly Adkins;
- 3. ii. Parker V. Adkins (1720 – 1792) – Parker was born in 1720 in Machumps Creek, Henrico, Virginia, married Mary "Polly" Fry in 1754 in Halifax County, Virginia, and died in 1792 in Montgomery County, Virginia;
- 4. iii. William V. Adkins, Jr. (1721 – 1784) – William was born about 1721 in Machumps Creek, Henrico County, Virginia, married Lydia Owens about 1845, and died on March 15, 1784 in Pittsylvania County, Virginia. William served under Col. Preston at the Battle of Point Pleasant;
- 5. iv. Joseph Adkins (1723 – Unknown) – Joseph was born about 1723 in Goochland County, Virginia, married Sarah on December 23, 1783 in Montgomery County, Virginia, and died between 1789 and 1810;

6.   v.   Jacob Adkins (1725 – 1791) – Jacob was born in 1725 in Goochland County, Virginia, married Judah in 1759 in Halifax County, Virginia, and died on 1791 in Franklin County, Virginia;
  7.   vi.   Sherwood 'Sherrod' Adkins (1728 – 1780) – Sherrod was born in 1728 in Goochland County, Virginia and died about 1780;
  8.   vii. Henry Adkins (1730 – Unknown) – Henry was born in 1730 in Goochland County, Virginia and married Rachel Hutchins on January 20, 1756 in Goochland County, Virginia;
  9.   viii. Elizabeth Ann Adkins (1732 – Unknown) – Elizabeth was born about 1732 in Henrico County, Virginia, married Zachariah Doss before 1754, and died before 1780; and
+ 10. ix.   Mary Adkins (1735 – 1820).

Second Generation

10. Mary Adkins (1735 – 1820) - Mary Adkins was born on October 12, 1735 in Richland, Goochland County, Virginia, the daughter of William V. Atkinson/Adkins and Elizabeth Parker. Mary first married Thomas J. Stephens, who passed away shortly after their marriage. Jacob Harley (known as the "Earl of Oxford"), the son of the third Earl of Oxford, a Royalist, by a common law marriage lived with Mary and together they had several children.

Jacob was sent to America as a tax collector for the Crown. It was said that Mary's brothers did not like him and fought with him. When the American Revolutionary War broke out with England, Jacob was called back to England and did not take Mary and their children with him. He never returned to America. When he died, he left some money for Mary and the children, but they would have had to go to England and present a claim to receive it. They never did. Mary raised her children alone and they all took her name of "Adkins".

Mary died about 1820 in Cabell County, Western Virginia and is buried in an unmarked gave on Beech Fork at the mouth of Bowen's Creek.

Children on Jacob Harley and Mary Adkins:
  11.   i.   David Adkins (1754 – Unknown) – David was born in 1754 in Snow District, Lunenberg, Virginia, married Judith on May 27, 184 in Henry County, Virginia, then Sylvaneous Adkins on May 19, 1807, and died in Louisa, Lawrence County, Kentucky;

12.	ii.	Mary Adkins (1756 – 1778) – Mary was born in 1756 in Halifax County, Virginia and died in 1778 in Henry County, Virginia;
13.	iii.	John Adkins (1758 – Unknown) – John was born about 1758 in Halifax County, Virginia;
14.	iv.	Christina Adkins (1759 – 1822) – Christina was born on January 5, 1759 in Halifax County, Virginia. married James Drake on October 24, 1793, then Sherrod B. Adkins on February 11, 1798, and died in 1822 in Beech Fork, Cabell County, Western Virginia;
15.	v.	Jacob Oxford Adkins (1761 – 1857) – Jacob was born about 1761 in Snow Creek, Halifax County, Virginia, married Phoebe Bradshaw on March 28, 1791 in Franklin County, Virginia, and died September 20, 1857 in Wayne County, Western Virginia;
+ 16.	vi.	Sherrod Adkins, Sr. (1765 – 1854); and
17.	vii.	Nancy Adkins (1767 – 1846) – Nancy was born about 1767 in Pittsylvania County, Virginia, married Littleberry Adkins on May 29, 1790 in Franklin County, Virginia, and died on January 18, 1846 in Lick Creek, Summers County, Western Virginia.

Third Generation

16. Sherrod Adkins, Sr. (1765 – 1854) - Sherrod Adkins, Sr. was born on March 2, 1765 in Story Creek, Halifax County, Virginia, the son of the Earl of Oxford and Mary Adkins. Sherrod married Sarah O. "Sally" Lucas, the daughter of Charles Lucas and Anne Kathleen Kaewood, on October 18, 1793 in Sinking Creek, Montgomery County, Virginia. Sarah was born in 1771 in Fincastle County, Virginia.

Sherrod would pass away on June 12, 1854 in Wayne County, Western Virginia.

Children of Sherrod Adkins, Sr. and Sarah O. Lucas.:

18.	i.	Nancy Anna Adkins (1794 – 1853) – Nancy was born about 1794 in Blueston River, Montgomery County, Virginia, married Jesse Adkins on January 18, 1813 in Cabell County, Western Virginia, and died on March 10, 1853 in Wayne County, Western Virginia;
19.	ii.	John R. Adkins (1796 – Unknown) – John was born about 1796 in Montgomery County, Virginia and married on June 3, 1819 in Cabell County, Western Virginia;
20.	iii.	Rebecca Adkins (1800 – 1874) – Rebecca was born on October 29, 1800 in Montgomery County, Western Virginia, married William Bartram, and died on August 31, 1874 in Wayne County, West Virginia;

+	21.	iv.	Edward Adkins (1803 – 1833);
	22.	v.	Delphia Adkins (1805 – Unknown) – Delphia was born 1805 in Montgomery County, Virginia, married Littleberry Adkins, Jr. in 1822 in Lawrence County, Kentucky;
	23.	vi.	Elizabeth Adkins (1808 – Unknown) – Elizabeth was born about 1808 and married Govey "Grover" Adkins on December 20, 1825 in Greenbrier County, Western Virginia;
	24.	vii.	Sherrod Adkins, Jr. (1810 – Unknown) – Sherrod was born on March 2, 1810 in Cabell County, Western Virginia; and
	25.	viii.	Margaret 'Peggy' Adkins (1812 – Unknown) – Peggy was born about 1812 in Cabell County, Western Virginia and married George Adkins on July 23, 1829 in Cabell County, Western Virginia.

Fourth Generation

21. Edward Adkins (1803 – 1833) - Edward Adkins was born on March 15, 1803 in Montgomery County, Virginia, the son of Sherrod Adkins, Sr. and Sarah O. Lucas. Edward married Nancy Jane "Gincy" Bartram, the daughter of John P. and Mary Polly (Davis) Bartram. Nancy was born in 1804 in Cabell County, Western Virginia.

Edward would pass away on March 24, 1833 in Beech Fork, Wayne County, Western Virginia and buried in Bloss Cemetery. Nancy then married James Cole.

Children of Edward Adkins and Nancy Jane Bartram:

+	26.	i.	Nancy Hanks Adkins (1821 – 1904) – Nancy was born on September 30, 1821 in Cabell County, Western Virginia, married John Hansford Watts about 1846, then Allen Trig Brumfield, and died May 13, 1904 on Wolf Creek, Wayne County, West Virginia;
	27.	ii.	Margaret 'Peggy' Adkins (1823 – Unknown) – Peggy was born about 1823 in Cabell County, Western Virginia;
	28.	iii.	Attison Adkins (1826 – Unknown) – Attison was born in December 1826 in Cabell County, Western Virginia and married Martha Patsy Asbury about 1845 in Wayne County, Western Virginia;
	29.	iv.	Mary Elizabeth 'Polly' Adkins (1829 – Unknown) – Polly was born about 1829 in Cabell County, Western Virginia;
	30.	v.	Harvey Adkins (1831 – Unknown) – Harvey was born on October 17, 1831 in Cabell County, Western Virginia and married Elizabeth "Betsy" Asbury about 1847; and
	31.	vi.	Calvery Adkins (1832 – Unknown) – Calvery was born on December 5, 1832 in Cabell County, Western Virginia and married Eliza.

Children of James Cole and Nancy Jane Adkins:
- 32. i. John Henderson Cole (1837 – 1864) – John was born on June 2, 1837 in Cabell County, Western Virginia, married Martha Fry, and died on July 15, 1864;
- 33. ii. Hawkins Cole (1840 – Unknown);
- 34. iii. George W. Cole (1842 – Unknown); and
- 35. iv. Elisha Cole (1843 – Unknown).

Fifth Generation

26. Nancy Hanks Adkins (1821 – 1904) – See Allen Trig Brumfield, page 258.

Descendents of Dr. Richard Parker and Mary Perkins

First Generation

1. Dr. Richard Parker (1630 – 1679) - Richard Parker was christened on November 29, 1630 at Warlegon in England, the son of James Parker and Katherine Buller, a knight and gentleman. Their home was at Browlshome Hall in Yorkshire England. The Buller family was an ancient and respectable family seated in Cornwall, dating back to the reign of Elizabeth (1558-1603). Katherine was a descendant of Geoffrey Plantagent. Richard's grand-father, William Parker, was Arch Deacon of Blisland, whose lineage is traced back to Giles Parker through his son, Edmund Parker, who died 1547, and to Monk William Le Parker, seated at Lancashire, England. William Le Parker received land 1395 and was styled "De Monk Hall in Extwistle".

Rowland Parker, a younger son of James, left an account of the family written on September 1, 1673. The account was found in an old Common Place Book now at Browsholme, the home of the Parker family in Yorkshire. He stated: *"Richard, ye 9th, Dr. of Physick went to Virginy, married a Londoner and had issue six children, liveth upon Saint James River, in ye Uplands of Virginy, hath been High Sheriff of sd County."*

English law dictated that the eldest son was to inherit the estate of the father, so Richard could expect little from his father. Thus, he became a doctor and left for the American Colonies to make his fortune as a landowner and Doctor. On July 27, 1652 Capt. Francis Morgan was granted a patent of land in Gloucester County, Virginia. This patent had ten headrights, and among these was Richard Parker. Richard was in Charles City County by 1678. With the patent, there was a stipulation that you must put up a small cabin (called seating) put a small stock of cattle to range in the woods for 12 months, and you had to remain in Virginia for three years. In addition, you also had to plant at least an acre of corn or tobacco.

Richard married Mary Perkins (the "Londoner" as Rowland put it), the widow of Nicholas Perkins, on July 31, 1656 in Charles City County. Mary had one son by Nicholas, Nicholas, Jr., born in 1647 in London, England and Nicholas had two other children from a previous marriage, Lydia and Elizabeth. Richard and his new family lived on his plantation of 110 acres at "Diggs His Hundred" until they move to Henrico County.

Richard practiced as a doctor in Charles City County, Virginia:

> "*April 21, 1656 Richard Parker was ordered to perfect the cure of the legge of John Matthew that he had treated for two years.*"

> "*June 22, 1656 William Fisher, orphan of John, indentured himself to Richard Parker, Cheurgeon, to learn the profession. This indenture was to last two years and ten months.*"

August 2, 1659, Dr. Parker leased or sold his 110 acre plantation at Westover to John Beauchamp, Merchant. In 1660, Dr. Richard Parker was still living in Charles City County, as he was serving as Sheriff.

By 1664, Richard and his family had moved to Henrico County, Virginia. In October of 1664, Dr. Parker was called back to Charles City County to serve as a juror, along with five others from Henrico County. To be a juror, one had to be worth at least 100 pounds sterling. In this case, the jurors had to "review" the body of George Bullington who had fallen from a horse and dragged to his death in the area of Charles City County.

On October 29, 1669, he was granted a patent for 350 acres of land on North Side of James River at the head of Four Mile Creek. This patent was near "Upland Brook."

Dr. Richard Parker died sometime between 1679 and 1682.

Children of Dr. Richard Parker and Mary Perkins:
2. i. Mary Parker, who married John Cannon;
3. ii. Susan Parker, who married Thomas Holmes and then Robert Smith;
+ 4. iii. Richard Parker, Jr. (1659 – 1726);
5. iv. Elizabeth Parker, who married John Crissey;
6. v. Thomas Parker (1666 – Unknown) – Thomas married Mary; and
7. vi. William Parker, who married Lucy Turner.

Second Generation

4. Richard Parker, Jr. (1659 – 1726) - Richard Parker was born about 1659 or 1660 in Charles City County, Virginia, the son of Dr. Richard and Mary Parker. He settled on a farm on the James River at the head of Four Mile Creek in the Henrico Parrish. Richard was a planter. He married Elizabeth "Mitha" Ballard and together they had four children. After the death of Elizabeth, he then married Myra.

Richard died sometime between February 27, 1726 (date of his will) and March 6, 1726, the date his will was recorded.

Children of Richard and Elizabeth Parker:
- 8.   i.   Ann Parker, who married James Daniel;
- + 9.   ii.   Elizabeth Parker (1695 – Unknown);
- 10.   iii.   Mary Parker, who married Lewis Jinkins; and
- 11.   iv.   Richard Parker.

Third Generation

9. Elizabeth Parker (1695 – Unknown) – See William V. Atkinson, page 265.

Descendents of William Lucas and Ann Scarbouch

First Generation

1. William Lucas (1630 – 1659) - William Lucas was born around 1630. Young William's father, William Lucas of Cornwall, England, was a merchant and was the owner of record in 1628 for the sailing ship *"Supply."* The *Supply* had sailed to the American Colonies (Virginia) in 1625 and 1626. It is likely that young William was born in the American Colonies. On August 16, 1644, provision was made by the Virginia Council for William Lucas and his family. William was granted 800 acres in Lower Norfolk County in 1647, after his marriage to the widow of Caesaar Hugget.

   Young William married Ann Scarbouch and together they had the three (3) children. William would die in 1659.

   Children of William Lucas and Ann Scarbouch:
   + 2. i. William Lucas (1654 – 1717);
     3. ii. A daughter, who married Abraham Evans; and
     4. iii. A daughter, who married John Harris

Second Generation

2. William Lucas (1654 – 1717) - William Lucas was born in 1654 in Surry County, Virginia, the son of William and Ann (Scarbouch) Lucas. William married Grace Beckwith, the daughter of Marmaduke Beckwith and Maudlin Creed of Surry County, Virginia. William acquired 30 acres in Surry County, Virginia 1680 from Ann Dennis. Together William and Grace would have seven (7) children.

   William made his will on October 1, 1716 in Surry Co, Virginia naming his wife and children. He died sometime in 1717 in Surry County, Virginia.

Children of William Lucas and Grace Beckwith:
+ 5. i. William Lucas (1688 – 1739);
  6. ii. Ann Lucas;
  7. iii. Elizabeth Lucas;
  8. iv. Grace Lucas;
  9. v. Hannah Lucas;
  10. vi. Mary Lucas; and
  11. vii. Charles Lucas.

Third Generation

5. William Lucas (1688 – 1739) - William Lucas was born in 1688, the son of William and Grace (Beckwith) Lucas. William married Martha and together they would have five (5) children.

On July 5, 1738, William bought 100 acres of land on the south side of Meherrin River in Brunswick County, Virginia, from Richard Smith.

William made his will in 1739 mentioning his wife Martha and his five sons by name, and his lands at Meherrin River, Little Creek and Miles Creek. William would die sometime in 1739 in Brunswick County, Virginia.

Children of William and Martha Lucas:
+ 12. i. Charles Lucas (1719 – 1793);
  13. ii. Nathaniel Lucas;
  14. iii. James Lucas;
  15. iv. Edmund Lucas; and
  16. v. Fredrick Lucas.

Fourth Generation

12. Charles Lucas (1719 – 1793) - Charles Lucas was born on December 25, 1719 in Spotsylvania County, Virginia, the son of William and Martha Lucas. Charles married Ann Kathleen Kaewood sometime prior to 1847. Ann Kathleen was born in New York about 1723.

Charles served during the Revolutionary War as a soldier for Giles County. Charles would serve as the constable in the Sinking Creek neighborhood. He passed away on November 18, 1793 in Sinking Creek, Giles County, Virginia.

Children of Charles Lucas and Ann Kathleen Kaewood:

17. i. Charles Lucas, Jr.(1747 – 1787) – Charles was born about 1747 in Sinking Creek, Augusta County, Virginia, married Catherine Fry, then Ester Barnett, and died in 1787 Greensville, Virginia. Charles was an American Revolutionary War Soldier from Giles County, Virginia. Charles, along with his brothers John and William would serve under Col. Preston at the Battle of Point Pleasant;

18. ii. Parker Lucas (1748 – 1835) – Parker was born in 1748 in Sinking Creek, August County, Virginia, married Margaret E. Price about 1778 in Montgomery County, Virginia, and died on March 27, 1835. Parker was an American Revolutionary War Soldier from Giles County, Virginia;

19. iii. John Lucas (1749 – 1836) – John was born on July 15, 1749 in Sinking Creek, August County, Virginia, married Mary Elizabeth Wilson on February 15, 1775 in Sinking Creek, Montgomery County, Virginia, and died on August 8, 1836 in Montgomery County, Virginia. John was a Captain in the American Revolutionary War from Giles County, Virginia;

20. iv. William Lucas (1749 – 1834) – William was born on July 15, 1749 in Sinking Creek, Augusta County, Virginia, married Elizabeth Price on October 2, 1782 in Montgomery County, Virginia, and died in 1834 in Cabell County, Western Virginia. William was a Captain in the American Revolutionary War from Giles County, Virginia;

21. v. George Lucas (1750 – Unknown) – George was born about 1750 in Sinking Creek, Augusta County, Virginia;

22. vi. Mary Lucas (1751 – Unknown) – Mary was born about 1751 in Sinking Creek, Augusta County, Virginia and married John Cline on June 5, 1798;

23. vii. David Lucas (1754 – Unknown) – David was born about 1754 in Sinking Creek, Augusta County, Virginia and married Mary Hale on November 7, 1809 in Montgomery County, Virginia;

24. viii. Randolph 'Ralph' Lucas (1770 – 1842) - Ralph was born about 1770 in Sinking Creek, Augusta County, Virginia, married Patience Williams on December 25, 1709 in Montgomery County, Virginia, and died in 1842 in Giles County, Virginia; and

+ 25. ix. Sarah O. 'Sally' Lucas (1771 – Unknown).

Fifth Generation

25. Sarah O. 'Sally' Lucas (1771 – Unknown) – See Sherrod Adkins, Sr., page 267.

Descendents of Stephen Bartram and Elizabeth Swearingen

First Generation

1. Stephen Bartram (1752 – 1821) - Stephen was born about 1752 in Edinburgh, Scotland, where as Elizabeth was born about 1756 in Dublin, Ireland, the daughter of Van Swearingen and Lucy Davis, who settled in Bath County, Virginia. They were married in Dublin, Ireland. Being a Protestant Preacher, he was not well received in Ireland and thus, moved on to the American Colonies. He arrived around the time of the American Revolutionary War and became a Revolutionary Soldier. He was supposeably at Valley Forge with George Washington's Army. Serving 7 years and 2 months, after leaving the army he had trouble finding his wife. He finally found her living near Philadelphia. They then settled near Appomattox, Virginia and started their family.

It was said *"that Betty Swangran Bartram could shoot like a trooper, and wore a bright red hunting shirt. She is said to have shot a raven on the wing."* She died in 1794 in Montgomery County, Virginia. Stephen then married Jane Peery.

Stephen owned land on the Maiden Spring Fork of the Clinch River sometime prior to 1804. During frequent Indian attacks, Stephen's family would have taken refuge in what became the historical Maiden Spring Fort, erected by Lt Rees Bowen. Stephen died on May 1, 1821 in Cabell County, Western Virginia

Children of Stephen Bartram and Elizabeth Swearingen:
+ 2.   i.   John P. Bartram (1784 – 1845);
   3.   ii.   David Bartram (1786 – 1864) – David was born October 28, 1786 in Appomattox, Virginia, married Rebecca Blue on July 19, 1810 in Cabell County, Western Virginia, then married Lucy Sperry on March 27, 1825 in Lawrence County, Kentucky, and died on April 28, 1864 in Catlettsburg, Boyd County, Kentucky;
   4.   iii.   Mary Bartram (1792 – 1820) – Mary was born about 1792 in Wythe County, Virginia and died before 1820; and
   5.   iv.   James P. Bartram (1794 – 1875) - James was born about 1794, married Delilah Wilson on May 5, 1813, and died before September 27, 1875 in Boyd County, Kentucky.

Children of Stephen and Jane (Peery) Bartram:
- 6. i. Betsy Bartram (1796 – 1820) – Betsy was born about 1796 in Maiden Spring, Wythe County, Virginia and died in 1820.

Second Generation

2. John P. Bartram (1784 – Unknown) - John P. Bartram was born in May 1784 in Appomattox,, Virginia, the son of Stephen and Elizabeth (Swearingen) Bartram. John married Mary "Polly" Davis on August 2, 1807 in Tazewell, Virginia. Polly was born about 1779 in Cabell County, Western Virginia.

John passed away in 1845 in Wayne County, Western Virginia, where as Mary passed away sometime after 1850.

Children of John P. Bartram and Mary Polly Davis:
- + 7. i. Nancy Jane 'Gincy' Bartram (1807 -1875);
- 8. ii. Stephen Bartram (1809 – Unknown) – Stephen was born about 1809 in Wayne County, Western Virginia, married Cynthia Adkins, and died sometime after 1880 in Catlettsburg, Boyd County, Kentucky;
- 9. iii. William Bartram (1810 – Unknown) – William married Rebecca;
- 10. iv. John Bartram (1814 – Unknown) – John married Mary;
- 11. v. Thomas Bartram (1816 – Unknown) - Thomas married Charlotte;
- 12. vi. Lewis Bartram (1818 – Unknown) – Lewis married Louisa;
- 13. vii. Charles Bartram (1822 – Unknown); and
- 14. viii. Joseph Bartram (1827 – Unknown) – Joseph married Marinda "Rinda" Bartram.

Third Generation

7. Nancy Jane 'Gincy' Bartram (1807 -1875) – See Edward Adkins, page 268.

Descendents of John Jacob and Ana-Eva Stehli, Sr.

First Generation

1. John Jacob Stehli Sr. (1690/95 – 1772) - John Jacob Stehli, Sr. was born between 1690 and 1695, probably in Germany. He married Ana-Eva between 1728 and 1738 in Germany. They left for America aboard the ship *"Priscilla, under Captain William Muir"* and arrived on September 11, 1749 with Johanes-Matthes Stroeher. They arrived in the Port of Philadelphia and settled in Shewsbury Twp, York County, Pennsylvania with their six children. After arriving in America, they would have one more son.

John Jacob would pass away on June 30, 1772 in Chanceford Twp, York County, Pennsylvania on his Icy Hill Plantation. Ana-Eva would died sometime after 1775.

Children of John Jacob and Ana-Eva Stehli, Sr.:

    2.   i.   Peter Stehli (1730 – 1791) – Peter was born sometime between 1730-1735, married Sara Salome between 1755-1760 in York County, Pennsylvania, and died January 15, 1791 in Berkeley County, Virginia;

    3.   ii.   Joseph Stehli (1739 -1808) – Joseph was born about 1739 and died about 1808 in Frederick County, Virginia;

    4.   iii.   Anna Marie Stehli (1742 – Unknown) – Anna was born about 1742, married Hans George Schaub about 1760, and then married Adam Hildebrand;

+   5.   iv.   John Jacob Stehli, Jr. (1744 – Unknown);

    6.   v.   Henry Stehli (1747 – Unknown) – Henry was born May 18, 1747 and died in Shrewsbury Twp, York County, Pennsylvania;

    7.   vi.   Andreas Stehli (1748 – Unknown) – Andreas was born about 1848, married Anna Maria (Unknown) about 1771, then married Anna Magaretha (Unknown) about 1784, and died in Shrewsbury Twp, York County, Pennsylvania; and

    8.   vii.   Stephen Stehli (1750 – 1791) – Stephen was born about 1750 Chanceford, York County, Pennsylvania, who married Mary Polly Unknown, then married Margaretha Gohn about 1775, and died before 1791 in York County, Pennsylvania.

Second Generation

5. John Jacob (Stehli) Staley, Jr. (1744 – 1793) - John Jacob (Stehli) Staley was born in Germany (possibly in the Moselle River Valley) about 1744, the son of John Jacob and Ana-Eva Stehli Sr. He immigrated to America with his family in 1749 aboard the ship *"Priscilla."* He married Catherine Elizabeth Goering, the daughter of Jacob Goering, about 1765 in York County, Pennsylvania. Together John Jacob and Catherine would have eight (8) children.

John Jacob served during the American Revolutionary War in the Seventh Battalion, Second Company, York Co Volunteers, 1775 - Captain Michael Doudel's Company 11/24/1776 - Captain Henry Miller's Company.

John Jacob died on August 11, 1793 and is buried in Reformed Cemetery, Mechlinburgh, Berkeley County, Virginia.

Children of John Jacob Staley, Jr. and Catherine Elizabeth Goering:
- 9. i. Catherine Marie Staley (1768 – 1841) – Catherine was born 1768 at Mulberry Hill Plantation, Chanceford Twp, York County, Pennsylvania, married John Nicholas Strayer, Jr. about 1785 in Mechlinburgh, Berkeley County, Virginia, died on July 3, 1841 in Logan County, Ohio, and is buried in Hurst Cemetery, Olive Chapel;
- 10. ii. Daniel Staley (1770 – 1814) – Daniel was born about 1770 in Chanceford Twp, York County, Pennsylvania and died about 1814 in Mechlinburgh, Berkeley County, Virginia;
- + 11. iii. Stephen Daniel Staley (1772 – 1826);
- 12. iv. John Staley (1775 – Unknown);
- 13. v. Sarah Staley (1777 – Unknown) – Sarah married a Fisher;
- 14. vi. Peter Staley (1779 – Unknown) – Peter was born on March 9, 1779 in Chanceford Twp, York County, Pennsylvania and married Sarah;
- 15. vii. Jacob Staley (1780 – Unknown) – Jacob was born November 16, 1780 in Chanceford Twp, York County, Pennsylvania; and
- 16. viii. Margaret Staley (1784 – 1793) – Margaret was born December 7, 1784 in Chanceford Twp, York County, Pennsylvania and died August 26, 1793 in Mechlinburgh, Berkeley County, Virginia.

Third Generation

11. Stephen Daniel Staley (1772 – 1826) - Stephen Daniel Staley was born in 1772 in Chanceford Twp, York County, Pennsylvania, the son of John Jacob and Catherine Elizabeth (Goering) Staley, Jr.

He married Barbara Yeasley, the daughter of Michael and Catherine (Welsh Norfenger Entler) Yeasley, about 1789 in Lynchburg, Berkeley County, Virginia. Around 1800, Stephen bought a farm along the Ohio River in Cabell County, Western Virginia, where he would die on February 2, 1826.

Children of Stephen Daniel and Barbara (Yeasley) Staley:
- 17. i. Jacob Staley (1789 – Unknown) – Jacob was born on October 11, 1789 in Jefferson County, Western Virginia and married Jemima;
- 18. ii. Catherine Staley (1791 – Unknown) – Catherine was born on March 19, 1791 in Berkeley County, Western Virginia and married Joseph Groves;
- 19. iii. Mary Marie Staley (1793 – 1864) - Mary was born on January 13, 1793 in Jefferson County, Western Virginia, married Solomon Thornburg on January 13, 1813 in Berkeley County, Western Virginia, and died on July 26, 1864;
- 20. iv. Sarah "Sally" Staley (1795 – Unknown) – Sally was born on December 1, 1795 in Jefferson County, Western Virginia and married George Hilyard on November 16, 1815 in Cabell County, Western Virginia;
- + 21. v. Stephen Staley, Jr. (1796 – 1851);
- 22. vi. Charles Staley (1798 – 1854) – Charles was born about 1798 and died August 31, 1854;
- 23. vii. Daniel Staley (1799 – 1883) – Daniel was born on February 11, 1799 in Shepherdstown, Jefferson County, Western Virginia, married Rebecca Bowen in Lawrence County, Ohio on February 27, 1820, and died on March 16, 1883 in Sangamon County, Illinois;
- 24. viii. Joseph Staley (1802 – Unknown) – Joseph was born in 1802 in Cabell County, Western Virginia and married Margaret Heizey on February 3, 1832 in Cabell County, Western Virginia; and
- 25. ix. Elizabeth A. Staley (1800 – 1877) – Elizabeth was born sometime between 1800 and 1815, married Benjamin Stephenson, died on May 31, 1877 in Cabell County, Western Virginia and is buried in Staley- Booth Cemetery.

Fourth Generation

21. Stephen Staley, Jr. (1796– 1851) - Stephen Staley, Jr. was born on March 6, 1796 in Berkeley County, Virginia, the son of Stephen Daniel and Barbara (Yeasley) Staley. He married Mary Peyton about 1817. Together they would have eleven (11) children.

Stephen died on June 11, 1851 in Wayne County, Western Virginia, while Mary passed away on September 30, 1873 in Wayne County. Both are buried in the Booth-Hines-Staley Cemetery in Wayne County, West Virginia.

Children of Stephen Staley, Jr. and Mary Peyton:
- 26. i. Jacob Staley (1817 – 1861) – Jacob was born on April 28, 1817 in White's Creek, Cabell County, Western Virginia, married Elizabeth Alice Burks, was a member of the 1st WV Cavalry, Company I, and died on June 22, 1861 of injuries during the Civil War;
- 27. ii. Rebecca A. Staley (1819 – Unknown) – Rebecca was born about 1819 and married Peres R. Polley on February 28, 1854 in Lawrence County, Ohio;
- 28. iii. Peyton Staley (1820 – 1917) – Peyton was born on December 9, 1820 in Wayne County, Western Virginia, married Martha A. Haynie, and died on February 10, 1917 on White's Creek in Wayne County, West Virginia;
- + 29. iv. Joseph Staley (1823 – Unknown);
- 30. v. Stephen Staley (1824 – 1906) – Stephen was born on May 28, 1824 in Wayne County, Western Virginia, married Anna H. Gardner on June 5, 1853 in Lawrence County, Ohio, and died on January 23, 1906 in Brookland, Craighead County, Arkansas;
- 31. vi. Daniel L. Staley (1826 – Unknown) – Daniel was born between 1826 and 1827 and married Mary Francis Deering on November 25, 1855 in Lawrence County, Ohio;
- 32. vii. Elisha Reynolds 'Rufus' Staley (1826 – 1900) – Elisha was born about 1829, married Rutha Ann Ballengee about 1852, and died after 1900 in Wayne County, West Virginia;
- 33. viii. Solomon P. Staley (1831 – 1891) – Solomon was born about 1831 on White's Creek, Cabell County, Western Virginia, married Nancy C. Fuller on April 12, 1866, and died in 1891 in Wayne County, West Virginia;
- 34. ix. Barbara Ann 'Baberry' Staley (1833 – 1919) – Baberry was born in January 1833 and died on May 1, 1919 in Wayne County, West Virginia;
- 35. x. Andrew J. Staley (1835 – Unknown) – Andrew was born about 1835 and married Elizabeth Caroline Fuller on August 30, 1860 in Wayne County, Western Virginia; and
- 36. xi. Mary E. Staley (1837 – Unknown) – Mary was born on March 19, 1837 in Cabell County, Western Virginia, married Granville D. Shingleton, and then married William Lett on June 10, 1866 in Wayne County, West Virginia.

Fifth Generation

29. Joseph Staley (1824– Unknown) - Joseph Staley was born about 1824 in Virginia, the son of Stephen and Mary (Peyton) Staley, Jr. He married Harriet Hinds, the daughter of Elias and Mary Polly (Bailey) Hinds. Harriet was born about 1828 in Cabell County, Western Virginia. Together Joseph and Harriet would have eleven (11) children.

    Children of Joseph Staley and Harriet Hinds:
	37.	i.	William Staley (1846 – Unknown);
	38.	ii.	Margaret Staley (1847 – Unknown) – Margaret was born sometime between 1847 and 1848 and married John Riggs on February 10, 1871 in Wayne County, West Virginia;
	39.	iii.	Albert Staley (1850 – 1853) – Albert was born about 1850 and died October 16, 1853 in Wayne County, Western Virginia;
	40.	iv.	Mary Staley (1853 – 1853) – Mary was born on May 20, 1853 in Wayne County, Western Virginia and died on July 1, 1853 in Wayne County, Western Virginia;
	41.	v.	Ezra Staley (1854 – Unknown) – Ezra was born on October 5, 1854 in Wayne County, Western Virginia and married Susan E. Rice on February 15, 1878 in Wayne County, West Virginia;
+	42.	vi.	Clarissa Staley (1856 – Unknown);
	43.	vii.	Solomon T. Staley (1860 – 1892) – Solomon was born on April 27, 1860 in Wayne County, Western Virginia and died on June 1, 1892;
	44.	viii.	Anthony Staley (1863 – Unknown) – Anthony was born in 1863 in Western Virginia and married Fannie Cyrus on May 8, 1881 in Wayne County, West Virginia;
	45.	ix.	Olivea 'Leva' Staley (1866 – Unknown) – Leva was born in 1866 in West Virginia and married Joseph Adkins on October 3, 1889 in Wayne County, West Virginia;
	46.	x.	Geneva Staley (1868 – Unknown) – Geneva was born on July 26, 1868 in Wayne County, West Virginia; and
	47.	xi.	Charles E. Staley (1872 – Unknown) – Charles was born on February 28, 1872 in Wayne County, West Virginia.

Sixth Generation

42. Clarissa Staley (1856 – Unknown) – See Milton D. Brumfield, page 261.

Descendents of Michael Yeasley and Catherine Welsh Norfsenger Entler

First Generation

1. Michael Yeasley (1730 – 1808) - Michael Yeasley was born in 1730, possibly in Pennsylvania or Virginia, the son of Nicholas and Julia Ann Yeisley. Michael married Catherine Welsh Norfsenger Entler in Virginia on June 6, 1752. Michael and Catherine would settle down in Shepherdstown, Jefferson County, Virginia, where they started their family. Together they would have seven daughters.

Michael served as a soldier during the Revolutionary War in the German Battalion from Shepherdstown under Capt. William Morgan's Co. (1776). After the war, Michael was a merchant in Shepherdstown, Virginia.

Both passed away in Shepherdstown, Jefferson County, Virginia, Catherine during May of 1801 and Michael on September 1, 1808.

Children of Michael and Catherine Welsh Norfsenger (Entler) Yeasley
- 2. i. Elizabeth Yeasley (1770 – Unknown);
- 3. ii. Catherine Yeasley (1774 – Unknown);
- 4. iii. Eva Yeasley (1776 – 1809) – Eva was born on July 2, 1776 in Jefferson Co, Virginia, married Martin Sheetz on January 20, 1799, and died January 17, 1809 in Jefferson Co, Virginia;
- + 5. iv. Barbara Yeasley (1770 – Unknown);
- 6. v. Sarah Yeasley (1778 – 1846) – Sarah was born on July 21, 1778 in Berkeley Co, Virginia, married Jacob Welshans on September 28, 1798, and died on November 27, 1846 in Virginia
- 7. vi. Maria Yeasley (1781 – Unknown) - Maria married Henry Cookus III; and
- 8. vii. Magdalena Yeasley (1783 – Unknown) - Magdalena married Solomon Ropp.

Second Generation

5. Barbara Yeasley (1770 – Unknown) – See Stephen Daniel Staley, page 282.

Descendents of Elias Hinds and Mary Polly Bailey

First Generation

1.   Elias Hinds (1793 – Unknown) - Elias Hinds was born about 1793 in New York and married Mary Polly Bailey. Mary was born about 1808 in North Carolina. Together Elias and Mary would have twelve children.

    Children of Elias Hinds and Mary Polly Bailey:

	2.	i.	Emeline Hinds (1821 – Unknown);
	3.	ii.	William Lewis Hinds (1821 – 1896) – William was born on September 14, 1821 in Virginia, married Catherine Ann Brumfield, and died April 7, 1896 in Lincoln County, Missouri;
	4.	iii.	Clarissa Hinds (1823 – Unknown) – Clarissa was born in 1823 and married Milton D. Brumfield on September 30, 1849;
+	5.	iv.	Harriet Hinds (1828 – Unknown);
	6.	v.	Ezra Hinds (1832 – Unknown) – Ezra married Elizabeth Jane Hatton in 1851;
	7.	vi.	John Hinds (1835 – Unknown) - John married Lucretia Lett on January 16, 1855;
	8.	vii.	Sarah A. Hinds (1837 – Unknown);
	9.	viii.	James Hinds (1838 – Unknown);
	10.	ix.	Lucrectia F. Hinds (1841 – Unknown) - Lucrectia married James Russell on December 16, 1860;
	11.	x.	Rebecca Hinds (1844 – Unknown);
	12.	xi.	Lehu Hinds (1846 – Unknown) – Lehu served in the 13th West Virginia Volunteer Infantry, Company I, during the Civil War. He was wounded in the left clavicle and spinal column and received a pension; and
	13.	xii.	Elias Hinds (1849 – Unknown).

William Lewis Hinds

Second Generation

5.   Harriet Hinds (1828 – Unknown) - See Joseph Staley, page 285.

Descendants of George Abel and Anna Elizabeth Rockerfeller West

First Generation

1. George Washington Abel (1810 – 1911) – George Washington Abel was born August 10, 1810 in Bucks County, Pennsylvania near the Delaware River, the son of John and Jane (Lewis) Abel. At the age of six (6), George was taken to a home in Bucks County where his mother was Matron for several years. He was orphaned early in life, and at age seven (7), was bound out to John Keppard, 16 miles from Philadelphia. He lived there until he was 22, knowing nothing but hardships. He was a broom maker by trade. In 1831, he went to New Jersey. In 1842, in the fall, he married Anna Elizabeth Rockerfeller West. Elizabeth was born in 1825 in New Jersey. In 1856, he moved his family to Ohio. He was Yankee Dutch Irish. He was not even five (5) feet tall. George lived to be over 101 years old.

Children of George Washington Able and Anna Elizabeth Rockerfeller West:

    2.   i.   Ellen M. Abel (1847 – Unknown) – Ellen was born in 1847 in Mercer County, New Jersey;

+ 3.   ii.   William H. Abel (1849 – 1932);

    4.   iii.   Mary Abel (1850 – Unknown) – Mary was born in 1849 in Mercer County, New Jersey;

    5.   iv.   George W. Abel (1851 – Unknown) – George was born in 1851 in Mercer County, New Jersey;

    6.   v.   Anna M. Abel (1853 – Unknown) – Anna was born in 1853 in Mercer County, New Jersey;

    7.   vi.   Charles F. Abel (1855 – Unknown) – Charles was born in 1855 in Mercer County, New Jersey;

    8.   vii.   Joseph Abel (1855 – Unknown) – Joseph was born in 1855 in Mercer County, New Jersey;

    9.   viii.   John M. Abel (1857 – Unknown) – John was born in 1857 in Mercer County, New Jersey;

    10.   ix.   Robert Abel (1859 – Unknown) – Robert was born in 1859 in Wheeling, Belmont, Ohio;

    11.   x.   Margaret Abel (1860 – Unknown) – Margaret was born in 1860 in Wheeling, Belmont, Ohio;

+ 12.   xi.   David Wesley Abel (1861 – Unknown); and

    13.   xii.   Emma L Abel (1869 – Unknown) – Emma was born in 1869 in Wheeling, Belmont, Ohio.

Second Generation

3. William H. Abel (1850 – 1932) – William H. Abel was born on October 27, 1850, the son of George Washington and Anna Elizabeth Rockerfeller (West) Abel. William married Elizabeth A Mansfield on October 31, 1872 in Tuscarawas County, Ohio. Elizabeth was born on July 8, 1856 in Cadiz, Harrison County, Ohio. William passed away on December 16, 1932, while Elizabeth would pass away on February 13, 1933.

Children of William H. Abel and Elizabeth A. Mansfield:
- 14. i. Emma M Abel (1873 – 1939) – Emma was born on December 13, 1873, married William Rinkus on September 9, 1891, and died on November 30, 1939;
- 15. ii. Margaret Elizabeth Abel (1875 – 1963) – Margaret was born on March 30, 1875, married Thomas Culp on January 18, 1894, and died on July 3, 1963;
- 16. iii. Thomas Marion Abel (1877 – 1962) – Thomas was born on June 1, 1877, married Bess J. Hocker on August 1, 1900, and died on August 13, 1962 in Belmont County, Ohio;
- 17. iv. William Milford Abel (1879 – 1948) – William was born on July 20, 1879, married Cora A. Ferguson on September 13, 1901, and died on September 9, 1948;
- 18. v. Lorena M 'Laura' Abel (1881 – 1959) – Laura was born on September 6, 1881, married Charles Gordon on March 30, 1898, and died on November 11, 1959;
- 19. vi. Bessie Abel (1883 – 1947) – Bessie was born on August 19, 1883, married John Humphrey on February 14, 1901, and died on July 13, 1947;
- 20. vii. Anna Jane Abel (1885 – 1963) – Anna was born on September 28, 1885, married Brady Frazier on June 24, 1903, and died November 6, 1963 in Stow, Summit County, Ohio;
- 21. viii. Eugene Hacket Abel (1889 – 1943) – Eugene was born on March 23, 1889 in Fairpoint, Belmont County, Ohio, married Golda Hines in June 1913, and died on January 15, 1943;
- 22. ix. Joseph Erman Abel (1891 – 1977) – Joseph was born on November 19, 1891 in Fairpoint, Belmont County, Ohio, married Hazel Robinson on June 2, 1915, and died on May 2, 1977 in Belmont County, Ohio;
- 23. x. Raymond Ross Abel (1893 – 1969) – Raymond was born on November 7, 1893, married Sarah Edith Fox on June 5, 1917, and died on February 28, 1969 in Bucyrus, Crawford County, Ohio;
- 24. xi. Sherman Hart Abel (1896 – 1972) – Sherman was born on July 7, 1896 in Uniontown, Ohio, married Anna Burghy on September 10, 1915, and died on May 16, 1972; and

25. xii. Lucy Belle Abel (1899 – 1975) – Lucy was born on June 21, 1899, married Frank E. Harris on August 17, 1918, and died on April 4, 1975 in Saint Clairsville, Belmont County, Ohio.

12. David Wesley Able (1864 – Unknown) – David Wesley Abel was born on September 17, 1864 in Belmont County, Ohio, the son of George and Anna Elizabeth Rockerfeller (West) Abel. David married Elma Steele, the daughter of Thomas and Nancy (Anderson) Steele, on September 17, 1885. Elma was born on October 15, 1865 in Old Washington, Guernsey County, Ohio.

George Thomas Abel, David Wesley Able, and Nancy Rozella (Able) Hodder in 1945

Children of David Wesley Abel and Elma Steele:
+ 26. i. Harry Walter Abel (1886 – 1963);
+ 27. ii. Charles Ellsworth Abel (1888 – 1927);
+ 28. iii. George Thomas Abel (1892 – Unknown);
+ 29. iv. Nancy Rozella Mae Abel (1898 – 1953);
    30. v. Sarah Margaret Abel (1902 – Unknown) – Sarah was born on August 19, 1902 and married Oliver Rider;
    31. vi. Mary Augusta Able (1906 – Unknown); and
    32. vii. Wilbur R. Abel (1908 – 1932) – Wilbur was born on August 26, 1908 and died on May 10, 1931.

Third Generation

26.   Harry Walter Abel (1886 – 1963) – Harry Abel was born on July 31, 1886 in Guernsey County, Ohio, the son of David Wesley and Elma (Steele) Abel. Harry married Hazel Shuttleworth. Harry passed away in 1963.

>   Children of Harry Abel and Hazel M. Shuttleworth:
>   33.   i.   Mary M. Abel (1908 – Unknown);
>   34.   ii.   Glen C. Abel (1911 – Unknown);
>   35.   iii.   Catherine H. Abel (1913 – Unknown);
>   36.   iv.   Margaret D. Abel (1915 – Unknown); and
>   37.   v.   Fern T. Abel (1917 – Unknown).

27.   Charles Ellsworth Abel (1888 – 1927) – See Pearl Navada Wright, page 99.

28.   George Thomas Abel (1892 – Unknown) – Thomas G. Abel was born on January 3, 1892 in Guernsey County, Ohio, the son of David Wesley and Elma (Steele) Abel. Thomas married and divorced Eulala Anders.

>   Children of Thomas G. Abel and Eulala Anders:
>   38.   i.   Eva M. Abel (1914 – Unknown); and
>   39.   ii.   Mary E. Abel (1915 – Unknown).

29.   Nancy Rozella Mae Abel (1898 – Unknown) – Nancy Rozella Mae Abel was born on May 23, 1898 in Guernsey County, Ohio, the daughter of David Wesley and Elma (Steel) Abel. Zella married Ralph Hodder. They would move to Los Angels, California prior to 1930.

>   Children of Ralph Hodder and Zella Mae Abel:
>   40.   i.   Marguerite Hodder (1818 – 1978);
>   41.   ii.   Lillian Hodder; and
>   42.   iii.   William Hodder.

Descendants of Richard Adam Steele and Rebecca Jane Makemie

First Generation

1. Richard Adam Steele (1690 – 1744) – Adam Steel was born in 1690 in Belfast, Ireland, the son of Adam Steele. He married Rebecca Jane Makemie, who was born in 1706 and together they had eight (8) children. Adam passed away in Mercersburg, Franklin County, Pennsylvania. Rebecca, along with his son, Richard and two daughters, Jane and Mary, left Pennsylvania and moved to Kentucky, first settling on Corn Island, then to a block fort near Louisville, Kentucky. They finally moved to a farm near Lexington, Kentucky in Fayette County. Makemie would pass away on August 1, 1795 in Lexington, Fayette County, Kentucky.

Children of Richard Adam Steele and Rebecca Jane Makemie:
+ 2. i. James Steele (1726 – 1780);
+ 3. ii. Mary Steele (1736 – 1809);
+ 4. iii. Agnes Steele (1843 -
+ 5. iii. Jane Steele (1745 – 1818; and
+ 6. iv. Richard Steele, Jr. (1848 – 1809)

Second Generation

2. James Steele (1726 -1780) – James Steele was born 1726 in Belfast Ireland, the son of Adam and Jane (Makemie) Steele. James married Martha, and died in 1780 in Frederick County, Virginia.

Children of James and Martha Steele:
7. i. Rebecca Steele (1746 – 1827) – Rebecca was born on October 5, 1746 in Nantmeal Twp. Chester County, Pennsylvania and married James Wynne about 1768 in St. Mary's Epics, Church, Warwick Twp, Chester County, Pennsylvania. James was the son of Jonathan Wynne II and Anne Warner. He was born March 28, 1736 in Nantmeal Twp, Chester County, Pennsylvania and died on December 30, 1817 in Nantmeal Twp, Chester County, Pennsylvania. Rebecca would pass away on September 25, 1827 in Nantmeal Twp, Chester County, Pennsylvania;

8.   ii.   Thomas Steele (1750 – 1834) - Thomas was born on May 12, 1750 in Belfast Ireland and married Sarah Melchoir, who was born on June 12, 1748 in Chester County Pennsylvania, and died August 22, 1824 in Stephens City, Virginia. Thomas died on November 23, 1834 in Stephens City, Virginia;
+ 9.   iii. Adam Steele (1776 – 1837);
   10.   iv.   Susan Steele (1778 – Unknown); and
   11.   v.   Mary Steele (1779 – Unknown).

3.   Mary Steele (1736 – 1809) – Mary Steele was born August 15, 1736, the daughter of Richard Adam Steele and Rebecca Jane (Makemie) Steele. Mary married Captain William Lytle, the son of John and Jane (McConnell) Litle, on October 29, 1761. William was born October 15, 1728 in Pennsylvania. William held a captain's commission in the Pennsylvania line during the French and Indian War, and immigrated to Kentucky in the year 1779.

Major General William Haines Lytle

William was a surveyor and was once captured by the Indians. William was a personal friend of Andrew Jackson, under whom, when Andrew Jackson was President, William held the office of Surveyor General of Public Lands.

William's great-great-grandson, William Haines Lytle who was born in Cincinnati, November 2, 1826, served in the Mexican war as captain; became a member of the Ohio legislature; ran for lieutenant-governor in 1857; was major-general of the Ohio militia; commanded the 4th Ohio Regiment in General O.M. Mitchel's Brigade during the Civil War; was killed at the Battle of Chickamauga (in Georgia), September 20, 1863.

Children of William Lytle and Mary Steele:
   12.   i.   Jane Lytle (1762 – 1796) – Jane was born on October 5, 1762 in Pennsylvania, married Robert Todd, and died on Nay 23, 1796;
   13.   ii.   Mary Lytle (1764 – 1808) – Mary was born on September 19, 1764 and died May 11, 1808;
   14.   iii. Isaac Lytle (1765 – Unknown);
   15.   iv.   John Lytle (1766 – 1843) – John was born on August 8, 1766, married Dorcas Waring, and died January 30, 1843;
   16.   v.   Sarah Lytle (1768 – Unknown) – Sarah was born on

August 14, 1768;
17. vi. William Haynes Lytle (1770 – 1813) – William was born on September 14, 1772 in Carlisle, Cumberland County, Pennsylvania, married Elizabeth Stahl on February 28, 1798 in Philadelphia, Pennsylvania, and died in 1813 near Cincinnati, Ohio;
18. vii. Agnes Lytle (1772 – 1843) – Agnes was born on September 14, 1772 in Derry Twp, Lancaster County, Pennsylvania, married Judge John Rowan, and died on July 14, 1843;
19. viii. Elizabeth Lytle (1774 – Unknown) – Elizabeth was born on September 1, 1774 in Pennsylvania and married Samuel Broadhead; and
20. ix. Josephine Lytle (1775 – Unknown) – Josephine married Nathaniel Foster.

4. Agnes Steele (1743 – 1813) – Agnes Steel was born in 1743 in Coleraine, County Derry, Ireland, the daughter of Richard Adam and Rebecca Jane (Makemie) Steele. In 1763, Agnes married Charles Pollock, the son of Thomas and Mary (Cochrane) Pollock. They were both from the neighborhood of Lewistown, Pennsylvania. Charles became a Private in the Cumberland County, Pennsylvania Militia during the American Revolutionary War. Charles died in March of 1795 at the age of 63 and was buried in Northumberland County, Pennsylvania. Shortly after the death of Charles, Mary, along with five of her sons and their families, moved to Erie County, Pennsylvania.

Children of Charles Pollock and Agnes Steele (all born in Northumberland County, Pennsylvania):
21. i. John Pollock (1765 – 1795;
22. ii. Adam Pollock (1767 – 1816) – Adam married Elizabeth Gilliland;
23. iii. James Pollock (1769 – 1857) – James married Mary Steele, his first cousin. James served as a Captain in 1795, when George Washington was President, and served under General Anthony Wayne, who achieved peace with the Indians with the "Treaty of Greenville" on August 3, 1795;
24. iv. Thomas Pollock (1772 – 1844) – Thomas married Margaret 'Mary' Fruit in 1796 and then married Eleanor Knox after 1817;
25. v. William Pollock (1773 – 1824) – William married Sarah 'Sally' Fruit in 1798
26. vi. Richard Pollock (1775 – Unknown);
27. vii. Charles Pollock (1780 – 1798);
28. viii. Mary Pollock (1782 – 1784);
29. ix. Jane Pollock (1784 – 1784); and

30. x. Robert Pollock (1785 – 1844) – Robert was born on May 22, 1785, married Margaret Anderson on December 12, 1810 and died on February 22, 1844.

5. Jane Steele (1745 – 1818) – Jane Steele was born in 1745 in Mercersburg, Franklin County, Pennsylvania, the daughter of Richard Adam and Rebecca Jane (Makemie) Steele. She married William Hueston about 1765. Jane passed away on January 1, 1818 in Lexington, Fayette County, Kentucky.

Children of William Hueston and Jane Steele:
- 31. i. Nancy Hueston, married John Graham of Pennsylvania;
- 32. ii. Sarah Hueston, married Benjamin Wood of New Jersey;
- 33. iii. Robert Hueston, married Mary Bartholomew Bodley of Fayette County, Kentucky;
- 34. iv. Susan Hueston, married James January of Marysville, Kentucky;
- 35. v. Jane Hueston, married James McNair of Pennsylvania;
- 36. vi. Mary Hueston;
- 37. vii. Elizabeth Hueston, married Robert Perry of Virginia; and
- 38. viii. William Hueston (1803 – Unknown) – William died unmarried in New Orleans in 1803.

6. Richard Adam Steel, Jr. (1748 – 1809) – Richard Adam Steel, Jr. was born about 1748, the son of Richard Adam and Rebecca Jane (Makemie) Steele. Richard, along with his mother and two sisters, Jane and Mary, left Pennsylvania and moved to Kentucky, first settling on Corn Island, then to a block fort near Louisville, Kentucky. They finally moved to a farm near Lexington, Kentucky in Fayette County. Richard married Martha Makemie, the daughter of John McCamey and niece of the Rev. Francis Makemie, the first Presbyterian preacher in America. Richard would become an elder of the Pisgah Presbyterian Church, on the Lexington and Versailles Roads. He was the first elder to attend the General Assembly from Kentucky, making the trip to New York with the Rev. Archibald Cameton, on horseback.

Richard would pass away in 1794. He left a will, and is buried in the Old Churchyard. Martha would pass away on September 22, 1822

Children of Richard Adam Steele, Jr. and Martha Makemie:
- 39. i. Adam Steel (1770 – Unknown) – Adam was born on September 4, 1770, married Brooke Beall, and then married Hannah Graham;

40.	ii.	Richard Steele (1775 – Unknown) – Richard was born on September 20, 1775 and married Amellia Neville;
41.	iii.	Joseph Steele (1779 – Unknown) – Joseph was born on July 7, 1779 and married Miriam Boone;
42.	iv.	Jane Steel (1781 – Unknown) – Jane was born on August 8, 1781;
43.	v.	John Rowan Steele (1783 – Unknown) – John was born on June 16, 1783 and married Thurza Howard Mayo;
44.	vi.	Mary Steele (1785 – Unknown) – Mary was born on May 22, 1785 and married John Sutherland;
45.	vii.	Martha Breckinridge Steele (1786 – Unknown) – Martha was born on June 23, 1786, married John Mendenhall, and then married Robert Beall;
46.	viii.	William Steele (1788 – Unknown) – William was born on January 1, 1788 and married Mary Rowan;
47.	ix.	Robert Steele (1790 – 1827) – Robert was born on September 14, 1790 and married Ellen Joel Lewis;
48.	x.	Ester Steele (1792 – 1822) – Ester was born on July 14, 1792, married William Kirkpatrick, and then married John Edwards; and
49.	xi.	Nancy Polk Steele (1795 – Unknown) – Nancy was born on February 7, 1795 and married John M. Talbott.

Third Generation

9.   Adam Steele (1776 – 1837) – Adam Steele was born about 1776 in Frederick County, Virginia, the son of James and Martha Steele. Adam married Hannah Stump in April 1802 in Frederick County, Virginia, then married Elizabeth Nicholls on October 23, 1813 in Frederick County, Virginia, later moved to Ohio, and died after 1837 in Ohio.

Children of Adam Steele and Hannah Stump:
50.	i.	Daniel Steele (1804 – 1874) – Daniel married Matilda Barrow on May 31, 1827 in Frederick County, Virginia;
51.	ii.	Barbara Ann Steele (1810 – Unknown) – Barbara Ann married Franklin Barrow on April 5, 1833 in Frederick County, Virginia;
52.	iii.	William Steele (1812 – Unknown); and
53.	iv.	David Steele (1813 – Unknown) – David married Lucinda Ellis on August 2, 1854 in Frederick County, Virginia.

Children of Adam Steele and Elizabeth Nicholls:
54.	i.	James Steele (1715 – Unknown) - James was born in 1815 in Frederick County, Virginia, and died after 1866 in Ross County, Ohio. He married Margaret Hamilton on August 16, 1838 in Ohio, then married Charlotte Mathews in 1843 in Ohio;

55.	ii.	John Steele (1816 – Unknown) – John married Cloa Barnard August 11, 1842 in Ohio and died after 1858 in Ohio;
56.	iii.	Unknown Steele was born 1818;
57.	iv.	Samuel Steele (1819 – Unknown) – Samuel was born in 1819 in Frederick County, Virginia;
58.	v.	Lucinda Steele (1822 – Unknown);
+ 59.	vi.	Thomas Steele (1825 – 1911);
60.	vii.	Vina Steele (1826 – Unknown);
61.	viii.	Peter Steele (1827 – 1865) – Peter was born in 1827 in Ohio and married Charity Perego October 14, 1853 in Ohio;
62.	ix.	David Steele (1829 – 1862) – David was born in 1829 in Ohio, married Sarah Ann Boyd November 18, 1857, and died November 17, 1862 in Bowling Green, Kentucky;
63.	x.	Prena Steele (1830 – Unknown) – Prena was born in 1830 in Frederick County, Virginia, married John Fleming November 16, 1848 in Ohio, and died after 1857 in Jackson Co. Illinois;
64.	xi.	Nancy Steele (1832 – 1870) – Nancy was born in 1832 in Frederick County, Virginia, married Aaron Stevens December 24, 1853 in Ohio, and died 1870 in Ohio;
65.	xii.	George Steele (1834 – 1909) - George was born in 1834 in Frederick County, Virginia, married Mariah Secrest November 24, 1857 in Ohio, and died November 3, 1909 in Ohio;
66.	xiii.	Joseph H. Steele (1835 – 1908) – Joseph was born in 1835 in Frederick County, Virginia, married Margaret Matilda Gordon November 13, 1860 in Ohio, and died August 5, 1908 in Ohio; and
67.	xiv.	Jane Steele (1837 –Unknown) – Jane was born in 1837 in Ohio, married James Stillion June 9, 1859 in Ohio, and died after 1875 in Ohio.

Fourth Generation

59. Thomas Steele (1825 – 1911) – Thomas Steele was born March 12, 1825 in Frederick County, Virginia, the son of Adam and Elizabeth (Nicholls) Steele. Thomas married Sarah Dayton on September 24, 1846 in Ohio, then married Nancy Anderson on June 17, 1858 in Ohio. Nancy was born in March 1831. Thomas was a barrel maker and farmer in Wills Township, Guernsey County. Ohio. Thomas died on April 7, 1911 in Guernsey County, Ohio and Nancy died in 1916. Both are buried in the Old Washington Cemetery.

Children of Thomas Steele and Sarah Dayton:

68.	i.	Mary E. Steele (1848 – Unknown) – Mary was born in 1848 in Ohio and married John B. Donaldson on July 16, 1882
69.	ii.	Ann Steele, died as an infant;

70.	ii.	Adam J. Steele (1850 – Unknown) – Adam married Julia Vance on October 31, 1872;
71.	iii.	Sarah Catherine Steele (1852 – Unknown) – Sarah married Levi Smith on July 1, 1872; and
72.	iv.	Samuel Steel (1855 – Unknown) – Samuel married Dora Smith on February 13, 1879.

Children of Thomas Steele and Nancy Anderson:

	73.	i.	Melvina Steele (1858 – Unknown) – Melvina was born in 1859 in Ohio and married Robert D. Lewis February 19, 1880 in Ohio;
	74.	ii.	Thomas Steele (1859 0 Unknown) – Thomas married Francis Isabella Sparrowgrove;
	75.	ii.	Susan Viola Steele (1861 – Unknown) - Susan was born in 1861 in Ohio and married William Barrett September 28, 1881;
	76.	iii.	Maggie Jane Steele (1863 – 1891) – Maggie was born in 1863 in Ohio, married W. S. Jones, and died on January 21, 1891;
+	77.	iv.	Elma Steele (1865 – 1946);
	78.	v.	Minnie Steele (1867 – Unknown) – Minnie was born in 1867 in Ohio and married Charles Bethel;
	79.	vi.	Charles Steele (1871 – Unknown) – Charles was born in 1871 in Ohio and married Inez Anderson;
	80.	vii.	Gladys Steele (1873 – Unknown) – Gladys married Terry Spears;
	81.	viii.	Una Mae Steele (1875 – Unknown) – Una was born in 1875 in Ohio and married Lewis Ogle; and
	82.	ix.	Rose Steele (1879 – Unknown).

Fifth Generation

77.   Elma Steele (1865 – 1946) – See David Wesley Abel, page 293.

Descendants of Samuel and Esther Harris

First Generation

1. Samuel Harris (Unknown – 1764) – Samuel Harris settled in Loudoun County, Virginia, where he married Esther. Together, they would have six (6) children.
    Samuel Harris, grantee, "of Fairfax" purchased land in Northern Neck, Prince William County, Virginia. Dated 21 April 1742. Description: 640 acres beginning at the corner of Joseph Dixon, on North Fork of Beaverdam Branch of Goose Creek, surveyed by Amos Janney. (Northern Neck Land Grants, Book E, 1736-1742, p. 454 --reel 291). Loudoun County, Virginia was formed out of Fairfax in 1757, and Fairfax, from Prince William County in 1742.
    Samuel was an early member of the Hopewell Monthly Meeting (MM), Virginia (the "American Quakers"). In 1744, when Fairfax MM was created, dividing the Hopewell and Fairfax boundaries along the Blue Ridge, the Friends in that locale west of the Blue Ridge, of which were largely members of Fairfax and Monoquesy Preparatory Meetings. Samuel was named a temporary overseer (along with Jacob Janney) of the Fairfax Men's Meeting, 26th, 4th month (June) 1745.
    Samuel passed away about 1764 in Loudoun County, Virginia.

    Children of Samuel and Esther Harris:
    + 2.   i.   Esther Harris, Jr. (1724 – 1807);
      3.   ii. David Harris, married a non-member of the Fairfax Monthly Meeting House in October 1764;
      4.   iii. Joseph Harris;
    + 5.   iv. Samuel Harris (Unknown – 1783);
    + 6.   v.   William Harris (1710 – 1767);
      7.   vi. Anne Harris.

Second Generation

2. Esther Harris, Jr. (1724 – 1807) – Esther Harris, Jr. was born about 1724 in Loudoun County, Virginia, the daughter of Samuel and Esther Harris. Esther married Henry Brown sometime between July 31 and August 23, 1745 in the Fairfax Meeting of Friends, Waterford,

Virginia. It was the first marriage for the Fairfax MM. Henry was born in 1720, the son of Richard and Hannah (Reynolds) Brown. Together they would have eight (8) children. Henry passed away in 1801, while Esther would pass away on April 17, 1807 in Loudoun County, Virginia.

    Children of Henry Brown and Esther Harris, Jr.:
- 8. i. Hannah Brown (1747 – 1806) – Hannah married Stacy Janny;
- 9. ii. John Brown (1749 – 1828) – John was born on November 15, 1749, married Phebe Harris, then Elizabeth Davis, then Martha Ball, and died June 2, 1828;
- 10. iii. Mary Brown (1752 – Unknown) – Mary married James Ball;
- 11. iv. Esther Brown (1755 – Unknown) – Esther married Jacob Sands;
- 12. v. Henry Brown (1758 – Unknown);
- 13. vi. Ann Brown (1761 – 1763);
- 14. vii. Mercer Brown (1765 – Unknown); and
- 15. viii. William Brown (1766 – 1829).

5.   Samuel Harris, Jr. (Unknown – 1783) – Samuel was the son of Samuel and Esther Harris. Samuel married Mary John, the daughter of Thomas John. Samuel died in 1783 in Loudoun County, Virginia, and his estate was probated on April 14, 1783, with a will dated May 10, 1782.

    Children of Samuel Harris, Jr. and Mary John:
- 16. i. Thomas Harris;
- 17. ii. Samuel Harris; and
- 18. iii. William Harris.

6.   William Harris (1710 – 1767) – William Harris was born between 1710 and 1720 in Loudoun County, Virginia, the son of Samuel and Esther Harris. William married Hannah Moore in Loudoun County, Virginia. Hannah was born between 1710 – 1720 in England. Together they would have eight (8) children.

William Harris, grantee, purchased land by deed, dated 6 Dec. 1742, located in Fairfax Co., VA (now Loudoun Co., VA) description: 670 ac. adjoining land of Samuel Harris and land of John Hanby. (Northern Neck Land Grants) William Harris was listed in Loudoun County, Virginia tithes tables in 1758. William Harris, Jr., (then age 16) is listed in 1765.

William and his family lived near present day Leesburg, Loudoun County, Virginia where records of him are found at Hopewell MM, Winchester, Virginia, Fairfax MM, Fairfax, Virginia. In 1762, there was some concern over William living on Indian Property Rights.

William passed away sometime before 1767, as Hannah, the "Widow" was dismissed by the Quakers on July 6, 1767. Both William and Hannah were buried in the Union Cemetery in Leesburg, Virginia.

Children of William Harris and Hannah Moore:
- 19. i. Hester 'Esther' Harris (1744 – 1810) – Esther was born on September 7, 1744 in Fairfax, Frederick County, Virginia, married Abraham Oldaker about 1766 in Loudoun County, Virginia, and died in 1810 in Fauquier County, Virginia;
- + 20. ii. Martha Harris (1746 – Unknown);
- 21. iii. William Harris (1748 – 1782) – William was born on October 19, 1748 in Fairfax, Frederick County, Virginia (Goose Creek Friends MM), married Elizabeth Holmes on October 22, 1772 in Fairfax, Frederick County, Virginia, living on Goose Creek, and died before 1782 in Leesburg, Loudoun County, Virginia;
- 22. iv. Daniel Harris (1751 – Unknown) – Daniel was born on November 14, 1751 in Loudoun County, Virginia;
- 23. v. Hannah Harris (1753 – Unknown) – Hannah was born on February 13, 1753 in Frederick County, Virginia, married Amon Updike on February 27, 1773, and died in Bedford County, Virginia;
- + 24. vi. Jesse Harris (1755 – 1825);
- 25. vii. Samuel Harris (1757 – 1783) – Samuel was born on March 22, 1757 in Fairfax, Frederick County, Virginia and died in 1782/83 in Fairfax, Frederick County, Virginia; and
- 26. viii. Mary Harris (1759 – Unknown) – Mary was born on April 7, 1759 in Fairfax, Frederick County, Virginia and died in Bedford County, Virginia.

Third Generation

20. Martha Harris (1746 – Unknown) – Martha Harris was born on September 29, 1746 in Fairfax, Frederick County, Virginia, the daughter of William and Hannah (Moore) Harris. Martha married John Oldaker about 1767 in Fairfax, Frederick County, Virginia. The Oldaker family would remove from Loudoun County, Virginia to Bedford County, Virginia about 1789 or 1790, and then on to the area of Kanawha, Mason, and Putnam Counties. Martha was disowned

December 7, 1767 from Hopewell MM to Fairfax MM, but she had already removed to Lost River MM.

    Children of John Oadaker and Martha Harris:
    27.   i.   Tamar Oldaker; and
    28.   ii.   Isaac Oldaker.

24.   Jesse Harris (1755 – 1825) – Jesse Harris was born on February 24, 1755 in Fairfax, Frederick County, Virginia, the son of William Harris and Hannah Moore. Jesse married Margaret 'Peggy' Nixon in 1776. Peggy was born in 1755 in Virginia. According to the Fairfax Monthly Meeting House, Peggy was a non-member. During the Revolutionary War, Jesse served in the Loudoun County, Virginia Militia, 57th Regiment, 2nd Battalion, under Lieut. Jones' Company.

In 1788, Jesse was listed on the Personal Property Tax List for Loudoun County, Virginia. Around 1805, Jesse moved his family to Ohio, as the family was listed on the 1820 US Census for Newton Twp, Licking County, Ohio. Jesse passed away on May 30, 1825 and is buried in the Marple Cemetery in Newton Twp, Licking County, Ohio. Peggy would pass away on May 1, 1835, and is also buried in the Marple Cemetery.

    Children of Jesse Harris and Margaret Nixon:
+   29.   i.   George Harris (1777 – Unknown);
    30.   ii.   David Harris (1778 – Unknown) – David was born in Virginia in 1778, erected a grist-mill on the Clearfork during the War of 1812, and participated in the War of 1812;
    31.   iii.   Amos Harris (1780 – 1813) – Amos was born in Virginia in 1780, died in 1813 in Licking County, Ohio, and is buried in the Marple Cemetery;
+   32.   iv.   Jesse Harris (1781 – 1812);
    33.   v.   William Harris (1783 – Unknown) – William was born in Virginia in 1783 and came to Ohio with the family around 1805;
    34.   vi.   John Harris (1786 – Unknown) – John was born in Virginia in 1786, came to Ohio with the family in 1805, and is listed in the 1820, 1840 and 1850 US Census for Ohio, Licking County, Mary Ann Twp;
    35.   vii.   Joshua Harris (1790 – Unknown) - Joshua was born in Virginia in 1790, came to Ohio with the family around 1805, and is listed in the 1820,1840 and 1850 US Census for Ohio, Licking County, Mary Ann Twp; and

36. viii. Isaac Harris (1794 – Unknown) - Isaac was born in Virginia in 1794, came to Ohio with the family around 1805, built a log school house on his farm about 1810, and is listed in the 1820, 1840 and 1850 US Census for Ohio, Licking County, Mary Ann Twp.

Fourth Generation

29. George Harris (1777 – 1860) – George Harris was born in Virginia in 1777, the son of Jesse and Margaret (Nixon) Harris. George married Catherine, most likely in Virginia. George moved his young family to Ohio in 1805 and settled in Newton Twp, Licking County, Ohio. George built a saw mill on the Clearfork about 1812. Catherine passed away in 1843 and is buried in the Marple Cemetery.

George would then marry Elizabeth McClane. Elizabeth was born in Virginia in 1798. George passed away after 1860, while Elizabeth would pass away after 1864. She is buried in the Marple Cemetery.

Children of George and Catherine Harris:
37. i. Mathias Harris (1799 – 1816) – Mathias is buried in the Maple Grove Cemetery in Newton Twp, Licking County, Ohio;
+ 38. ii. Isaac Harris (1803 – 1879);
39. iii. George Harris (1807 – 1860) – George is buried in the Marple Cemetery in Newton Twp, Licking County, Ohio;
40. iv. William Harris (1807 – 1866) – William was born on February 2, 1807, possibly a twin of George, married Margaret Trout, and is buried in the Philipps Cemetery in Granville, Licking County, Ohio;
41. v. Jonah Harris (1812 – Unknown) – Jonah was born in 1812 in Licking County, Ohio; and
42. vi. David Harris.

32. Jesse Harris (1781 – 1813) – Jesse Harris was born in Virginia in 1781, the son of Jesse and Margaret (Nixon) Harris. Jesse married Elizabeth B. Robinson on April 28, 1806 in Licking County, Ohio. Elizabeth was born in 1790 in Lost River, Hardie County, Western Virginia, the daughter of Stephen and Sarah (Oldaker) Robinson. These families all came to Ohio during 1805 to settle in Licking County. Jesse died sometime before 1812 and is buried in the Marple Cemetery in Licking County, Ohio. Elizabeth then married John Whitmire about 1813 in Licking County, Ohio. They moved to Sidney, Shelby County, Ohio. Elizabeth would pass away sometime before 1830.

Children of Jesse Harris and Elizabeth B. Robinson:
  43. i. Celia Nixon Harris (1810 – 1888); and
  44. ii. Stephen Harris (1812 – Unknown).

Children of John Whitmire and Elizabeth B. (Robinson) Harris:
  45. i. Mahala Hoy Whitmire (1814 – 1855);
  46. ii. David Oldaker Whitmire (1816 – Unknown);
  47. iii. James Smith Whitmire (1821 – Unknown);
  48. iv. Zachariah Hoy Whitmire (1823 – 1897);
  49. v. Sarah Jane Whitmire (1825 – Unknown); and
  50. vi. Margaret Ann Whitmire (1827 – Unknown).

Fifth Generation

38. Isaac Harris (1803 – 1879) – Isaac Harris was born on September 3, 1803 in Loudoun County, Virginia, the son of George and Catherine Harris. Isaac came with his family to Licking County, Ohio in 1805. Isaac married Rachel Haas on November 24, 1825 in Licking County, Ohio. Rachel was born on May 25, 1801 in Virginia, the daughter of John and Elizabeth (Wilkins) Haas. Rachel passed away on August 19, 1869 in Licking County, Ohio and is buried in Wilson Cemetery. Isaac then married Sarah Graham Loder sometime before 1870. Sarah was born on April 20, 1825 in Ohio. Isaac would pass away on August 6, 1879, while Sarah would pass away on January 17, 1893. Both are buried in Wilson Cemetery in Licking County, Ohio.

Children of Isaac Harris and Rachel Haas (all born in Licking County, Ohio:
+ 51. i. Mary Harris (1825 – Unknown);
  52. ii. Elizabeth Harris (1827 – Unknown);
  53. iii. John Harris (1829 – Unknown);
+ 54. iv. Absolom W. Harris (1837 – 1896);

Sixth Generation

51. Mary Harris (1825 – Unknown) – Mary Harris was born in 1825 in Licking County, Ohio, the daughter of Isaac and Rachel (Haas) Harris. Mary married James N. Armstrong sometime in 1851. James was born in 1825.

Children of James N. Armstrong and Mary Harris:
- 55. i. Emmit E. Armstrong (1854 – Unknown);
- 56. ii. Alfred Armstrong (1857 – Unknown); and
- 57. iii. Harris N. Armstrong (1859 – Unknown).

54. Absolom W. Harris (1837 – 1896) – Absolom W. Harris was born in 1837 in Licking County, Ohio, the son of Isaac and Rachel (Haas) Harris. Absolom married Victoria Philipps sometime before 1864. Victoria was born on March 21, 1842 in Licking County, Ohio, the daughter of Samuel Griffith and Susannah (Reily) Philipps. Victoria would pass away on February 19, 1875, shortly after giving childbirth. She was buried in the Wilson Cemetery in Newark, Ohio. Absolom then married the widow, Mary A. (Nutter) Cramer, sometime before 1880. Mary was born in 1844. Absolom would die from typhoid fever on November 15, 1896, along with two of his daughters. He was buried in Wilson Cemetery in Newark, Ohio.

Lydia J. Harris

Children of Absolom Harris and Victoria Philipps:
- 58. i. Samuel E. Harris (1864 – 1902) – Samuel married Hannah and died on February 26, 1902 in Licking County, Ohio;
- 59. ii. Clifton E. Harris (1865 – 1926) – Clifton passed away on March 26, 1926 in Licking County, Ohio;
- + 60. iii. Laura Elizabeth Harris (1867 – 1946);
- 61. iv. Susannah W. Harris (1869 – Unknown) – Susannah married Carl E. Bagent and passed away sometime before 1946;
- 62. v. Lydia J. Harris (1871 – 1961) – Lydia was born on April 19, 1871 in Newton Twp, Licking County, Ohio, passed away on December 27, 1961 in Newark, Ohio, and is buried in Cedar Hill Cemetery; and
- 63. vi. An infant, who was born and died on February 9, 1875 in Licking County, Ohio.

Children of Absolom Harris and Mary A. (Nutter) Cramer;
- 64. i. Edward H. Harris (1879 – 1938) – Edward was born in Bladensburg, Ohio on November 5, 1879, he was a painter, passed away in the Licking County Home on January 22, 1938, and is buried in Maple Grove Cemetery, Licking County;
- 65. ii. Harry F. Harris (1879 – 1961) – Harry was born in Licking County and died sometime after 1961;
- 66. iii. Lulu R. Harris (1880 – 1896) – Lulu died of typhoid fever on November 8, 1896 and is buried in Wilson Cemetery, Newark, Ohio; and
- 67. iv. Daisy D. Harris (1887 – 1896) – Daisy died of typhoid fever on November 20, 1896 and is buried in Wilson Cemetery, Newark, Ohio.

Children of Mary A. (Nutter) Cramer:
- 68. i. Matilda Cramer (1868 – Unknown);
- 69. ii. Lotta D. Cramer (1872 – Unknown);
- 70. iii. Lillie Cramer (1874 – Unknown); and
- 71. iv. Minnie Cramer (1876 – Unknown).

Seventh Generation

Olaf and Laura E. (Harris) Wetterholm

60. Laura Elizabeth Harris (1867 – 1946) – Laura Elizabeth Harris was born on January 27, 1867 in Chatham (previously called "Harrisburgh"), Licking County, Ohio, the daughter of Absolom W. and Victoria (Philipps) Harris. She was not married when she had her two children and it is thought the father was a Hancock.

On February 10, 1902, the Newark Advocate reported the following regarding a major wholesale shoplifting ring in Newark, Ohio: *"Mrs. Laura Harris and Mrs. Ella Haughey appeared before Mayor Atherton at 2 o'clock this afternoon, for their preliminary hearing on the charge of receiving stolen goods, in connection with the recent shoplifting cases. By their attorneys Smythe & Smythe, the defendants waved a trial by jury, and submitted to be tried by the court only. A plea of guilty was entered and the defendants were sentenced to five days each in jail, and to pay the costs of prosecution."*

On June 16, 1904, the Newark Advocate reported the following: *"POLICE COURT – Laura Harris was fined $25 and costs for keeping a house of prostitution, two girls were fined $5 and costs and a third $1 and costs for being inmates."*

On September 28, 1904, the Newark Advocate reported the following: *"POLICE COURT – Laura Harris was fined $5 and costs for visiting a wine room, in police court this morning by Mayor Crilly. A warrant was also served on her charging her with keeping her saloon open on Sunday, and which charge she will have a hearing later."*

Laura married Olaf Wetterholm on January 28, 1911 in Newark, Ohio. Olaf was born on January 27, 1871 in Gongheeping, Sweden, the son of Charles and Mary Wetterholm. Olaf served in the Army of the United States, Battery B of the Second Regiment Field Artillery. He was in Cuba from October 14, 1906 to February 1909, and was discharged on August 7, 1909. When he enlisted, he was 23 years old, had blue eyes, brown hair, ruddy complexion, and was 5 feet 6 and ¼ inches tall.

Olaf was an employee of the Pharis Rubber Company in Newark, Ohio. He was a member of the Eagles Lodge and of the Druids in Newark, Ohio.

Olaf passed away at Newark City Hospital on March 27, 1944. Laura passed away in the Eshelman Nursing Home on August 27, 1946 in Newark, Ohio and is buried in Wilson Cemetery. .

Children of Laura Elizabeth Harris:
+ 72. i. Arthur Harris (1892 – 1981); and
   73. ii. Harold Charles Harris (1900 – 1948) – Harold was born in Newark, Ohio on July 16, 1900, was a brakeman for the Baltimore & Ohio Railroad, was a World War II veteran, was killed by a train on January 24, 1948 near Barnesville, Ohio, and buried in Wilson Cemetery, Newark, Ohio.

Eighth Generation

72. Arthur Harris (1892 – 1981) – Arthur 'Art' Harris was born on February 21, 1892 in Newark, Licking County, Ohio, the son of Laura Elizabeth Harris. Art, along with his brother Harold, were raised in the Children's' Home in Newark, Ohio. He was dismissed from the Children's Home on April 1, 1908 by reason of age limit, and released to Oscar Fairall, Claylick, Ohio (likely, his employer.) Art

Arthur and Flora C. (Carter) Harris

married Flora 'Floy' Christine Carter, the daughter of Bert C. and Mary (Wilson) Carter, sometime in 1918, prior to entering the military.

Art served in the United States Army during World War I, from May 27, 1918 to April 4, 1919.

Flory passed away on November 24, 1956 in Newark, Ohio and is buried in the Wilson Cemetery. Art passed away in May of 1981 in Newark, Ohio and is buried in the Wilson Cemetery.

Children of Arthur Harris and Flora C. Carter:
+ 74. i. Arthur Eugene Harris (1920 – 1986); and
+ 75. ii. Laura Mae Harris (1922 – Living).

Ninth Generation

Arthur Eugene Harris

74. Arthur Eugene Harris (1920 – 1986) – Arthur Eugene 'Gene' Harris was born on January 31, 1920 in Newark, Ohio, the son of Arthur and Flora Christine (Carter) Harris. Gene married Norma Bertene Juniper on December 14, 1940 in Newark, Ohio. Norma was born in Glouster, Athens County, Ohio on July 26, 1924, the daughter of Pearl and Daisy Mae (Rankin) Juniper. Gene would serve in the United States Army during World War II, from October 21, 1944 to April 13, 1946. After returning he was employed by

Rockwell Axle Plant for 21 years and retired at the age of 55 due to poor health. He and Norma would divorce in 1980.

Norma then married Albert Cherubini in May of 1984 and divorced him in 1986. Gene passed away of a heart attack on February 10, 1986 in Newark, Ohio and was cremated, with his ashes spread on his property by his sons. A marker is located in Wilson Cemetery.

Children of Arthur Eugene Harris and Norma Bertene Juniper:
- + 76. i. Gary Eugene Harris (Living);
- + 77. ii. Larry Richard Harris (Living);
- + 78. iii. Norma Marlene Harris (Living);
- + 79. iv. Thomas Edward Harris (Living);
- + 80. v. Michael David Harris (Living);
- + 81. vi. Robert Kenneth Harris Living);
- + 82. vii. Timothy Wayne Harris (1953 – 2001);
- + 83. viii. Susan Annette Harris (Living); and
- + 84. ix. James Arthur Harris (Living).

Norma Bertene Juniper

75. Laura Mae Harris (1922 – Living) – Laura 'Sis' Mae Harris was born on October 8, 1922 in Newark, Ohio, the daughter of Arthur and Flora Christine (Carter) Harris. Sis married Charles E. Barrett on October 26, 1945.

Children of Charles E. Barrett and Laura Mae Harris:
- + 85 i. Maurice Barrett (Living).

Tenth Generation

76. Gary Eugene Harris (Living) – Gary Harris was born in Newark, Ohio, the son of Arthur Eugene and Norma Bertene (Juniper) Harris. Gary married Patty Starkey.

Children of Gary Harris and Patty Starkey:
86. i. Denver Lee Harris (Living)
87. ii. Holly Jo Harris (Living)

77. Larry Richard Harris (Living); – Larry 'Bub' Richard Harris was born in Newark, Ohio, the son of Arthur Eugene and Norma Bertene (Juniper) Harris. Tim married Rose Jean Moran, the daughter of Benjamin Moran and Juanita Chedester Moran never married. Jean went by the name of Arbaugh, although not adopted.

Children of Larry Richard Harris and Rose Jean Moran:
88. i. Molly Jean Harris (Living);
89. ii. Robyn Rene Harris (Living);
90. iii. Michael Richard Harris (Living); and
91. iv. Kelly Sue Harris (Living).

78. Norma Marlene Harris (Living); – Norma Marlene Harris was born in Newark, Ohio, the daughter of Arthur Eugene and Norma Bertene (Juniper) Harris. Marlene married James Hunt, the son of John and Pauline Hunt.

Children of James Hunt and Norma Marlene Harris:
92. i. Matthew B. Hunt (Living); and
93. ii. Helen Christine Hunt (Living).

79. Thomas Edward Harris (Living); – Thomas 'Tom' Harris was born in Newark, Ohio, the son of Arthur Eugene and Norma Bertene (Juniper) Harris. Tom married and divorced Victoria Norman, the daughter of Jim and Juanita Norman. Tom served in the United States Marine Corp. Tom then married Ora Watts, the daughter of Floyd and Lucy Watts.

Children of Thomas Edward Harris and Victoria Norman:
94. i. Julie Harris (Living); and
95. ii. Janette Harris (Living).

Children of Thomas Edward Harris and Ora Watts:
96. i. Jerry Edward Harris (Living); and
97. ii. Jacquline Lee Harris (Living).

80. Michael David Harris (Living); – Michael 'Rusty' Harris was born in Newark, Ohio, the son of Arthur Eugene and Norma Bertene (Juniper) Harris. Rusty married Jenny Hammond on July 1, 1974, the daughter of Clayton and Ethel Hammond. Rusty served in the United States Air Force.

    Children of Michael David Harris and Jenny Hammond:
        98.   i.   Joshua Harris (Living); and
        99.   ii.   Patrick Harris (Living).

81. Robert Kenneth Harris Living); – Robert 'Bob' Harris was born in Newark, Ohio, the son of Arthur Eugene and Norma Bertene (Juniper) Harris. Bob married and divorced Priscilla Ann Jessup, the daughter of Charles Howard and Edith Rose (Wray) Jessup. Bob then married Katherine Ann (Staugh) Harris.

    Children of Robert Kenneth Harris and Priscilla Ann Jessup:
        100.   i.   Wendy Sue Harris (Living).

    Children of Robert Kenneth Harris and Katherine Ann (Staugh) Harris:
        101.   ii.   Justine Harris (Living).

82. Timothy Wayne Harris (1953 – 2001) – Timothy 'Tim' Wayne Harris was born in Newark, Ohio, the son of Arthur Eugene and Norma Bertene (Juniper) Harris. Tim married and divorced Katherine Ann Staugh, the daughter of James Frederick and Pauline (McDonald) Staugh. Tim would pass away from cancer on July 25, 2001 in Licking County, Ohio.

    Children of Timothy Wayne Harris and Katherine Ann Staugh:
        102.   i.   Stacy DeLynn Harris (Living).
        103.   ii.   Amber Michelle Harris (Living); and

83. Susan Annette Harris (Living) – See William D. Comisford, Jr., page 31.

84. James Arthur Harris (Living) – James 'Jim' Arthur Harris was born in Newark, Ohio, the son of Arthur Eugene and Norma Bertene (Juniper) Harris. Jim married Barbara Ann Bickel, the daughter of James George and Margaret June (Killen) Bickel.

Children of James Arthur Harris and Barbara Ann Bickel:
    104.   i.   Nathan Arthur Harris (Living); and
    105.   ii. James Clay Harris (Living).

85.   Maurice Barrett (Living) – Maurice Barrett was born in Newark, Ohio, the son of Charles E. and Laura Mae (Harris) Barrett. Maurice married Debra.

    Children of Maurice and Debra Barrett:
    106.   i.   Leslie Barrett (Living).

The Arthur and Norma Harris Family Children
Front Row: Norma Marlene, James Arthur, Susan Annette;
Back Row: Timothy Wayne, Larry Richard, Gary Eugene, Robert Kenneth, Michael David, Thomas Edward

Descendants of Jacob and Christina Haas

First Generation

1. Jacob and Christina Haas.

   Children of Jacob and Christina Haas:
   + 2. i. John Haas (1730 – 1801)
     3. ii. Jacob Haas
     4. iii. Isaac Haas
     5. iv. George Haas
     6. v. Jonathan Haas
     7. vi. Elizabeth Haas
     8. vii. Rebecca Haas
     9. viii. Catharine Haas, married John Attdoerffer
     10. ix. Polly Haas

Second Generation

2. John Haas (1730 – 1801) – John Haas was born before 1830, the son of Jacob and Christina Haas. John married Maria Catharine Kelp before 1856. Catharine was born on September 28, 1729 in Wolferlingen, Germany, the daughter of John and Maria (Sonner) Kolb. John passed away in 1801 in Shenandoah County, Virginia, leaving a will dated April 15, 1793. Christina passed away in 1837.

   Children of John Haas and Maria Catharine Kelp:
   + 11. i. John Haas (1756 – 1827);
   + 12. ii. Jacob Haas (1760 – 1819);
     13. iii. Anna Marie Haas (1762 – 1845) – Anna Marie married John Heise;
   + 14. iv. Christena Haas, married Abraham Gochenour;
     15. v. Elizabeth Haas, married Philip Crousdorf;
     16. vi. Maria Haas, married Henry Geeding

Third Generation

11. John Haas (1756 – 1827) – John Haas was born in 1756 in Shenandoah County, Virginia, the son of John and Maria Catharine (Kelp) Haas. John married Elizabeth Wilkins on October 5, 1774 in Shenandoah County, Virginia. Elizabeth was born in 1759 in Shenandoah County, Virginia, the daughter of Johann Gottfried

"Godfrey" and Christina (Nonemacher) Wilkins. John and his family came to Washington Twp, Licking County, Ohio around 1808. John passed away in 1827, while Elizabeth passed away in 1837, both in Licking County, Ohio.

Children of John Haas and Elizabeth Wilkins:
- 17. i. Catherine Haas (1785 – 1848);
- + 18. ii. John Haas (1787 – 1874);
- 19. iv. Mary 'Margaret' Haas (1789 – 1851) – Margaret was born on August 12, 1789 in Shenandoah County, Virginia and married John Grabiel on February 7, 1807 in Shenandoah County, Virginia;
- 20. v. Christena Haas (1791 – Unknown) – Christena was born on November 10, 1791 in Shenandoah County, Virginia and married Martin Robinson on December 2, 1816 in Licking County;
- 21. vi. Elizabeth Haas (1791 – Unknown) – Elizabeth was born on November 10, 1791 in Shenandoah County, Virginia and married Philip Smoots on February 1, 1812 in Shenandoah County, Virginia;
- + 22. vii, William Haas (1794 – 1869);
- 23. viii. Sarah Haas (1796 – 1832) – Sarah was born in July of 1796, married Joseph F. Parrett on August 6, 1814, and died on October 7, 1832 in Ross, Virginia;
- 24. ix. Adam Haas (1798 – Unknown) – Adam was born on December 25, 1798 and married Savanah Robinson on July 8, 1819;
- + 25. x. Rachel Haas (1801 – 1869);
- 26. xi. Rebecca Haas (1803 – 1829);
- 27. xii. Absolom W. Haas (1805 – 1887) – Absolom was born on November 21, 1805 in Virginia, married Ruhama E. Sells in 1849 in Licking County, Ohio, died in 1887 in Burlington Twp, Licking County, Ohio, and both are buried in Maple Grove Cemetery; and
- 28. xiii. Simon Haas (1810 – 1874) – Simon was born on September 9, 1810 in Woodbridge, Virginia, married Hannah Marple, died on June 16, 1874 in Licking County, and is buried in the Maple Grove Cemetery.

12. Jacob Haas (1760 – 1819) – Jacob Haas was born in 1760 in Shenandoah County, Virginia, the son of John and Maria Catharine (Kelp) Haas. Jacob married Christina Sonner on June 10, 1788. The minister was Rev. Simon Haar and the witness was Andrew Summer. Christina was born in 1768 near Strasburg, Virginia in Shenandoah County, the daughter of Johann Philip and Anna Elizabeth (Wendle) Sanner. Jacob and Christina lived on Narrow Passage Creek northwest of Woodstock. Jacob died in 1819 in Shenandoah County,

Virginia, while Christina would pass away sometime between 1838 and 1854 in Strasburg, Shenandoah, Virginia or in Indiana.

The March 10, 1819 issue of the Woodstock Herald states, *"Died Sunday last Mr. Jacob Haas, an old worthy inhabitant of this County. He has left a disconsolate number of relatives and friends to mourn his irreparable loss."*

    Children of Jacob Haas and Christina Sonner:

29. i. John Haas (1789 – Unknown) – John married Sarah Koontz on April 10, 1815, John was the Sheriff of Shenandoah County in the 1850's. He was appointed an Ensign in the Light Infantry of the 1st Battalion, 18th Regiment May 10, 1814. He was one of the men selected March 3, 1834 to solicit funds in the Woodstock area for the Valley Pike. He was appointed trustee for the Woodstock Female Seminary March 13, 1847;

30. ii. Jacob Haas (1790 – 1889) – Jacob was born on November 10, 1790, married Catherine Pitman, the daughter of Emanuel and Esther (Funkhouser) Pitmann of Mt. Olive, Shenandoah County, Virginia, on April 7, 1819, Jacob and Catherine moved to Harrison County Indiana. Jacob established the "Haas Chapel" there. Jacob Haas was licensed to preach at Mill creek in April 1831. Both buried in Haas Cemetery Harrison County, Indiana;

31. iii. Elizabeth Haas (1792 – 1828);

32. iv. Philip Haas (1794 – Unknown) – Philip married Magdalena Phillips on November 5, 1825;

33. v. Catherine Haas, married John Altdorffer on December 23, 1817, married by the Rev. Schmucker;

34. vi. Rebecca Haas, married William Nagel on September 8, 1823;

35. vii. Isaac Haas (1800 – 1873) – Isaac was born on December 2, 1800 and died in Indiana on January 23, 1873;

36. viii. Mary Haas (1802 – Unknown) – Mary married William Coffman on March 30, 1822;

37. ix. George Haas (1804 – Unknown); and

38. x. Jonathan Haas (1806 – 1853) – Jonathan married Regina Coffman on March 30, 1830 and died on August 9, 1853.

14.   Christena Haas (1764 – 1812) – Christena Haas was born about 1764 in Frederick County, Virginia, the daughter of John and Maria Catharine (Kelp) Haas. Christena married Abraham Gochenour on October 18, 1782 in Shenandoah County, Virginia. Abraham was born in 1771 in Frederick County, Virginia, the son of Jacob and Margaret (Good) Gochenour. Christena passed away sometime before 1812.

Children of Abraham Gochenour and Christena Haas:
- 39. i. Elizabeth Gochenaur (1784 – 1846);
- 40. ii. Henry Gochenaur (1791 – 1856);
- 41. iii. Catharine Gochenaur (1794 – 1857);
- 42. iv. Mary Gochenaur (1796 – 1844);
- 43. v. Samuel Gochenaur (1796 – 1828); and
- 44. vi. Abraham Gochenaur (1806 – 1838).

Fourth Generation

18.   John Haas (1787 – 1874) – John Haas was born on March 4, 1787 in Shenandoah County, Virginia, the son of John and Elizabeth (Wilkins) Haas. John married Mary Ann Boyd on January 15, 1821 in Licking County, Ohio, and died on May 3, 1874. Mary passed away in 1843.

Children of John Haas and Mary Ann Boyd:
- 45. i. J. K. Haas;
- 46. ii. William Haas;
- 47. iii. J. W. Haas; and
- 48. iv. Simon L. Haas (1842 – Unknown) – Simon was born on December 21, 1842 in Western Virginia, married Delia Harris, and died sometime after 1909).

22.   William Haas (1794 – 1869) – William Haas was born on January 2, 1794 in Shenandoah County, Virginia, the son of John and Elizabeth (Wilkins) Haas. John married Isabella, who was born in Ireland.

Children of William and Isabella Haas:
- 49. i. Mary E. Haas;
- 50. ii. Martha Haas; and
- 51. iii. Finney Haas (1851 – 1908).

25.   Rachel Haas (1801 – 1869) – See Isaac Harris, page 308.

Descendants of Thomas Phillips and Mary Philipps

First Generation

1. Thomas Phillips (1735 – 1813) – Thomas Phillips was born in 1735 in Llandilo Twp, Carmarthenshire, South Wales. Phillip married Mary Philipps and adopted the spelling of her surname. Mary was born in Picton Castle, Pembrokeshire, Wales, the daughter of Thomas and Mary Philipps. Mary was also the sister of Erasmus Philippps, who was head counselor of the King Bench.

In 1787, Thomas's son's: Thomas; John H.; Erasmus; were seized on Board a ship by the English press gang to put them in the engineer service, but they were not compelled to go, owing to the fact their mother was the sister of Erasmus Philipps, who had much influence in England. John H. was the reputed author of some seditious or treasonable literature, and, to avoid arrest and punishment, he decided to immigrate to America. He sailed for Philadelphia, accompanied by his brothers, who were more or less implicated with him.

With some persuasion Thomas's sons asked their father, and a man of some wealth, to close his business affairs, and follow them to America. Shortly afterwards, Thomas and an associate, Theophilus Rees, sailed to America. They arrived in America on May 14, 1795 after a voyage of 44 days from Liverpool, aboard a British armed ship, the *Amphion*, manned by Royal Navy sailors, and Captain Williams. The ship was chartered by Theophilus and Thomas and they brought with them family and friends. They settled for a short time in Beulah near Ebensburg, Cambria County, Pennsylvania, where Thomas operated wagon trains. In and around 1796, Thomas, along with Theophilus, became the two original founders of the Welsh settlement in Licking County, Ohio, that is now referred to as the "Welsh Hills'" in Granville, when they purchased nearly three thousand acres from Sampson Davis, a Welshman of Philadelphia.

Mary passed away in Philadelphia, Pennsylvania about 1804, prior to the families move to Ohio. Thomas passed away on May 20, 1813 in Licking County, Ohio.

Children of Thomas Phillips and Mary Philipps:
- 2. i. John H. Philipps (Unknown – 1832) – John died in Cincinnati, Ohio;
- 3. ii. Thomas Philipps (Unknown – 1801) – Thomas married Elizabeth Legg and died in Beulah, Somerset County, Pennsylvania;
- 4. iii. Erasmus Philipps (Unknown – 1801) – Erasmus died after 1801 in New York;
- + 5. iv. Martha Philipps (1769 – 1842);
- + 6. v. Samuel Jones Philipps (1777 – 1854);
- + 7. vi. Rachel Philipps (1784 – 1841);
- + 8. vii. Sallie Philipps, married William Morrison;
- 9. viii. Mary Philipps; and
- 10. ix. Anna Philipps, married Evan Griffith.

Second Generation

5. Martha Philipps (1769 – 1842) – Martha Philipps was born on October 12, 1769, the daughter of Thomas and Mary (Philipps) Phillips. Martha married Samuel White in 1797 in Pennsylvania. Samuel was born on March 4, 1762 in Peterborough, Massachusetts. Martha passed away on April 14, 1842 and is buried in the Philipps Cemetery in Licking County, Ohio, while Samuel passed away on September 13, 1851.

Children of Samuel White and Martha Philipps:
- 11. i. Jonathan White (1800 – 1827) – Jonathan was born in Cambria County, Pennsylvania and died is Stark County, Ohio;
- 12. ii. Joseph White (1810 – Unknown) – Joseph was born after 1810 in Licking County, Ohio; and
- 13. iii. Samuel White (1812 – 1844) – Samuel was born on March 3, 1812 in Licking County, Ohio and died on July 20, 1844.

6. Samuel Jones Philipps (1777 – 1854) – Samuel Jones Philipps was born in 1777 in South Wales, the son of Thomas and Mary (Philipps) Phillips. Samuel married Lydia Griffith, the daughter of Daniel and Anna Griffith. Lydia was born in 1775.

Lydia passed away on April 4, 1843 in Licking County, Ohio and is buried in the Philipps Cemetery. Samuel passed away on March 2, 1854 in Newark, Licking County, Ohio and is buried in the Philipps Cemetery.

Children of Samuel Jones Philipps and Lydia Griffith:
    14.   i.   Thomas Philipps (1800 – 1884);
    15.   ii.   John Philipps (1802 – 1832);
    16.   iii.   Mary Philipps (1804 – Unknown);
+ 17.   iv.   Samuel Griffith Philipps (1806 – 1899);
    18.   v.   Erasmus Philipps (1808 – Unknown);
    19.   vi.   Ann Philipps;
    20.   vii.   Ben Philipps;
    21.   viii.   Lydia Philipps;
    22.   ix.   Washington Philipps (1819 – 1842)
    23.   x.   Lucretia Philipps; and
    24.   xi.   Sallie Philipps.

7.   Rachel Philipps (1784 – 1841) – Rachel Philipps was born in 1784, the daughter of Thomas and Mary (Philipps) Phillips. Rachel married Thomas Owens. Thomas was born in 1761. Thomas passed away on May 29, 1820, while Rachel passed away on October 21, 1841. Both are buried in the Philipps Cemetery in Licking County, Ohio.

Children of Thomas Owens and Rachel Philipps:
    25.   i.   Erasmus Owens
    26.   ii.   Diana Owens
    27.   iii.   Esther Owens
    28.   iv.   Sallie Owens

8.   Sallie Philipps, the daughter of Thomas and Mary (Philipps) Phillips, married William Morrison. Together, they would have four (4) children.

Children of William Morrison and Sallie Philipps:
    29.   i.   Tom Morrison
    30.   ii.   Julia Morrison
    31.   iii.   William Morrison
    32.   iv.   Sallie Morrison

Third Generation

17.   Samuel Griffith Philipps (1806 – 1899) – Samuel Griffith Philipps was born on November 17, 1806 in Beulah, Cambria County, Pennsylvania, the son of Samuel Jones and Lydia (Griffith) Philipps. Samuel married Susannah Reily in October of 1829. Susannah was born on May 23, 1807 at Tilton Fort, Jefferson County, Ohio, the daughter of Jacob and Sallie (Tilton) Reily. Samuel was a teacher and in 1855 went to Kansas, where he helped make government

surveys. Susannah passed away on September 22, 1893 in Granville Twp, Licking County, Ohio and is buried in the Philipps Cemetery. Samuel passed away on December 26, 1899 in Granville Twp. Licking County, Ohio and is buried in the Philipps Cemetery.

    Children of Samuel Griffith Philipps and Susannah Reily:
- 33. i. Joseph Philipps (1831 – 1832) – Joseph was born in November 1831, died on July 1, 1932, and is buried in the Philipps Cemetery;
- 34. ii. Sarah Philipps (1833 – Unknown) – Sarah married David D. Jones of Morrow County, Ohio;
- 35. iii. Persilla Philipps (1838 – Unknown) – Persilla was born on November 8, 1836, married E.L. Rose, and died on May 28, 1897;
- 36. iv. Martha Philipps (1841 – Unknown) – Martha married S. J. White;
- + 37. v. Victoria Philipps (1842 – 1875);
- + 38. vi. Ellen 'Nellie' M. Philipps (1844 – Unknown);
- + 39. vii. Samuel Jones Philipps (1845 – 1910);
- 40. viii. Thomas Wendell Philipps (1849 – 1902) – Thomas was born on August 28, 1849 in Licking County, Ohio, died on November 3, 1902 in Licking County, Ohio, and is buried in the Philipps Cemetery; and
- 41. ix. Lydia Philipps, died at age 12.

Fourth Generation

37. Victoria Philipps (1842 – 1875) – See Absolom W. Harris, page 309.

38. Ellen M. Philipps (1844 – Unknown) – Ellen 'Nellie' M. Philipps was born in 1844 in Ohio, the daughter of Samuel Griffith and Susannah (Reily) Philipps. Nellie married Jacob G. Frederick on May 20, 1865, where they would live in Granville, Ohio. Jacob was born in 1836 in Ohio. Jacob was a painter.

    Children of Jacob G. Frederick and Ellen M. Philipps:
- 42. i. Arthur J. Frederick (1866 – Unknown);
- 43. ii. Ada G. Frederick (1872 – 1902); and
- 44. iii. Nellie N. Frederick (1876 – Unknown).

39. Samuel Jones Philipps (1845 – 1910) – Samuel Jones Philipps was born on December 28, 1845 in a little log house in McKean Twp, Licking County, Ohio, the son of Samuel Griffith and Susannah (Reily) Philipps. Samuel attended school at the "old stone school house", which still stands today, about 2 miles northeast of Granville. It was erected by the Rev. Thomas Hughs in 1825, on his farm. On September 6, 1864, Samuel enlisted in the Union Army as a member of Company D, 22nd Ohio Volunteer Infantry, being mustered out August 18, 1865. Upon returning, he attended Denison University and for a number of years engaged successfully in teaching in the county schools.

Samuel married Wilhelmina Williams on June 15, 1876 in Licking County, Ohio, the daughter of John and Ester (Jones) Williams. Wilhelmina was born in Granville Twp, Licking County, Ohio on March 2, 1857.

Samuel Jones Philipps

Wilhelmina passed away on June 23, 1898, while Samuel would pass away on December 10, 1910. Both are buried in the Philipps Cemetery.

Children of Samuel Jones Philipps and Wilhelmina Williams:
- 45. i. Mamie O. Philipps (1877 – Unknown) – Mamie married Samuel Wheeler of Montclair, New Jersey, and who was a graduate of Wellesley College, near Boston;
- 46. ii. Victoria B. Philipps (1879 – Unknown) – Victoria married Daniel Jones, of Cincinnati;
- 47. iii. Pearl L. Philipps (1882 – Unknown) – Pearl married and divorced George Hottinger; then married Vernon Taylor;
- 48. iv. Bertha N. Philipps (1884 – Unknown) – Bertha married Mr. Boles;
- 49. v. Susie E. Philipps (1886 – Unknown) – Susie married G.P. Barber, of Newark
- 50. vi. Thomas Warren Philipps (1888 - 1941) – Thomas was born on July 23, 1888, attending Law School in New Jersey, taught school in Baltimore, Ohio, and at Newark High School, married Rhea Grace Evans on August 25, 1914, was elected Licking County Engineer in 1941, and died from a head injury on June 27, 1941;
- 51. vii. Samuel J. Philipps (1890 – Unknown) – Samuel married Olive;

52. viii. Winifred W. Philipps (1892 – Unknown) – Winfred married her sisters ex-husband, George Hottinger;
53. ix. Edith D. Philipps (1895 – Unknown) – Edith married Saul (Marx) Markawitz; and
54. x. Philip Philipps (1897 – Unknown) - Philip married Elsie Hankinson.

Descendants of Johann Gottfried Wilkins and Christina Nonemacher

First Generation

1. Johann Gottfried Wilkins (1721 – Unknown) – Johann Gottfried 'Godfrey' Wilkins was born in 1721 in Weiler, Baden, Germany. Godfrey immigrated to the American Colonies around 1727. Godfrey married Christina Nonemacher on November 6, 1746 in Philadelphia, Pennsylvania. Christina passed away about 1761. Godfrey then married Catherine Heller on January 14, 1762 in Philadelphia, Pennsylvania. Godfrey would pass away on May 26, 1785 in Frederick County, Virginia.

    Children of Johann Gottfried Wilkins and Christina Nonemacher:
- 2. i. Mathias Wilkins (1747 – 1803) – Mathias was born in 1847 in Shenandoah County, Virginia, married Margaret Hottel Keller on July 27, 1769, and died on October 12, 1803 in Lost River, Hardy County, Western Virginia;
- 3. ii. George Wilkins (1750 – 1821) – George was born about 1750 in Frederick County, Virginia, married Lydia Wise in 1769, then Barbara Travel in 1775, and died in Hardy County, Western Virginia;
- 4. iii. Henry Wilkins (1756 – 1803) – Henry was born in Frederick County, Virginia, married Rachel Skilit in 1782, and died on January 3, 1803 in Highland County, Ohio;
- \+ 5. iv. Elizabeth Wilkins (1759 – 1837);
- 6. v. Godfrey Wilkins (1760 – 1810) – Godfrey was born in Frederick County, Virginia, married Catherine Layman on June 13, 1786 in Woodstock, Shenandoah County, Virginia, and died in 1810 in Shenandoah County, Virginia.

    Children of Johann Gottfried Wilkins and Catherine Heller:
- \+ 7. i. John Wilkins (1762 – 1814).

Second Generation

5. Elizabeth Wilkins (1759 – 1837) – See John Haas, page 317.

7. John Wilkins (1762 – 1814) – John Wilkins was born on August 26, 1762 in Lost River, Hardy County, Western Virginia, the son of Johann Gottfried and Catherine (Heller) Wilkins. John married Hannah Craybill around 1783 in Virginia. Hannah was born on July 1, 1768 in Rockingham Co., Virginia. John moved his family to Newark, Ohio in 1812. John passed away on September 26, 1814 in Licking County, Ohio and is buried in the Wilkins Cemetery (the "Avery Fisher Farm) in Licking County, Ohio. His epitaph carved in his tombstone reads *"Stop my friend and take my view of death's cold grave allowed you. Remember that you are born to die, and turn to dust as well as I."* Hannah would pass away on August 1, 1834 in Ohio.

Children of John Wilkins and Hannah Craybill:
8. i. Levi Wilkins, died in Iowa or Missouri;
9. ii. Catherine Wilkins;
10. iii. Sarah Wilkins;
11. iv. David Wilkins (1783 – Unknown) – David died in Jersey, Ohio;
12. v. Daniel Wilkins (1785 - 1847) – Daniel married Rebecca Barnes;
13. vi. Samuel Wilkins (1789 – 1865) – Samuel married Wedlena Swisher;
14. vii. Elizabeth Wilkins (1791 – 1857);
15. viii. John Wilkins (1792 - Unknown);
16. ix. Jacob Wilkins (1795 - 1856);
17. x. George Wilkins (1799 - 1825); and
18. xi. Hannah Wilkins (1806 – 1886) – Hannah married Abraham Swisher on March 9, 1826.

Descendants of Daniel and Anna Griffith

First Generation

1.   Daniel Griffith (1753 – 1831) – Daniel Griffith was born in August 1753 in Wales. Daniel married Anna. He died on September 24, 1831 in Licking County, Ohio and is buried in the Old Colony Burying Grounds.

    Children of Daniel and Anna Griffith:
- \+   2.   i.   Lydia Griffith (1775 – 1843);
-     3.   ii.   John H. Griffith (Unknown – 1850) – John married Ann Jones and passed away soon after arriving in California during the Gold Rush;
- \+   4.   iii.   Esther Griffith (1795 – 1883);
-     5.   iv.   Mary Griffith;
-     6.   v.   Ann Griffith;
-     7.   vi.   William Thomas Griffith (1802 – 1875) – William was born on August 21, 1802 in Wales, married Elizabeth Charlotte Jones, in Wales, sometime before 1829, died June 1, 1875 in Licking County, Ohio ;
-     8.   vii.   Hannah Griffith; and
-     9.   viii.   Catherine Griffith.

Second Generation

2.   Lydia Griffith (1775 – 1843) – See Samuel Jones Philipps, page 322.

4.   Esther Griffith (1795 – 1883) – Esther Griffith was born on February 1, 1795 in Carmarthenshire, Wales, the daughter of Daniel and Anna Griffith. Esther married Edmund James on January 28, 1814 in Licking County, Ohio. Esther passed away on July 18, 1883 in Morrow County, Ohio.

    Children of Edmund James and Esther Griffith:
- \+   10.   i.   Ebenezer R. James (1814 – Unknown);
-     11.   ii.   David James (1817 – Unknown);
-     12.   iii.   William James (1817 – Unknown);
-     13.   iv.   Mary James;
-     14.   v.   Ann James;
-     15.   vi.   Thomas James (1823 – Unknown);
-     16.   vii.   Daniel James (1826 – Unknown);

17. viii. Joseph James (1828 – Unknown);
18. ix. Davis E. James (1837 – Unknown);
19. x. John H. James; and
20. xi. Benjamin James.

Third Generation

11. Ebenezer R. James (1814 – Unknown) – Ebenezer R. James was born on November 10, 1814 in Licking County, Ohio, the son of Edmund James and Esther Griffith. Ebenezer married Phoebe Bockover on April 27, 1837.

    Children of Ebenezer James and Phoebe Bockover:
    21. i. Flora A. James (1839 – Unknown);
    22. ii. Wesley K. James (1842 – Unknown);
    23. iii. Infant James; and
    24. iv. Lewis J. James (1845 – Unknown).

Descendants of Jacob Reily and Sally Tilton

First Generation

1. Jacob Reily (1779 – 1851) – Jacob Reily was born about 1779 in Delaware, the son of Isaac and Martha (Bazaleel) Reily. Isaac Reily was an Irish minister of considerable wealth and importance in public affairs residing near Philadelphia. He lost all his possessions during the Revolution and died near the close of the War leaving his widow penniless. Martha came to Ohio in 1785 with her son Jacob, where she married Jimmie Johnson for her second husband. She and Jimmy came to the Welsh Hills in 1802. Jacob would marry Sallie Tilton, the daughter of John and Susannah (Jones) Tilton. Sallie was born about 1773 in Tilton Fort, Jefferson County, Ohio. Sallie was thought to be the first white child born in the Northwest Territory (Ohio). Jacob and Sallie reached the Welsh Hills around the fall of 1807 or the spring of 1808. They built their cabin at the north east corner of the Rees purchase at the headwaters of the Sharon run on a farm now familiarly known as the "Old Booher Place". Sally passed away on September 8, 1849 in Licking County, Ohio, while Jacob passed away on October 3, 1851 in Licking County, Ohio. Both are buried in the Old Colony Burying Ground.

Children of Jacob Reily and Sally Tilton:
+   2.   i.   Susannah Reily (1807 – 1893);
    3.   ii. Bazaleel Reily (1809 – 1836) – Bazaleel passed away on December 20, 1836 and is buried in the Old Colony Burying Ground in Licking County, Ohio;
    4.   iii. Priscilla Reily (1814 – 1832) – Priscilla passed away on December 26, 1832 and is buried in the Old Colony Burying Ground in Licking County, Ohio; and
    5.   iv. Isaac Reily (1820 – 1822) – Isaac passed away in July 1, 1822 and is buried in the Old Colony Burying Ground in Licking County, Ohio.

Second Generation

2. Susannah Reily (1807 – 1893) – See Samuel Griffith Philipps, page 323.

Descendants of John Tilton and Mary Pearsall

First Generation

1. John Tilton (1612 – 1688) – John Tilton was born on March 4, 1612 or 1613 in Wolston, Warwickshire, England, the son of William Tilton III and Ursela Pycroft. John married Mary Pearsall. Mary was born in Wolston, Warwick, England in 1620. Mary passed away on May 23, 1683, while John passed away on April 3, 1688, both are buried in Gravesend, Kings County, New York.

Children of John Tilton and Mary Pearsall:

	2.	i.	John Tilton (1639 – 1700) – John was born on January 4, 1639 or 1640 in Lynn, Essex County, Massachusetts and passed away on November 20, 1700 in Middleton, Monmouth County, New Jersey;
+	3.	ii.	Peter Tilton (1642 – Unknown)
	4.	iii.	Sarah Tilton (1644 – Unknown) – Sarah was born on May 4, 1644 in Gravesend, Kings County, New York;
	5.	iv.	Esther Tilton (1647 – 1703) – Esther was born on May 21, 1647 in Gravesend, Kings County, New York and passed away on September 24, 1703 in Gravesend, Kings County, New York;
	6.	v.	Abigail Tilton (1650 – Unknown) – Abigail was born in Gravesend, Kings County, New York;
	7.	vi.	Thomas Tilton (1651 – Unknown) – Thomas was born on March 1, 1651 or 1652 in Gravesend, Kings County, New York and died in Kent, New Castle County, Delaware; and
	8.	vii.	Mary Tilton (1654 – Unknown) – Mary was born on June 4, 1654 in Gravesend, Kings County, New York.

Second Generation

3. Peter Tilton (1642 – Unknown) – Peter Tilton was born on November 16, 1642 in Lynn, Essex County, Massachusetts, the son of John Tilton and Mary Pearsall. Peter married Rebecca Brazier, the daughter of Henry and Susan (Spicer) Brazier, on April 22, 1665. Rebecca was born on April 24, 1648. Rebecca passed away on October 6, 1700, while John passed away on December 15, 1700, both in Middleton, Monmouth County, New Jersey.

Children of Peter Tilton and Rebecca Brazier:
- 9. i. Rebecca Tilton (1665 – 1710) – Rebecca was born on July 6, 1665 in Gravesend, Kings County, New York;
- 10. ii. John Tilton (1668 – 1731);
- 12. iii. Peter Tilton (1671 – 1731) – Peter was born on February 10, 1671 or 1672 in Shrewsbury, Monmouth County, New Jersey and died about 1731 in Middleton, Monmouth County, New Jersey;
- 13. iv. Mary Tilton (1675 – 1678) – Mary was born on September 8, 1675 and passed away on August 31, 1678 in Shrewsbury, Monmouth County, New Jersey;
- 14. v. Thomas Tilton (1676 – 1677) – Thomas was born on July 20, 1676 in Middleton, Monmouth County, New Jersey and passed away in May of 1677 in Monmouth County, New Jersey;
- 15. vi. Esther Tilton (1678 – 1704) – Esther was born on June 5, 1678 in Middleton, Monmouth County, New Jersey, married Richard Stout, and died in 1704 in Middleton, Monmouth County, New Jersey;
- 16. vii. Daniel Tilton (1679 – 1748) – Daniel was born on July 9, 1679 in Middleton, Monmouth County, New Jersey, married Sarah Wyckoff, and died on May 31, 1748 in Freehold, Monmouth County, New Jersey;
- 17. viii. Mary Tilton (1681 – 1749) – Mary was born on February 2, 1681 in Middleton, Monmouth County, New Jersey, married Richard Stout, and died in 1749 in Middleton, Monmouth County, New Jersey;
- 18. ix. Catherine Tilton (1684 – 1765) – Catherine was born on July 14, 1684 in Middleton, Monmouth County, New Jersey, married Hugh Hartshorne, and passed away on June 18, 1765 in Middleton, Monmouth County, New Jersey;
- 19. x. Henry Tilton (1686 – 1707) – Henry was born on November 24, 1686 in Middleton, Monmouth County, New Jersey and passed away on December 1, 1707 in Middleton, Monmouth County, New Jersey;
- 20. xi. Samuel Tilton (1689 – 1743) – Samuel was born on January 17, 1689 or 1690 in Middleton, Monmouth County, New Jersey, first married about 1715, then married Elizabeth Willet on February 4, 1744 in New Jersey, and passed away on February 4, 1743 or 1744 in Middleton, Monmouth County, New Jersey;
- 21 xii. William Tilton (1696 – Unknown); and
- + 22. xiii. Joseph Tiltlon (1704 – 1746).

Third Generation

22. Joseph Tilton (1704 – 1791) – Joseph Tilton was born in 1704 in Middleton, Monmouth County, New Jersey, the son of Peter and Rebecca (Ebtharpe) Tilton. Joseph married Elizabeth Ebtharpe, the daughter of Francis and Elinor Ebtharpe. Elizabeth was born on February 24, 1707 in Cecil County, Maryland. Elizabeth would pass away in 1768, while Joseph passed away on October 30, 1746 in Maryland.

Children of Joseph Tilton and Elizabeth Ebtharpe:
- 23.   i.   Elizabeth Tilton (1736 – Unknown);
- + 24. ii. John Tilton (1738 – 1810);
- 25.   iii. Thomas Tilton (1740 – 1793) – Thomas was born in Cecil County, Maryland, married Deborah Farrell in 1766 in Maryland, and died in February 1793 in Washington City, Washington County, Pennsylvania;
- 26.   iv. Elijah Tilton; and
- 27.   v.   Richard Tilton, married Nancy Ann Lum in 1774 in Mason County, Kentucky.

Fifth Generation

24. John Tilton (1738 – 1810) – John Tilton was born in 1738 in Cecil County, Maryland, the son of Joseph and Elizabeth (Ebtharpe) Tilton. John married Susannah Jones in 1759 in Maryland. Susannah was born on February 25, 1748 or 1749 in Elkridge, Howard County, Maryland. John passed away on July 10, 1810 in Warren Twp, Jefferson County, Ohio, while Susannah would pass away on October 15, 1838 in Tiltonville, Jefferson County, Ohio.

Children of John Tilton and Susannah Jones:
- 28.   i.   Joseph Tilton (1766 – 1800) – Joseph was born on December 30, 1766 on Buffalo Creek, Washington County, Pennsylvania and passed away on April 16, 1860 in Tiltonville, Jefferson County, Ohio;
- 29.   ii. Thomas Tilton (1768 – 1828) – Thomas was born in 1768 on Buffalo Creek, Washington County, Pennsylvania and passed away in 1828 in Tiltonville, Jefferson County, Ohio;
- 30.   iii. Jackson Tilton (1769 – 1791) – Jackson was born in 1769 on Buffalo Creek, Washington County, Pennsylvania and died on May 3, 1791 in the Northwest Territory;
- 31.   iv. Susannah Tilton (1769 – 1854) – Susannah was born on January 24, 1769 on Buffalo Creek, Washington County, Pennsylvania and died on February 1, 1854;

	32.	v.	Polly Tilton (1771 – Unknown) – Polly was born on Buffalo Creek, Washington County, Pennsylvania;
+	33.	vi.	Sally Tilton (1773 – Unknown);
	34.	vii.	Pricilla Tilton (1776 – Unknown) – Pricilla was born on October 30, 1776 on Buffalo Creek, Washington County, Pennsylvania;
	35.	viii.	Lorenzo Tilton (1777 – Unknown) – Lorenzo was born on Buffalo Creek, Washington County, Pennsylvania;
	36.	ix.	John Tilton (1781 – 1781) – John was born and died on Buffalo Creek, Washington County, Pennsylvania;
	37.	x.	Caleb Tilton (1783 – 1847) – Caleb was born in the Northwest Territory (Warren Twp, Jefferson County, Ohio) and passed away in 1847 in Tiltonville, Jefferson County, Ohio;
	38.	xi.	Elijah Tilton (1785 – Unknown) – Elijah was born on Buffalo Creek, Washington County, Pennsylvania;
	39.	xii.	William Tilton (1787 – Unknown) – William was born on April 3, 1787 in the Northwest Territory (Warren Twp, Jefferson County, Ohio);
	40.	xiii.	Ann Tilton (1789 – Unknown) - Ann was born in February 1789 in the Northwest Territory (Warren Twp, Jefferson County, Ohio);
	41.	xiv.	Susan Tilton (1790 – 1790) – Susan was born and died in 1790 in the Northwest Territory (Warren Twp, Jefferson County, Ohio);
	42.	xv.	Druscilla Tilton (1792 – 1861) - Druscilla was born in 1792 in the Northwest Territory (Warren Twp, Jefferson County, Ohio) and passed away in 1861 in Warren Twp, Jefferson County, Ohio; and
	43.	xvi.	John Tilton (1799 – 1831) – John was born on July 14, 1799 in the Northwest Territory (Warren Twp, Jefferson County, Ohio) and passed away on July 22, 1831 in Warren Twp, Jefferson County, Ohio.

Sixth Generation

33. Sally Tilton (1773 – Unknown) – See Jacob Reily, page 331.

Descendants of Henry Brazier and Susan Spicer

First Generation

1. Henry Brazier (1624 – Unknown) – Henry Brazier or Brasier was born in 1624. Henry was an Englishman from the shire of Essex and was in New Amsterdam (New York City) as early as 1644, when he married Susan Spicer on October 9, 1644 in New Amsterdam, New York. Susan was born in 1624, the daughter of Thomas and Ann Spicer.

Their early home was on Manhattan Island at "Deutil Bay" or "Hopton." Henry later obtained land on Long Island on the East River. Then In 1659 Henry purchased land at Gravesend.

In 1659, the town of "The Cove" (in Kings County, New York) agreed to give Henry Brazier 500 gilders for building a mill.

Children of Henry Brazier and Susan Spicer:
- 2. i. Mary Brazier (1645 – Unknown);
- 3. ii. Willem Brazier (1646 – Unknown);
- + 4. iii. Rebecca Brazier (1648 – 1700);
- 5. iv. Breser Brazier (1653 – Unknown);
- 6. v. Machtelt Brazier (1655 – Unknown);
- 7. vi. Susannah Brazier (1656 – 1716) – Susannah was born in Manhattan, New York, married William Churchill on March 10, 1672 in Manhattan, New York;
- 8. vii. Martha Brazier (1657 – Unknown);
- 9. viii. Sarah Brazier (1659 – Unknown);
- 10. ix. Henry Brazier (1663 – Unknown);
- 11. x. Isaac Brazier (1666 – Unknown); and
- 12. xi. Abraham Brazier (1668 – Unknown).

Second Generation

4. Rebecca Brazier (1648 – 1700) – See Peter Tilton, page 333.

Descendants of Charles Carter and Rachel Sharp

First Generation

1. Charles Carter (1821 – 1888) – Charles Carter was born in 1821 in Hampshire County, England. Charles immigrated to America around in 1836 and would settle in Perry County, Ohio. Charles served an apprenticeship at carpentering in Putnam, Perry County, Ohio. He followed that trade but a few years, before becoming a farmer. Charles married Rachel Sharp on April 16, 1840 in Pleasant Twp, Perry County, Ohio. Rachel was born in 1722 in Virginia, the daughter of Daniel Sharp. Charles was the postmaster in Moxahala and a farmer. Rachel would pass away in 1859. Charles then married Mary A. Berry in 1861. Mary was born in 1830 in Ohio. Charles passed away on July 4, 1888 in Moxahala, Perry County, Ohio and was reported as follows in the newspaper:

> *"Prepared His Own Grave: New Lexington, July 9 – Charles Carter, aged sixty-eight, died on the Fourth at Moxahala, and was buried. About a year ago he fixed up his own grave, underlaying it with cinders, upon which he was to be placed, and a stone slap to be laid upon him with no coffin, so that as his body moldened away, it would press through the cinders into the earth. Directions for his funeral were duly made by him, and were carried out."*

Children of Charles Carter and Rachel Sharp:
```
     2.    i.   Mary Carter (1846 – Unknown);
     3.   ii.   George Carter (1846 – Unknown);
     4.  iii.   Margaret Carter (1848 – Unknown);
+    5.   iv.   James Carter (1849 – Unknown);
     6.    v.   Charles Carter (1851 – Unknown);
     7.   vi.   William Carter (1854 – Unknown); and
     8.  vii.   Thomas Carter (1856 – Unknown).
```

Children of Charles Carter and Mary A. Berry:
```
     9.    i.   Jerome Carter (1863 – Unknown);
    10.   ii.   Martha E. Carter (1869 – Unknown); and
    11.  iii.   Culley 'Callie' M. Carter (1870 – Unknown).
```

Second Generation

5.   James Carter (1849 – Unknown) – James Carter was born on December 29, 1849 in Perry County, Ohio, the son of Charles and Rachel (Sharp) Carter. James married Ella around 1878 in Perry County, Ohio. Ella was born in 1845 in Ohio. James was a farmer in Perry County, Ohio.

    Children of James and Ella Carter:
+   12. i. Bert C. Carter (1879 - 1936);

Third Generation

12.   Bert C. Carter (1879 – 1936) – Bert C. Carter was born on May 6, 1879 in Moxahala, Perry County, Ohio, the son of James and Ella Carter. Bert married Mary Sylvania Wilson on December 4, 1900 in Columbus, Franklin County, Ohio at the residence of Harry Cunningham, 455 Third Avenue. Mary was born on July 7, 1879 in Newark, Licking County, Ohio, the daughter of George and Nettie (Miller) Wilson. Bert was a painter and the family lived at 1006 Weiant Avenue, Newark, Ohio. The family was a member of Neal Avenue M. E. Church. Bert passed away on April 15, 1936 and is buried in the Wilson Cemetery in Newark, Ohio. Mary passed away on July 23, 1938 in Newark and is buried in the Wilson Cemetery.

    Children of Bert C. Carter and Mary Sylvania Wilson:
+   13. i. Flora C. Carter (1901 - 1956);
+   14. ii. Helen D. Carter (1904 – Unknown);
      15. ii. Ethel L. Carter (1904 – 1975) – Ethel was born on September 28, 1904, never married, was living at Worley Terrace when she passed away on April 9, 1975;
      16. iii. Adeline L. Carter (1906 – 1975) – Adeline was born on February 28, 1906, never married and died sometime after 1975;
      17. iv. Robert B. Carter (1909 – 1979) – Robert was born on July 31, 1908 in Newark, Ohio;
      18. v. Barbara Ann Carter (1914 – 1914) – Barbara Ann died as a stillborn;
+   19. v. Marjorie J. Carter (1915 – 1962); and
      20. vi. Dorothy E. Carter (1917 – 1934) – Dorothy was born on February 23, 1917 in Newark, Ohio, never married, died on July 12, 1934 in Newark, Ohio of complications from an operation for appendicitis, and is buried in Wilson Cemetery.

Bert C. and Mary S. (Wilson) Carter

Forth Generation

13. Flora C. Carter (1901 - 1956) – See Arthur Harris, page 311.

14. Helen D. Carter (1904 – Unknown) – Helen D. Carter was born in 1904, the daughter of Bert C. and Mary Sylvania (Wilson) Carter. Helen married Earl C. Inlow, the son of C. Bert and Oriel Inlow. Earl was born in 1904 in Ohio. They would move their family to Maywood, California.

       Children of Earl C. Inlow and Helen D. Carter:
- 21. i. Harold I. Inlow (1923 - Unknown);
- 22. ii. Geraldine Inlow (1923 – Unknown);
- 23. iii. Dorris M. Inlow (1925 – Unknown); and
- 24. iv. Eileen C. Inlow (1928 – Unknown).

19. Marjorie J. Carter (1915 – 1962) – Marjorie J. Carter was born on June 14, 1914 in Newark, Ohio, the daughter of Bert C. and Mary Sylvania (Wilson) Carter. Marjorie married James L. Fairley. The family lived at 1054 Weiant Avenue in Newark, Ohio. Marjorie died on February 26, 1962, and is buried in Wilson Cemetery, Newark, Ohio.

    Children of James L. Fairley and Marjorie J. Carter:
       25.   i.   Mrs. Roy D. Waldeck of Utica;
       26.   ii.   Mrs. Larry W. Lane of Newark; and
       27.   iii. Judith Kay Fairley.

Descendants of Thomas Wilson and Mary Riley

First Generation

1. Thomas Wilson (1725 – 1764) – Thomas was born before 1725 in Edinburgh, Scotland. Thomas immigrated to Ireland where he met and married Mary Riley sometime before 1737. Mary was born about 1715 in Northern Ireland. They immigrated to Nova Scotia, where they found the weather too severe to their liking and moved to Pipes Creek, Frederick/Carroll County, Maryland. According to the records, "...*on the 29th of January 1757, Thomas Wilson, Farmer of Pipe Creek, made a payment of 22 pounds 10 shillings sterling money of Great Britain, and gave a mortgage in one year on Margos Fancy - 445 acres to James Dickson, Gentleman.*" It appears that he resided on the west side of Monocacy in the Taneytown neighborhood.

Thomas died about February or March of 1764 leaving a will dated March 24, 1764, while Mary would pass away between 1805 and 1810.

Children of Thomas Wilson and Mary Riley:

    2.   i.   Joseph Wilson (1737 – 1810) – Joseph was born about 1737 in Pipe Creek, Monocacy, Frederick County, Maryland, married Catherine Miller in 1755 in Frederick County, Maryland, and died after 1810;

+ 3.   ii.   Thomas Wilson II (1740 – 1824);

    4.   iii.   James Wilson (1744 – 1814) – James was born in Frederick County, Maryland and married Elizabeth Stevenson;

    5.   iv.   William Wilson (1755 – 1821) – William was born on April 17, 1755 in Frederick County, Maryland, married Esther Fickle on February 22, 1774 in Bedford County, Pennsylvania, and died on December 6, 1821 in Fairfield County, Ohio;

    6.   v.   Susanna Wilson, born in Frederick County, Maryland, married Bigger Head, and died sometime after 1810, possibly in Kentucky;

    7.   vi.   Mary Polly Wilson, born in Frederick County, Maryland, married Benjamin Ogle, and died sometime after 1810;

    8.   vii.   Esther Wilson, born in Frederick County, Maryland, married Amos Smith, and died sometime after 1810;

    9.   viii.   Elizabeth Wilson, born in Frederick County, Maryland, married a McLain, and died sometime after 1810;

10. ix. Michael Wilson (1761 – 1818) – Michael married Oprphey Grimes; and
11. x. Priscilla Wilson (1763 – 1858) – Priscilla was born in Frederick County, Maryland, married John Biggs on November 20, 1782, and died in Ohio

Second Generation

3. Thomas Wilson II (1740 – 1824) – Thomas Wilson was born on April 5, 1740 in Frederick County, Maryland, the son of Thomas and Mary (Riley) Wilson. Thomas married Elizabeth Elliot Hays, the daughter of Jonathan C. Hays III and Mary Henderson. Elizabeth was born on November 15, 1755 in Taneytown, Frederick County, Maryland.

Thomas was an American Revolution Patriot serving under Capt George Richard Bird of the County of Frederick, Detachment, Maryland Troops (enlisted 4th Company, Frederick Detachment, 4th Battalion, Maryland Troops, May 2, 1782, under Capt. George Richard Byrd.)

Elizabeth was buried in the family plot on their property in Garrett County, Maryland, while Thomas passed away in 1824 in Allegany/Garrett County, Maryland and was buried in the Wilson Cemetery in Altamont, Garrett County, Maryland. Thomas has a government marker which was dedicated on July 30, 1972.

Children of Thomas Wilson II and Elizabeth Elliott Hays:
12. i. Thomas Wilson III (1777 - 1864) – Thomas was born on April 25, 1777 in Frederick County, Maryland, married Susan Bowman on November 21, 1801 Kitzmiller, Maryland, and died on November 3, 1864 in Kitzmiller, Maryland;
13. ii. Joseph Wilson (1779 – Unknown) – Joseph was born on February 15, 1779 and married Elizabeth Shinn;
+ 14. iii. James W. Wilson (1781 – 1852);
15. iv. Johnathen Hays Wilson (1784 – 1855) – Johnathen was born on April 5, 1784 in Maryland, married Elizabeth Inskeep on March 29, 1814 in Allegany County, Maryland, and passed away on November 25, 1855;
16. v. Mary Wilson (1786 – Unknown) – Mary was born on July 4, 1786, married William Williams Ashby, and died sometime after 1886;
17. vi. Michael Wills Wilson (1788 – 1856) – Michael was born on November 17, 1788 in Rawlings, Allegany County, Maryland, married Harriet Cresap on July 6, 1824 in Allegany County, Maryland, and died in April 1856;

18	vii.	Elizabeth Hays Wilson (1791 – 1878) – Elizabeth was born on November 12, 1791, married Jesse Ashby on September 18, 1813 in Allegany County, Maryland, and passed away in 1878 in Washington County, Iowa;
19	viii.	Esther Wilson (1794 – 1881) – Esther was born on June 22, 1794 in Allegany County, Maryland, married Charles Duval in September 1842, and died on May 10, 1881 in Perry County, Ohio; and
20	ix.	William R. Wilson (1797 – Unknown) – William was born on May 7, 1797 in Allegany County, Maryland, married Elizabeth Jones on December 16, 1845 in Allegany County, Maryland, and died before 1871.

Third Generation

14. James W. Wilson (1781 – 1852) – James W. Wilson was born on March 6, 1781, the son of Thomas Wilson II and Elizabeth Elliott Hays. James married Martha Ann Ashby, the daughter of William Wilton and Sarah (Williams) Ashby. Martha was born on February 10, 1786.

The family settled near Somerset, Perry County, Ohio and established what later would become known as the "Wesley Farm." James became a widely respected judge for Perry County, Ohio.

James passed away on March 31, 1852, while Martha passed away on March 6, 1880. Both passed away in Perry County, Ohio.

Children of James W. Wilson and Martha Ann Ashby:

	21.	i.	Jonathon Hays Wilson (1807 - 1879) – Jonathon was born on April 5, 1807 in Allegany County, Maryland, married Alice Marshall, and died on November 18, 1879;
	22.	ii.	Michael Wills Wilson (1808 – 1891) – Michael was born on August 13, 1808 in Allegany County, Maryland, married Catherine Hood, and passed away in 1891 in Washington, Iowa;
	23.	iii.	James Riley Wilson (1810 – Unknown);
	24.	iv.	Sarah Ashby Wilson, married Israel Moore on February 16, 1832;
+	25.	v.	Thomas Wilson (1811 – Unknown);
	26.	vi.	Elizabeth Hays Wilson (1816 – 1895) – Elizabeth was born on September 16, 1816 in Perry County, Ohio, married Robert E. Huston on June 24, 1847, and died in November 1895;
	27.	vii.	William Ashby Wilson;
	28.	viii.	Michael Wilson; and
	29.	ix.	Martha Wilson.

Fourth Generation

25. Thomas Wilson (1811 – Unknown) – Thomas Wilson born in 1811, the son of James W. and Martha Ann (ashby) Wilson. Thomas married Barbara Cotterman on May 3, 1837 in Perry County, Ohio. Barbara was born about 1811 in Ohio, the daughter of Johan Michael and Catherine (Hetrich) Coderman. The family was listed in the 1850 US Census – Ohio, Perry County, Hopewell Twp.

Children of Thomas Wilson and Barbara Cotterman:
- 30   i.   Mary Wilson (1838 - Unknown);
- 31.   ii.   Samuel Wilson (1839 – Unknown) – married Mary A.
- + 32.   iii.   George W. Wilson (1840 – 1919);
- 33.   iv.   Mahalia E. Wilson (1843 – Unknown);
- 34.   v.   Nancy Wilson (1846 – Unknown);
- 35.   vi.   Elijah Wilson (1847 – Unknown) – married Mary E.;
- + 36.   vii.   Martha 'Mattie' Wilson (1849 – 1933);
- 37.   viii.   Sarah Wilson (1852 – Unknown); and
- 38.   ix.   Frances Wilson (1857 – Unknown).

Fifth Generation

32. George W. Wilson (1840 – 1919) – George W. Wilson was born on September 1, 1840 in Thornport, Perry County, Ohio, the son of Thomas and Barbara (Coderman) Wilson.

George served as a private in Company G of the 31st Ohio Volunteer Infantry during the Civil War (1861-1865). It was on the 23rd of November, 1863, the 31st OVI moved out of their works near Chattanooga, Tennessee, to attack the rebels on Mission Ridge (across the Tennessee River from Chattanooga). On the 24th General Joseph Hooker drove the rebels from Lookout Mountain, and the Army of the Cumberland drove them from their front into their works near the foot of the ridge. The 31st Ohio did the skirmishing that day, and occupied Orchard Knob. On the 25th, the whole Union line advanced, driving the rebels from their works at the foot of the Ridge, and with a yell and cheer, the Union Army, drove the enemy up the Ridge, captured all of their artillery, and a great number of prisoners – the Battle of Mission Ridge. George was njured during the battle, but inspite of having one eye shot out, a part of his nose torn away, and his other eye injured so seriously that he would afterwards loose sight in it, George would serve for the remainder of the war.

After the war, George married Jenett 'Nettie' C. Miller. Nettie was born in 1846, the daughter of Enoch Miller. George returned to farming, until he became almost totally blind. The family attended the Holy Trinity Evangelical Lutheran Church. Nettie passed away from dropsy on July 7, 1919 in Newark, Ohio and is buried in Cedar Hill Cemetery. Upon the death of Nettie, George resided at his son's house, at 45 Riley Street in Newark, Ohio. After being blind for nearly 38 years and ill for 21 months, George passed away at the age of 79 from dropsy on October 26, 1919 in Newark, Ohio and is buried in Cedar Hill Cemetery.

Children of George W. Wilson and Jenett C. Miller:
- 39. i. Ella Wilson (1873 – Unknown) – married Frank Ingram and lived in Columbus, Ohio;
- 40. ii. Frank A. Wilson (1877 – Unknown) – lived in Dayton, Ohio; and
- + 41. iii. Mary Sylvania Wilson (1879 - 1938);

36. Martha Wilson (1849 – 1933) – Martha 'Mattie' Wilson was born in 1849, the daughter of Thomas and Barbara (Coderman) Wilson. Mattie married Conrad Robert Kissinger. Conrad served in Company K of the 87th Pennsylvania Volunteer Infantry during the Civil War. He was mustered in York, Pennsylvania in September 1861. He was wounded at Mine Run, Virginia on November 30, 1863. Conrad was a blacksmith. Conrad passed away on October 12, 1902 in Hebron, while Mattie passed away on July 13, 1933 in Hebron, Ohio. Both are buried in the Hebron Cemetery.

Children of Conrad Robert Kissinger and Martha Wilson:
- 42. i. Thomas Kissinger (1871 – Unknown);
- 43. ii. Rose Kissinger (1872 – Unknown);
- 44. iii. William Kissinger (1875 – 1941);
- 45. iv. Robert Kissinger (1877 – 1902); and
- 46. iii. Bessie May Kissinger (1882 – Unknown) - Bessie married a Mr. Craw.

Sixth Generation

41. Mary Sylvania Wilson (1879 - 1938) – See Bert C. Carter, page 340.

Descendants of Johann Uhrich Kotterman and Agnes Katherina Kuhlewein

First Generation

1. Johann Uhrich Kotterman – Johann Uhrich Kotterman married Agnes Katherina Kuhlewein.

   Children of Johann Uhrich Kotterman and Agnes Katherina Kuhlewein:
   +   2.   i.   Johann Philip Kotterman (1732 – 1799).

Second Generation

2. Johann Philip Kotterman (1732 – 1799) – Johann Philip Kotterman was born on January 2, 1732 or 1733, the son of Johann Uhrich Kotterman. Johann passed away in 1799 in Rebuck, Washington Twp, Northumberland County, Pennsylvania.

   Children of Michael Kotterman:
   +   3.   i.   Johan Michael Cotterman (1777 – 1867).

Third Generation

3. Johan Michael Cotterman (1777 – 1867) – Johan Michael Cotterman was born on April 8, 1777 in Stouchberg, Berk County, Pennsylvania, the son of Michael Kotterman. Johann married Catherine Hetrich in on November 24, 1798 in Zion Lutheran Church, Harrisburg, Dauphin Co., Pennsylvania. Catherine was born on November 11, 1777, the daughter of Johan Nicholaus and Anna Katarina (Broscious) Hetterich. The family was German Lutheran. Johan would move his family to Ohio around 1811. They would have six (6) children born in Northumberland County, Pennsylvania and another five (5) born in Hopewell Twp, Perry County, Ohio. Catherine would pass away on April 10, 1853, while Johan would pass away on November 30, 1867 in Hopewell Twp, Perry County, Ohio. Both are buried in Glenford, Perry County, Ohio in the St. Paul's Lutheran-Reform Cemetery.

Children of Johan Michael Coderman and Catherine Hetrich:
- 4. i. Lydia Cotterman (1800 – Unknown) – Lydia was born in 1800 in Northumberland County, Pennsylvania, married Isaac Ridenour on January 19, 1817 in Lima, Allen County, Ohio;
- 5. ii. Barbara Cotterman;
- 6. iii. John Cotterman (1801 – 1843) – John was born in 1801 in Northumberland County, Pennsylvania, married Elizabeth Rarick in 1825 in Thornville, Perry County, Ohio, and died on March 27, 1843;
- 7. iv. Catherine Cotterman, married George Cokensparger in 1836 in Perry County, Ohio;
- 8. v. Elizabeth Cotterman (1804 – Unknown) – Elizabeth married Frederick Mechling
- 9. vi. Michael Cotterman (1805 – Unknown) – Michael was born on July 5, 1805, married Sarah King in 1831 in Perry County, Ohio, and lived in Wyandotte County, Ohio;
- + 10. vii. Daniel Cotterman (1809 – Unknown);
- + 11. viii. Barbara Cotterman (1811 – Unknown);
- 12. ix. Salome Sarah Cotterman (1815 – 1896) – Salome was born in 1815, married Fredrick Martzloff, and died in 1896;
- + 13. x. Samuel Cotterman (1817 – Unknown);
- + 14. xi. Philip Cotterman (1822 – Unknown); and
- 15. xii. Mary Elizabeth Cotterman (1823 – 1890) – Mary married Rev. Jacob Weimer.

Fourth Generation

10. Daniel Cotterman (1809 – Unknown) – Daniel Cotterman was born in 1809 in Pennsylvania, the son of Johan Michael and Catherine (Hetrich) Cotterman. Daniel married Elizabeth Garrison. Daniel was a farmer.

Children of Daniel Cotterman and Elizabeth Garrison:
- 16. i. Israel Cotterman (1830 – Unknown) – Israel served during the Civil War;
- 17. ii. Royal Cotterman (1833 – Unknown);
- 18. iii. Samuel Cotterman (1835 – Unknown);
- 19. iv. Amos Cotterman (1837 – Unknown);
- 20. v. Amy Cotterman (1840 – Unknown);
- 21. vi. James W. Cotterman (1843 – Unknown) – James served during the Civil War in the 31st OVI, Company A;
- 22. vii. Margaret J. Cotterman (1847 – Unknown);
- 23. viii. John H. Cotterman (1852 – Unknown) – John served during the Civil War;

24. ix. Maria E. Cotterman (1852 – Unknown); and
25. x. Silama Cotterman (1858 – Unknown)

11. Barbara Cotterman (1811 – Unknown) – See Thomas Wilson, page 346.

12. Samuel Cotterman (1817 – Unknown) – Samuel Cotterman was born in 1817 in Perry County, Ohio, the son of Johan Michael and Catherine (Hetrich) Cotterman. Samuel married Margaret Foreman. Samuel was a farmer.

Children of Samuel Cotterman and Margaret Foreman:
26. i. Isaac Cotterman (1841 – Unknown) – Isaac served during the Civil War;
27. ii. Alfred Cotterman (1842 – Unknown) – Alfred served as a private during the Civil War in the 31st OVI, Company G;
28. iii. Harvey Cotterman (1844 – Unknown) – Harvey served as a private during the Civil War in the 31st OVI, Company G;
29. iv. Franklin Cotterman (1846 – Unknown) – Franklin served as a private during the Civil War in the 160th OVI (National Guard), Company G;
30. v. George Cotterman (1848 – Unknown);
31. vi. Mary Jane Cotterman (1850 – Unknown);
32. vii. Henry Cotterman (1853 – Unknown) – Henry served during the Civil War;
33. viii. Martha E. Cotterman (1856 – Unknown);
34. ix. John Cotterman (1859 – Unknown);
35. x. James Cotterman (1861 – Unknown); and
36. xi. Noah Cotterman (1862 – Unknown).

13. Philip Cotterman (1822 – 1904) – Philip Cotterman was born in February 3, 1822 in Perry County, Ohio, the son of Johan Michael and Catherine (Hetrich) Cotterman. Philip married Mary Bender, the daughter of Yost and Catharine (Heeke) Bender. Mary was born in 1827 in Germany. Philip was a farmer. Mary passed away on February 17, 1903 in Hopewell Twp, Perry County, Ohio, while Philip would pass away on April 4, 1904.

Children of Philip Cotterman and Mary Bender:
37. i. Almeda Cotterman (1852 – Unknown);
38. ii. Gilbert Leroy Cotterman (1854 – Unknown);
39. iii. William Henry Cotterman (1858 – Unknown);
40. iv. Charles Clinton Cotterman (1860 – Unknown); and
41. v. Elmore Cotterman (1868 – Unknown).

Descendants of Enoch and Emetine Miller

First Generation

1. Enoch Miller (1804 – 1873) – Enoch Miller was born in 1804 in Virginia or Pennsylvania. Enoch married Emetine sometime before 1830. She would pass away before 1850. Enoch occupation was a cooper. Enoch then married Emily. Emily was born about 1825 in Ohio. Enoch passed away on September 13, 1873 in Newark, Ohio and is buried in the Cedar Hill Cemetery.

    Children of Enoch and Emetine Miller:
      2.   i.   Jane Miller (1830 – Unknown);
      3.   ii.   Albert Miller (1833 – Unknown);
      4.   iii. George Miller (1834 – Unknown);
      5.   iv. Mary Miller (1840 – Unknown);
+   6.   v.   Jenett C. Miller (1846 – 1919);

    Children of Enoch and Emily Miller:
      7.   i.   Laymont Miller (1852 – 1924) – Laymont married Catherine 'Kate' Fessler, worked in a gas house, died June 19, 1924; and
      8.   ii.   Charles E. Miller (1859 – Unknown) – Charles worked in a foundry.

Second Generation

6. Jenett C. Miller (1846 – 1919) – See George W. Wilson, page 346.

Descendants of George H. Juniper

First Generation

1. George Juniper (1802 – Unknown) – George Juniper was born in 1802 in Maryland. Came to Ohio and settled in York Twp, Athens County sometime before 1824.

    Children of George Juniper:
- 2.   i.   Huldah Juniper (1823 – Unknown);
- 3.   ii.   Thomas Juniper (1824 – Unknown) – Thomas married Charlotte Taylor, daughter of John and Drusilla (Fling) Taylor;
- 4.   iii.   George Juniper (1827 – Unknown) – George married Eleanorre;
- 5.   iv.   Mary Juniper (1832 – Unknown);
- 6.   v.   Rebecca Juniper (1832 – Unknown);
- 7.   vi.   Absalom Juniper (1836 – Unknown) – Absalom served as a private during the Civil War, 20th OVI, Company H;
- 8.   vii.   Jeremiah Juniper (1838 – Unknown) - Jeremiah served as a private during the Civil War, 18th OVI, Company G;
- 9.   viii.   Matilda Juniper (1839 – Unknown);
- 10.   ix.   Reuben Juniper (1842 – Unknown) – Reuben served as private during the Civil War, 18th OVI, Company G; and
- + 11.   x.   James Juniper (1845 – 1912).

Second Generation

11. James Juniper (1845 – 1912) – James Juniper was born in 1845, the son of George Juniper. George married Minerva. Minerva was born in 1842. James served as a private during the Civil War in the 75th OVI, Company D. James passed away on January 29, 1912 and is buried in Nye Cemetery near Chauncey, Athens County, Ohio.

    Children of James and Minerva Juniper:
- 12.   i.   Anna Juniper (1864 – Unknown);
- 13.   ii.   Samuel Juniper (1865 – Unknown);
- + 14.   iii.   Silas Juniper (1870 – Unknown); and
- 15.   iv.   Frankie Juniper (1874 – Unknown).

Third Generation

14. Silas Juniper (1870 – Unknown) – Silas Juniper was born in February 1870 in Ohio, the son of James and Minerva Juniper. Silas married Mary J. McClelland. Mary was born in March 1878 in Ohio. Silas was a coal miner.

    Children of Silas Juniper and Mary J. McClelland:

	16.	i.	Clyde H. Juniper (1892 – Unknown);
	17.	ii.	Zina Juniper (1893 – Unknown);
	18.	iii.	Bert L. Juniper (1894 – 1975) – Bert was born on March 24, 1894 and passed away in December 1975 in Glouster, Athens County, Ohio;
	19.	iv.	Foster P. Juniper (1899 – Unknown);
+	20.	v.	Pearl Juniper (1902 – 1977);
	21.	vi.	Effie Juniper (1906 – 1996)- Effie married a Mr. Harris and passed away on August 1, 1996 in Glouster, Athens County, Ohio;
	22.	vii.	Minerva Juniper (1910 – Unknown) – Minerva married a Mr. Anderson;
	23.	viii.	Olive C. Juniper (1913 – Unknown) – Olive married a Mr. Hayden;
	24.	ix.	Helen Juniper (1917 – Unknown) – Helen married a Mr. Souders;
	25.	x.	Male Juniper

Fourth Generation

20. Pearl Juniper (1902 – 1977) – Pearl Juniper was born on May 13, 1902 in Glouster, Athens County, Ohio, the son of Silas and Mary J. (McClelland) Juniper. Pearl married and divorced Daisy Mae Rankin, the daughter of Wallace A. and Sarah M. (Stanley) Rankin. Daisy was born on June 4, 1904. Pearl then married Ethel McFarland, while Daisy went on to marry Clarence Winchel. Peal passed away on May 11, 1977 in Newark, Ohio and is buried in Newark Memorial Gardens. Daisy passed away November 3, 2001 in Zanesville, Muskingum County, Ohio.

Children of Pearl Juniper and Daisy Mae Rankin:
    26.   i.   Gerald Ernest Juniper (1922 – 1961) – Gerald was born on June 19, 1922, married Mildred Plant, then Dorothy in 1947, died on December 21, 1961, and is buried in the Lutheran Cemetery; and
+   27.   ii.   Norma Bertene Juniper (1924 – Living).

Pearl and Daisy Mae (Rankin) Juniper

Fifth Generation

27. Norma Bertene Juniper (1924 – Living) – See Arthur Eugene Harris, page 312.

Descendants of William Rankin and Jane Steen

First Generation

1. William Rankin (1745 – 1833) – William Rankin was born in 1745 in Ireland, the son of Samuel and Rachel Rankin. William married Jane Steen about 1770. William and his brother Benjamin Rankin lived on adjoining farms in Dromore Townland on the "Abercorn Donegal Estate" in County of Donegal, Ireland in 1806. These two farms were purchased by a descendant of Benjamin's in 1887 and were still owned by the Rankin family in 1954. William passed away in 1833 in Ulster, County of Derry, Ireland.

Children of William Rankin and Jane Steen:
+ 2. i. William Rankin (1770 – Unknown);
+ 3. ii. David Rankin (1772 – 1813);
+ 4. iii. Joseph A. Steen Rankin (1774 – 1839);
+ 5. iv. Benjamin Rankin (1777 – 1845); and
   6. v. James Rankin (1779 – 1859) – James was born in April of 1779 in Ireland, married Margaret Steen, and passed away on November 15, 1859 in Ireland.

Second Generation

2. William Rankin (1770 – Unknown) – William Rankin was born in Ireland in 1770, the son of William and Jane (Steen) Rankin. Willaim, along with his brothers David, Joseph, and Benjamin landed in Boston, Massachuetts on June 18, 1798. William was in Toby Twp, Armstrong County, Pennsylvania during the taking of the 1840 US Census.

Children of William Rankin:
   7. i. William Rankin (1802 – Unknown);
   8. ii. James Rankin;
   9. iii. David Rankin; and
   10. iv. Catherine Rankin.

3. David Rankin (1772 – 1813) – David Rankin was born in 1772 in the County of Cork, Ireland. David, along with his brothers landed in the Port of Boston on June 18, 1798. They would move on and settle in Clarion County, Pennsylvania by 1806. David married

Elizabeth Wallace. David passed away on March 15, 1813 in Fairview Twp, Butler County, Pennsylvania. Elizabeth passed away in April 1869.

>   Children of William Rankin and Elizabeth Wallace:
>   11. i. William Rankin (1808 – 1883) – William married Sarah Levier;
>   + 12. ii. Jane Rankin (1809 – 1890);
>   + 13. iii. Joseph D. Rankin (1811 – 1872); and
>   + 14. iv. David Rankin (1813 – 1902).

4.   Joseph A. Steen Rankin (1774 – 1839) – Joseph was born in 1774 on Abercom Estate, Laggan Valley, County of Donegal, Ireland, the son of William and Jane (Steen) Rankin. Joseph married Elizabeth Jane Johnson in 1802 in New Jersey. Joseph would serve as an Armstrong County Commissioner and an Associate Judge. He served one term in the Pennsylvania State Legislature. He was appointed an Associate Judge in 1829. In 1808, Joseph helped organize a congregation which was designated as the Associate Congregation of Cherry Run. Joseph was chosen ruling elder of the Seceder Cemetery. Joseph passed away on June 20, 1839 in Clarion County, Pennsylvania.

>   Children of Joseph A. Steen Rankin and Elizabeth Jane Johnson:
>   15. i. James Rankin (1803 – 1863);

5.   Benjamin Rankin (1777 – 1845) – Benjamin Rankin was born in June of 177 in Dromore, County of Dondgal, Ireland, the son of William and Jane (Steen) Rankin. Benjamin married Letticie Johnson. Letticie was born in 1776. Letticie would pass away in 1835, while Benjamin would passed away on December 17, 1845 in Toby, Clarion County, Pennsylvania

>   Children of Benjamin Rankin and Letticie Johnson:
>   16. i. William Rankin (1802 – 1881);
>   17. ii. Jane Rankin (1805 – 1888);
>   18. iii. Benjamin McClellan Rankin (1816 – 1883) – Benjamin served as a private during the Civil War in the 103rd Pennsylvania Infantry, Company B; and
>   19. iv. Samuel Rankin.

Third Generation

12. Jane Rankin (1809 – 1890) – Jane Rankin was born on January 18, 1809 in Pennsylvania, the daughter of David and Elizabeth (Wallace) Rankin. Jane married Josiah Somerville. Josiah was born on January 29, 1810 in Pennsylvania, the son of James and Sarah (Scott) Somerville. Josiah would pass away on February 15, 1881, while Jane would pass away on May 23, 1890.

    Children of Josiah Somerville and Jane Rankin:
- 20. i. David Rankin Somerville – David served as a private during the Civil War in the 82nd Pennsylvania Infantry, Company C;
- 21. ii. Samuel Somerville (1839 – Unknown) – Samuel served as a private during the Civil War in the 5th Pennsylvania Heavy Artilery;
- 22. iii. Sarah Somerville (1838 – Unknown);
- 23. iv. Rachel Somerville (1841 – Unknown);
- 24. v. James Harvey Somerville;
- 25. vi. Elizabeth Somerville;
- 26. vii. Frances Somerville; and
- 27. viii. Samantha Somerville.

13. Joseph D. Rankin (1811 – 1872) – Joseph D. Rankin was born on July 25, 1811 in Pennsylvania, the son of David and Elizabeth (Wallace) Rankin. Joseph married Rachel Thompson. Rachel was born about 1817 in Pennsylvania. Rachel passed away sometime before August 13, 1870. Joseph then married Fannie Somerville. Joseph passed away on October 4, 1872 in Clarion County, Pennsylvania.

    Children of Joseph D. Rankin and Rachel Wallace:
- 28. i. Samuel Rankin (1840 – Unknown) – Samuel was born in Pennsylvania;
- + 29. ii. David Rankin (1843 – Unknown);
- 30. iii. Mary Rankin (1845 – Unknown); and
- 31. iv. Clurry Rankin (1848 – Unknown).

    Children of Joseph Rankin and Fannie Somerville:
- 32. i. Hannah Rankin (1852 – 1918);
- 33. ii. Joseph Addison Rankin (1854 – 1937); and
- 34. iii. Sarah Rankin (1856 – 1913).

14. David Rankin (1813 – 1902) – David Rankin was born in 1813 in Pennsylvania, the son of David and Elizabeth (Wallace) Rankin. David married Nancy Moore. Nancy was born about 1817 in Pennsylvania. Nancy passed away sometime in 1897, while David passed away in 1902.

    Children of David Rankin and Nancy Moore:
        35.   i.   James Rankin (1846 – 1926).

Fourth Generation

29. David Rankin (1842 – 1888) – David Rankin was born in 1842 in Pennsylvania, the son of Joseph D. and Rachel (Thompson) Rankin. David married Lavina C. McGee on August 18, 1864. Lavina was born on October 6, 1843 in Madison Twp, Clarion County, Pennsylvania, the daughter of Jacob and Catherine (Lefever) McGee. David passed away in 1888 in Pennsylvania, while Lavina would pass away on September 27, 1906.

    Children of David Rankin and Lavina C. McGee:
+   36.   i.   Wallace A. Rankin (1866 – 1913).
+   37.   ii.   Joseph David Rankin (1869 – 1963); and
     38.   iii. Daniel B. Rankin (1879 – Unknown) – Daniel was born in Clarion County, Pennsylvania.

Fifth Generation

36. Wallace A. Rankin (1866 – 1913) – Wallace Rankin was born on June 16, 1865 in Pennsylvania, the son of David and Lavina C. (McGee) Rankin. Wallace married Sarah M. Stanley on February 16, 1890 in Clarion County, Pennsylvania. Wallace and his young bride then moved to Athens County, Ohio, settling in Trimble Twp. Wallace was a coal miner. Wallace was killed on October 23, 1913 when he fell from a coal train. Sarah passed away on April 16, 1932.

    Children of Wallace A. Rankin and Sarah M. Stanley:
        39.   i.   Cora F. Rankin (1890 – Unknown) – Cora was born in December 1890;
        40.   ii.   Nellie L. Rankin (1892 – Unknown) – Nellie was born in December 1892;
        41.   iii. David W. Rankin (1895 – Unknown) – David was born in March 1895;
        42.   iv. James L. Rankin (1897 – Unknown) – James was born in May 1897;

	43.	v.	Ernest T. Rankin (1899 – Unknown) – Ernest was born in May 1899; and
+	44.	vi.	Daisy Mae Rankin (1904 – 2001).

37.   Joseph David Rankin (1869 – 1963) – Joseph David Rankin was born on August 6, 1869 in Pennsylvania, the son of David and Lavina C. (McGee) Rankin. Joseph would move to Athens County, Ohio sometime before 1890. Joseph married Laura Mae McGee on February 11, 1890 in Glouster, Athens County, Ohio. Laura Mae was born on November 22, 1872 in Pennsylvania, the daughter of Daniel S. and Adaline McGee. Joseph was a coal miner. Lavina would pass away on December 26, 1918. Joseph passed away in Columbus, Ohio on October 19, 1963, and is buried in the Glouster Cemetery in Athens County, Ohio

Children of Joseph David Rankin and Laura Mae McGee:

45.	i.	Olive Rankin (1890 – Unknown) – Olive was born deaf on August 4, 1890 in Pennsylvania;
46.	ii.	Lillian Leota Rankin (1892 – 1977) – Lillian was born on June 28, 1892 in Glouster, Athens County, Ohio, married Harry Breakey, and died March 1977 in Ohio;
47.	iii.	Daisy Rankin (1894 – Unknown) – Daisy was born on July 19, 1894 in Ohio; and
48.	iv.	Adeline Rankin (1897 – Unknown) – Adeline was born on January 16, 1897 in Ohio.

Sixth Generation

44.   Daisy Mae Rankin (1904 – 2001) – See Pearl Juniper, page 356.

Descendants of John McGee and Mary E. Woods

First Generation

1. John McGee (1765 – 1845) – John McGee was born in 1765 in Northern Ireland. John immigrated to America and settled in Toby, Twp, Armstrong County, Pennsylvania. John married Mary E. Woods about 1789. John passed away in 1845 in Madison Twp, Clarion County, Pennsylvania.

    Children of John McGee and Mary E. Woods:
	2.	i.	James McGee (1794 - 1831);
	3.	ii.	Female McGee (1800 – Unknown);
	4.	ii.	Adam Nicely McGee (1802 – 1870) – Adam was born on April 19, 1802 in Westmoreland County, Pennsylvania, married Eleanor Lykes in 1823, and passed away on September 30, 1870 in Madison Twp, Clarion County, Pennsylvania;
+	5	iii.	Jacob McGee (1804 – 1873); and
	6.	iv.	John McGee (1805 – 1850) – John was born about 1805 in Toby Twp, Armstrong County, Pennsylvania and died before 1850.

Second Generation

5   Jacob McGee (1804 – 1873) – Jacob McGee was born about 1804 in Toby Twp, Armstrong County, Pennsylvania, the son of John McGee. Jacob married Catherine Lefever. Catherine was born about 1807 in Pennsylvania. Jacob passed away about August 1873 in Brady Twp, Clarion County, Pennsylvania

    Children of Jacob McGee and Catherine Lefever:
+	7.	i.	Elizabeth McGee (1826 – 1907);
+	8.	ii.	Joseph L. McGee (1828 – Unknown);
	9.	iii.	James L. McGee (1831 – 1899) – James was born on January 31, 1831 in Tope Twp, Armstrong County, Pennsylvania, married Nancy Mortimer about 1852 in Clarion County, Pennsylvania, then Mary A. Lefever, and passed away on February 2, 1899 in Oakdale, Athens County, Ohio;
	10.	ii.	Nancy McGee (1832 – Unknown);
+	11.	iii.	John McGee (1833 – 1913);
	12.	iv.	Mary McGee (1836 – Unknown);

	13.	v.	Fannie McGee (1839 – Unknown) – Fannie married John Anderson around 1864;
+	14.	vi.	Lavina McGee (1842 – 1906);
+	15.	vii.	Daniel S. McGee (1845 – Unknown);
	16	viii.	Samuel McGee (1848 – Unknown); and
	17	ix.	William H. McGee (1853 – Unknown).

Third Generation

7. Elizabeth McGee (1826 - 1907) – Elizabeth McGee was born on September 16, 1826 in Redbank, Armstrong County, Pennsylvania, the daughter of Jacob and Catherine (Lefever) McGee. Elizabeth married John Armitage Ganoe. John was born about 1824 in Pennsylvania. Elizabeth passed away on June 21, 1907 in Parker, Armstrong County, Pennsylvania.

Children of John Armitage Ganoe and Elizabeth McGee:
18.	i.	Catherine Ganoe (1839 – Unknown);
19.	ii.	Mary Delilah Ganoe (1847 – 1935);
20.	iii.	Nancy J. Ganoe (1850 – Unknown);
21.	iv.	Joseph Ganoe (1853 – 1938);
22.	v.	Malissa Ganoe (1855 – 1940);
23.	vi.	Sarah Ganoe (1858 – Unknown);
24.	vii.	Kiane 'Kttie' Ganoe (1860 – Unknown); and
25.	viii.	Thomas Alfred Ganoe (1866 – Unknown).

8. Joseph L. McGee (1828 – Unknown) – Joseph L. McGee was born in June 1828 in Toby Twp, Armstrong County, Pennsylvania, the son of Jacob and Catherine (Lefever) McGee. Joseph married Mary Jane Phillips in 1850 in Pennsylvania. Mary was born in September of 1837. Joseph passed away sometime after 1900.

Children of Joseph L. McGee and Mary Jane Phillips:
26.	i.	Albert McGee (1853 – Unknown);
27.	ii.	William S. McGee (1857 – Unknown);
28.	iii.	Alcena C. McGee (1858 – Unknown);
29.	iv.	Eliza Jane McGee (1862 – Unknown);
30.	v.	Mary S. McGee (1865 – Unknown);
31.	vi.	Lauretta Catherine McGee (1867 – 1904);
32.	vii.	Frances K. McGee (1873 – Unknown); and
33.	viii.	Jessie May McGee (1878 – 1903).

11. John McGee (1833 – 1913) – John McGee was born on June 21, 1833 in Pennsylvania, the son of Jacob and Catherine (Lefever) McGee. John married Lovenia. Lovenia was born in 1837. John passed away December 24, 1913 in Trimble Twp, Athens County, Ohio.

    Children of John and Lovenia McGee:
        34.   i.   Lizzie McGee (1863 – Unknown);
        35.   ii.   Samuel McGee (1865 – Unknown);
        36.   iii, Addison McGee (1871 – Unknown);
        37.   iv. Jessey McGee (1878 – Unknown); and
        38.   v.   Bertha McGee (1879 – Unknown).

14. Lavina McGee (1842 – 1906) – See David Rankin, page 362.

15. Daniel S. McGee (1845 – Unknown) – Daniel McGee was born about March 1845 in Pennsylvania, the son of Jacob and Catherine (Lefever) McGee. Daniel married Adaline about 1866.

    Children of Daniel S. and Adaline McGee:
        39.   i.   Jacob McGee (1864 – Unknown);
        40.   ii.   Adam McGee (1868 – Unknown);
        41.   iii. Clara McGee (1870 – Unknown);
        42   iv. Jessie McGee (1871 – Unknown);
+   43   v.   Laura Mae McGee (1872 – Unknown);
        44   vi. Minty McGee (1873 – Unknown);
        45   vii. Cora McGee (1877 – Unknown); and
        46   viii. Olive McGee (1880 – Unknown).

Fourth Generation

43. Laura Mae McGee (1872 – Unknown) – See Joseph David Rankin, page

List of Military Service

As proud Americans, ancestors of this Comisford family have helped preserved the American way of life through participation in the Colonial Wars against the Indians, the French and Indian Wars, the Dunmore War of 1774, the American Revolution, the War of 1812, the Mexican War, the American Civil War, Spanish American War, World War I, World War II, the Korean War and the Vietnam War.

Colonial Wars:
   King Phillip's War (1675-1676)
      Benedict Arnold
      Richard Arnold
      John Ballard
      Nathaniel Ballard
      William Ballard
      James Barker
      Joseph Belcher, a soldier and quartermaster
      Josiah Belcher
      Roger Burlingame
      John Jenckes, under Capt. John Whipple of Ipswich
      Ebenezer Owen, Massachusetts Regiment, Fourth Company, under Captain Isaac Johnson
      Stephen Paine, the First Plymouth Colony Company, under Major Bradford

King William's War (1689-1697):
   James Carder, Captain – Rhode Island
   Nathaniel Jenckes, a Major in the Massachusetts Militia
   Ebenezer Owen, Naval Forces commanded by Sir William Phipps of Maine
   Philip Tillinghast, member of Captain Gallup's Expedition against Canada

List of Military Service

French and Indian War (1755-1758)
    Captain Lewis Bonnett, Virginia Militia
    Captain William Lytle, Pennsylvania Militia
    Captain John Wetzel, Virginia Militia

Dunmore War of 1774:
    Captain Lewis Bonnett
    Captain John Wetzel

American Revolutionary War (1776-1781)
    Thomas Angell
    Major General Benedict Arnold,
    William Aplin, Rhode Island
    Stephen Bartram
    Ephraim Blackburn
    Nathaniel Blackburn
    Captain Lewis Bonnett
    Humphery Brumfield
    James Brumfield III
    James Brumfield IV
    Robert Brumfield
    Joseph Gray
    William Green , Minutemen of Culpeper County, Virginia
    Jesse Harris, Loudoun County, Virginia Militia, 57th Regiment, 2nd Battalion, under Lieut. Jones' Company
    Charles Lucas, Jr. – Giles County, Virginia
    Charles Lucas, Sr. – Giles County, Virginia
    John Lucas, Captain – Giles County, Virginia
    Parker Lucas – Giles County, Virginia
    William Lucas, Captain – Giles County, Virginia
    Johannes Lantz
    Oswald Newby
    Charles Pollock, Private, Pennsylvania Militia
    John Jacob Staley, Jr. - Seventh Battalion, Second Company, York Co Volunteers, 1775 - Captain Michael Doudel's Company, 11/24/1776 - Captain Henry Miller's Company
    Captain John Wetzel

List of Military Service

American Revolutionary War (1776-1781) - continued
    Johannes Michael Waggoner, served under Captain John Harness and Colonel Riddel in General McIntosh's Campaign, and served as a Ranger under Captain Owen Davy and Colonel Charles Martin
    Thomas Wilson II, enlisted 4th Company, Frederick Detachment, 4th Battalion, Maryland Troops, May 2, 1782, under Capt. George Richard Byrd
    General Joseph Winlock - Virginia
    Francis Wright
    Michael Yeasley, German Battalion from Shepherdstown, Capt. William Morgan's Co.-1776

War of 1812 (1812-1814)
    General Joseph Winlock
    Captain Lewis Bonnett, Jr.
    Byrd Brumfield, 2nd Reg. (Evans) Virginia Militia
    Captain William Wirt Brumfield, 167th Militia, Wayne County, Virginia
    David Haas
    John Haas, Ensign in the Light Infantry of the 1st Battalion, 18th Regiment May 10, 1814
    Daniel C. Mills, Roll of Capt. John Spencer's Company, Ohio Spies – Licking Co
    Captain James Pollock
    Thomas Russell
    Jacob Staley, 57th Reg. Virginia Militia
    John Staley, 4th Reg. Virginia Militia
    Peter Staley, Flying Camp (McDonalds) Virginia Militia
    Fielding Winlock Wright, 6th Reg. 4th Co, detached from Rockingham Regiment

Mexican War (1847)
    Gordon Brumfield – Captain Elisha McComan, Company C
    William Haines Lytle

List of Military Service

The American Civil War (1861-1865)
  Albert M. Aplin, Orderly in 31st OVI, Company B
  Benjamin Aplin, 90th OVI, Company E
  John Aplin, 129th OVI, Company A
  Alfred Cotterman, a private in 31st OVI, Company G
  Franklin Cotterman, a private in 160th OVI (National Guard), Company G
  Harvey Cotterman, a private in 31st OVI, Company G
  Henry Cotterman
  Isaac Cotterman
  Israel Cotterman
  James W. Cotterman, 31st OVI, Company A
  John H. Cotterman
  Wesley Davis, 1st OVI, Company B
  Philander R. Hand, 31st OVI, Company H
  Lehu Hinds, 13th Reg, WV Infantry
  Absalom Juniper, a private in 20th OVI, Company H
  James Juniper, a private in 75th OVI, Company D
  Jeremiah Juniper, a private in 18th OVI, Company G
  Reuben Juniper, a private in 18th OVI, Company G
  William Longstreth, 3rd Regiment, Pennsylvania Provisional Cavalry
  Major General William Haines Lytle, Commanded the 4th Ohio Regiment
  Charles Case Marsh, 31st, OVI, Company F & S
  John R. McCulloch, a private in 31st OVI, Company A
  Ashford Mills, a private in 3rd OVI, Company H
  Daniel G. Mills, a private in 31st OVI, Company H
  Jacob Thomas Mills, 3rd OVI, Company F&S, Physician (Hospital Steward)
  Captain Warner Mills, 32nd OVI, Company G
  Benjamin McClellan Rankin, a private in 103rd Pennsylvania Infantry, Company B
  Sgt. Nathan Smith, 76th OVI, Company H
  David Rankin Somerville, a private in 82nd Pennsylvania Infantry, Company C
  Samuel Somerville, a private in 5th Pennsylvania Heavy Artilery

List of Military Service

The American Civil War (1861-1865) - continued
    Jacob Staley, 1st WV Cavalry, Company I, and died on June 22, 1861 of injuries
    John L. Tygard, a private in 1st WV Cavalry, Company A & G
    George W. Wilson, a private in 31st OVI, Company G

Spanish American War (1898-1899)
    Charles F. Tygard, a in the Seventh Regiment Ohio Volunteer Infantry, Company K

World War I (1917-1919)
    Benjamin Rue Comisford, American Expeditionary Forces
    Francis Flavia Comisford, United States Marine Corp
    Arthur Harris, United States Army
    William Joseph (Benjamin) Stichter, United States Navy
    Olaf Wetterholm, United States Army, Battery B of 2nd Reg Field Artillery

World War II (1941–1945)
    General Douglas MacArthur of World War II, Congressional Metal of Honor Recipient
    Homer Paris Comisford, United States Navy, World War II
    Ernie Fouts, United States Navy
    Arthur Eugene Harris, United States Army
    Harold Charles Harris
    Wallace C. Lappen, United States Navy
    Bruce Smith, United States Army
    William Joseph (Benjamin) Stichter, United States Navy

Korean War (1950-1953)
    Robert Charles Comisford, United States Marine Corp
    Thomas Perry Comisford, United States Marine Corp
    William Davis Comisford, Sr., United States Air Force
    Willam Joseph Stichter, Jr., United States Air Force

List of Military Service

Vietnam War (1957-1975) - continued
    Ronald Carter, United States Air Force
    Steven Charles Comisford, United States Navy
    Mark Andrew Comisford, United States Army
    Richard Anthony Comisford. United States Army
    Jon Brent Comisford, United States Army
    Gary Eugene Harris, United States Marine Corp
    Michael David Harris, United States Air Force
    Thomas Edward Harris, United States Marine Corp

Our Famous American Cousins
Presidents of the United States of America

1st United States of America
President George Washington
(1732 – 1799)

3rd United States Of America
President Thomas Jefferson
(1743 – 1826)

16th United States of America
President Abraham Lincoln
(1809 -1865)

25th United States of America
President William McKinley
(1843 – 1901)

Our Famous American Cousins
Presidents of the United States of America

26th United States of America
President Theodore Roosevelt
(1858 – 1919)

32nd United States of America
President Franklin Delano
Roosevelt
(1882 – 1945)

41st United States of America
President George Herbert Walker Bush
(1924 – Living)

43rd United States of America
President George Walker Bush
(1946 – Living)

Our Famous American Cousins

**Benedict Arnold
Governor of Rhode Island
(1615 – 1678)
Elected first Governor of
Rhode Island in 1663 and
re-elected in 1664, 1669, 1677,
and 1678**

**Benedict Arnold
(1741 – 1801)
Committed treason against
America during the American
Revolutionary War**

**Daniel Boone
(1734 – 1820)
American Pioneer and Trailblazer**

Our Famous American Cousins

Lewis Wetzel
(1764 – 1808)
Frontiersman and Indian Fighter

Major General William H. Lytle
(1826 – 1863)
Fourth Ohio Regiment in General O.M. Mitchel's brigade in the Civil War, was killed at the Battle of Chickamauga (in Georgia), September 20, 1863.

Clarissa Harlowe Barton
"Angel of the Battlefield"
(1821 – 1912)
Civil War Nurse (1861 – 1865)
Founder and President of the American National Red Cross (1883 - 1905)

Our Famous American Cousins

Wyatt Berry Sapp Earp
((1848 – 1929)
Lawman and Gambler
Famous for the "Gunfight at the OK Corral" in Tombstone, Arizona in 1881

General of the Army Douglas MacArthur
(1880 – 1964)
Commander of Allied forces in the Southwest Pacific Area during World War II
Metal of Honor Recipient
"...I shall return."

Robert Taliaferro Relationship to President George Washington

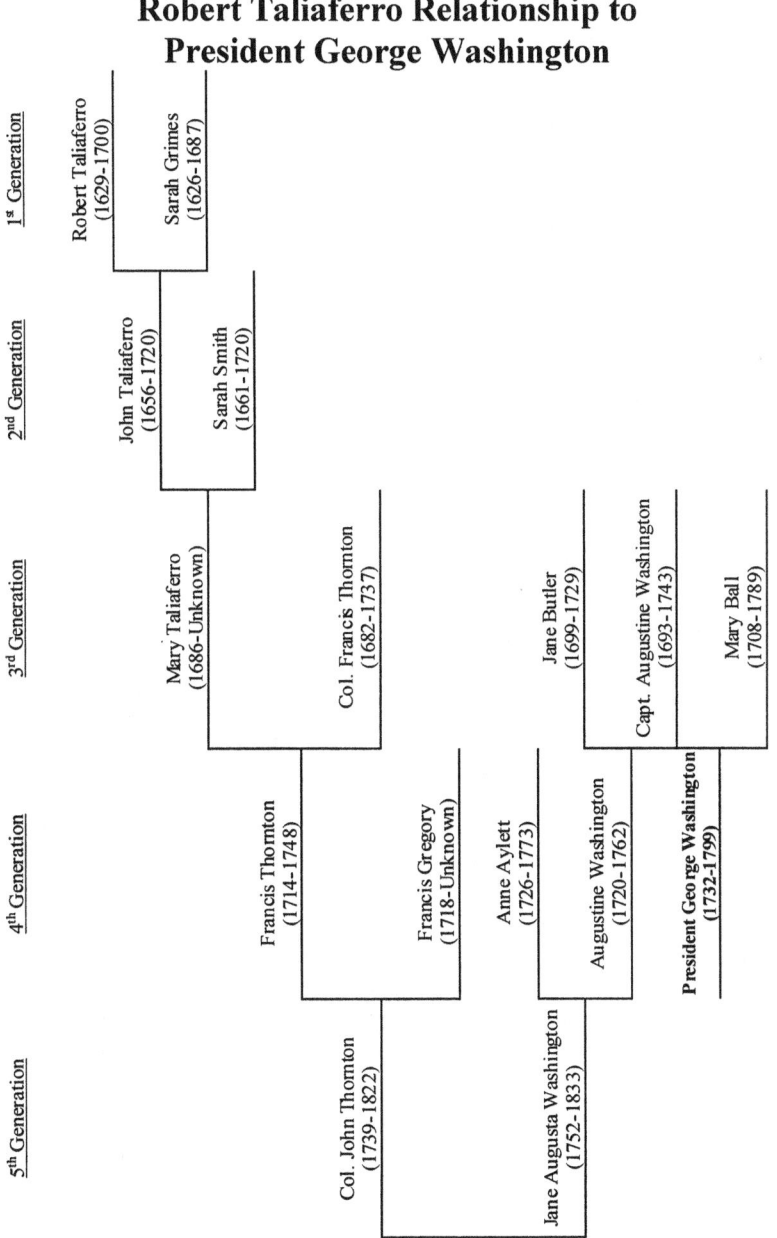

Robert Taliaferro Relationship to President Thomas Jefferson

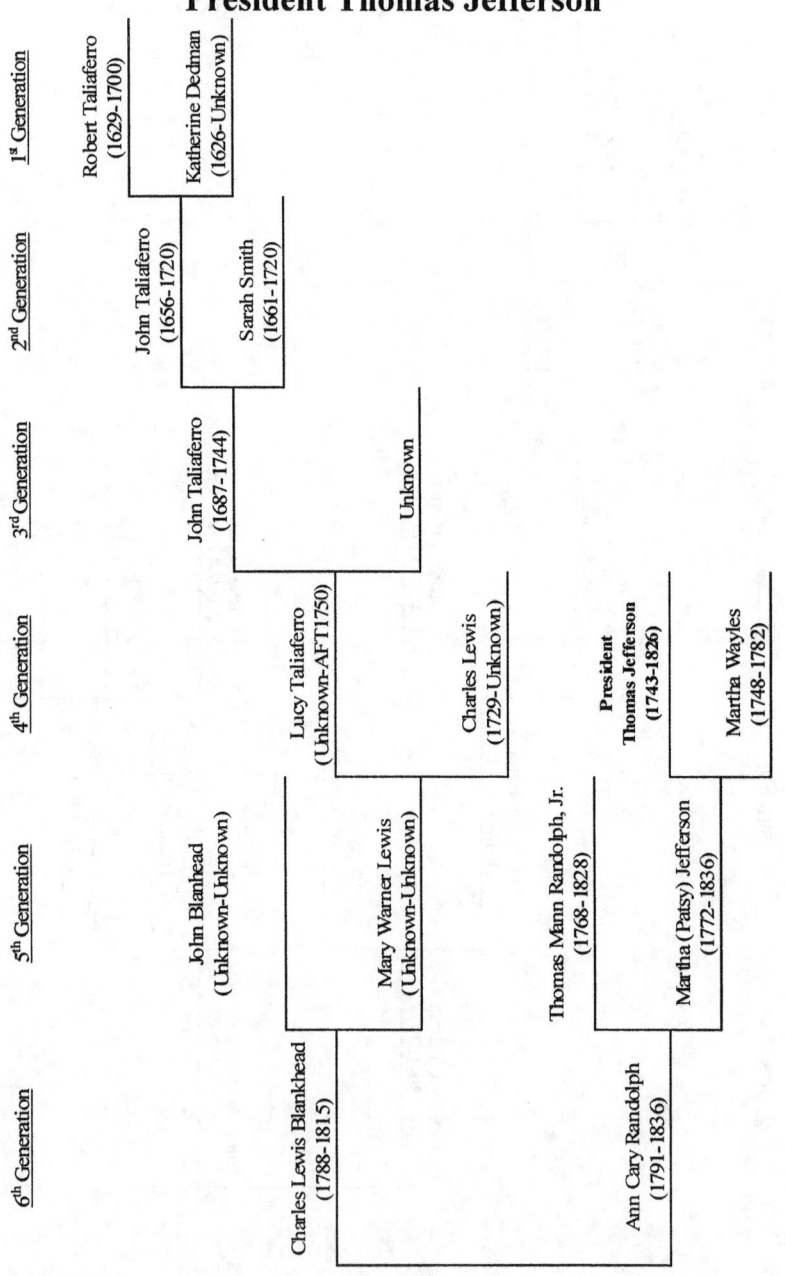

Sources

Allman, C.B., *Lewis Wetzel, The Life and Times of a Frontier Hero*, 2000 (originally published as *The Life and Times of Lewis Wetzel*, 1939).

Arnold, Elisha Stephen, *The Arnold Memorial: William Arnold of Providence and Pawtuxet, 1587-1675, and a Genealogy of his Descendants*. 1935.

Articles and Obituaries published in the Columbus Dispatch

Articles and Obituaries published in the Newark Dailey Advocate, the Newark Advocate, the Newark American Tribune

Baptist Piety, "The Last Will & Testimony of Obadiah Holmes", Edwin S. Gaustad, Christian University Press, Wm. B. Eerdmans Publishing, 1978

Bartlett, Joseph Gardner, *Belcher Families in New England*. 1906.

Biographical Review Publishing Co., Chicago, *Biographical Review of Cass, Schuyler and Brown Counties, Illinois*, 1892

Brister, E.M.P., *1909 Centennial History of the City of Newark and Licking County Ohio*. 1909

Census of the United States – (1790-1930)

Colket, Meridith B., Jr., *Genealogy of the Jenks Family of America*, 1952.

De Hass, Wills, *History of the Settlement and Indian Wars of Western Virginia*. 1851.

Genealogy of the Families of Braintree, Mass., 1640-1850, by Waldo Chamberlain Sprague, AB

Graham, A.A., *History of Fairfield and Perry Counties, Ohio*. 1883

Hill, N.N. Jr., *History of Licking County, Ohio Its Past and Present.* 1881

Hintgen, William, *The Border Wars of the Upper Ohio Valley* (1769-1794) 1999.

History of Belmont and Jefferson Counties, Ohio. 1880

History of Woonsocket, 1641 – 1876 by E. Richardson, Woonsocket: S. S. Foss, Printer, 1876

Information from the Civil War Military Files in the National Archives and Records Administration, Washington, D.C.

Interstate Publishing Chicago, *Biographical and Historical Record of Wayne and Appanoose Counties.* 1886

Kenamond, Alva Dayne, *Prominent Men of Shepherdstown During Its First 200 Years.* 1963.

Licking County, Ohio 1982: A collection of historical sketches and family histories, compiled by members and friends of the Licking County Genealogy Society, Newark, Ohio. 1982

Lobdell, Jared, *Recollections of Lewis Bonnett, Jr.* 1991

Martzolff, Clement L., *History of Perry County*, Ohio, 1902

Portrait and Biographical Record of Guernsey County, Ohio, Owen & Co., 1895

Probate Records, Licking County, Ohio

Sarchet, *History of Guernsey County, Ohio.* 1911.

Savage, James, *A Genealogical Dictionary of The First Settlers of New England, Before 1692.*

State of Ohio Department of Health Division of Vital Statistics Certificates of Death

Sutor, J. Hope, *Past & Present of the City of Zanesville & Muskingum Co.* 1905

The Great Migration: Immigrants to New England, 1634-1635 by Robert Charles Anderson

The Pioneers of Massachusetts (1620-1650) by Charles Henry Pope

The Tenmile Country and Its Pioneer Families: A Genealogical History of the Upper Monongahela Valley, by Howard L Leckey

Various Cemetery Listings and Records

Wagoner, Crystal V., *John Waggoner (1751-1842) and Margaret (Bonnet) Waggoner: Ancestors, Families, and Descendants.* 1995.

W. H. Venable, *Beginnings of Literary Culture in the Ohio Valley: Historical and Biographical Sketches* 284-85 (Cincinnati: Robert Clarke & Co., 1891)

1844 Providence Directory (Rhode Island).

And a multitude of other information obtained through visits, phone calls, emails, and other sources.

Name Index

Abel, Anna Jane, 292
Abel, Anna M., 291
Abel, Austin Charles, 136, 137
Abel, Bernadine Madge, 137
Abel, Bessie, 292
Abel, Catherine H., 294
Abel, Charles Ellsworth, 20, 135, 137, 293
Abel, Charles F., 291
Abel, David Wesley, 135, 291, 293, 294, 301
Abel, Ellen M., 291
Abel, Emma L., 291
Abel, Emma M., 292
Abel, Eugene Hacket, 292
Abel, Eva M., 294
Abel, Fern T., 294
Abel, George, 293
Abel, George Thomas, 293
Abel, George W., 291
Abel, George Washington, 291
Abel, Glen C., 294
Abel, Harry Walter, 293, 294
Abel, John, 291
Abel, John M., 291
Abel, Joseph, 291
Abel, Joseph Erman, 292
Abel, Lorena M., 292
Abel, Lucy Belle, 293
Abel, Marcia Muyetta, 137
Abel, Marcia Muyette, 20, 21, 24, 25
Abel, Margaret, 291
Abel, Margaret D., 294
Abel, Margaret Elizabeth, 292
Abel, Mary, 291
Abel, Mary Augusta, 293
Abel, Mary E., 294
Abel, Mary M., 294
Abel, Nancy Rozella, 293
Abel, Raymond Ross, 292
Abel, Robert, 291
Abel, Sarah Delores, 137
Abel, Sarah Margaret, 293
Abel, Sherman Hart, 292
Abel, Thomas Marion, 292

Abel, Wilbur R., 293
Abel, William, 136
Abel, William H., 291, 292
Abel, William Mead, 137
Abel, William Milford, 292
Able, Melissa Irene, 30
Adamson, Cassandra, 42
Adcocke, John, 149
Adcocke, Nelle Rose, 149, 150
Adkins, Attison, 268
Adkins, Calvery, 268
Adkins, Christina, 267
Adkins, Cynthia, 280
Adkins, David, 266
Adkins, Delphia, 268
Adkins, Edward, 258, 268, 280
Adkins, Elizabeth, 268
Adkins, Elizabeth Ann, 266
Adkins, George, 268
Adkins, Govey, 268
Adkins, Havey, 268
Adkins, Henry, 266
Adkins, Jacob, 266
Adkins, Jacob Oxford, 267
Adkins, Jesse, 267
Adkins, John, 267
Adkins, John R., 267
Adkins, Joseph, 265, 285
Adkins, Littleberry, 267
Adkins, Littleberry, Jr., 268
Adkins, Margaret, 268
Adkins, Mary, 266, 267
Adkins, Mary Elizabeth, 268
Adkins, Mary Polly, 265
Adkins, Nancy, 267
Adkins, Nancy Ann, 267
Adkins, Nancy Hanks, 258, 261, 268, 269
Adkins, Parker V., 265
Adkins, Polly Ann, 259
Adkins, Rebecca, 267
Adkins, Richard, 265
Adkins, Sherrod, 267
Adkins, Sherrod B., 267
Adkins, Sherrod, Jr., 268

Adkins, Sherrod, Sr., 267, 268, 277
Adkins, Sherwood, 266
Adkins, Sylvaneous, 266
Adkins, William V., 265
Albright, Willard, 136
Aldis, Daniel, 151
Allan, Sarah J., 10
Allcock, Catharine, 155, 156, 158
Allen, Mary, 164
Allen, Mr., 204
Altdorffer, John, 319
Amspach, Nettie May, 70, 71
Anders, Eulala, 294
Anderson, George, 145
Anderson, Inez, 301
Anderson, Margaret, 298
Anderson, Nancy, 293, 300, 301
Andrews, John, 229
Andrews, William, 174
Angell, Alice, 224
Angell, Amphillis, 224
Angell, Deborah, 224
Angell, Elizabeth, 153
Angell, James, 218, 224
Angell, John, 224
Angell, Margery, 224
Angell, Mary, 208, 224
Angell, Thomas, 208, 218, 224
Ankrom, Mr., 42
Aplin, Albert C., 143, 147
Aplin, Albert M., 142
Aplin, Alice, 145, 147
Aplin, Alice E., 147
Aplin, Ann Russel, 142
Aplin, Anna Oliva H., 148
Aplin, Arthur S., 147
Aplin, Benjamin, 140, 141, 142, 143, 144, 147, 148, 201
Aplin, Benjamin Baker, 142
Aplin, Brenda, 148
Aplin, Charles B., 148
Aplin, Charles F., 144
Aplin, Charles J., 147
Aplin, Charles Joseph, 143, 148
Aplin, Clara J., 147
Aplin, Clarance, 147
Aplin, Edward Allen, 142
Aplin, Eliza Jane, 145
Aplin, Elizabeth, 148
Aplin, Elizabeth Gray, 142, 143

Aplin, Emily, 145, 147
Aplin, Emma, 147
Aplin, Esther, 145
Aplin, Everet, 145
Aplin, Hannah, 140, 142
Aplin, Henrietta, 141
Aplin, Henry Seymore, 142, 143
Aplin, Ida, 147
Aplin, Ira E., 144
Aplin, James, 140
Aplin, John, 139, 140, 141, 145, 154
Aplin, John M., 148
Aplin, John Turpin, 142, 143, 147
Aplin, John, Jr., 140, 141, 142, 177
Aplin, Joseph, 140
Aplin, Laura H., 147
Aplin, Lydia, 145, 147
Aplin, Lydia Gray, 142
Aplin, Mahala C., 148
Aplin, Mahala Ellen, 134, 135, 144, 148
Aplin, Maria, 144
Aplin, Mariah, 147
Aplin, Mary, 141
Aplin, Mary Miller, 147
Aplin, Maurice H., 148
Aplin, Oliver, 141
Aplin, Rebecca, 140
Aplin, Robert, 141
Aplin, Samuel, 141
Aplin, Sarah, 141, 145
Aplin, Sarah Cook, 142
Aplin, Stephen Arnold, 141
Aplin, Thomas, 141
Aplin, Walter, 145
Aplin, Welcome C., 148
Aplin, Welcome Gray, 134, 142, 143, 144
Aplin, William, 140, 141, 142, 147
Aplin, William Henry, 143, 144, 145
Archer, David Megary, 145
Arkron, William, 42
Armstrong, Alfred, 309
Armstrong, Emmit E., 309
Armstrong, Harris N., 309
Armstrong, James N., 308, 309
Arnold, Anne, 153
Arnold, Barbara, 175
Arnold, Benedict, 173
Arnold, Benjamin, 176

Arnold, Christopher, 176
Arnold, Eleazer, 208
Arnold, Elisha, 175
Arnold, Elizabeth, 141, 142, 171, 174, 175, 176, 177, 207, 209
Arnold, Elizabeth Peake, 172
Arnold, Ester, 174
Arnold, Freelove, 209
Arnold, Grace, 207
Arnold, Ichabod, 207
Arnold, Israel, 174, 175, 176, 177, 182
Arnold, James, 175
Arnold, Joanna, 171, 173, 193, 194, 196, 208
Arnold, Job, 209
Arnold, John, 208
Arnold, Jonathan, 209
Arnold, Joseph, 175
Arnold, Josiah, 175
Arnold, Lydia, 176
Arnold, Margery, 171
Arnold, Mary, 175, 176, 177, 208, 209
Arnold, Nicholas, 171, 173, 207
Arnold, Phebe, 174, 176
Arnold, Richard, 207, 208, 224
Arnold, Richard, Jr., 208
Arnold, Sarah, 174, 175, 200, 204, 205, 209
Arnold, Simon, 176
Arnold, Sion, 176
Arnold, Stephen, 141, 173, 174, 175, 176, 177, 180, 186
Arnold, Susanna, 207
Arnold, Tamzen, 171
Arnold, Thomas, 204, 207, 208, 209, 213, 217
Arnold, William, 171, 172, 175, 193
Asbury, Elizabeth, 268
Asbury, Martha Patsy, 268
Ashby, Jesse, 345
Ashby, Martha Ann, 345
Ashby, William Williams, 344
Ashby, William Wilton, 345
Ashton, Alice, 208, 218, 224
Ashton, John, 218
Atkinson, William V., 265, 273
Attdoerffer, John, 317
Atwood, Amos, 39

Atwood, Harry, 39
Atwood, Ray, 39
Atwood, Wilmer, 39
Audrey, John, 185
Ayers, Sarah, 185
Aylesworth, Arthur, 235
Bagent, Carl E., 309
Bailey, Joseph, 127
Bailey, Mary Polly, 260, 285, 289
Bailey, Mr., 130
Baker, John, 57
Ball, James, 304
Ball, Martha, 304
Ballard, Ann, 231
Ballard, Anne, 231
Ballard, Catharine, 231
Ballard, Elizabeth, 231, 273
Ballard, Henry, 231
Ballard, Hester, 227, 228, 232
Ballard, John, 232
Ballard, Nathaniel, 232
Ballard, Phillip, 231
Ballard, Thomas, 231
Ballard, William, 227, 231, 232
Ballengee, Rutha Ann, 284
Barber, G.P., 325
Barbour, Matthew, 199
Barbour, Robert, 199
Barclay, Alexander, 82
Barker, Christiana, 181, 282
Barker, Elizabeth, 182
Barker, James, 174, 181, 182
Barker, Joseph, 182
Barker, Mary, 95, 174, 175, 179, 182
Barker, Peter, 182
Barker, Sarah, 182
Barker, William, 182
Barlingstone, Mary Elizabeth, 215, 217
Barlingstone, William, 215
Barnard, Cloa, 300
Barnett, Ester, 277
Barrett, Charles E., 313, 316
Barrett, Leslie, 316
Barrett, Maurice, 313, 316
BarretT, William, 301
Barrick, Elizabeth, 112
Barrow, Franklin, 299
Barrow, Matilda, 299
Barry, Mary, 134

Bartholomew, Abigail, 151
Bartram, Betsy, 280
Bartram, Charles, 280
Bartram, David, 279
Bartram, James P., 279
Bartram, John, 280
Bartram, John P., 268, 279, 280
Bartram, Joseph, 280
Bartram, Lewis, 280
Bartram, Marinda, 280
Bartram, Mary, 279
Bartram, Nancy Jane, 258, 268, 280
Bartram, Stephen, 279, 280
Bartram, Thomas, 280
Bartram, William, 267, 280
Battale, John, 126
Bauer, Christopher Michael, 26
Bauer, John E., 26
Bauer, Michael Stephen, 26
Bayse, Emily, 107
Bayse, Harriet, 107
Beall, Brooke, 298
Beall, Robert, 299
Beauchamp, John, 272
Beaver, Jacob, 6
Beaver, Rebecca, 6
Bebout, Kathleen, 25
Beckwith, Grace, 275, 276
Beckwith, Marmaduke, 275
Beecher, Captain Thomas, 181
Beem, Nora Janett, 89
Belcher, Abigail, 159
Belcher, Anna, 158
Belcher, Benjamin, 159
Belcher, Dorothy, 159
Belcher, Edward, 158
Belcher, Elizabeth, 152, 153, 156, 158, 159
Belcher, Gregory, 155, 156, 158
Belcher, Hannah, 153, 168, 169
Belcher, John, 155, 156, 158, 168
Belcher, Jonathan, 158
Belcher, Joseph, 156, 158
Belcher, Josiah, 152, 156, 158, 165
Belcher, Margery, 155
Belcher, Mary, 156
Belcher, Moses, 156
Belcher, Nathan, 159
Belcher, Rebecca, 158
Belcher, Ruth, 159

Belcher, Samuel, 156
Belcher, Sarah, 168
Belcher, Thomas, 155
Bell, Elizabeth M., 37
Bell, Felix, 36
Bell, George Washington, 34, 36
Bell, Jason, 36
Bell, Josephine, 37
Bell, Julia A., 36
Bell, Margaret, 36
Bell, Maria, 36
Bell, Mary, 36
Bell, Sarah J., 36
Bell, Susan Rebecca, 37
Bell, William H., 36
Bender, Mary, 351
Bender, Yost, 351
Bennett, Frances, 108
Berelsman, Theodore W., 23
Berry, Joannah, 254
Berry, Mary A., 339
Bethel, Charles, 301
Bias, Roland, 256
Bickel, Barbara Ann, 315, 316
Bickel, James George, 315
Bickley, Dorothy, 55
Bicknell, Haphet, 204
Bicknell, Thomas, 204
Bieber, Esther M., 16
Biggs, John, 344
Billings, Mary, 156
Binckley, Elizabeth Catherine, 27, 29, 30
Binckley, Robert, 27
Binkley, Edith, 83
Binkley, George S., 84
Binkley, George W., 84
Binkley, Harriet E., 84
Binkley, Homer, 84
Binkley, Louisa, 84
Binkley, Nancy C., 84
Binkley, Pharsalia, 84
Binkley, Rebecca, 84
Binkley, Warren, 84
Bird, Capt. George Richard, 344
Blackburn, Cassandra, 48
Blackburn, Ephram, 45, 47
Blackburn, Jehu, 47, 48
Blackburn, John, 41, 45, 47, 48
Blackburn, Margaret Amelia, 48

Blackburn, Mary, 33, 41, 47, 48
Blackburn, Mary E., 48
Blackburn, Rachel, 48
Blackburn, Rebecca, 33
Blackburn, Susannah, 47
Blackburn, Uriah, 47, 48
Blair, William, 199
Blount, Jane, 175
Blue, Rebecca, 279
Board, Ruby, 2
Bochover, Phoebe, 330
Bodley, Mary Bartholomew, 298
Boitnott, Sylvia, 147
Boles, Mr., 325
Bonet, Jaques, 54
Bonnet, Jean, 56
Bonnett, Anna Mary, 54
Bonnett, Barbara, 61
Bonnett, Catherine, 55
Bonnett, Christina, 55
Bonnett, Daniel, 54
Bonnett, David Daniel, 53, 54
Bonnett, Elizabeth, 34, 50, 51, 52, 55, 61
Bonnett, Jacob, 54, 56, 58
Bonnett, James, 54
Bonnett, Jean Jacques, 54, 55
Bonnett, Jean Pierre, 53
Bonnett, Jeanne Coliver, 54
Bonnett, Johan Martin Simon, 55
Bonnett, Johann Adam Issak, 55
Bonnett, John, 61
Bonnett, Lewis, 50, 55, 56, 58, 59, 61, 64
Bonnett, Lewis, Jr., 61
Bonnett, Louis, 53
Bonnett, Margaret, 64
Bonnett, Marguerite Catharine, 55
Bonnett, Mary, 55, 56, 61
Bonnett, Peter, 54
Bonnett, Samuel, 55, 64
Bonnett, Susanna Magdeline, 55
Bonticore, Mary, 54
Boone, Miriam, 299
Borden, Sarah, 242
Boren, Emily, 95
Bosworth, Hannah, 227
Bouchet, Petronella, 54
Bourne, Andrew, 119, 120, 123, 126
Bourne, Ann, 119

Bourne, Christian, 101, 114, 116, 120, 121, 123, 126
Bourne, Francis, 120
Bourne, Henry, 120
Bourne, James, 120
Bourne, John, 114, 119, 120, 123
Bourne, Peter, 120
Bourne, Robert, 120
Bourne, Sarah, 120
Bowen, Ceres, 259
Bowen, James, 103
Bowen, Rebecca, 283
Bowman, Susan, 344
Boyd, Mary Ann, 318
Boyd, Sarah Ann, 300
Boyer, Anita Louise, 137
Boyer, James Edward, 137
Boyer, John Steven, 137
Boyer, Joseph William, 137
Boyer, Judith Eileen, 137
Boyer, Margaret Ellen, 137
Boyer, Sarah, 139
Boyer, Thomas Allen, 137
Bradford, Major, 151
Bradshaw, Phoebe, 267
Brazier, Abraham, 337
Brazier, Breser, 337
Brazier, Henry, 333, 337
Brazier, Isaac, 337
Brazier, Machtelt, 337
Brazier, Martha, 337
Brazier, Mary, 337
Brazier, Rebecca, 333, 334, 337
Brazier, Sarah, 337
Brazier, Susannah, 337
Brazier, Willem, 337
Bread, Allen, 232
Breakey, Harry, 363
Brintnall, Mary, 151
Bristol, John, 132
Broadhead, Samuel, 297
Broscious, Ann Katarina, 349
Brown, Ann, 304
Brown, Arthur, 233
Brown, Esther, 304
Brown, Hannah, 304
Brown, Henry, 303, 304
Brown, John, 304
Brown, Mary, 304
Brown, Mercer, 304

Brown, Mr., 204
Brown, Nathaniel, 227
Brown, Rebecca, 85
Brown, Rev. Frederick, 28
Brown, Richard, 304
Brown, Tamara, 131, 132, 133
Brown, William, 304
Browne, Chaddus, 233, 234
Browne, Daniel, 234
Browne, Deborah, 234, 236
Browne, Hannah, 235
Browne, James, 234, 235
Browne, Jeremiah, 234
Browne, John, 228, 234, 235, 242
Browne, Judah, 234
Browne, Major John, 242
Browne, Martha, 203, 228, 229, 235, 236
Browne, Mary, 235, 236
Browne, Moses, 235
Browne, Obadiah, 236
Browne, Phebe, 235
Browne, Sarah, 183, 211, 235
Browning, Maria, 144
Brumfield, Allen Trig, 257, 258, 261, 269
Brumfield, Angeline, 259
Brumfield, Ann, 253, 256, 257
Brumfield, Anthony, 260
Brumfield, Bostic, 257
Brumfield, Bostic C., 258
Brumfield, Bryd, 256
Brumfield, Caroline, 260
Brumfield, Catherine Ann, 258, 289
Brumfield, Celly, 256
Brumfield, Charles, 262
Brumfield, Christopher Columbus, 259
Brumfield, Clyde, 262
Brumfield, Commodore P., 259
Brumfield, Dicy, 256
Brumfield, Elenor, 260
Brumfield, Emaline, 260
Brumfield, Euella, 260
Brumfield, Fanny, 256
Brumfield, George, 256
Brumfield, George B., 259
Brumfield, Gordon P., 260
Brumfield, Henderson P., 257
Brumfield, Henry Clay, 259

Brumfield, Herman, 262
Brumfield, Humphrey, 255
Brumfield, Inez Marie, 28, 250, 251, 262, 263
Brumfield, Isabel, 253
Brumfield, James, 253
Brumfield, James Cephas, 250, 261, 262
Brumfield, James II, 253, 254
Brumfield, James III, 254, 255, 256
Brumfield, James IV, 255, 256, 257
Brumfield, Joanna, 260
Brumfield, Joel, 256
Brumfield, John Humphrey, 257
Brumfield, John J., 260
Brumfield, John Watson, 254
Brumfield, Jordan, 257, 259
Brumfield, Latimer R., 261
Brumfield, Levinia, 255
Brumfield, Louisa, 259
Brumfield, Lucinda, 260, 261
Brumfield, Lydia, 259
Brumfield, Maggie E., 261
Brumfield, Major, 254
Brumfield, Malinda, 260
Brumfield, Margaret Ann, 257, 260
Brumfield, Margeret Ellen, 259
Brumfield, Martha, 253
Brumfield, Mary, 256, 262
Brumfield, Mary Ann, 260
Brumfield, Mary E., 261
Brumfield, Mary Polly, 254, 255, 256
Brumfield, Micajah, 256
Brumfield, Milton D., 257, 258, 260, 261, 285, 289
Brumfield, Milton J., 260
Brumfield, Morgan G., 260
Brumfield, Nathaniel, 260
Brumfield, Oliver C., 261
Brumfield, Ona, 262
Brumfield, Peneton H., 261
Brumfield, Robert, 253, 254
Brumfield, Sarah, 255, 256
Brumfield, Sina, 256
Brumfield, Susan, 257
Brumfield, Susan M., 260
Brumfield, Susannah, 256, 257
Brumfield, Theadore, 260
Brumfield, Thomas, 253
Brumfield, Thurman, 262

Brumfield, William, 253, 254, 260
Brumfield, William H., 260
Brumfield, William Wirt, 256, 257, 258, 259, 261
Brumfield, William Wirt, Jr., 258, 261
Bucklin, Benjamin, 229
Buckner, Margaret, 126
Buller, Katherine, 271
Bullington, George, 272
Burch, David Pierce, 75, 77
Burch, Hazel, 77
Burchard, Thomas, 187
Burchell, Amelia Houston, 91
Burgess, Garland, 255
Burgess, James W., 260
Burghy, Anna, 292
Burks, Elizabeth Alice, 284
Burlingame, Alice, 217
Burlingame, Elizabeth, 204, 208, 209, 217
Burlingame, Jane, 217
Burlingame, John, 217
Burlingame, Mary, 217
Burlingame, Mercy, 217
Burlingame, Patience, 217
Burlingame, Peter, 217
Burlingame, Roger, 208, 215, 216, 217
Burlingame, Thomas, 215, 217
Burns, Tamson, 132
Bush, Cyrena, 95
Butler, Mary Mildred, 107
Butt, Elisha Swearington, 95
Butt, Elizabeth Johnson, 95
Butt, Hazel Green, 95
Butt, John Frances, 95
Butt, John Swearington, 94, 95
Butt, Johnson Crofford, 95
Butt, Nancy, 95
Butt, Richard Calvin, 95
Butt, Ruebin Pinkney, 95
Butt, William Alfred, 95
Butterworth, Henry, 183
Butterworth, Mary, 227
Butterworth, Sarah, 183, 185
Calvin, John, 53
Cameton, Rev. Archibald, 298
Cannon, John, 272
Carder, Hannah, 197

Carder, James, 198
Carder, John, 198
Carder, Joseph, 197
Carder, Mary, 186, 196, 197, 198
Carder, Richard, 196, 197
Carder, Sarah, 197
Carder, Susanna, 197
Carpenter, Benjamin, 175, 185
Carpenter, Hannah, 175
Carpenter, Lydia, 175
Carpenter, Mr., 176
Carpenter, Silas, 174, 175
Carpenter, William, 172
Carr, Elizabeth, 234
Carroll, James T. Birdie, 259
Carter, Adeline L., 340
Carter, Barbara Ann, 340
Carter, Bert C., 312, 340, 341, 342, 347
Carter, Charles, 339, 340
Carter, Culley M., 339
Carter, Dorothy E., 340
Carter, Elizabeth, 133, 134
Carter, Ella, 340
Carter, Ethel L., 340
Carter, Flora C., 340, 341
Carter, Flora Christine, 312, 313
Carter, George, 339
Carter, Helen D., 340, 341
Carter, Ivan F., 251
Carter, James, 339
Carter, Jerome, 339
Carter, Margaret, 339
Carter, Marjorie J., 340, 342
Carter, Martha E., 339
Carter, Mary, 126
Carter, Mary A., 339
Carter, Michael, 251
Carter, Patrica Ann, 251
Carter, Rachel, 133
Carter, Rev. Thomas, 211
Carter, Richard, 133
Carter, Robert B., 340
Carter, Ronald I., 251
Carter, Scott D., 251
Carter, Thomas, 339
Carter, Truman F., 251
Carter, William, 339
Case, Elizabeth Stafford, 176
Castleman, John Stephen, 91

Castleman, Sarah, 91
Castleman, William Albert, 92
Catlett, Elizabeth, 125
Catlett, Sarah, 126
Cayton, Frederick Allen, 137
Cayton, James, 137
Cayton, Lois Lynn, 137
Chaffee, Dorothy, 151
Chalfant, Clementine, 34
Chalfant, Elijah, 34
Chalfant, Margaret, 34
Chalfant, Mary A., 34
Chalfant, Robert, 34
Chalfant, William H., 34
Chandler, Mr., 51
Chedell, Betsey, 201
Chedester, Juanita, 314
Cherubini, Albert, 313
Chickering, Anne, 150, 151, 152
Chickering, Francis, 150
Christ, Ester May, 40
Christ, Solomon, 40
Church, Elizabeth, 200
Church, Richard, 200
Churchill, William, 337
Clark, Alice, 132
Clark, Jean, 199
Clark, William, 91
Clarke, Elisha, 186
Cleaveland, Josiah, 153
Cline, John, 277
Cobbs, Ann, 254
Cochrane, Mary, 297
Coderman, Johan Michael, 346
Coen, Delilah, 51
Coffelt, Mary, 57
Coffman, Regina, 319
Coffman, William, 319
Cokensparger, George, 350
Cole, Elisha, 269
Cole, George W., 269
Cole, Hawkins, 269
Cole, James, 268
Cole, John Henderson, 269
Cole, William, 37
Coleman, Elijah James, 34
Collins, Mahala, 148
Collins, Sarah, 131
Comisford, A.T., 9
Comisford, Alisha Augusta, 8, 19, 20

Comisford, Amanda Nichelle, 29
Comisford, Andrew Thomas, 2, 4, 5,
    6, 7, 11, 15, 17, 37
Comisford, Anthony Binckley, 27, 30
Comisford, Benjamin Rue, 16
Comisford, Brandon William, 31
Comisford, Brent, 25
Comisford, Brian, 25
Comisford, Catherine Ann, 2, 4, 5
Comisford, Charles Benne, 19, 20,
    21, 24, 25, 137
Comisford, Charles Brants, 7, 11, 12,
    13, 14, 15
Comisford, Charles Bruce, 21, 24
Comisford, Charles Bruce, Jr., 24
Comisford, Clara, 4, 5, 8, 10
Comisford, Cody Rae, 30
Comisford, Cora, 8
Comisford, Cynthia, 25
Comisford, David Michael, 21, 24
Comisford, David Paris, 29
Comisford, David William, 27, 29
Comisford, Dustin Joseph, 31
Comisford, Ellen July, 4
Comisford, Esther, 16
Comisford, Francis Flavia, 19, 21,
    22, 26
Comisford, Gerald Scott, 21, 25
Comisford, Heather Lea, 30
Comisford, Helen Lillian, 22, 26
Comisford, Homer Paris, 24, 26, 27,
    28, 29, 30
Comisford, Homer Whitcome, 19,
    22, 23, 24, 26, 27, 28, 137
Comisford, Janet Sue, 24
Comisford, Jeffery Scott, 24
Comisford, Jeremy Patrick, 29
Comisford, Jon Brent, 21, 25
Comisford, Joseph, 4, 8
Comisford, Joseph Paris, 8, 9
Comisford, Julia Rosealie, 8
Comisford, Katherine Jordan, 30
Comisford, Kathleen Melissa, 21, 25
Comisford, Kirk Matthew, 27, 29, 30
Comisford, Lacie Dawn, 30
Comisford, Laura Lea, 25
Comisford, Lori Jeanne, 26
Comisford, Marcia Lynn, 24
Comisford, Margaret, 4, 5, 8, 9, 10
Comisford, Mark Andrew, 27, 30

Comisford, Mary M, 2, 4, 5, 7, 19
Comisford, Melissa Brooke, 31
Comisford, Michael Anthony, 25
Comisford, Nicole Diane, 30
Comisford, Paris P., 8
Comisford, Paris Patrick, 1, 2, 4, 5
Comisford, Patricia, 26
Comisford, Patrick Henry, 4, 7, 8, 19
Comisford, Patrick Paris, 30
Comisford, Penny Mechael, 24
Comisford, Perry, 11
Comisford, Perry Paris, 7, 17, 18, 19, 20, 21, 22, 27, 71
Comisford, Randy Scott, 29, 31
Comisford, Richard Anthony, 21, 25
Comisford, Robert, 26
Comisford, Robert Charles, 22
Comisford, Rosa, 8
Comisford, Rosette Helene, 4, 5
Comisford, Ryan Steven, 30
Comisford, Sadie, 16, 17
Comisford, Sandra Lea, 24
Comisford, Scott James, 31
Comisford, Seth Foster, 30
Comisford, Shane Mathew, 31
Comisford, Shirley Ellen, 27, 30, 31
Comisford, Steven Charles, 27, 29, 30
Comisford, Thomas, 24
Comisford, Thomas Brent, 25
Comisford, Thomas Perry, 22, 26
Comisford, Tracy Scott, 25
Comisford, Virginia, 25
Comisford, William Davis, 24, 27, 28, 29, 31, 251
Comisford, William Davis, Jr., 29, 31, 315
Comisford, William Flavia, 7, 15
Comstock, Samuel, 207
Connors, Margaret, 246
Cook, Joyce, 262
Cooke, Elizabeth, 242
Cooke, Esther, 188
Cooke, John, 188
Cookus, Henry III, 286
Cooper, Allen, 82
Cooper, Caroline, 82
Cooper, Elizabeth, 82
Cooper, Hannah, 82
Cooper, Hiram, 82
Cooper, James A., 82
Cooper, Jasper F., 82
Cooper, Louisa, 82
Cooper, Rebecca A., 82
Cooper, Sarah E., 82
Corp, Rebecca, 153
Cotterman, Alfred, 351
Cotterman, Almeda, 351
Cotterman, Amos, 350
Cotterman, Amy, 350
Cotterman, Barbara, 346, 350, 351
Cotterman, Catherine, 350
Cotterman, Charles Clinton, 351
Cotterman, Daniel, 350
Cotterman, Elizabeth, 350
Cotterman, Elmore, 351
Cotterman, Franklin, 351
Cotterman, George, 351
Cotterman, Gilbert Leroy, 351
Cotterman, Harvey, 351
Cotterman, Henry, 351
Cotterman, Isaac, 351
Cotterman, Israel, 350
Cotterman, James, 351
Cotterman, James W., 350
Cotterman, Johan Michael, 349, 350, 351
Cotterman, John, 350, 351
Cotterman, John H., 350
Cotterman, Lydia, 350
Cotterman, Margaret J., 350
Cotterman, Maria E., 351
Cotterman, Martha E., 351
Cotterman, Mary Elizabeth, 350
Cotterman, Mary Jane, 351
Cotterman, Michael, 350
Cotterman, Noah, 351
Cotterman, Philip, 350, 351
Cotterman, Royal, 350
Cotterman, Salome Sarah, 350
Cotterman, Samuel, 350, 351
Cotterman, Silama, 351
Cotterman, William Henry, 351
Coulson, Margaret, 48
Coulson, Thomas, 48
Cousine, Christine, 53, 54
Cowgill, Evan, 131
Cox, Jane, 187, 191
Cramer, Lillie, 310
Cramer, Lotta D., 310

Cramer, Mary A. (Nutter), 309, 310
Cramer, Matilda, 310
Cramer, Minnie, 310
Craw, Mr., 347
Crawford, Ada, 70
Craybill, Hannah, 328
Creed, Maudlin, 275
Cresap, Harriet, 344
Crigler, Catherine, 92
Crimeans, Linsy, 256
Crissey, John, 272
Cromwell, Oliver, 183
Crosby, Bessie, 78
Crousdorf, Philip, 317
Crump, Hiram B., 105
Crundy, Alice, 211
Culp, Thomas, 292
Cumberledge, George Fielding, 50
Cunningham, Henry, 340
Cunningham, John, 116
Cunningham, Lizzie, 107
Cusac, Carrie Pearl, 40
Cyrus, Fannie, 285
Dalany, Daniel, 54
Danford, Rev. C.M., 27
Dare, John, 91
Darling, Elizabeth, 225, 226
Davies, Elizabeth, 167, 168
Davies, Margaret, 167
Davis, Albert Perry, 70
Davis, Charles Joseph, 68, 70, 71
Davis, Clara May, 70
Davis, Clarence Clay, 70, 73
Davis, Dennis M., 73
Davis, Dolores Ann, 73
Davis, Eliza E., 71
Davis, Elizabeth, 67, 85, 304
Davis, Ellen Eleanor, 120
Davis, Evelyn M., 73
Davis, Georgia Emma, 70, 72, 73
Davis, Hannah J., 134, 135
Davis, Harold J., 73
Davis, Huldah, 165
Davis, Jesse N., 70
Davis, Jessie Helen, 17, 18, 19, 20, 21, 22, 27, 70, 71
Davis, Jessie Ronald, 73
Davis, John, 127
Davis, John William, 70
Davis, Lillie Belle, 70, 71
Davis, Lucy, 279
Davis, Lula B., 70
Davis, Marcus Whitcome, 17, 67, 68, 69, 70, 71, 72, 77
Davis, Margaret, 127
Davis, Mary, 152
Davis, Mary Marie, 68, 71
Davis, Mary Polly, 268, 280
Davis, Myrtle I., 70
Davis, Newton Jerod, 67, 70, 73
Davis, Owen, 71
Davis, Raymond Thomas, 70
Davis, Robert G., 73
Davis, Sampson, 321
Davis, Sarah Ann, 127, 128
Davis, Scintha Paralee, 258
Davis, Thomas, 67, 68, 134
Davis, Wesley Perry, 67, 68, 70, 71
Davy, Capt. Owen, 64
Davy, Clara Mae, 10
Davy, Florence, 10
Davy, George C., 10
Davy, Nellie, 10
Davy, William C., 10
Dayton, Sarah, 300
De Coursey, Mary, 93
Dedman, Henry, 125
Dedman, Katherine, 125
Deering, Mary Francis, 284
Denton, Nancy, 25
Desreux, Abram, 54
Desreux, Ann Marie, 54, 55, 56, 58
Deweese, Emma Alice, 40
Deweese, Samuel, 40
Dexter, Alice, 229
Dexter, James, 174
Dexter, John, 229
Dillee, Elizabeth, 158, 161, 164
Dixon, Joseph, 303
Dod, Daniel, 235
Donaldson, John B., 300
Doss, Zachariah, 266
Dove, Elder Adam, 72
Drake, James, 267
Drummond, Van Leer, 132
Dungan, Barbara, 174, 181, 182
Dungan, William, 181
Dunning, John David, 135
Dunning, Margaret Belle, 135
Dupler, Donna, 25

Durham, John C., 97
Durham, Nora, 97
Duval, Charles, 345
Eagon, Catherine, 41, 43
Eagon, Clementine, 41, 42
Eagon, David, 43
Eagon, Delilah, 42
Eagon, Elizabeth, 42, 43
Eagon, Henry, 43
Eagon, James, 41, 43
Eagon, John, 43
Eagon, Lucy, 42
Eagon, Margaret, 42
Eagon, Mary, 41, 43, 44
Eagon, Mary Polly, 42
Eagon, Rebecca, 43
Eagon, Richard, 41
Eagon, Sally, 43
Eagon, Sampson, 41, 43, 44
Eagon, Sarah, 33, 34, 36, 37, 41, 42, 44
Eagon, Solomon, 33, 41, 48
Eagon, Susannah, 41, 42, 44
Eagon, Thomas I., 42
Eagon, Uriah B., 42
Eagon, William, 43
Earp, Mariah Ann, 147
Easton, Nicholas, 181, 182
Ebtharpe, Elinor, 335
Ebtharpe, Elizabeth, 335
Ebtharpe, Francis, 335
Ebtharpe, Rebecca, 335
Eddy, John, 167
Edwards, William, 40
Eggleston, Elizabeth, 126
Eggleston, Laura Belle, 147
Eldred, Elizabeth, 149
Eliot, Jacob, 161
Ellis, Lucinda, 299
Entler, Catherine, 283, 286
Esten, Jemina, 153
Evans, Abraham, 275
Evans, Rhea Grace, 325
Fairley, James L., 342
Fairley, Judith Kay, 342
Farrell, Deborah, 335
Ferguson, Catherine, 92
Ferguson, Cora A., 292
Fessler, Catherine, 353
Fickle, Esther, 243

Ficklin, Joseph, 128
Field, Ruth, 224
Fielding, Margaret, 93
Fiske, Ann, 150
Fitch, Marian E., 73
Fitzgerald, Sammie Jean (Fortner), 24
Flagg, Sarah, 200
Fleischer, Agnes, 49, 63, 64
Fleming, John, 300
Flint, Thomas, 128
Flowers, Linda, 24
Foreman, Margaret, 351
Fortner, M. Cornellia, 25
Fortner, Thurman, 24, 25
Foster, Lynn E., 30
Foster, Nathaniel, 297
Fouts, Ernie, 251
Fox, Sarah Edith, 292
Frazier, Brady, 292
Frederick, Ada G., 324
Frederick, Arthur J., 324
Frederick, Jacob G., 324
Frederick, Nellie N., 324
Freenough, Mr., 165
French, Asa T., 132
Friend, Augusta Ellen, 87
Friend, Charles, 86, 87
Fruit, Margaret, 297
Fruit, Sarah, 297
Fry, Catherine, 277
Fry, Martha, 269
Fry, Mary, 265
Frye, Charles W., 148
Frye, John, 148
Fullen, Rebecca A., 31
Fuller, Elizabeth Caroline, 284
Fuller, Joseph, 158
Fuller, Mary, 141
Fuller, Nancy C., 284
Fulwater, Sarah, 225
Funkhouser, Esther, 319
Fuschain, Adam, 49
Fuschain, Clara, 49, 50
Gaffney, Rosette Helene, 1, 2
Ganoe, Catherine, 366
Ganoe, John Armitage, 366
Ganoe, Joseph, 366
Ganoe, Kiane, 366
Ganoe, Malissa, 366

Ganoe, Mary Delilah, 366
Ganoe, Nancy J., 366
Ganoe, Sarah, 366
Ganoe, Thomas Alfred, 366
Gardner, Anna H., 284
Garrison, Elizabeth, 350
Garrison, Nancy, 66
Gary, Thankful, 140
Geeding, Henry, 317
Gilbert, Elizabeth, 141
Gilbert, Thomas, 156
Gill, Augustis, 39
Gill, Fidilia, 39
Gill, Minnie, 39
Gill, Rebecca, 156
Gilliland, Elizabeth, 297
Gnat, Elias Ann, 92
Gochenour, Abraham, 317, 319, 320
Gochenour, Catharine, 320
Gochenour, Elizabeth, 320
Gochenour, Henry, 320
Gochenour, Jacob, 319
Gochenour, Mary, 320
Gochenour, Samuel, 320
Goering, Catherine Elizabeth, 282
Goering, Jacob, 282
Gohn, Margaretha, 281
Good, Carlton Frances, 78
Good, Francis Marion, 78
Good, Harry E., 78
Good, James, 78
Good, Margaret, 319
Goodin, Victoria Spring, 29
Goodrich, Nathan, 58
Goodrich, Rev. Jay, 135
Goodwin, Ira, 6
Gordon, Charles, 292
Gordon, Margaret Matilda, 300
Gordon, Susan Cassandra, 34, 37
Grabiel, John, 318
Graham, Hannah, 298
Graham, John, 116, 298
Grant, President Ulysses S., 35
Grant, Sarah Ellen, 90
Grass, George, 7
Gray, Amasa, 142, 200, 201, 205
Gray, Catherine, 200
Gray, Elizabeth, 199, 200, 201
Gray, Hannah, 200
Gray, James, 199, 200

Gray, John, 199, 200, 201
Gray, Jonas, 200
Gray, Joseph, 200
Gray, Lydia, 142, 143, 144, 147, 148, 201
Gray, Mary, 199
Gray, Matthew, 199, 200
Gray, Robert, 199, 200
Gray, Samuel, 199
Gray, Sarah, 199, 201
Gray, Susanna, 200
Gray, Welcome, 201
Gray, William, 199
Green, Aaron, 105
Green, Almira, 109
Green, Amanda, 106, 109
Green, Amelia Frances, 108
Green, Andrew Jackson, 107
Green, Angeline, 109
Green, Ann G., 109
Green, Augustine, 106
Green, Aylette F., 107
Green, Bird, 106
Green, Boargenes, 106
Green, Brunetta Taylor, 108
Green, Caroline, 88
Green, Cassander E., 107
Green, Celinda E., 109
Green, Edward Augustus, 108
Green, Edward Churchman, 107, 108
Green, Elimira, 107
Green, Eliza Ann, 106
Green, Elizabeth, 96, 97, 103, 105, 106, 110
Green, Elizabeth Valentine, 108
Green, Felix, 106
Green, Ferdinand E., 107
Green, George T. W., 106
Green, George W., 107, 109
Green, Harriet, 107
Green, Henry R., 88
Green, Hiram, 106, 109
Green, Isaac, 7, 19
Green, James, 101, 102, 105, 117
Green, James Bayse, 107
Green, James W., 105, 107
Green, John, 96, 105, 106, 109, 130
Green, Joseph, 7
Green, Joseph Thomas, 108
Green, Julia Ann, 105

Green, Juliet, 109
Green, Louisa, 107
Green, Lovey Mariah, 109
Green, Lucy E., 106
Green, Lydia, 176
Green, Margaret S., 105
Green, Maria L., 108
Green, Mary, 101, 102, 105, 106, 107, 108
Green, Mary Jane, 107, 109
Green, Mary L., 107
Green, Mary Polly, 105
Green, Moses, 106, 107
Green, Murlie Rosa, 7, 19
Green, Nancy, 103
Green, Nancy Ann, 105
Green, Olive, 109
Green, Philadelphius, 108
Green, Purlina, 109
Green, Rebecca, 105
Green, Rebecca Catherine, 107
Green, Rev. Benjamin, 15
Green, Richard A., 106
Green, Robert W., 106
Green, Robert William, 107
Green, Sally, 103
Green, Sarah, 105, 109
Green, Sarah Ann, 107
Green, Selina Frances, 106
Green, Selucas, 108
Green, Sophia Ball, 108
Green, Susan Elizabeth, 107
Green, Susan Smith, 106, 108
Green, Taylor Bayse, 107
Green, Theodore, 7
Green, Thilbert, 107
Green, Thomas, 105, 106, 107
Green, Thomas W., 106
Green, Virginia Felix, 107
Green, William, 102, 103, 105, 106, 107, 108
Green, William Andrew Jackson, 106, 107
Green, William F., 109
Greene, John, 174
Greene, Peter, 174
Greene, Sarah, 175
Greenfield, James, 42
Gretchell, Pricilla, 164
Grice, Charles, 167

Griffith, Anna, 322, 329
Griffith, Catherine, 329
Griffith, Daniel, 322, 329
Griffith, Elizabeth, 83
Griffith, Elizabeth Marie, 89
Griffith, Esther, 329
Griffith, Evan, 322
Griffith, Hannah, 329
Griffith, John, 329
Griffith, Lydia, 322, 323, 329
Griffith, Mary, 329
Griffith, Reuben, 48
Griffith, William Thomas, 329
Grimes, Oprphey, 344
Grimes, Sarah, 125
Gross, Edmund, 159
Groton, Benjamin, 197
Groves, Amelia, 95
Groves, David, 2
Groves, John, 131
Groves, Joseph, 283
Groves, Samuel, 2
Grymes, Rev. Charles, 125
Guerit, Judith, 54
Gulley, Alice, 171
Gulley, John, 171
Haar, Rev. Simon, 318
Haas, Absolom W., 318
Haas, Adam, 318
Haas, Anna Marie, 317
Haas, Catharine, 317, 318
Haas, Christena, 317, 318, 319, 320
Haas, Christina, 317
Haas, Elizabeth, 317, 318, 319
Haas, George, 317, 319
Haas, Isaac, 317, 319
Haas, Isabella, 318
Haas, Jacob, 317, 318, 319
Haas, John, 308, 317, 318, 319, 327
Haas, Jonathan, 317, 319
Haas, Maria, 317
Haas, Mary, 318, 319
Haas, Philip, 319
Haas, Polly, 317
Haas, Rachel, 308, 318, 320
Haas, Rebecca, 317, 318, 319
Haas, Sarah, 318
Haas, Simon, 318
Haas, William, 318
Haie, Marion Bennett, 125

Haines, Elizabeth, 91
Hale, John, 186
Hale, Mary, 277
Hale, Wiley, 259
Hall, Bridgette, 25
Hall, Earl Lester, 25
Hall, Hannah, 91
Hall, Wayne D., 25
Halton, Elizabeth, 256
Hamilton, Margaret, 299
Hammond, Clayton, 315
Hammond, Ethel, 315
Hammond, Jenny, 315
Hammontree, Elizabeth, 133
Hanby, John, 304
Hand, Alberta, 89
Hand, George I., 77
Hand, Jennings R., 77
Hand, Philander R., 89
Hankinson, Elsie, 326
Hanna, Elizabeth, 68, 70, 71
Hanna, Joseph, 68
Hardesty, Edna A., 142
Hardin, Matilda, 106
Hared, John, 215
Harley, Jacob, 266, 267
Harmon, Eli Ferinand, 260
Harmon, Elizabeth, 260
Harmon, William H., 260
Harness, Capt. John, 64
Harper, Frances, 179
Harris, Absolom W., 308, 309, 310, 324
Harris, Amber Michelle, 315
Harris, Amos, 306
Harris, Anne, 303
Harris, Arthur, 311, 312, 313
Harris, Arthur Eugene, 31, 312, 313, 314, 315, 357
Harris, Athur, 341
Harris, Catherine, 307
Harris, Celia Nixon, 308
Harris, Clifton E., 309
Harris, Daisy D., 310
Harris, Daniel, 305
Harris, David, 303, 306, 307
Harris, Denver, 314
Harris, Edward H., 310
Harris, Elizabeth, 308
Harris, Esther, 303, 304
Harris, Esther, Jr., 303, 304
Harris, Frank E., 293
Harris, Gary Eugene, 313, 314
Harris, George, 306, 307
Harris, Hannah, 305
Harris, Harold Charles, 311
Harris, Harry F., 310
Harris, Hester, 305
Harris, Holly Jo, 314
Harris, Isaac, 307, 308, 320
Harris, Jacquline Lee, 314
Harris, James Arthur, 313, 315, 316
Harris, James Clay, 316
Harris, Janette, 314
Harris, Jerry Edward, 314
Harris, Jesse, 305, 306, 307, 308
Harris, John, 275, 306, 308
Harris, Jonah, 307
Harris, Joseph, 303
Harris, Joshua, 306, 315
Harris, Julie, 314
Harris, Justine, 315
Harris, Kelly Sue, 314
Harris, Larry Richard, 313
Harris, Laura Elizabeth, 309, 310, 311, 312
Harris, Laura Mae, 312, 313, 316
Harris, Lulu R., 310
Harris, Lydia J., 309
Harris, Martha, 305, 306
Harris, Mary, 305, 308, 309
Harris, Mathias, 307
Harris, Michael David, 313, 315
Harris, Michael Richard, 314
Harris, Molly Jean, 314
Harris, Nathan Arthur, 316
Harris, Norma Marlene, 313
Harris, Patrick, 315
Harris, Phebe, 304
Harris, Robert Kenneth, 313, 315
Harris, Robyn Rene, 314
Harris, Samuel, 303, 304
Harris, Samuel E., 309
Harris, Samuel, Jr., 304
Harris, Stacy DeLynn, 315
Harris, Stephen, 308
Harris, Susan Annette, 31, 313, 315
Harris, Susannah W., 309
Harris, Thomas, 304
Harris, Thomas Edward, 313, 304

Harris, Thomas, Jr., 235
Harris, Timothy Wayne, 313, 315
Harris, Wendy Sue, 315
Harris, William, 188, 303, 304, 305, 306, 307
Harris, William, Jr., 304
Harrison, General William Henry, 93
Harter, Charles, 70
Hartong, Dorothy Arlene, 100
Hartong, Effie, 100
Hartong, Madison, 100
Hartshorne, Hugh, 334
Hartwell, Eleanor, 256
Harvey, Mary, 261
Harvey, Narcissus, 250, 261, 262
Harvey, Thomas, 261
Haskins, Rachel, 257
Hatfield, John, 257
Hatfield, William, 256
Hatton, Elizabeth Jane, 289
Hatton, Malinda, 257
Hawkings, Mr., 204
Hawkins, Benjamin, 108
Hawkins, Edward, 174
Hawkins, Henry Clinton, 108
Hawkins, James Alexander, 108
Hawkins, John William, 108
Hawkins, Keisah, 209
Hawkins, Madeline, 194
Hawkins, Margaret Ann, 108
Hawkins, Mary, 106, 107
Hawkins, Mary Jane, 108
Hawkins, Sarah Martha, 108
Hawkins, Susan Frances, 108
Hawkins, Winfield Scott, 108
Haynes, Truman Herman, 4
Haynie, Martha A., 284
Hays, Elizabeth Elliot, 344, 345
Hays, Jonathan C., III, 344
Hayward, Hannah, 208
Head, Bigger, 243
Hearn, George, 225
Hearn, Joan, 225, 226
Hearndon, Alice, 234
Heeke, Catharine, 351
Heinlein, Sarah M., 85
Heise, John, 317
Heisse, George H., 42
Heizey, Margaret, 283
Heller, Catherine, 327, 328

Helson, Martha, 19
Henderson, Mary, 344
Henkins, Margaret, 34
Hennan, Enoch, 34
Henton, Elizabeth, 95
Heskett, Mary J., 133, 134
Hetrich, Catherine, 346, 349, 350, 351
Hetterich, Johan Nicholaus, 349
Hickey, Edward, 9, 10
Hickey, Florence, 9
Hickey, Karl, 9, 10
Hickey, Lillian, 9, 10
Hickey, Marie, 9, 10
Hickle, Stephen V., 133
Hickle, Walter C., 133
Hildebrand, Adam, 281
Hilyard, George, 283
Hinds, Clarissa, 260, 289
Hinds, Elias, 260, 285, 289
Hinds, Emeline, 289
Hinds, Ezra, 289
Hinds, Harriet, 261, 285, 289, 290
Hinds, James, 289
Hinds, John, 289
Hinds, Lehu, 289
Hinds, Lucretia, 289
Hinds, Rebecca, 289
Hinds, Sarah A., 289
Hinds, William, 258
Hinds, William Lewis, 289
Hines, Golda, 292
Hocker, Bess J., 292
Hodder, Lillian, 294
Hodder, Marguerite, 294
Hodder, Ralph, 294
Hodder, William, 294
Hoffman, Pearl Ethel, 21
Holden, Francis, 243
Holden, Mary, 198
Holmes, Elizabeth, 305
Holmes, Hopestill, 243
Holmes, Joan, 237
Holmes, John, 237, 242, 243
Holmes, Jonathan, 242
Holmes, Joseph, 237, 242
Holmes, Lydia, 242
Holmes, Martha, 185, 242
Holmes, Mary, 228, 234, 235, 242, 243

Holmes, Nathaniel, 237
Holmes, Obadiah, 234, 237, 239, 240, 242,
Holmes, Robert, 237, 239
Holmes, Samuel, 237, 242
Holmes, Sarah, 243
Holmes, Thomas, 272
Holstein, Mary, 260
Holt, Betsy, 94
Homeric, Eleanor Jeanne, 26
Hommond, Rollie, 23
Hone, Amy, 86
Hone, Anna E., 85
Hone, Eliza J., 85
Hone, Elizabeth J., 85
Hone, Harriet A., 85
Hone, Henry, 85
Hone, James, 85
Hone, James Brown, 85
Hone, John Henry, 85
Hone, Mariam C., 85
Hone, Mary Ellen, 85
Hone, Rebecca Mae, 85
Hone, Ruth E., 85
Hone, Safety M., 85
Honeychurch, Mary, 218
Hood, Catherine, 345
Hook, Jessee, 42
Hooker, General Joseph, 346
Hooper, Phebe, 91
Hoover, Eleanor, 257, 258, 259, 261
Hoover, Thomas, 257
Hopkins, Thomas, 172
Hopkins, William, 171
Hottinger, George, 325, 326
House, Ada Bell, 76
House, Elizabeth Belle, 78
House, George R., 76, 78
House, Gracie, 76
House, Harry Allen, 76, 77, 78
House, Jefferson, 76, 77, 78
House, John, 76
House, Mamie Rachel, 76, 78
House, Margaret Louisa, 78
House, Mary Eleanor, 78
Houseman, Carol, 29
Howard, Elizabeth, 215
Howe, Damaris, 141
Huber, Elizabeth, 26
Hubner, Anna, 21

Hubner, Elizabeth, 21, 22
Hudson, Benjamin T., 145
Hudson, Rebecca, 232
Hueston, Elizabeth, 298
Hueston, Jane, 298
Hueston, Mary, 298
Hueston, Nancy, 298
Hueston, Robert, 298
Hueston, Sarah, 298
Hueston, Susan, 298
Hueston, William, 298
Huffaker, Dr. A., 15
Hughes, Leah, 41
Hughes, Nathaniel, 41
Hughs, Rev. Thomas, 324
Humphrey, John, 292
Humphrey, Martha, 91, 92
Hunt, Christine, 314
Hunt, Deborah, 155
Hunt, Eli, 91
Hunt, Enoch, 151
Hunt, James, 314
Hunt, John, 314
Hunt, Matthew, 314
Hunt, Pauline, 314
Hunt, Peter, 151
Huntingdon, Jacolyn, 215, 217
Hurt, John, 255
Huston, Robert E., 345
Hutchins, Rachel, 266
Hutton, Betty, 128
Hyde, Catharine, 239, 240, 242, 234
Hyde, Gilbert, 239
Hyde, Patience, 175
Inghram, Arthur, 42
Inlow, C. Bert, 341
Inlow, Doris M., 341
Inlow, Earl C., 340
Inlow, Eileen C., 341
Inlow, Geraldine, 341
Inlow, Harold I., 341
Inlow, Oriel, 341
Inskeep, Elizabeth, 344
Isabee, Emily, 259, 260
Jackson, President Andrew, 296
Jackson, William, 91
Jacobs, Thomas, 235
James, Ann, 329
James, Benjamin, 330
James, Daniel, 329

James, David, 329
James, Davis E., 330
James, Ebenezer R., 329
James, Edmund, 329
James, Flora A., 330
James, Infant, 330
James, John H., 330
James, Joseph, 330
James, Lewis J., 330
James, Mary, 329
James, Thomas, 329
James, Wesley K., 330
James, William, 329
Jane, Effie, 90
Janney, Amos, 303
Janney, Stacy, 304
January, James, 298
Jarvis, Richard Walter, 40
Jenckes, Abigail, 228
Jenckes, Catharine, 203, 204, 229
Jenckes, Daniel, 226
Jenckes, Deborah, 226
Jenckes, Ebenezer, 227
Jenckes, Elizabeth, 226, 227
Jenckes, Ester, 227, 229
Jenckes, George, 226
Jenckes, Joanna, 227
Jenckes, John, 225, 226, 229
Jenckes, Joseph, 203, 225, 226, 227, 228, 229, 232
Jenckes, Joseph, Jr., 227, 228, 229, 236
Jenckes, Lydia, 229
Jenckes, Martha, 229
Jenckes, Mary, 227, 229
Jenckes, Nathaniel, 227, 229
Jenckes, Obadiah, 229
Jenckes, Samuel, 226
Jenckes, Sarah, 226, 227
Jenckes, William, 228
Jenks, Daniel, 227
Jessup, Charles Howard, 315
Jessup, Priscilla Ann, 315
Jett, Mary Mollie, 116
John, Mary, 304
John, Thomas, 304
Johnson, Abraham, 258
Johnson, Andrew, 256
Johnson, Ann, 123
Johnson, Captain Isaac, 168
Johnson, Catherine, 123
Johnson, Charlie, 254
Johnson, Elizabeth, 114, 120, 123
Johnson, Elizabeth Jane, 360
Johnson, Henry, 119, 120, 123, 126
Johnson, Joseph, 158
Johnson, Katherine, 237, 239
Johnson, Letticie, 360
Johnson, Martha, 258
Johnson, Richard, 120, 123
Johnson, Sarah, 123
Johnson, William, 51
Jones, Daniel, 325
Jones, David D., 324
Jones, Elizabeth, 345
Jones, John, 42
Jones, Susannah, 331, 335
Jones, W.S., 301
Jones, William H., 108
Jordan, John, 256
Jordan, Lesley Elise, 30
Juniper, Absalom, 355
Juniper, Anna, 355
Juniper, Bert L., 356
Juniper, Clyde H., 356
Juniper, Effie, 356
Juniper, Foster P., 356
Juniper, Frankie, 355
Juniper, George, 355
Juniper, George H., 355
Juniper, Gerald Ernest, 357
Juniper, Helen, 356
Juniper, Huldah, 355
Juniper, James, 355, 356
Juniper, Jeremiah, 355
Juniper, Mary, 355
Juniper, Matilda, 355
Juniper, Minerva, 355, 356
Juniper, Norma B., 31, 312, 313, 314, 315, 357
Juniper, Norma Marlene, 315
Juniper, Olive C., 356
Juniper, Pearl, 312, 356, 357, 363
Juniper, Rebecca, 355
Juniper, Samuel, 355
Juniper, Silas, 355, 356
Juniper, Thomas, 355
Juniper, Zina, 356
Kaewood, Ann Kathleen, 267, 276, 277

Kains, Bea, 16
Keech, Mary, 185
Keller, Margaret Hottel, 327
Kelp, Maria Catharine, 317, 318, 319
Kelso, Joan, 200
Kent, Ann, 44
Kent, Ephraim, 44
Kent, George, 44
Kent, George Layton, 44
Kent, James B., 42
Kent, Minerva, 51
Kent, Sarah, 44
Kent, Solomon, 44
Kent, Susannah, 44
Kent, Thomas, 44
Kent, Uriah, 44
Kent, William, 44, 51
Killen, Margaret June, 315
King, Sarah, 350
Kirk, Alice B., 15, 16
Kirk, Mr. and Mrs. Elijah, 15
Kirk, William, 75
Kirkpatrick, William, 299
Kirton, Mary, 161
Kissinger, Bessie May, 347
Kissinger, Conrad Robert, 347
Kissinger, Robert, 347
Kissinger, Rose, 347
Kissinger, Thomas, 347
Kissinger, William, 347
Klein, George, 24
Klein, Marie, 24
Knight, William, 232
Knower, Daniel, 140
Knox, Eleanor, 297
Kolb, John, 317
Koontz, Sarah, 319
Kotterman, Johann Philip, 349
Kotterman, Johann Uhrich, 349
Kratzenburg, Gertrude Ann, 245
Kratzenburg, Johanna, 245, 246
Kratzenburg, Stephen, 245
Kuhlewein, Agnes Katherina, 349
Kyles, Hannah, 65
Ladley, Mary, 83, 86, 87
Lambotham, Mary, 183
Lamson, Molly, 200
Lane, Mrs. Larry W., 342
Lantz, Alexander, 50, 51
Lantz, Amelia, 52

Lantz, Andrew, 49
Lantz, Andrew, 50
Lantz, Catherine, 50
Lantz, Delilah, 51
Lantz, Elias, 51
Lantz, Elizabeth, 50, 51, 52
Lantz, Ellis P., 52
Lantz, Emma, 51
Lantz, Emma B., 52
Lantz, George, 49
Lantz, Hans George, 49
Lantz, Harriet, 51
Lantz, Jacob, 49, 50, 51
Lantz, Johannes, 49, 50
Lantz, John, 51, 52
Lantz, John George, 50
Lantz, John, Jr., 34, 50, 51, 52, 61
Lantz, Lewis, 50, 51
Lantz, Margaret, 51
Lantz, Margaretha, 49
Lantz, Mary, 50, 51
Lantz, Nancy, 51
Lantz, Remembrance, 52
Lantz, Samuel, 50
Lantz, Sarah, 52
Lantz, Sarah Elizabeth, 6, 34, 35, 38, 39, 40, 51
Lantz, Simon, 51
Lantz, Thomas, 51
Lantz, Ulysses, 51
Lantz, William, 50, 51, 52
Lappen, Charles, 251
Lappen, Frieda, 251
Lappen, Larry, 251
Lappen, Mark, 251
Lappen, Nancy, 251
Lappen, Wallace C., 251
Latham, Francis, 181
Latham, Lewis, 181
Lathum, Jane, 188
Layman, Catherine, 327
Leary, Elizabeth T., 108
Lecrone, Isaac, 19
Lecrone, Leo Bruce, 19
Lecrone, Pauline M., 19
Lecrone, Samuel, 19
Lee, Edward, 54
Lee, Elizabeth, 227, 231, 232
Lees, Frank S., 71
Lees, Howard George, 71

Lees, Lillie, 71
Lees, Mildred, 71
Leete, Phebe, 207, 211
Leete, Robert, 211
Lefever, Catherine, 367
Lefever, Mary A., 365
Legg, Elizabeth, 322
Lemly, Anna J., 108
Lester, Hiram, 34
Lett, Lemuel C., 144
Lett, Lucretia, 289
Lett, Mary Francis, 144, 145
Lett, William, 284
Levier, Sarah, 360
Lewis, Colonel, 64
Lewis, Ellen Joel, 299
Lewis, Jane, 291
Lewis, Robert D., 301
Lightly, Maria, 40
Lincoln, Albert Aplin, 143
Lincoln, Benjamin Aplin, 143
Lincoln, Charles James, 143
Lincoln, Edward Henry, 143
Lincoln, Elisha, 143
Lincoln, Elizabeth Pray, 143
Lincoln, Julian Welcome, 143
Lincoln, Lucy Webb, 143
Lincoln, Lydia Ann, 143
Lincoln, Marea Marie, 143
Lincoln, Sanford Elisha, 143
Lincoln, Sarah Adeline, 143
Lincoln, William Stowell, 143
Lippitt, Martha, 217
Lippitt, Mary, 208
Lippitt, Mary Knowles, 217
Litle, John, 296
Loder, Sarah Graham, 308
Longstreth, Albert P., 37
Longstreth, Daniel, 37
Longstreth, Fanny A., 37
Longstreth, John, 37
Longstreth, Malinda A., 37
Longstreth, Samuel, 37
Longstreth, William, 37
Lorentz, Mary, 64
Lorentz, Mary Elizabeth, 55
Low, Anthony, 175
Low, John, 194
Lowther, Colonel William, 64
Lucas, Ann, 276

Lucas, Charles, 267, 276, 277
Lucas, Charles, Jr., 277
Lucas, David, 277
Lucas, Edmund, 276
Lucas, Elizabeth, 276
Lucas, Fredrick, 276
Lucas, George, 277
Lucas, Grace, 276
Lucas, Hannah, 276
Lucas, James, 276
Lucas, John, 277
Lucas, Martha, 276
Lucas, Mary, 276, 277
Lucas, Nathaniel, 276
Lucas, Parker, 277
Lucas, Randolph, 277
Lucas, Sarah O., 267, 268, 277
Lucas, William, 275, 276, 277
Luke, George, 119
Lum, Nancy Ann, 335
Luther, Adeline, 259
Lykes, Eleanor, 365
Lytle, Agnes, 297
Lytle, Elizabeth, 297
Lytle, Isaac, 296
Lytle, Jane, 296
Lytle, John, 296
Lytle, Josephine, 297
Lytle, Mary, 296
Lytle, Sarah, 297
Lytle, William, 296
Lytle, William Haines, 296
Lytle, William Haynes, 297
MacDean, Dr. Donald, 15
Makemie, Martha, 298
Makemie, Rebecca Jane, 295, 297, 298
Makemie, Rev. Francis, 298
Mala, William, 108
Malay, Joannem, 5
Malone, Elizabeth, 7
Malone, Joseph, 246
Malone, Mary Connors, 246, 247, 249
Mansfield, Elizabeth A., 292
March, Alexander, 155
Markawitz, Saul, 326
Marple, Hannah, 318
Marsh, Alexander, 156
Marsh, Charles Case, 84, 90

Marsh, Olive Mabel, 90
Marsh, Roswell, 84, 90
Marshall, Alice, 345
Martin, Colonel Charles, 64
Martin, John, 149
Martzloff, Frederick, 350
Mason, Christopher, 229
Mason, Mr., 176
Masters, Abraham, 192
Masters, Elizabeth, 191
Masters, Jane, 192
Masters, John, 187, 191
Masters, Lydia, 183, 187, 188, 191, 192
Masters, Nancy, 51
Masters, Nathaniel, 187, 191, 192
Masters, Sarah, 191
Mather, Joseph C., 147
Mathews, Charlotte, 299
Mauk, Anthony Wayne, 85
Mawney, Elizabeth T., 186
Mayes, John Hendricks, 95
Mayes, Susanna, 95
Mayhew, Thomas, 187
Mayo, Thurza Howard, 299
McCarney, John, 298
McClain, Jane, 61
McClane, Elizabeth, 307
McClelland, Mary J., 356
McConnell, Jane, 296
McCoy, Clark, 147
McCulloch, Jessie, 39
McCulloch, John R., 38, 39
McCulloch, William, 39
McDaniel, Francis, 94
McDaniel, Philisia, 94
McDonald, Kirk Matthew, 31
McDonald, Pauline, 315
McDonald, Tracy Lynn, 30, 31
McFarland, Elemor, 199
McFarland, Ethel, 356
McGee, Adaline, 363, 367
McGee, Adam Nicely, 365, 367
McGee, Addison, 367
McGee, Albert, 366
McGee, Alcena C., 366
McGee, Bertha, 367
McGee, Clara, 367
McGee, Cora, 367
McGee, Daniel, 363

McGee, Daniel S., 366, 367
McGee, Eliza Jane, 366
McGee, Elizabeth, 365, 366
McGee, Fannie, 366
McGee, Female, 365
McGee, Frances K., 366
McGee, Jacob, 362, 365, 366, 367
McGee, James, 365
McGee, James L., 365
McGee, Jessey, 367
McGee, Jessie, 367
McGee, Jessie May, 366
McGee, John, 365, 366, 367
McGee, Joseph L., 365, 366
McGee, Laura Mae, 363, 367
McGee, Lauretta, 366
McGee, Lavina, 366
McGee, Lavina C., 362, 363
McGee, Lizzie, 367
McGee, Lovenia, 367
McGee, Mary, 365
McGee, Mary S., 366
McGee, Minty, 367
McGee, Nancy, 365
McGee, Oive, 367
McGee, Samuel, 366, 367
McGee, William H., 366
McGee, William S., 366
McGinnis, Julia Ann, 67
McGinnis, Sam, 67
McGinnis, Sarah, 67, 68
McGreath, Eleanor, 132
McGreath, Joseph P., 132
McIntyre, Ellen, 92
McKenzie, Murdock, 255
McKinley, Aaron, 131, 132, 134, 135, 148
McKinley, Alice Orpha, 135
McKinley, Andrew, 131, 132
McKinley, Byron, 135, 136
McKinley, Celte, 133
McKinley, Charles, 134
McKinley, Clarinda J., 132
McKinley, Claro G., 135
McKinley, Claudia, 135
McKinley, Ebenezer, 131, 132, 133, 134
McKinley, Ebenezer Hayden, 132
McKinley, Elizabeth, 132
McKinley, Elza, 132

McKinley, Fern, 134
McKinley, Forest E., 23, 99, 134, 135, 136
McKinley, Fred L., 135
McKinley, George W., 133
McKinley, Grace, 135
McKinley, Irene B., 133
McKinley, Israel, 131
McKinley, Jane, 132
McKinley, Jenevieve, 136
McKinley, John, 132
McKinley, John R., 133, 134
McKinley, Lucinda, 132
McKinley, Majestic Eileen, 136
McKinley, Mary, 131, 134
McKinley, Mildred Ada, 23, 24, 26, 27, 28, 135, 136, 137
McKinley, Oliver, 135
McKinley, President William, 131
McKinley, Rachel, 132
McKinley, Rachel A., 133
McKinley, Ruth, 132
McKinley, Sarah, 131
McKinley, Sarah A., 132, 133
McKinley, Thamer E., 132
McKinley, Thomas L., 135
McKinley, Thomas W., 132, 133, 134
McKinley, Uncle Piedmond, 131
McKinley, Walter M., 135
McKinley, Walter Ray, 134
McKinley, William, 131, 132, 133
McKinley, William A., 132, 133
McKinley, Willoughby, 131, 133, 134, 135
McNair, James, 298
McPherson, Judge, 38
Mechling, Frederick, 350
Meek, E.L., 148
Melchoir, Sarah, 296
Melletti, Rhea, 21
Mendenhall, John, 299
Mercer, Sarah C., 135
Mercy, Esther, 142
Merry, Joseph, 211
Michell, Rebecca Ann, 251
Miller, Albert, 353
Miller, Ann, 127
Miller, Benjamin F., 108
Miller, Charles E., 353

Miller, Elizabeth Ann, 147
Miller, Emetine, 353
Miller, Emily, 353
Miller, Enoch, 347,353
Miller, George, 353
Miller, George W., 40
Miller, Howard, 136
Miller, Jane, 353
Miller, Jenett C., 347, 353
Miller, Laymont, 353
Miller, Mary, 353
Miller, Nettie, 340
Millison, Elizabeth, 131, 132
Mills, Adaline, 81, 84
Mills, Alcinda, 83, 86, 87
Mills, Anna E., 87
Mills, Ashford, 83
Mills, Ashford S., 75, 81, 84
Mills, Benjamin Lampton, 84, 89
Mills, Daniel G., 83
Mills, Daniel J., 89
Mills, Dave, 83
Mills, Earl, 87
Mills, Emily B., 68, 75, 76, 77, 82, 84
Mills, Francis W., 83, 89
Mills, Glen, 87
Mills, Isagueena, 87
Mills, Jacob, 75, 81, 82, 83, 84, 92
Mills, Jacob Thomas, 83, 87, 88
Mills, Kate, 87
Mills, Louisa, 81, 82
Mills, Mahlon, 87
Mills, Mary, 87
Mills, Mary Ann, 81, 83
Mills, Rebecca, 81, 82, 85, 86
Mills, Roger B., 89
Mills, Sarah E., 84
Mills, Sarah Jane, 82, 84, 90
Mills, Thomas, 81
Mills, Warner, 83
Mills, Warner W., 75, 81, 83, 86, 87, 89
Mills, Webb, 87
Minor, Margaret, 50
Minor, Minerva, 51
Minor, Theopylus, 51
Minor, William, 34, 51
Mohan, Mary R., 73
Moore, Elizabeth, 144

Moore, Hannah, 304, 305
Moore, Israel, 345
Moore, Jemina, 144
Moore, Joseph, 144, 148
Moore, Mahala (Collins), 134, 144
Moore, Rhoda, 144, 148
Moran, Benjamin, 314
Moran, Oma Lea, 25
Moran, Rose Jean, 314
Morgan, Captain Francis, 271
Morrison, Julia, 323
Morrison, Sallie, 323
Morrison, Tom, 323
Morrison, William, 322, 323
Mortimer, Nancy, 365
Morton, Ann, 120
Morton, Jane, 120
Moses, Marie, 16
Mowry, Mary, 208
Mowry, Uriah, 153
Murray, Mary J., 37
Myhill, Edward, 123
Napier, Cora, 261
Napier, Patrick, 256
Napier, Thomas Hugh, Jr., 256
Napier, Walter, 261
Napier, William, 261
Nash, John, 140
Nash, Mary, 156
Neel, Capt. Thomas, 64
Nelden, Lou, 23
Nester, Elizabeth, 258
Neville, Amelia, 299
Newby, Armistead, 130
Newby, Edward, 106, 128, 130
Newby, Elsey, 130
Newby, Esther, 128
Newby, Hannah, 127
Newby, Henry, 127, 130
Newby, Irene, 128
Newby, James, 127
Newby, Lucy, 130
Newby, Mary, 106, 128, 130
Newby, Oswald, 127, 128
Newby, Peggy, 128
Newby, Pollard, 130
Newby, Prichard, 128
Newby, Robert, 128
Newby, Sarah, 96, 106, 109, 127, 130
Newby, Sarah Ann, 128

Newby, Whaley, 127
Newby, William, 127
Newby, William P., 128, 130
Newell, Joseph, 209
Nicholls, Elizabeth, 299, 300
Nichols, Ruth, 142
Nixon, Margaret, 306, 307
Noble, Elizabeth, 200
Noll, Sarah, 36
Nonemacher, Christina, 318, 327
Norris, Richard, 128
Novak, Ruth, 252
Oadaker, Miss, 8
O'Byran, Peggy, 257
O'Day, Julia, 7
O'Day, Mary, 7, 8, 19
O'Day, Parker, 7
Odell, Polly, 91
Odenbaugh, Elizabeth, 51
Odlin, John, 242
Ogle, Benjamin, 243
Ogle, Lewis, 301
Oldaker, Abraham, 305
Oldaker, Isaac, 306
Oldaker, J.W., 75
Oldaker, John, 305, 306
Oldaker, Sarah, 307
Oldaker, Tamar, 306
Oldham, Mr., 191
Osborn, Richard, 92
Owen, Abigail, 139, 153, 154, 169
Owen, Daniel, 167
Owen, Deliverance, 167
Owen, Ebenezer, 153, 167, 168, 169
Owen, Elizabeth, 153
Owen, Hannah, 168
Owen, John, 167
Owen, Josiah, 168, 169
Owen, Mary, 169
Owen, Nathaniel, 167
Owen, Obadiah, 168
Owen, Thomas, 168
Owen, William, 167, 168
Owens, Diana, 323
Owens, Erasmus, 323
Owens, Esther, 323
Owens, Lydia, 265
Owens, Sallie, 323
Owens, Thomas, 323
Paddock, John, 167

Paine, Abigail, 153
Paine, Benjamin, 152, 153
Paine, Ebenezer, 154
Paine, Edward, 149
Paine, Elizabeth, 151, 152
Paine, Ezekial, 153
Paine, Gideon, 153
Paine, Hannah, 139, 140, 141, 154
Paine, John, 150, 151, 152, 153, 159
Paine, Joseph, 152
Paine, Josiah, 152
Paine, Mary, 151
Paine, Nathan, 153
Paine, Nathaniel, 149, 150, 151
Paine, Rebecca, 150, 151, 153
Paine, Samuel, 151, 153
Paine, Sarah, 151
Paine, Solomon, 139, 153, 154, 169
Paine, Stephen, 151, 152
Paine, Stephen, Jr., 149, 150, 151, 152
Paine, Stephen, Sr., 149, 150
Paine, Urania, 153
Paine, William, 153
Palmer, Catherine, 81, 91
Parent, Mary Ann, 54
Paris, Mary, 186
Parker, Alice, 150
Parker, Ann, 273
Parker, Clara, 137
Parker, Edmund, 271
Parker, Elizabeth, 265, 272, 273
Parker, Giles, 271
Parker, James, 271
Parker, Mary, 272, 273
Parker, Richard, 271, 272, 273
Parker, Richard, Jr., 265, 272, 273
Parker, Rowland, 271
Parker, Susan, 272
Parker, Thomas, 272
Parker, William, 150, 271, 272
Parker, William Le, 271
Parkhurst, Abigail, 211
Parkhurst, Caleb, 212
Parkhurst, Daniel, 212
Parkhurst, Deborah, 211
Parkhurst, Elizabeth, 211
Parkhurst, George, 207, 211, 212
Parkhurst, John, 211
Parkhurst, Joseph, 211
Parkhurst, Joshua, 212
Parkhurst, Mary, 211
Parkhurst, Phebe, 207, 211, 213
Parkhurst, Samuel, 211
Parrett, Joseph F., 318
Parsons, Captain, 64
Payne, Dann, 149
Paynr, Margaret, 149
Peake, Christian, 171, 172, 193
Peake, Thomas, 171
Pearsall, Mary, 333
Peck, Anne, 151
Peck, Samuel, 151
Pemberton, Elizabeth, 128
Pemberton, Larkin, 128
Pepper, Jacob, 151
Perego, Charity, 300
Perkins, Mary, 271, 272
Perkins, Nicholas, Jr., 271
Perkins, Nickolas, 271
Perry, Robert, 298
Pethtell, Eli, 36
Peyton, Mary, 283, 284, 285
Phelps, Elizabeth, 232
Philipps, Ann, 323
Philipps, Anna, 322
Philipps, Ben, 323
Philipps, Bertha N., 325
Philipps, Edith D., 326
Philipps, Ellen M., 324
Philipps, Erasmus, 321, 322, 323
Philipps, John, 323
Philipps, John H., 321, 322
Philipps, Joseph, 324
Philipps, Lucretia, 323
Philipps, Lydia, 323, 324
Philipps, Mamie O., 325
Philipps, Martha, 322, 324
Philipps, Mary, 321, 322, 323
Philipps, Pearl L., 325
Philipps, Persilla, 324
Philipps, Philip, 326
Philipps, Rachel, 322, 323
Philipps, Sallie, 322, 323
Philipps, Samuel Griffith, 309, 323, 324, 331
Philipps, Samuel J., 325
Philipps, Samuel Jones, 322, 323, 324, 325, 329
Philipps, Sarah, 324

Philipps, Susie E., 325
Philipps, Thomas, 321, 322, 323
Philipps, Thomas Warren, 325
Philipps, Thomas Wendell, 324
Philipps, Victoria, 309, 310, 324
Philipps, Victoria B., 325
Philipps, Washington, 323
Philipps, Winifred W., 326
Phillips, Belle, 51
Phillips, Magdalena, 319
Phillips, Richard, 152
Phillips, Thomas, 321, 322
Phillips, William, 182
Pickworth, Ruth, 192
Pierce, William, 142
Pierson, Thomas, 235
Pitman, Catherine, 319
Pitmann, Emanuel, 319
Plantagent, Geoffrey, 271
Platto, David K., 108
Pollard, Mary, 127
Polley, Peres R., 284
Pollock, Adam, 297
Pollock, Charles, 297
Pollock, James, 297
Pollock, Jane, 297
Pollock, John, 297
Pollock, Mary, 297
Pollock, Richard, 297
Pollock, Robert, 298
Pollock, Thomas, 297
Pollock, William, 297
Potter, Abel, 152
Potter, John, 176, 217
Power, Nicholas, 194
Power, Nicholas III, 186
Pratt, Ann, 203
Pray, John, 235
Price, Catherine, 70
Price, Christian, 119, 120
Price, Elizabeth, 277
Price, Hannah Ann, 70, 73
Price, Margaret E., 277
Price, Thomas, 70
Priest, Jane, 6
Priest, William, 6
Prikle, Alexander, 95
Pugh, Jim, 75
Pycroft, Ursela, 333
Quene, Mary, 24, 25

Rainsford, Anna, 165
Rainsford, David, 164
Rainsford, Edward, 158, 161, 164, 165
Rainsford, Elizabeth, 165
Rainsford, Hannah, 165
Rainsford, John, 164
Rainsford, Jonathan, 164
Rainsford, Josiah, 164
Rainsford, Mary, 164
Rainsford, Nathan, 164
Rainsford, Robert, 161
Rainsford, Solomon, 164
Rainsford, Urania, 152, 158, 164, 165
Ralph, Thomas, 215
Ralston, Ann, 44
Rankin, Adeline, 363
Rankin, Benjamin, 359, 360
Rankin, Benjamin McClellan, 360
Rankin, Catherine, 359
Rankin, Clurry, 361
Rankin, Cora F., 362
Rankin, Daisy, 363
Rankin, Daisy Mae, 312, 356, 363
Rankin, Daniel B., 362
Rankin, David, 359, 360, 361, 362, 363
Rankin, David W., 362
Rankin, Ernest T., 363
Rankin, Hannah, 361
Rankin, James, 359, 360, 362
Rankin, James L., 362
Rankin, Jane, 360, 361
Rankin, Joseph, 361, 362
Rankin, Joseph A., 359
Rankin, Joseph D., 360, 361
Rankin, Joseph David, 362, 363, 367
Rankin, Lillian Leota, 363
Rankin, Mary, 361
Rankin, Nellie L., 362
Rankin, Olive, 363
Rankin, Samuel, 360, 361
Rankin, Sarah, 361
Rankin, Wallace A., 356, 362
Rankin, William, 358, 360
Rarick, Elizabeth, 350
Reape, Samuel, 173, 193
Reckel, Charles, 30
Reckel, Christina, 29, 30
Reed, Aldie, 147

Rees, Stanley, 87
Rees, Theophilus, 321
Reily, Bazaleel, 331
Reily, Isaac, 331
Reily, Jacob, 323, 331, 336
Reily, Priscilla, 331
Reily, Susannah, 309, 323, 324, 331
Remington, Mary, 176
Reynolds, Hannah, 304
Rhoades, Elizabeth Jane, 86
Rhodes, Dorothy Whipple, 176
Rhodes, Elizabeth, 175, 194
Rhodes, Jeremiah, 194
Rhodes, John, 194
Rhodes, Malachi, 186, 194, 196, 198
Rhodes, Mary, 176, 194, 196
Rhodes, Peleg, 194
Rhodes, Rebecca, 194
Rhodes, Sarah, 177, 186, 196
Rhodes, Zachariah, 173, 193, 194, 196
Rice, Susan E., 285
Richards, Arnold, 65
Richards, Jim, 7
Richards, Susannah, 65, 66
Riddle, Colonel, 64
Ridenour, Isaac, 350
Ridenour, Vida Grace, 27
Rider, Oliver, 293
Riggs, John, 285
Riggs, Joseph, 235
Riley, John Robert, 108
Riley, Mary, 243, 344
Rinkus, William, 292
Roberts, Howard, 24
Robinson, Elizabeth B., 307, 308
Robinson, Hazel, 292
Robinson, Martin, 318
Robinson, Savanah, 318
Robinson, Stephen, 307
Rodeffer, John, 61
Rodeffer, Philip, 61
Rogers, James Alfred, 145
Ropp, Solomon, 286
Rose, E.L., 324
Roshon, Francis Austin, 20
Roshon, Henry, 20
Roshon, Wesley, 19, 20
Ross, Mary, 91
Rowan, Judge John, 297

Rowan, Mary, 299
Rowe, Sarah Virginia, 259
Rowe, Stephen, 259
Ruggles, Elizabeth, 156
Runyan, John, 65
Russell, James, 289
Russell, Lucinda, 132, 133, 134
Russell, Thomas, 132
Rutherford, Jane, 260
Sabeere, Mr., 224
Sager, Emily, 83
Sager, Jacob N., 83
Sager, Jerome, 83
Sager, Mary E., 83
Sager, Thomas, 83
Sager, William, 83
Salome, Sara, 281
Salton-stall, Sir Richard, 191
Samy, Mable, 24
Sands, Jacob, 304
Sanford, Walker J.L., 256
Sanner, Johann Philip, 318
Sartin, Sarah, 255
Sayles, Isabelle, 185
Sayles, John, 173
Sayles, Mary, 243
Scarbouch, Ann, 275
Scerest, Mariah, 300
Schaub, Hans Gerge, 281
Schenck, Rosana Lee, 30
Schmucker, Rev., 319
Schooley, Mary, 86
Scott, Catherine, 229
Scott, Sarah, 361
Scott, Sylvanus, 227
Seagrave, Susannah, 87
Seely, Ruth, 153
Sells, Ruhama E., 318
Shackelford, John, 128
Sharp, Daniel, 339
Sharp, Rachel, 339, 340
Sharparowe, Elizabeth, 233, 234
Sheetz, Martin, 286
Sheldon, Joseph, 176
Sheldon, Mary, 174
Sheldon, Nicholas Tanner, 185
Shepard, Ruhuma, 57
Shepherd, Catherine, 91
Shepherd, David, 91
Shepherd, Hannah, 91

Shepherd, Humphrey, 92
Shepherd, James, 91
Shepherd, John, 91
Shepherd, Jonah Humphrey, 92
Shepherd, Joseph Henry, 91
Shepherd, Marcy, 92
Shepherd, Martha, 92
Shepherd, Mary, 75, 81, 82, 83, 84, 91, 92
Shepherd, Moses, 91
Shepherd, Nancy Ann, 92
Shepherd, Parkinson Daniel, 92
Shepherd, Rebecca, 91
Shepherd, Sarah, 91
Shepherd, Tacy, 92
Shepherd, Thomas, 81, 91, 92
Shingleton, Frances Selena F., 259
Shingleton, Granville D., 284
Shinn, Elizabeth, 344
Shumaker, Judith Ann, 25
Shumaker, Robert, 25
Shuttleworth, Hazel, 294
Simmons, Jonathan Ellis, 141
Simpson, Susanna Gaylord, 211, 212
Sims, Caroline Matilda, 87
Sims, Simeon Walter, Sr., 87
Six, John Conrad, 55
Skilit, Rachel, 327
Slabuagh, Franklin E., 70
Slocum, Mary, 234
Smith, Abigail, 209
Smith, Amey, 209
Smith, Amos, 243
Smith, Benjamin, 174, 175
Smith, Benjamin, Jr., 196
Smith, Captain John, 111, 112
Smith, Chloe Opal, 98, 99
Smith, Dora, 301
Smith, E., 147
Smith, Edward, 173, 179, 224
Smith, Eleanor, 208
Smith, Elisha, 179
Smith, Elizabeth, 175, 176, 177
Smith, Elizabeth Jerusha, 107
Smith, Fred, 25
Smith, George, 7
Smith, James Willie, 97, 98, 100
Smith, John, 211, 229
Smith, John Rudolph, 147
Smith, Julia Henrietta, 77, 78

Smith, Levi, 301
Smith, Loren Wilson, 98, 100
Smith, Major Lawrence, 125
Smith, Martha, 152
Smith, Miss, 204
Smith, Mr., 167
Smith, Nathan, 97
Smith, Phebe, 179
Smith, Philip, 179
Smith, Richard, 276
Smith, Robert, 272
Smith, Sandra Josephine, 100
Smith, Sarah, 126, 173, 174, 179, 180
Smith, Sharon, 25
Smoots, Philip, 318
Solinger, George, 8
Somerville, David Rankin, 361
Somerville, Elizabeth, 361
Somerville, Fannie, 361
Somerville, Frances, 361
Somerville, James, 361
Somerville, James Harvey, 361
Somerville, Josiah, 361
Somerville, Rachel, 361
Somerville, Samantha, 361
Somerville, Samuel, 361
Somerville, Sarah, 361
Sonner, Christina, 318, 319
Sonner, Maria, 317
Soulice, John, 54
Sparrowgrove, Francis Isabella, 301
Spears, Terry, 301
Spencer, William, 209
Sperry, Lucy, 279
Spicer, Ann, 337
Spicer, Susan, 337
Spicer, Susanna, 333
Spicer, Thomas, 337
Sprague, Patience, 228
Stacye, Francis, 149
Stafford, Amos, 217
Stafford, Freelove, 186
Stahl, Elizabeth, 297
Staley, Albert, 285
Staley, Andrew J., 284
Staley, Anthony, 285
Staley, Barbara Ann, 284
Staley, Catherine, 283
Staley, Catherine Marie, 282
Staley, Charles, 283

Staley, Charles E., 285
Staley, Clarissa, 285
Staley, Clarissa A., 261
Staley, Daniel, 282, 283
Staley, Daniel L., 284
Staley, Elisha Reynolds, 284
Staley, Elizabeth A., 283
Staley, Ezra, 285
Staley, Geneva, 285
Staley, Jacob, 282, 283, 284
Staley, John, 282
Staley, John Jacob, Jr., 282
Staley, Joseph, 261, 283, 284, 285, 290
Staley, Margaret, 282, 285
Staley, Mary, 285
Staley, Mary E., 284
Staley, Mary Marie, 283
Staley, Olivea, 285
Staley, Peter, 282
Staley, Peyton, 284
Staley, Rebecca A., 284
Staley, Sarah, 282, 283
Staley, Solomon P., 284
Staley, Solomon T., 285
Staley, Stephen, 284
Staley, Stephen Daniel, 282, 283, 286
Staley, Stephen, Jr., 283, 284, 285
Staley, William, 285
Stanley, Sarah M., 356, 362
Starkey, Patty, 313, 314
Starr, Landon, 132
Staten, Charles, 259
Staugh, James Frederick, 315
Staugh, Katherine Ann, 315
Steele, Adam, 295, 296, 298, 299, 300
Steele, Adam J., 301
Steele, Agnes, 295, 297
Steele, Ann, 300
Steele, Barbara Ann, 299
Steele, Charles, 301
Steele, Daniel, 299
Steele, David, 299, 300
Steele, Elma, 135, 293, 294, 301
Steele, Ester, 299
Steele, George, 300
Steele, Gladys, 301
Steele, James, 295, 299
Steele, Jane, 295, 298, 299, 300

Steele, John, 300
Steele, John Rowan, 299
Steele, Joseph, 299
Steele, Joseph H., 300
Steele, Lucinda, 300
Steele, Maggie Jane, 301
Steele, Martha, 295, 299
Steele, Martha Breckinridge, 299
Steele, Mary, 295, 296, 297
Steele, Mary E., 300
Steele, Melvina, 301
Steele, Minnie, 301
Steele, Nancy, 300
Steele, Nancy Polk, 299
Steele, Peter, 300
Steele, Prena, 300
Steele, Rebecca, 295
Steele, Richard, 299
Steele, Richard Adam, 295, 297, 298
Steele, Richard Adam, Jr., 298
Steele, Richard, Jr., 295
Steele, Robert, 299
Steele, Rose, 301
Steele, Samuel, 300, 301
Steele, Sarah Catherine, 31
Steele, Susan, 296
Steele, Susan Viola, 301
Steele, Thomas, 293, 296, 300, 301
Steele, Una Mae, 301
Steele, Vina, 300
Steele, William, 299
Steen, Jane, 359, 360
Steen, Margaret, 359
Steere, Thomas, 208
Stehli, Ana-Eva, 281, 282
Stehli, Andreas, 281
Stehli, Anna Marie, 281
Stehli, Henry, 281
Stehli, John Jacob, Jr., 281
Stehli, John Jacob, Sr., 281, 282
Stehli, Joseph, 281
Stehli, Peter, 281
Stehli, Stephen, 281
Stephens, Thomas J., 266
Stephenson, Benjamin, 283
Stevens, Aaron, 300
Stevens, Rebecca, 232
Stevenson, Elizabeth, 243
Stewart, J. Harvey, 36
Stewart, Jessie, 37

Stichter, Agnes, 247
Stichter, Alfred, 247
Stichter, Ann, 245
Stichter, Anna Marie, 245, 246, 247, 249, 251
Stichter, Barbara Ann, 245
Stichter, Barbara K., 245
Stichter, Catherine, 247
Stichter, Catherine V., 247
Stichter, Delores, 247
Stichter, Elizabeth M., 245, 246, 249
Stichter, Frank, 247
Stichter, George A., 245, 247
Stichter, George A., Jr., 247
Stichter, James Adam, 245, 247
Stichter, Jeffery, 252
Stichter, Joseph T., 246, 247, 248, 249
Stichter, Josephine Theresa, 28, 29, 31, 251
Stichter, Lillian, 247
Stichter, Margaretta Genevieve, 246, 248, 249
Stichter, Marjorie Elizabeth, 251
Stichter, Michelle, 252
Stichter, Phillip John F., 245
Stichter, Sean, 252
Stichter, Serovica, 247
Stichter, William, 247, 252
Stichter, William Adam, 245, 246, 247, 249
Stichter, William Adam, Jr., 245, 246
Stichter, William J., 28, 246, 249, 250, 251, 263
Stichter, William Joseph, Jr., 251, 252
Stillion, James, 300
Stillwell, Alice, 242
Stilwell, Charles, 96
Stilwell, Dellie, 97
Stilwell, Everett, 96
Stilwell, Flora, 96
Stilwell, George, 96
Stilwell, James W., 97
Stilwell, Jesse, 97
Stilwell, Jessie T., 97
Stilwell, Joseph, 96
Stilwell, Myrtle, 97
Stith, Elenor, 256
Stoneking, David, 36

Story, Susan, 232
Stout, Richard, 334
Strawn, Alice, 85
Strawn, Amanda, 82
Strawn, Charles, 86
Strawn, Charles F., 85
Strawn, Clark U., 86
Strawn, David Oakley, 82, 86
Strawn, Eliza J., 86
Strawn, Elizabeth, 82
Strawn, Ellen, 86
Strawn, Ellen Jane, 82
Strawn, George, 86
Strawn, George Washington, 82, 85, 86
Strawn, Harriet J., 85
Strawn, Hattie, 86
Strawn, Isaac, 82, 86
Strawn, Isaac N., 86
Strawn, Isaac Newton, 86
Strawn, John, 85
Strawn, John B., 82, 85, 86
Strawn, Martha, 85
Strawn, Mary A., 85
Strawn, Mary Ann, 82, 85
Strawn, Mary Catherine, 86
Strawn, Moses, 82
Strawn, Nelson, 82, 86
Strawn, Olive, 86
Strawn, Roswell, 86
Strawn, Sherman, 86
Strawn, Susan A., 86
Strawn, Thomas Jefferson, 86
Strawn, Thomas, Jr., 82
Strawn, Walter C., 86
Strayer, John Nicholas, Jr., 282
Stump, Hannah, 299
Styles, Jonathan, 50
Summer, Andrew, 318
Sunderland, Mary, 164
Sutherland, John, 299
Sutton, Patience, 253
Swearingen, Elizabeth, 279
Swearingen, Van, 279
Sweet, Sarah Eleanor, 217
Swick, Melvina Ann, 108
Taber, Esther, 188
Taber, John, 188
Taber, Joseph, 188

Taber, Lydia Masters, 183, 185, 186, 188, 190
Taber, Philip, 183, 186, 187, 188, 192
Taber, Thomas, 188
Taggart, Arthur W., 72, 73
Taggart, Frank, 73
Taggart, Frederick, 73
Taggart, Karl Arthur, 73
Taggart, Lawrence, 73
Taggart, Thelma Elmira, 73
Talbott, John M., 299
Taliaferro, Catherine, 126
Taliaferro, Charles, 126
Taliaferro, Christian, 125
Taliaferro, Francis, 125
Taliaferro, John, 126
Taliaferro, Mary, 120, 126
Taliaferro, Mary Catherine, 123
Taliaferro, Richard, 126
Taliaferro, Robert, 125, 126
Taliaferro, Sara, 126
Talliaferro, Francis, 125
Tapp, Alice, 116
Tapp, Ann, 116
Tapp, Charity, 114
Tapp, Elizabeth, 101, 102, 112, 116, 117
Tapp, Lewis, 116
Tapp, Mary, 116
Tapp, Sarah, 116
Tapp, Vincent, 114, 116
Tapp, William, 101, 116
Tapp, William III, 114, 116, 121
Tapptico, Elinor, 111, 112
Tapptico, Elizabeth, 112, 114
Tapptico, William, 113
Tapptico, William I, 111, 112
Tapptico, William II, 112, 114
Taptico, Elizabeth, 112
Taygart, Clementine, 34, 36
Taygart, Elizabeth, 34, 37
Taygart, John, 33
Taygart, Julia Ann, 33, 34
Taygart, Mary, 34
Taygart, Rebecca, 34
Taygart, Sarah Ann, 34
Taygart, Susan, 34
Taygart, William, 33, 34, 36, 37, 42, 44
Taygart, William, Jr., 34
Taylor, Augustus, 133
Taylor, George W., 107
Taylor, Mr., 243
Taylor, Vernon, 325
Taylor, Wayne D., 40
Teff, Samuel, 227
Tenolds, Thomas, 254
Thacker, Joseph, 260
Thacker, Mary Etta, 260
Thacker, Sarah Roya, 259
Thomas, Sarah, 52
Thompson, Aaron, 235
Thompson, Elizabeth, 191
Thompson, Rachel, 361, 362
Thomson, Elizabeth, 127
Thornburg, Solomon, 283
Thorton, Dinah, 208
Tibbles, Venson, 145
Tight, Caroline, 88
Tillinghast, Abigail, 185, 186
Tillinghast, Benjamin, 177, 185, 186, 196
Tillinghast, Elisha, 186
Tillinghast, Elizabeth, 186
Tillinghast, Hannah, 186
Tillinghast, James, 186
Tillinghast, John, 185
Tillinghast, Joseph, 186
Tillinghast, Lydia, 176, 185, 186
Tillinghast, Marcie, 141
Tillinghast, Mary, 185, 186
Tillinghast, Mercy, 177, 186
Tillinghast, Pardon, 183, 188, 190
Tillinghast, Pardon III, 185
Tillinghast, Philip, 185
Tillinghast, Rev. Pardon Elisha, 183, 185, 186
Tillinghast, Sarah, 185, 186
Tilton, Abigail, 333
Tilton, Ann, 336
Tilton, Caleb, 336
Tilton, Catherine, 334
Tilton, Daniel, 334
Tilton, Druscilla, 336
Tilton, Elijah, 335, 336
Tilton, Elizabeth, 335
Tilton, Esther, 333, 334
Tilton, Henry, 334
Tilton, Jackson, 335

Tilton, John, 331, 333, 334, 335, 336
Tilton, Joseph, 334, 335
Tilton, Lorenzo, 336
Tilton, Mary, 333, 334
Tilton, Peter, 333, 334, 335, 337
Tilton, Polly, 336
Tilton, Pricilla, 336
Tilton, Rebecca, 334
Tilton, Richard, 335
Tilton, Sallie, 323, 331, 336
Tilton, Samuel, 334
Tilton, Sarah, 333
Tilton, Susan, 336
Tilton, Susannah, 335
Tilton, Thomas, 333, 334, 335
Tilton, William, 334, 336
Tilton, William III, 333
Todd, Robert, 296
Tolle, James, 109
Tolle, Lovey, 109
Tolle, Nancy, 109
Tolman, Benjamin, 159
Tomblin, Joseph, 256
Tomlins, Timothy, 232
Townsend, Elizabeth, 231
Tracy, Jesse, 132
Travel, Barbara, 327
Trout, Jeri, 252
Trout, Margaret, 307
Turner, Ann, 204
Turner, Josiah, 152
Turner, Lucy, 272
Turner, Mary, 173
Turpin, Anne, 204
Turpin, Catharine, 204
Turpin, Elizabeth, 204, 205
Turpin, Esther, 204
Turpin, John, 200, 204, 205, 209
Turpin, Joseph, 204
Turpin, Lydia, 204
Turpin, Martha, 204
Turpin, Mary, 204
Turpin, Sarah Lydia, 142, 200, 201, 205
Turpin, William, 203, 204, 229
Tussing, Elder George N., 5
Tygard, Abraham, 33
Tygard, Charles Edwards, 37
Tygard, Charles F., 40

Tygard, Eagon Blackburn, 6, 7, 33, 34, 35, 38, 39, 40, 52
Tygard, Estel, 39
Tygard, Flavius, 39
Tygard, Flavius Josephus, 35, 38
Tygard, Fred C., 37
Tygard, Gurtrude Ester, 39
Tygard, James Wallace, 37
Tygard, John L., 35, 39
Tygard, John Rinehart, 33, 37
Tygard, Lorie Mildred, 40
Tygard, Mariah, 35, 38, 39
Tygard, Marinda, 40
Tygard, Marrion M., 37
Tygard, Mary, 39
Tygard, Melissa, 5, 6, 7, 11, 15, 17, 25, 35, 37
Tygard, Perry Eagon, 35, 40
Tygard, Perry L., 37
Tygard, Sarah, 7
Tygard, Sarah E., 35, 37, 39
Tygard, Vera, 40
Tygard, William F., 35, 39
Tygart, Perrigan L., 34
Updike, Amon, 305
Vallet, Sarah, 152
Van horn, Elder J.J., 17
Vance, Julia, 301
Vergoose, Susanna, 164
Vess, Hiram A., 82
Waggoner, Anna Elizabeth, 50, 58, 59, 61, 63, 64
Waggoner, Barbara, 49, 50, 63, 64
Waggoner, Catherine, 66
Waggoner, Elijah, 66
Waggoner, Elizabeth, 65
Waggoner, George, 66
Waggoner, Henry, 66
Waggoner, Jacob, 66
Waggoner, Johannes Michael, 63, 64, 65, 66
Waggoner, John, 66
Waggoner, John Peter, 63, 64
Waggoner, Mariah, 66
Waggoner, Mary, 63, 64, 65
Waggoner, Paul, 66
Waggoner, Peter, 65
Waggoner, Polly Marie, 43
Waggoner, Samuel, 66
Waggoner, Susannah, 66

Waggoner, Willheim, 58, 63, 64
Waggoner, William, 49, 66
Wagnerin, Anna Elizabeth, 58, 63, 64
Wait, Thomas, 152
Waldeck, Mrs. Roy D., 342
Wallace, Elizabeth, 360, 361, 362
Ward, James S., 258
Ward, Rev. W.D., 40
Ward, Samuel, 235
Waring, Dorcas, 296
Warner, Anne, 295
Warner, Charles D., 71
Warner, Margaret Marie, 71
Warner, Russell William, 71
Warner, William P., 71
Washington, Catherine F., 130
Washington, George, 64
Washington, President George, 297
Waterman, Charles, 141
Waterman, Nathaniel, 197
Waterman, Waite, 194
Watson, Elizabeth Francis, 253, 254
Watts, Floyd, 314
Watts, James, 258
Watts, John Hansford, 258, 268
Watts, Lucy, 314
Watts, Ora, 314
Watts, Vienna, 261
Waybright, Thomas, 145
Wayne, General Anthony, 297
Webb, Daniel A., 94
Webb, John Wesley, 94
Weber, Olive, 2
Webster, Polly, 95
Weimer, Rev. Jacob, 350
Wells, Ms., 34
Welshans, Jacob, 286
Wendle, Anna Elizabeth, 318
West, Elizabeth Rockerfeller, 291, 293
Westcott, Damaria, 173
Westfall, William Henderson, 145
Wetterholm, Charles, 311
Wetterholm, Mary, 311
Wetterholm, Olaf, 311
Wetzel, Eva Christine, 57
Wetzel, George, 57
Wetzel, Jacob, 57
Wetzel, John, 58
Wetzel, John Martin, 56, 57

Wetzel, John, Jr., 58
Wetzel, Lewis, 57, 58
Wetzel, Magdalena Elizabeth, 57
Wetzel, Martin, 54, 57
Wetzel, Nicholas, 55
Wetzel, Susan, 58
Whaley, Mary, 127
Whaley, Oswald, 127
Wheeler, Samuel, 325
Whipple, Capt. John, 235
Whipple, Deliverance, 175
Whipple, Dorothy, 196
Whipple, Elzear, 224
Whipple, Jonathan, 224
Whipple, Mary, 198
Whipple, Otis, 177
Whipple, Sarah, 229
Whipple, Thomas, 228
White, Jonathan, 322
White, Joseph, 322
White, L., 67
White, S. J., 324
White, Samuel, 322
White, Thomas M., 77
Whitefield, Rev. George, 153
Whiting, Samuel, 232
Whitmire, David Oldaker, 308
Whitmire, James Smith, 308
Whitmire, John, 307, 308
Whitmire, Mahala Hoy, 308
Whitmire, Margaret Ann, 308
Whitmire, Sarah Jane, 308
Whitmire, Zachariah Hoy, 308
Wickersham, Mary, 252
Wiley, Martha, 48
Wiley, Sarah, 199, 200
Wiley, William, 51
Wilkins, Catherine, 328
Wilkins, David, 328
Wilkins, Elizabeth, 308, 317, 318, 327, 328
Wilkins, George, 327, 328
Wilkins, Godfrey, 327
Wilkins, Hannah, 328
Wilkins, Henry, 327
Wilkins, Jacob, 328
Wilkins, Johann Gottfried, 317, 327, 328
Wilkins, John, 327, 328
Wilkins, Levi, 328

Wilkins, Mathias, 327
Wilkins, Samuel, 328
Wilkins, Sarah, 328
Willard, Samuel, 227
Willet, Captain Thomas, 149, 152
Willet, Elizabeth, 334
William, Wilhelmina, 325
Williams, Daniel, 194
Williams, Eleanor, 58
Williams, Elizabeth, 151
Williams, Josephine, 97
Williams, Lucy, 85
Williams, Maude, 78
Williams, Owen, 167
Williams, Patience, 277
Williams, Roger, 171, 218, 233, 235
Williams, Sarah, 345
Williamson, Carol Sue, 29, 30
Williamson, Margaret, 29
Williamson, Wade, 29
Willis, Ralph, 99
Wills, Virginia Evelyn, 99
Wills, William Ralph, 99
Wilson, Delilah, 279
Wilson, Elijah, 346
Wilson, Elizabeth, 343
Wilson, Elizabeth Hays, 345
Wilson, Ella, 347
Wilson, Esther, 343, 345
Wilson, Francis, 346
Wilson, Frank A., 347
Wilson, George, 340
Wilson, George W., 346, 347, 353
Wilson, James, 343
Wilson, James Riley, 345
Wilson, James W., 344, 345
Wilson, Johnathen Hays, 344, 345
Wilson, Joseph, 343, 344
Wilson, Mahalia, 346
Wilson, Martha, 345, 346, 347
Wilson, Mary, 312, 344, 346
Wilson, Mary Elizabeth, 277
Wilson, Mary Polly, 343
Wilson, Mary Sylvania, 340, 341, 342, 347
Wilson, Michael, 344
Wilson, Michael Wills, 344, 345
Wilson, Nancy, 346
Wilson, Priscilla, 344
Wilson, Samuel, 346
Wilson, Sarah, 346
Wilson, Sarah Ashby, 345
Wilson, Susanna, 343
Wilson, Thomas, 343, 344, 345, 346, 351
Wilson, Thomas II, 343, 344, 345
Wilson, Thomas III, 344
Wilson, William, 343
Wilson, William Ashby, 345
Wilson, William R., 345
Winchel, Clarence, 356
Wingfield, Martha Sarah, 126
Winlock, General Joseph, 93
Winlock, Joseph, 93
Winlock, Sarah, 93, 94, 95
Winthrop, John, 161
Wise, Lydia, 327
Wiseman, Mary, 40
Wolf, Eva, 61
Wolf, Jacob, Jr., 65
Wolfe, John Jacob, 57
Wood, Benjamin, 298
Woods, Mary E., 365
Woods, Ms., 41, 45, 47, 48
Woods, Shirley (Roberts), 24
Woodward, John, 169
Woodward, Mary, 208
Wray, Edith Rose, 315
Wright, Annie M., 96
Wright, Bernice, 97, 98
Wright, Bernice, 100
Wright, Charles, 94
Wright, Charles H., 95, 96
Wright, Columbia Jane, 95, 97, 109
Wright, Elizabeth, 96
Wright, Emily Jane, 95, 97
Wright, Fielding Winlock, 94
Wright, Francis, 93, 94, 95
Wright, Francis DeCoursey, 94
Wright, Horace, 96
Wright, Isaac Newton, 94
Wright, James, 95
Wright, James F., 96
Wright, John, 109
Wright, John G., 109
Wright, Joseph W., 95
Wright, Lemuel, 95, 96, 97, 110
Wright, Lucinda, 95, 96, 97
Wright, Margaret, 94
Wright, Martha, 94, 95, 96

Wright, Mary, 93
Wright, Mary Watson, 94
Wright, Nancy, 94, 95
Wright, Pearl Navada, 20, 23, 97, 99, 135, 136, 137, 294
Wright, Peter, 95
Wright, Reuben, 94
Wright, Robert, 109
Wright, Sarah Amanda, 96, 97, 98, 135
Wright, Solomon, 93
Wright, Stella G., 96
Wright, Thornton, 94, 95, 96, 97
Wright, William, 93, 94
Wrolens, Mary, 76
Wyckoff, Sarah, 334
Wykoff, Abram, 37
Wynne, James, 295
Wynne, Jonathan II, 295
Yeasley, Barbara, 283, 286
Yeasley, Catherine, 286
Yeasley, Elizabeth, 286
Yeasley, Eva, 286
Yeasley, Magdalena, 286
Yeasley, Maria, 286
Yeasley, Michael, 283, 286
Yeasley, Sarah, 286
Yost, Henry, 43
Yost, Rebecca, 43
Young, Isabella T., 75, 77
Young, Jane Emily, 17, 68, 69, 70, 71, 72, 75, 77
Young, John, 68, 75, 76, 77, 84
Young, Lavonia, 75, 76, 77, 78
Young, Mary Adele, 75, 77
Young, Orriel, 75, 76
Zimmerman, Abraham, 42

www.ingramcontent.com/pod-product-compliance
Lightning Source LLC
Chambersburg PA
CBHW050830230426
43667CB00012B/1945